TRINITY AND ELECTION

TRINITY AND ELECTION

The Christocentric Reorientation of Karl Barth's Speculative Theology, 1936–1942

Shao Kai Tseng

LONDON • NEW YORK • OXFORD • NEW DELHI • SYDNEY

T&T CLARK
Bloomsbury Publishing Plc
50 Bedford Square, London, WC1B 3DP, UK
1385 Broadway, New York, NY 10018, USA
29 Earlsfort Terrace, Dublin 2, Ireland

BLOOMSBURY, T&T CLARK and the T&T Clark logo are
trademarks of Bloomsbury Publishing Plc

First published in Great Britain 2023
Paperback edition published 2024

Copyright © Shao Kai Tseng, 2023

Shao Kai Tseng has asserted his right under the Copyright, Designs and
Patents Act, 1988, to be identified as Author of this work.

Cover design: Terry Woodley
Cover image: The Isenheim Altarpiece, Grünewald, Matthias (c. 1470–1528).
Found in the collection of MuséeUnterlinden, Colmar.
(Photo by Fine Art Images/Heritage Images/Getty Images)

All rights reserved. No part of this publication may be reproduced or
transmitted in any form or by any means, electronic or mechanical, including
photocopying, recording, or any information storage or retrieval system,
without prior permission in writing from the publishers.

Bloomsbury Publishing Plc does not have any control over, or responsibility for,
any third-party websites referred to or in this book. All internet addresses given in this
book were correct at the time of going to press. The author and publisher regret any
inconvenience caused if addresses have changed or sites have ceased to exist,
but can accept no responsibility for any such changes.

A catalogue record for this book is available from the British Library.

Library of Congress Cataloging-in-Publication Data

Names: Tseng, Shao Kai, 1981- author.
Title: Trinity and election : the Christocentric reorientation of Karl
Barth's speculative theology, 1936-1942 / Shao Kai Tseng.
Description: London ; New York : T&T Clark, 2023. | Includes
bibliographical references and index. |
Identifiers: LCCN 2022036173 (print) | LCCN 2022036174 (ebook) | ISBN
9780567709318 (hb) | ISBN 9780567709356 | ISBN 9780567709301 (epdf) |
ISBN 9780567709349 (epub)
Subjects: LCSH: Barth, Karl, 1886-1968. | Trinity. | God (Christianity) | Metaphysics.
Classification: LCC BX4827.B3 T777 2023 (print) | LCC BX4827.B3 (ebook) |
DDC 230/.044–dc23/eng/20230109
LC record available at https://lccn.loc.gov/2022036173
LC ebook record available at https://lccn.loc.gov/2022036174

ISBN: HB: 978-0-5677-0931-8
PB: 978-0-5677-0935-6
ePDF: 978-0-5677-0930-1
eBook: 978-0-5677-0934-9

Typeset by Integra Software Services Pvt. Ltd.

To find out more about our authors and books visit www.bloomsbury.com
and sign up for our newsletters.

*to George Hunsinger
who taught me how to read Barth*

CONTENTS

Preface	viii
Abbreviations: Works by Karl Barth	xiv
INTRODUCTION	1
Chapter 1 SKETCHING THE BACKGROUND: THE POST-KANTIAN PARADIGM REEXAMINED	25
Chapter 2 SKETCHING THE BACKGROUND: BARTH AND THE HISTORY OF SPECULATIVE THEOLOGY	53
Chapter 3 SKETCHING THE CONTOURS: ACTUALISTIC ONTOLOGY AND SPECULATIVE THEOLOGY	83
Chapter 4 PAINTING THE PORTRAIT: JESUS CHRIST AS *SPECULUM ELECTIONIS* (1936)	117
Chapter 5 PAINTING THE PORTRAIT: JESUS CHRIST AS *SPECULUM TRINITATIS* (1940)	149
Chapter 6 PAINTING THE PORTRAIT: JESUS CHRIST AS ELECTING, ELECTED, AND ELECTION (1942)	179
Chapter 7 FRAMING THE PICTURE: ELECTION AND NATIONHOOD— CHRISTOCENTRIC REFLECTIONS FROM 1936 TO 1938	203
EPILOGUE	233
Bibliography	241
Index	255

PREFACE

This book is dedicated to George Hunsinger, my erstwhile Th.M. supervisor at Princeton Theological Seminary in 2008–9. Through the years he has remained one of my most important theological mentors, and the present study in large part consists of reflections on what he taught me about Barth, especially what he calls the Anselmian and Hegelian "moments" regulating Barth's mature theology. Following Professor Hunsinger, I portray Barth as a theologian who critically brings classical theology to bear on distinctively modern problems while drawing eclectically on modern philosophy and theology. I hope to show in the footsteps of Professor Hunsinger that the trinitarian and Christological dogmas defined and clarified at Nicaea, Constantinople, Ephesus, and Chalcedon as well as the faith-seeking-understanding program developed by classical theologians like Augustine and Anselm remain ever pertinent in our day.

The portrait that I paint of Barth as a "speculative" theologian is significantly indebted to Sigurd Baark. He and I arrived in Princeton in the same year, when he was admitted as a doctoral candidate. In many ways he helped me wrap my mind around Barth when I was a novice. Though we did not stay in touch after I graduated, it is unsurprising that the thesis and arguments of my 2018 monograph on Barth and Augustine matched the results of Sigurd's research published earlier in the same year. Correspondences ensued from the publication of our respective volumes, and these exchanges have again proved edifying to my work on Barth. Following Sigurd, I have adopted the term "speculative" to describe Barth's mature theology as a whole.

In this book I build on and challenge a dominant model of post-Kantian Barth interpretation that downplays the Anselmian moment of his theology. If, despite the best of my efforts, I happen to misrepresent any part of the views of the proponents of this paradigm, I ask for their forgiveness. I hope they would understand my disagreements with their views as expressions of deep admiration for their work.

The theology of nationhood is my chosen frame for the portrait I paint of Barth in this book. This framing is not an imitation of Baroque art, in which the picture might look as if it were painted to fit a pre-existing frame. The topic of nationalism is treated in the final chapter, the draft of which I did not write up until those of the first four chapters were completed.

I could well have chosen to present my portrait of Barth in another frame or without a frame at all. However, I believe that the continuing relevance of the Christocentric reorientation of his speculative theology in the 1930s can be best appreciated among contemporary readers when it is framed within the context of the surge of nationalisms across Europe and parts of Asia in the first half of the twentieth century, not least the mystical nationalism developed in Germany as an expression of an essentially pantheistic form of speculative metaphysics.

This framing is especially personal to me as the author. I am a Taiwanese-Canadian working as an academic at a public university in China, the ancestral land of my maternal grandparents and the country in which my paternal grandparents were born and raised. I find myself in a situation reminiscent of Barth's experience from the 1920s and early 1930s, when he worked in Germany as a Swiss national.

This experience is partly reflected in an open letter that Barth polemically addressed to Emanuel Hirsch, Barth's erstwhile colleague from Göttingen, in 1932. Barth writes: "It is my destiny that in Switzerland I have my homeland and in Germany the work of my lifetime, and … I strive to be a good German without ceasing to be a good Switzer."[1]

This statement brings sharply to the foreground the question: what is it that makes a "good German"? For Hirsch, being a "good German" entails embracing an ideology and civil religion that "makes Germany great again," so to speak (no pun intended). Barth, on the other hand, deemed all forms of nationalism idolatrous and firmly rejected them.

Being a good German meant for Barth honoring the unique and universal Lordship of Jesus Christ *in Germany*, which entails, *inter alia*, the refusal to be a *German Christian*. Barth would have wholeheartedly agreed with what Professor Jürgen Moltmann said to my Chinese friends in an interview from 2019 (which, incidentally, was recorded at his home when I happened to be presenting on Augustine at the nearby Tübingen *Stift*): "I am not a German Christian, but a Christian in Germany."[2]

In the footsteps of Barth, albeit without becoming a Barthian (which would have been against his own wish anyway), I, as a Christian in China, strive to honor both my Chinese and Taiwanese-Canadian identities. This is challenging, not only because my commitment to the Lordship of Christ forbids me to sing along with the nationalistic choir of worship in this part of the world, or anywhere in God's good creation for that matter, but also because of the temptation to deny and despise God's gift of nationhood to all peoples in the face of nationalistic idolatries and national sins. For a long time, I gave in to the temptation of being embittered by the thuggish wickedness of the nations in our world today.

As a neo-Calvinist, I found in Barth's theology a powerful source of encouragement and consolation in this sorry state of affairs. Barth, as a speculative theologian in the Anselmian tradition, consistently—more consistently than Anselm himself—refused to allow the philosophical tail to wag the theological dog, so to speak. This means that he did not allow the socio-political and cultural contexts of his time to dictate the terms of his theology.

---

1. Offener Brief Karl Barths, Bonn, April 17, 1932. In *GA* 35, 205. Translation mine.

2. The documentary was directed and produced by Christian filmmakers Xin Wang and Leilei Pan under the guidance of Professor Moltmann's former *Doktorsöhne*, Hong-Hsin Lin and Liang Hong. See https://v.youku.com/v_show/id_XNDIwNDY2OTAwNA==.html (last accessed September 3, 2021).

With his Christocentric doctrine of election, he repudiated every form of nationalistic idolatry, but affirmed nationhood as God's gift to all peoples in Jesus Christ. At the same time, Barth recognized human nature in the dimension of nationhood, as in every other dimension, as a determination by the flesh of Jesus Christ, in which the negation of sin in reprobation is sublated by God's gracious election. The church in every nation, per Barth, must recognize the particularities of the sins of her nation and repent for these sins in order to re-enact the gracious election that Christ has already accomplished once for all.

It serves well to remember that Barth's Christocentric reorientation of the doctrine of election was completed at the height of the Second World War. It was a time when the great British pianist Dame Myra Hess would perform the music of Bach, Mozart, Beethoven, and Schumann in the accompaniment of the sound of German bombshells dropped on the City of London. This served to remind her compatriots that the Allies were fighting not against a wicked people, but a wicked regime that hijacked a great nation. This was also the basic tone that the British government under both Neville Chamberlain and Winston Churchill tried to set for the struggles of the Allies against the Third Reich.

Barth would have basically agreed with this "noble" characterization of Germany as a *Kulturnation*, but as Carys Mosely rightly points out, this depiction of the German nation was too "simplistic" for Barth.[3] Barth affirmed Germany's cultural-nationhood as God's gift to the German people and to the world, but he also saw in its sinful edifice a *Nichtiges* that threatened to dissolve God's good creation. He insisted that no human individual can escape such national "edifice of error and conceit" apart from the Holy Spirit's re-enactment of the work of reconciliation accomplished in Jesus Christ.[4]

Barth's sophisticated view of German nationhood is reflected in a letter to French Protestants written in December 1939:

> The German people are not wicked as a people, are not at any rate more wicked than any other people. The idea that to-day they must be punished as a whole is an idea which is impossible both from a Christian and from a human point of view. But Hitler's National Socialism is most certainly the wicked expression of the extraordinary political stupidity, confusion, and helplessness of the German people.[5]

Despite the national edifice of sin and pride that Barth identified in the German people, however, he still strived to be a "good German" in his lifetime work as

---

3. Carys Moseley, *Nations and Nationalism in the Theology of Karl Barth* (Oxford: Oxford University Press, 2013), 146.

4. *Gottes Gnadenwahl*, 38.

5. Karl Barth, "First Letter to the French Protestants," in Karl Barth, *Letters to Great Britain from Switzerland*, ed. Alec Vidler (London: Sheldon Press, 1941), 36. Cited in Moseley, *Nations and Nationalism in the Theology of Karl Barth*, 146.

a theologian, even after his return to Switzerland in 1935. No nation, however depraved she may have become, can flee from the grace of Jesus Christ who has already triumphed over nothingness. This grace may existentially turn out to be her temporal punishment or even the termination of her existence, but the Christian is called not to pray for judgment, but for God's forgiveness even for Sodom, Gomorrah, and Nineveh.

I have to admit that for a long time, I was so engrossed in bitterness against the wickedness of earthly nations and regimes, that I neglected to pray Abraham's prayer for the sinful cities. This experience has led to profound admiration for Barth's theology on my part. From his letters, one can easily discern his anger and frustration in the face of Hitler's rise to power, not least in view of the fact that so many of his friends and colleagues, like Hirsch and Paul Althaus, came out one after another in support of the *Führer* as God's gift to the nation.

Still, Barth stood his ground and resisted the temptation to demonize the German nation. This is truly remarkable in view of my own experience. He consistently called for priestly intercession on the part of Christians in Germany—who refused to be German Christians—on behalf of the great yet sinful nation. In this fact alone, I believe, Barth has a lot to teach to Christians around a world torn apart by international conflicts of interests and values.

The venerable Dieter Borchmeyer, world-leading *Germanistiker*, in a lecture tour through China in 2018, highlighted the tensions between global and national identities amidst competing claims between globalism and nationalism in the European context. In the 2020 foreword to the published lectures, printed in Chinese, Professor Borchmeyer laments how in his home country the passion for German nationhood accompanying the 1989 *Mauerfall* has "dissipated" and come to be "spat upon" in our day.[6] "Authoritative politicians and intellectuals [in Germany] today repeatedly remind everyone that what is important is not the German identity, but the European."[7]

The question is, as Professor Borchmeyer rightly points out, "Can people really tear apart these two identities?"[8] Barth would have agreed with Professor Borchmeyer that treating the two identities as "antithetical" is

> quite unedifying ... When we travel to France or Italy, we first sense that the other party is French or Italian, and only thereafter do we perceive them as European. Frankly speaking, what we are primarily looking for and trying to experience in these countries is not their European-ness, but rather something that constitutes their own respective national auras; not something that we also possess, but rather the alterity that constitutes their differences from us. Europe

---

6. Dieter Borchmeyer, *Was heisst deutsche Musik?* [什么是德意志音乐], trans. Linjing Jiang [姜林静)] and Mingfeng Yu [余民峰] (Beijing: Commercial Press, 2020), 4. Translation mine henceforth.
7. Borchmeyer, *Was heisst deutsche Musik?*, 4.
8. Borchmeyer, *Was heisst deutsche Musik?*, 4.

is an abstract entity, and only when different national auras are given the room to become concrete will it be possible for a true Europe to emerge from the gradual development of historical progress. Only in the midst of differences between states, nations, and spirits will we be able to have a unified Europe.[9]

The problem is, on what "ontological"—to use the word in its broadest sense—ground may we speak of and hope for a genuinely *inter*-national unity-in-diversity achieved through historical progress? The speculative proposal given by the apparently dissonant symphony of Goethe, Schiller, Fichte, Novalis, the Schlegel brothers, Schleiermacher, Hegel, Schelling, Feuerbach, Heine, Marx, and Wagner, among others, as we shall see in this book, was one that ultimately and perhaps inevitably deified the German nation by an essentially pantheistic immanentization and secularization of the Christian doctrines of election and providence. Thomas Mann, who was ever critical of the nationalism reflected through Wagner's later works, did not do much to reverse or correct this ontology either, an ontology essentially composed of an anthropology elevated to the status of theology.

The European Anthem today still worships Schiller's *Götterfunken* through Beethoven's celebrated tune. The Wagnerian combination of universal Christian values with ancient Teutonic paganism has come to characterize the European ethos as a whole today, and not just the German nation. German nationalism has evolved into European nationalism under the guise of globalism. The mystical nationalism of early twentieth-century Germany has become the *Volksreligion* of the European "nation" of the early twenty-first century, only that this time the same idolatry has returned with a New Age twist. "*Er ist wieder da*": not only in the form of narrow-minded right-wing nationalism, but also in the form of seemingly open-minded left-wing globalism that tries to establish a global order by downplaying the particularities of the nations.

In view of this situation, I think Barth would have basically agreed with Professor Borchmeyer's proposal and fleshed it out with Christological content. From a Christian viewpoint, history is indeed teleological and progressive (*pace* Bultmann), and we should by all means strive to establish a unified world in which diversity may genuinely thrive. This history, however, must not be taken to be the sinful *Weltgeschichte* of Adamic hubris. It has to be understood as the history of Jesus Christ, the history in which God-in-and-for-Godself became God-for-us without ceasing to be God-in-and-for-Godself.

The nations are *one* important, though not *the* most central, dimension of the external basis of this history. The enactment of this history through the election of the community, the *una sancta ecclesia*, is *the* internal basis of both nationhood and global humanity. Amidst the sins and heresies manifested through both nationalism and globalism as expressions of our history *in Adamis*, Barth's theology has reminded me in profoundly personal ways that as a member of Christ's body, I am called, not least in my capacity as a professional theologian, but certainly

---

9. Borchmeyer, *Was heisst deutsche Musik?*, 4.

not in this capacity alone, to live and work as a witness for the redemptive history accomplished *in Christo*.

In the language of neo-Calvinism, but with a Barthian grammar: redemptive history is the internal basis of world-history, and world-history is the external basis of redemptive history. When the first Roman Imperator who assumed the divine title of Augustus made Virgil's *Aeneid* the official folklore of the Roman Empire, Jesus Christ was born in Bethlehem to bring to us the gospel that is the only true narrative of historical progress. Make no mistake: Christ was born in Bethlehem both under an imperial edict from Caesar Augustus and by the eternal decision of the triune God. There is, however, no balanced equilibrium between Christ and Caesar. There is only a path, an organic one, from Octavius to Jesus of Nazareth, which is the path from death to resurrection, from sin to regeneration, from unheeding deafness to faith. And he who inaugurated the kingdom of God on earth has taught us to pray the prayer that I pray I may always have the faith, hope, and love to pray: "Your kingdom come. Your will be done on earth as it is in heaven."

Shao Kai Tseng
Summer 2022, Shanghai

ABBREVIATIONS: WORKS BY KARL BARTH

Anselm: *Anselm: Fides Quaerens Intellectum, Anselm's Proof of the Existence of God in the Context of His Theological Scheme.* Trans. Ian Robertson. London: SCM, 1960.

CD: *The Church Dogmatics*, 12 Part-Volumes (I/1-IV/4). Eds. G. W. Bromiley and T. F. Torrance. Trans. G. W. Bromiley. Edinburgh: T&T Clark, 1956–75.

GA: *Karl Barth Gesamtausgabe*, 45 Volumes. Zurich: Theologischer Verlag Zürich, 1973–2008.

GD: *The Göttingen Dogmatics*, Vol. 1. Ed. Hannelotte Reiffen. Trans. G. W. Bromiley. Grand Rapids: Eerdmans, 1990.

Gottes Gnadenwahl: *Gottes Gnadenwahl*. Munich: Chr. Kaiser Verlag, 1936.

KD: *Die Kirchliche Dogmatik*, 12 Part-Volumes (I/1-IV/4). Zurich: Theologischer Verlag Zürich, 1980.

MD (*Münster Dogmatics*): *Die christliche Dogmatik im Entwurf, 1. Band: Die Lehre vom Worte Gottes, Prolegomena zur christlichen Dogmatik, 1927.* Zurich: Theologischer Verlag Zürich, 1982.

Protestant Theology: *Protestant Theology in the Nineteenth Century*. Trans. Brian Cozens and John Bowden. Grand Rapids: Eerdmans, 2002.

Romans II: *The Epistle to the Romans*, 1922 Edition. Trans. Edwyn Hoskyns. London: Oxford University Press, 1933.

INTRODUCTION

General Approach and Objectives

"Barth's Speculative Theology": A New Interpretative Model

This book is on the Trinity and election in the Christocentric phase of the theology of Karl Barth (1886–1968). Since the publication of Bruce McCormack's 1995 masterpiece, *Karl Barth's Critically Realistic Dialectical Theology: Its Genesis and Development 1909–1936*, the scholarly consensus has been by and large that Barth's Christocentric revision of the doctrine of election in 1936 marks, in one way or another, the beginning of the mature phase of his theology.[1] The present study is a re-examination of Barth's turn to Christocentrism in the hitherto untranslated 1936 *Gottes Gnadenwahl* and further developments up to the 1942 *CD* II/2 within a new interpretative framework that Sigurd Baark and I advanced independently of one another in 2018.[2]

The new interpretative model, which describes Barth as a "speculative" theologian (a term first adopted by Baark), makes two basic claims. First, the *Denkform* of Barth's mature theology is retrieved from the speculative tradition handed down from classical Latin theology to modern German idealism. Second, his innovative development of a basically Anselmian mode of speculation in the late 1920s and early 1930s constitutes an affirmation of the "unsublatable subjectivity" of the triune God against the anthropological, egocentric mode of speculation that culminated in G. W. F. Hegel (1770–1831).[3]

The "speculation" model of Barth interpretation was developed against a dominant paradigm that came to be described as "post-Kantian" in recent

---

1. Bruce McCormack, *Karl Barth's Critically Realistic Dialectical Theology* (Oxford: Clarendon Press, 1995), 455.
2. See Sigurd Baark, *The Affirmations of Reason: On Karl Barth's Speculative Theology* (Cham: Palgrave Macmillan, 2018). Also see my *Barth's Ontology of Sin and Grace: Variations on a Theme of Augustine* (London: Routledge, 2018).
3. A term coined by Baark. See Baark, *The Affirmations of Reason*, 256.

scholarship.⁴ McCormack's monumental work from 1995 represents the beginning of the dominance of this paradigm. In this work, he presents Barth as a theologian whose critical realism and dialectical *Denkform* find their intellectual origins in Marburg neo-Kantianism.

The central theological implication of this intellectual-biographical account is what McCormack in his 2021 *Humility of the Eternal Son* calls "Barth's 'rule.'"⁵ McCormack explains:

> Barth's "rule" is this: "statements about the divine modes of being antecedently in themselves cannot be different in content from those that are to be made about their reality in revelation." Taken seriously, this means at a minimum that no statements can be made about the immanent Trinity that do not find a firm and clear root in the economy. Even more: Barth's "rule" entails the claim that the immanent Trinity and the economic Trinity do not differ in content; that no metaphysical "gap may be introduced that would make the immanent Trinity to be somehow "more" than what is given to be known in the economy. What *is* permissible, I would say, is a quasi-transcendental method that asks, for example, what must God be in God's Self if it is true that Jesus is Lord?⁶

Here McCormack reads into a statement taken from *CD* I/1 a certain "quasi-transcendental" *Denkform* with supposed Marburg neo-Kantian origins. The statement in quotation marks that he calls "Barth's 'rule,'" however, is in fact a distorted paraphrase rather than a direct quote. The passage that McCormack references here states the very opposite view. What Barth himself says in this passage is:

> We cannot define the Father, the Son, and the Holy Ghost, i.e., we cannot delimit them the one from the other. We can only state that in revelation three who delimit themselves from one another are present, and if in our thinking we are not to go beyond revelation we must accept the fact that these three who delimit themselves from one another are antecedently a reality in God Himself.⁷

---

4. See Thomas Xutong Qu, "Kritischer musste Kants Kritik sein: Eine nachkantische Interpretation von Barths Beziehung zu Kant unter besonderer Berücksichtigung der Religionskritik Barths," in *Gottes Gegenwarten: Festschrift für Günter Thomas zum 60. Geburtstag*, ed. Markus Höfner and Benedikt Friedrich (Leipzig: Evangelische Verlagsanstalt, 2020), 53–68.

5. Bruce McCormack, *The Humility of the Eternal Son* (Cambridge: Cambridge University Press, 2021), 1.

6. McCormack, *The Humility of the Eternal Son*. Paraphrasing *CD* I/1, 479.

7. *CD* I/1, 479. Original: "wir müssen, wenn wir nicht über die Offenbarung hinausdenken wollen, dabei bleiben, daß diese drei sich selbst gegenseitig Abgrenzenden auch zuvor in Gott selber Wirklichkeit sind." *KD* I/1, 511.

McCormack's imposition of a "quasi-transcendental" *Denkform* on Barth, then, is not a fruit of faithful interpretation of Barth's texts. Rather, it is an attempt to fit a distorted picture of Barth's writings into McCormack's intellectual-biographical framework set forth in *Barth's Dialectical Theology*.

The thrust of McCormack's intellectual-biographical account of Barth is that Barth's so-called critical realism and dialectical theology first originated from Marburg neo-Kantianism, and that the epistemological presuppositions of (neo-) Kantianism continued to inform his thought through to the end of his career. Part and parcel of this intellectual-biographical account is a rejection of the received view up to the early 1990s, espoused most famously by Hans Urs von Balthasar and Thomas F. Torrance, that Barth's theology underwent a turn from dialectics to analogy in the late 1920s and early 1930s as a result of his discovery of Anselm's *fides quaerens intellectum* program.[8]

The post-Kantian paradigm, notwithstanding its immense contribution to the literature, has for the most part neglected the broader intellectual-historical context and lexical framework of Barth's writings. Its dismissal of his own acknowledgment of an Anselmian *Denkform* undergirding the *Church Dogmatics* has frustrated readers who insist on the primacy of the author's express intent in the text over secondary accounts of the author's intellectual biography. After all, Barth explicitly stated: "The real work that documents my conversion ... from the residue of a philosophical or anthropological ... grounding of Christian doctrine ... is ... my 1931 book on Anselm of Canterbury's proofs of the existence of God."[9]

The proposal that Baark and I advanced separately in 2018 does not constitute a naïve return to the Balthasar paradigm, which, in our view, does not sufficiently attend to the speculative heritage of Barth's basically Anselmian *Denkform*. Baark's work, as far as I am aware, offers the first intellectual-historical account that successfully explicates the German idealist background of Barth's appeal to Anselm. My own study painted a similar portrait by way of a lexical study of Barth's dialectical employment of the vocabularies of historic Latin theology and modern German philosophy, especially that of Hegel. In a related article, I demonstrated that Barth's mature theological ontology is of a largely Hegelian form and a basically Anselmian core.[10]

---

8. See Hans Urs von Balthasar, *The Theology of Karl Barth*, trans. Edward Oakes (San Francisco: Ignatius, 1992); Thomas F. Torrance, *Karl Barth: An Introduction to His Early Theology 1910–1931* (Edinburgh: T&T Clark, 1962).

9. See Karl Barth, "Parergon," *Evangelische Theologie* 8 (1948): 272. Quoted in Balthasar, *The Theology of Karl Barth*, 93. I address McCormack's treatment of Balthasar's quotation in chapter 2.

10. Published in German: Shao Kai Tseng, "Karl Barths aktualistische Ontologie: Ihre Substanzgrammatik des Seins und Prozessgrammatik des Werdens," *Neue Zeitschrift für Systematische Theologie und Religionsphilosophie* 60 (2019): 32–50. And in Chinese: "Karl Barth's Actualistic Ontology: A Dialectic of Process and Substance Grammars," *Logos and Pneuma: Chinese Journal of Theology* 52 (2020): 263–89. The shorter English version does

The matching results of our independent inquiries carry the implication that Barth was not simply the kind of "post-Kantian" thinker described in McCormack's 1995 game-changer. Barth was not primarily concerned with the problems to which Immanuel Kant (1724–1804) directly gave rise, nor did he rely primarily on some (neo-)Kantian critical realism or *Realdialektik* to tackle those problems. Rather, Barth engaged primarily with the speculative idolatry of German idealism, and appealed to Anselm to maintain against idealist speculation what Baark rightly describes as the "unsublatable subjectivity" of the triune God.

In the first two chapters of this study, I will first defend the speculation model against the post-Kantian paradigm with an intellectual-historical account of Barth's appeal to Anselm. It is through Hegel and the idealisms of the post-Kantian era, I will argue, that Barth retrieves and renovates Anselm's speculative *Denkform* in an attempt to overcome their challenges. Chapters 3–6 comprise lexical-exegetical and historical-analytical expositions of the basically Anselmian mode of speculation underlying Barth's Christocentric reorientation of his theology in 1936–42. Barth's struggles against the nationalistic dimension of idealist speculation will be a prominent feature of this study, which concludes with a chapter on Barth's doctrine of election and theology of nationhood.

Both Baark and I agree with McCormack's view that the Christocentric "doctrine of election," which Barth began to develop in 1936, marked "the culmination of Barth's development as a theologian."[11] While McCormack's account of the maturation of Barth's theology denies the importance that Barth himself attaches to *Anselm: Fides Quaerens Intellectum* (1931), however, I will argue that Barth's mature Christocentrism was indeed a full-fledged expression of his speculative theology.

In particular, I will demonstrate that Barth's emendatory use of Hegel's logic of mediation within a basically Anselmian *Denkform* entails a mediated—rather than immediate—identity between Jesus Christ and the electing God, and that Barth uses this *Denkform* to distinguish between God-in-and-for-Godself and God's self-determined being as God-for-us. Election is for Barth not merely a contingent exercise of God's will. Jesus Christ who *is* election in its subjectivity, objectivity, and activity *is* the secondary mode of God's absolute being, grounded in and made possible by the primary mode of God's absolute being qua Trinity. As both the *speculum Trinitatis* and *speculum electionis*, Jesus Christ is the very subject God who remains ever unsublated in his history of covenantal relationship with us. As Baark puts it most aptly: "The unsublatable subjectivity of God, wherein God remains sovereign in all modes of revelation, is an affirmation of the inner, triune life of God in a form suitable to be known by his creatures."[12]

---

not stress the speculative aspect of Barth's actualistic ontology: Shao Kai Tseng, "Barth on Actualistic Ontology," in *The Wiley-Blackwell Companion to Karl Barth*, ed. George Hunsinger and Keith Johnson (Oxford: Wiley-Blackwell, 2020), 739–51. I take my cue from George Hunsinger, *Reading Barth with Charity: A Hermeneutical Proposal* (Grand Rapids: Baker Academic, 2015), 136.

11. Baark, *The Affirmations of Reason*, 4.
12. Baark, *The Affirmations of Reason*, 236.

The Speculation Model: Questions Yet to Be Answered

Baark's 2018 monograph is to be credited as the first work that sets forth the intellectual-historical underpinnings of the speculation model of Barth interpretation. While my previous monograph resonated with Baark's work in our shared interpretative trajectory, I did not give an extended account of the history of ideas underlying the development of Barth's speculative theology.

Still, a number of key questions remain to be answered in Baark's work, if the basic intellectual historiography underlying our interpretative model is to be adequately established. Baark's narration of Barth's intellectual-historical background is limited to German idealism, and focuses only on three philosophers, namely, Kant, Fichte, and Hegel.[13] He presents Kant's critical philosophy and the speculative responses from Fichte and Hegel by in-depth analyses of the primary literature. An overall accurate picture of the German idealist background of Barth's speculative theology is painted thereby.

On important question that awaits an answer is: How did Barth himself interpret Kant, Fichte, and Hegel in the 1920s and 1930s? The best way to answer this question would be to compare the writings of the philosophers to *Protestant Theology in the Nineteenth Century* (first published in 1946), which consists of written lectures that Barth composed in the late 1920s and 1930s. Baark's presentation of German idealism, however, basically leaves *Protestant Theology* out of sight. He only discusses this work briefly in his discussion of the early dialectical theology of Barth and Eduard Thurneysen.[14]

Furthermore, how was Barth's understanding of German idealism shaped by its nineteenth-century *Rezeptionsgeschichte*? And how was Barth's own speculative theology in turn shaped by his reception of this *Rezeptionsgeschichte*? More specific questions would include: Which interpretation of Kant did Barth inherit—an empirical realist one or a phenomenalist one? What was Barth's understanding of the reception of Kant in later German idealism? And how does that shed light on his speculative program as a critical response to idealist speculation?

Another missing link yet to be established in Baark's account of Barth's German idealist background is the role of Descartes in modern speculative philosophy. As we shall see, there is a strong sense of urgency in Barth's writings to set the Anselmian mode of speculation apart from the Cartesian, which, on Barth's view, culminated in Hegel. To make sense of this fact, we must deal with a number of questions: How did popular German historiographies of ideas in the nineteenth century come to regard Anselm as the founder of modern speculative philosophy? How did nineteenth-century German historiographies come to interpret Anselm, Descartes, and Hegel as representatives of the same pantheistic tradition of speculative metaphysics in different historical periods? And what did all of this have to do with German Christianity as a mystical form of nationalism and nationalistic form of pantheism?

---

13. Baark, *The Affirmations of Reason*, 33–111.
14. Baark, *The Affirmations of Reason*, 115–18.

Finally, the last but perhaps most significant piece of the puzzle is Barth's Christocentric revision of the doctrine of election in 1936. As we saw, Baark acknowledges that "Barth's doctrine of election was the culmination of Barth's development as a theologian."[15] How the doctrine of election developed in 1936 fits into the larger picture of Barth's speculative theology is a question yet untapped in Baark's publications, and my own treatment of this topic has only appeared in the Chinese language so far.[16] This is one main task that I take up in this volume, in preparation of which I will attempt to answer the array of questions raised above in the first three chapters.

Barth's Speculative Theology: The Problems of Identity and Extension

In the sixth chapter of his monograph, Baark presents the very form of Barth's speculative theology.[17] There is again very little in this chapter—if anything—to quarrel with from my standpoint. The missing links in the intellectual-historiographical part of Baark's work, however, imply that there are still some important features of Barth's speculative *Denkform* that we have yet to attend to.

Central among these, I will argue in Chapter 2, are the themes of *speculative identity* and *speculative extension*. These are especially prominent in Barth's treatment of the Cartesian mode of speculation, which, as he saw it, culminated in Hegel.

As a note of explanation, the term "speculation" originated from *speculum*, the Latin for "mirror." This Latin word also carries the extended meanings of "reflected image" and "copy." In the Western theological tradition, "speculative theology" is a mode of theologizing that treats God's work(s) as analogical reflections of God's essence.

It has escaped the notice of most experts in the field that Barth explicitly characterizes his own *credo ut intelligam* program as "speculative."[18] He identifies two diametrically opposites modes of speculation, namely, the Cartesian and the Anselmian. Cartesian metaphysics posits an *immediate identity* between *my* thinking (*cogito*) and *my* being (*sum*) in connection with a *speculative identity* (i.e., ontological analogy) between God's being and *my* conception of God. Faith in these identities serves as the starting point of Descartes's *credo ut intelligam* program. The deficiency of *my* thinking and *my* being is for Descartes a mirror image—an ontic *speculative extension*—of the perfection of God, allowing for noetic speculative extensions from the human intellect to God's knowledge of all things, thus attaining to what the venerated Kant scholar Henry Allison calls

---

15. Baark, *The Affirmations of Reason*, 4.

16. My treatment of this topic has only been published in Chinese so far: Shao Kai Tseng, "The Christocentric Reorientation of Karl Barth's Actualistic Ontology in Gottes Gnadenwahl (1936)," *Sino-Christian Studies* 31 (2021): 149–90.

17. Baark, *The Affirmations of Reason*, 171–229.

18. *Anselm*, 167.

a "putative ... God's-eye view of things."[19] What this implies—perhaps against Descartes's own intent—is, according to Barth, that divine nature is no more than the perfection of human attributes. The essence of Cartesian theology, on Barth's view, is anthropology; the Cartesian god is but a Feuerbachian projection.

Put another way, what Barth seeks to repudiate is the rationalist and idealist notion of some innate idea of divinity in creatures as an ontic speculative extension of God's essence that allows for noetic extension from creatures to God. For Barth, *a priori* concepts such as infinitude, eternality, immutability, and being serve to facilitate our *understanding* of God's revelation, but they do not reveal God to us. If we try to fit God into these *a priori* concepts and categories, then we fall into Feuerbach's charge of idolatry. Knowledge of God through revelation sheds light on and explicates these concepts for us. These concepts do not reveal God to us—they are not speculative extensions of God's being.

As Barth sees it, what went wrong with the Cartesian mode of speculation that culminated in Hegel is the philosophical presupposition of the *conceivability* of God, that is, the *speculative identity* between God and human conceptions of divinity. Anselmian speculation is, per Barth, diametrically opposed to Cartesian speculation. Anselm does not try to fit God into the human concept of infinite being. Rather, Anselm proceeds from faith in the God self-revealed to the church in Scripture, and tries to explicate the concept of infinite being in light of knowledge of God given through the *analogia fidei*. Anselm's God cannot be reduced to the noetic speculative extension of a human concept, and his conception of infinite being cannot be elevated to the status of an ontic speculative extension of God's essence.

In the form of a prayer, Anselm declares that God is *inconceivable*: "Therefore, O Lord, thou art not only that than which a greater cannot be conceived, but *thou art a being greater than can be conceived*."[20] Barth comments on this passage: "God is He than whom no greater can be conceived. But an inconceivable is, as such, conceivable. If it were not identical with God, then it would be a greater than God. Therefore, since no greater than He can be conceived, God is Himself the inconceivable (*Prosl.* 15)."[21]

Faith in some speculative identity (i.e., a reflected identity between the original and the mirror image, so to speak), of course, is necessary as the starting point of any *Denkform* properly described as "speculative." Barth allows no room for faith in any self-identity within the creature, but he has to accept some immediate self-identity and mediated speculative identity as his theological point of departure. For Barth, immediate self-identity is to be found in the *I AM* alone as being-itself, *ipsum esse*. More concretely: the immediate identity of subject, object,

---

19. Henry Allison, *Kant's Transcendental Idealism: An Interpretation and Defense* (New Haven: Yale University Press, 2004), xvi–xvii.

20. Anselm of Canterbury, *Proslogion*, in *St. Anselm: Basic Writings*, trans. Sidney Norton Deane (Chicago: Open Court, 1962), 68.

21. *CD* I/1, 185.

and act is to be found in the immanent Trinity alone, which Barth calls God's primary absoluteness (see Chapters 3 and 5). This identity on its own, however, is insufficient for the establishment of human knowledge of God.

There has to be a speculative identity and extension—a mirror image as it were—through which the creature may contemplate God. On the Anselmian principle of divine inconceivability, Barth insists that this speculative identity is not between God's being and any human conception of God. Rather, the speculative extension is from God's primary absoluteness *a se* to God's secondary mode of absolute being *in Christo* and *pro me*, in which God remains unsublated as the subject God. This extension constitutes the mediated identity between *Deus absconditus* and *Deus revelatus*, that is, the subject and being of God in the modes of aseity and promeity.

Barth's basically Anselmian mode of speculation, in other words, posits two self-identities. The first is the immediate identity between being and act, namely, God's essence and *opera ad intra* qua Trinity. The second is the speculative identity between God's being-in-act *ad intra* and God's being in the act of revelation *ad extra*.

One problem that Barth had to overcome in adopting this basically Anselmian *Denkform* is the problem of the image of God as speculative extension. In *Monologion*, Anselm, adopting Augustine's analogical notion of the *imago* or *speculum Trinitatis*, asserts that "if the mind itself alone among all created beings is capable of remembering and conceiving of and loving itself," then it proves itself to be "the true image of that being which, through its memory and intelligence and love, is united in an ineffable Trinity."[22]

This rendition of the human mind as a speculative image of God's very triune essence, as Barth sees it, stands in sharp tension with Anselm's later assertion in *Proslogion* that God is greater than can be conceived. Barth acknowledges that this is not necessarily an irresolvable contradiction and in fact sets out to resolve it in *CD* II/1.

In any case, speculative extension is a *sine qua non* for human contemplation of God. If no creature can be described as *imago Dei* in any sense whatsoever, then there can be no human knowledge of God at all. This is a problem that remains to be resolved in Anselm. Anselm could not identify that image except in something within the human mind that appears analogous to God's triune essence. In doing so, however, he would risk contradicting his own axiom of divine inconceivability.

Barth came to be aware of this problem as early as *CD* I/1, where he states in a section on the *vestigium Trinitatis* that "no matter how pleasing and credible it seems at first in the words of an Anselm," the

> moment it is taken seriously it leads plainly and ineluctably into an ambivalent sphere in which in a trice, even with the best will in the world, we are no longer

---

22. Anselm of Canterbury, *Monologium*, in *St. Anselm: Basic Writings*, trans. Sidney Norton Deane (Chicago: Open Court, 1962) 132.

speaking of the God of whom we want to speak and whose traces we meant to find but of some principle of the world or humanity, of some alien God. The original intention was to speak of God's revelation. But what happened was talk about the world and man, and this talk, understood as talk about God's revelation, necessarily wound up by being talk against God's revelation.[23]

In I/1, Barth had only spotted the problem, but he did not find a solution yet. His Christocentric reorientation of the doctrine of election was the final step that he took in revising the *basically* Anselmian program that he adopted. I say "basically," because he did not adopt this program *tout court*. At least as early as I/1, he had come to see the need to flesh out this program Christologically.

In *Gottes Gnadenwahl*, Barth exploits the full meaning of the historic expression of Christ as "*speculum praedestinationis*."[24] No human essence or thinking can in and of itself serve as the speculative image or extension of the triune God who is unknowable *per essentiam*. Christ alone is the *speculum Trinitatis*. In *CD* III/1, Barth speaks of the correspondence or analogy (*Entsprechung*) between God's primary and secondary absoluteness in terms of an "*analogia relationis*."[25]

Because Christ is very human and fully human in his historical agency, not as an appearance (*Schein*) of the divine but as very God and fully God, the speculative self-extension of God in the act of election allows for our speculative (i.e., mediated and reflected) knowledge of God. The mediacy of this speculative knowledge is twofold. Election as a secondary mode of God's absolute being is the mirror of God's primary absoluteness *ad intra*, the *speculum Trinitatis*, and the enacted history of the incarnation is the mirror of God's secondary absoluteness, the *speculum electionis*.

Put another way, there is an immediate identity between act and essence in God's triune being *ad intra*, to which the mediated identity between Jesus Christ and the electing God corresponds. Knowledge of the history of Jesus Christ mediates to us knowledge of God's eternal election. Knowledge of election, in turn, mediates to us knowledge of the triune God who is unknowable *per essentiam*. Every step of the way in the process of revelation, the *speculum Dei* is none other than Jesus Christ who is and never ceases to be the very unsublatable subject God.

The Christocentric doctrine of election, in other words, allows Barth to identify none other than Jesus Christ as the *imago Dei*, for Christ is both the *speculum Trinitatis* and *speculum electionis*. It was Barth's speculative theology that demanded the Christological revision of the doctrine of election. Conversely, it was his Christological doctrine of election that marked the completion of his basically Anselmian program and of his Copernican revolution against Cartesian-Hegelian speculation.

---

23. *CD* I/1, 344.
24. *Gottes Gnadenwahl*, 49.
25. *CD* III/1, 373.

Overview of the Study

Chapter 1

The first chapter of this study offers a survey and assessment of received paradigms in Barth studies, and discusses the strengths and weaknesses of McCormack's dominating post-Kantian model. One of McCormack's most significant contributions is his accentuation of the post-Kantian background of Barth's theological development, which also happens to be at the same time its Achilles' heel.

By "post-Kantian," I have in mind a specific intellectual-historical description of the nineteenth century in European thought and culture as an era that sought to respond to Kant's challenges and/or complete his philosophical project by accepting fundamental philosophical ideas and principles variously attributed to him. This era is characterized by a distinctively modern consciousnesses of historical progress. Karl Ameriks's authoritative narration describes the modern "historical turn" in two stages, namely, "a stage-setting Kantian prehistory," followed by the "early post-Kantian 'founders' era.'"[26] According to this view, Kant's critical philosophy, especially the difficult doctrine of transcendental idealism, played a crucial role in providing the intellectual-historical conditions for the rise of modern historical consciousness in the generations of Johann Gottlieb Fichte (1762–1814), Friedrich Schleiermacher (1768–1834), Friedrich Schelling (1775–1854), Hegel, and Karl Marx (1818–83).

McCormack's characterization of Barth as a "modern" theologian echoes this description of modernity as "post-Kantian." For McCormack, "it was the rise of 'historical consciousness'—by which ... [he] mean[s] the awareness that all human thinking is conditioned by historical (and cultural) location—that was most basic to the emergence of what we tend to think of as 'modern' theology today."[27] The "first" of the "most significant preconditions necessary for the emergence of historical consciousness as a culturewide phenomenon in Germany," McCormack explains, is "Kant's limitation of what may be known by the theoretical reason in phenomenal reality."[28]

It is of course difficult to quarrel with this account of Kant's importance. However, the description of the modern era as "post-Kantian" sometimes runs the danger of reductionism and, in McCormack's case, of underestimating what Ameriks calls the "founders' era." It carries a strong tendency to portray "modern"

---

26. Karl Ameriks, *Kant and the Historical Turn: Philosophy as Critical Interpretation* (Oxford: Oxford University Press, 2006), 15.

27. Bruce McCormack, *Orthodox and Modern: Studies in the Theology of Karl Barth* (Grand Rapids: Baker, 2008), 10–11.

28. McCormack, *Orthodox and Modern*, 11.

thinkers, Barth included, as doing little more than attempting to "overcome Kant by means of Kant; not retreating behind him and seeking to go around him."[29]

Johannes Zachhuber has demonstrated that the turn to history in nineteenth-century German philosophy was much more than merely a reaction to Kant's philosophy. The Enlightenment principle of historical progress featured prominently in, say, the writings of Gotthold Lessing (1729–81) and Johann Gottfried Herder (1744–1803) as well.[30] Zachhuber's masterful narration of the development of theology as a science in the nineteenth century powerfully cautions us against understanding modern historical consciousness through the singular lens of Kantian philosophy.

In fact, it was almost a consensus among German-speaking scholars of Barth's generation that nineteenth-century views of historical progress arose from intellectually diverse developments of broad Enlightenment principles. One famous example of this intellectual-historical understanding is found in the ballyhooed volume by Karl Löwith (1897–1973), *From Hegel to Nietzsche: The Revolution in Nineteenth-Century Thought*, written in Japan in 1939 while in exile from Germany, and eventually published in Switzerland in 1941.[31]

If there was a reductionistic tendency among Christian thinkers of the generation of Barth and Löwith, it was to blame the rise of German nationalism and nationalisms across Europe on a certain view of historical destiny for which Hegel was chiefly responsible. Löwith describes Hegel's understanding of historical "progress directed toward a final elaboration and consummation of the established principle of the whole course of history" as largely a result of "reinterpreting" through "Enlightenment" categories "the theological tradition according to which" history is determined by God's purpose in election and providence.[32]

Barth, too, famously stated that "proper theology begins just at the point where the difficulties" of Hegel's idea of divine-human identity "disclosed by Strauss and Feuerbach are seen and then laughed at."[33] The final obstacle to "proper theology," for Barth, was not Kant, but Hegel. Hegel, on Barth's (mis)interpretation, represented the culmination of "Kant's transcendentalism."[34] McCormack's narrow focus on the (neo-)Kantian origins of Barth's theology has exhibited a striking neglect of the significance that Barth attaches to Hegel.

---

29. Bruce McCormack, *Karl Barth's Critically Realistic Dialectical Theology* (Oxford: Clarendon, 1995), 465.
30. See Johannes Zachhuber, *Theology as Science in Nineteenth-Century Germany* (Oxford: Oxford University Press, 2013), 7–9.
31. Karl Löwith, *From Hegel to Nietzsche: The Revolution in Nineteenth-Century Thought*, trans. David Green (New York: Columbia University Press, 1991).
32. Karl Löwith, *Meaning in History* (Chicago: University of Chicago Press, 1949), 60.
33. *Protestant Theology*, 554.
34. *Protestant Theology*, 379.

Barth explicitly states the view that Hegel, rather than Kant, represents the pinnacle of the distinctively modern difficulty that Christian theologians must overcome.

> It is possible to bypass Fichte and Schelling, but it is as impossible to pass by Hegel as it is to pass by Kant. And the promissory nature of the truth Hegel enunciated and the ease with which it lends itself to equalization will perhaps be even greater than in the case of Kant for someone who, as a theologian, must finally say "No" to Hegel.[35]

Of course, I freely acknowledge that Barth's intellectual-historical account of nineteenth-century Protestant theology carries some serious flaws. His misinterpretation of Kant's transcendental idealism as a phenomenalistic theory is a topic I discuss in the next chapter. His basically pantheistic interpretation of Hegel is also debatable. The way he sustains his reading is easily refuted by contemporary scholars like, say, Charles Taylor and Michael Rosen.[36] However, in the present study, I am not interested in evaluating Barth's interpretation of other thinkers. What I am interested in is how his own account of the history of ideas came to shape his development as a theologian.

This brings us to the salient point of the first chapter. McCormack's portrayal of the post-Kantian Barth is a Barth who was informed at once by Marburg neo-Kantianism and Kant's own philosophy. Kant's express intention in developing the doctrine of transcendental idealism was to safeguard empirical realism. He explicitly rejected phenomenalistic, two-object interpretations of his account of the thing-in-itself and its appearance. McCormack recognizes all of this about Kant, and interprets Kant as an empirical realist.

The problem is that Barth holds to a two-object interpretation of Kant, and yet McCormack imposes the empirical realist Kant on Barth. What is worse, McCormack is emphatic that Barth's dialectical *Denkform*, including his actualism—what McCormack deems to be *the* reigning principle of Barth's theological ontology—originated from Marburg neo-Kantianism. This is deeply problematic, precisely because the Marburg neo-Kantians, as McCormack himself acknowledges, explicitly rejected Kant's empirical realism and developed a highly idealistic and phenomenalistic version of Kantianism.

In other words, McCormack contradicts himself by claiming that Barth's theology has its origins in (1) an empirically realistic form of Kantianism and (2) the phenomenalistic version of Kantianism espoused by his Marburg teachers. Furthermore, McCormack's claim that the early Barth re-appropriated

---

35. *Protestant Theology*, 382–3.
36. For Barth's take on Hegel's philosophy of ultimate divine-human identity, see *Protestant Theology*, 370–407. Cf. Charles Taylor, *Hegel and Modern Society* (Cambridge: Cambridge University Press, 1979); Michael Rosen, *Hegel's Dialectic and Its Criticism* (Cambridge: Cambridge University Press, 1982).

Kant's empirical realism contradicts the fact that Barth adopted a two-object interpretation of Kant's transcendental idealism.

The fact is that Barth himself interpreted Kant as a phenomenalist thinker, and he rejected what he saw as Kant's subjective idealism. Therewith, Barth also rejected the idealistic rendition of Kantian philosophy that he learned from his Marburg teachers. To impose either Kant's own empirical realism or the positivistic phenomenalism of the Marburg school on Barth would amount to a contradiction to Barth's own account of his intellectual-historical background. Yet, McCormack imposes both of these on Barth, and so his paradigm not only misconstrues Barth's intentions, but is also inevitably inconsistent with itself.

Chapter 2

My refutation of McCormack's intellectual-biographical and intellectual-historical paradigm in Chapter 1 serves to prepare for my defense of the "speculation" model of Barth interpretation. I realize that the characterization of Barth as a "speculative" theologian needs to be defended, not least because of his express aversion to the term.

In Chapter 2, I will offer an intellectual-historical defense of the proposal to describe Barth's *fides quaerens intellectum* program as "speculative." Implicit in this description is a rejection of the various proposals to interpret Barth's theological *Denkform* as "transcendental," "critically realistic," or "dialectical" in any (neo-) Kantian sense.

As explained earlier, the term "speculation" originated from the Latin for "mirror" (*speculum*: a word that can denote other things in different contexts). This Latin word carries the extended meaning of "imitation" or "likeness," as in a mirror image. Sometimes it is synonymous with *imago*, which is employed in the speculative tradition to refer to the object that is reflected as a copy of the original, so to speak.

In the Western theological tradition, "speculation" refers to a mode of theologizing that honors the principle of God's unknowability *per essentiam*. The finite intellect of creatures cannot contain the infinite Creator. This is expressed most succinctly by the core statement of the *extra Calvinisticum* in the Reformed tradition: *finitum non capax infiniti*. God's self-revelation to the creature is like a mirror image of God's essence. In principle, human knowledge of God does not correspond immediately to God's essence (although the various proposals of analogical theology often tend to violate this principle). Human conceptions of God can only be analogous to the *speculum* of God's essence given in revelation. These conceptions cannot be univocal with God's essential being or self-knowledge. Human beings can only *after-think* (*nachdenken*) God's self-revelation within the creaturely realm and *reflect* on God's essence, in such a way that human knowledge of God can become *analogical* to God's self-knowledge.

On Barth's account, speculative theology took an anthropological turn in Descartes, and this anthropocentric mode of speculation culminated in Hegel. I will offer an analysis of Barth's intellectual-historical narrative in light of what

I like to call a "philosophical folklore" that accompanied the rise of Germany's mystical nationalism.

Descartes's faith, according to Barth, is in the immediate self-identity between the thinking (*cogito*) and essence (*sum*) of the rational ego, and in the speculative identity between God's essence and the human conception of perfect being. I will discuss how Kant dismantled Descartes's *cogito ergo sum* and ontological proof of God's existence, and the reception of and responses to Kant's critique in some representatives of the major intellectual movements in Germany, including Friedrich Schiller, Novalis, Johann Gottlieb Fichte, Friedrich Schleiermacher, G. W. F. Hegel, and others.

This intellectual history will be presented in three dimensions in an intertwined manner. First, I will offer my own readings of the primary literature, so as to try, to the best of my ability, to allow the players in this history to speak for themselves. Second, I will present the *Rezeptionsgeschichte* of some of these players in the nineteenth century. This includes, for example, how Fichte understood and reacted to Kant's critique of Descartes; how Hegel understood Kant to be an antimetaphysical philosopher, and how Hegel responded to and corrected Fichte's attempt to restore Cartesian speculation after Kant; and how this history came to be narrated in the generation of Hegel's students up to the early twentieth century through popular works like Heinrich Heine's *Zur Geschichte der Religion und Philosophie in Deutschland*.

Third, I will examine Barth's understanding of this intellectual history by looking into how his own account of the history reflects the influences of popular nineteenth-century historiographies of ideas and how he formed his own interpretations of the particular thinkers in this history. In a nutshell, Barth understood what he took to be Kant's phenomenalistic "transcendentalism" as demanding a modern renovation of Cartesian speculation. Kant himself, per Barth, did not begin the project of restoring speculative metaphysics. On Barth's view, the post-Kantian revival of the Cartesian mode of theological speculation culminated in Hegel.

Hegel is distinctively modern and post-Kantian in that he rejected the notion of immediate self-identity. All identities, per Hegel, are mediated and speculative. Hegel follows Descartes in asserting a speculative identity between God and human reason, but Hegel rejects both the Cartesian postulation of immediate identity between *cogito* and *sum* and the classical Christian doctrine of immediate self-identity in the triune Godhead. God, per Hegel, determines Godself as God through a process of self-sublation and self-reconciliation. That is, God becomes determinate as God by being reconciled to that which is not God. The subject and attributes of God are not immediately identical. The attributes of God in relation to the world determine what God is. The subject (God) does not determine the predicates (e.g., "is love," "is being," "is absolute," etc.). Rather, the predicates determine the subject. Thus, instead of saying "God is absolute," for instance, Hegel would say, "the absolute is God."

It was in Anselm, I will argue, that Barth found the antidote to the subject-predicate reversal in Hegelian speculation. Anselm describes God not only as that greater than which nothing can be conceived. Anselm is emphatic that God is greater than can be conceived. That is, God cannot be reduced to or identified with—immediately or speculatively—a rational *Begriff*. With Anselm and against Descartes and Hegel, Barth insists that the speculative identity giving rise to knowledge of God is the identity between God-in-and-for-Godself and God-for-us. On this basis, Barth is emphatic against Hegel that there is indeed an immediate self-identity revealed to us in Jesus Christ, namely, the identity between the subject, object, and act of love in freedom in God's triune Godhead. Speculative theology is genuinely theological only if the mirror, so to speak, reflects to us a true image of the original. This means that in becoming God-for-us, the same subject God does not cease to be the subject God in-and-for-Godself. In Hegelian language: God is unsublatably absolute in God's being-in-and-for-Godself, and the only way for God to be known to creatures is to become God-for-us without ceasing to be God-in-and-for-Godself.

Chapter 3

If the previous chapters serve to sketch the intellectual-historical background of Barth's theology, then the third chapter of this study is intended to illuminate the interpretative framework that I adopt in the ensuing chapters. In particular, I will focus on what has in recent Anglophone scholarship come to be called Barth's "actualistic ontology."

George Hunsinger helpfully reminds us that Barth rejects ontology in the strict sense of the term as a branch of metaphysics in the continental philosophical tradition. What Barth rejects is the Cartesian-Hegelian mode of speculation, which finds its starting point in philosophical preconceptions of the idea of divinity and proceeds to impose this abstract idea on God. Instead of altogether rejecting the study of the idea of being, however, Barth, in the footsteps of Anselm, wants to subjugate this intellectual inquiry to a starting point in faith in the Word of God— in the *regula fidei*. What Barth rejects, in other words, is the status of ontology as *praeambula fidei*, rather than the very study of being. In the present work, then, I will speak of Barth's "ontology" only in the extended meaning of the term to refer to any "general area of action, inquiry, or interest" that addresses the notion of being.[37]

My discussions will center on the notion of "being-in-act" (*Sein in der Tat*). The goal of this chapter is to explicate its grammars through an examination of key terms like "determination" (*Bestimmung*), "nature" (*Natur*), "essence" (*Wesen*), and "being" (*Sein/Dasein*), so as to illuminate the interpretive framework with which I proceed to comment on Barth's turn to Christocentrism in the subsequent chapter.

I will show that Barth is in partial agreement with Hegel against what has in recent scholarship come to be called the "substantialist" (a term I use with

---

37. See Hunsinger, *Reading Barth with Charity*, 2.

hesitation: see Chapter 3) tradition, that God is a living subject rather than abstract substance. God's subjectivity, however, is for Barth "unsublatable."

Here I borrow an originally Hegelian term that Baark employs in his reading of Barth, which I already alluded to earlier. "Sublation" is a term that Barth himself frequently uses, and is a keyword that will recur throughout this study. This word is one standard English translation of "*Aufhebung*." The German verb *heben* means "to lift," and *aufheben* in its ordinary usage can mean either "to abrogate" or "to elevate." Hegel combines both denotations to refer to the dialectical negation of the abstract moment of logic, not for the purpose of annihilating it, but rather to elevate it to the third moment that he characterizes as "positively rational."[38] Spirit, per Hegel, must undergo a process of sublation through the moment of objectivity (being-for-itself: *Für-sich-Sein*) in order to become the absolute subject (being-in-and-for-itself: *An-und-für-sich-Sein*).

Against Hegel, Barth insists that the subjectivity of the triune God in God's being-in-and-for-Godself is unsublatable. Barth's retainment of the substance grammar of the Latin tradition shows that he has dialectically incorporated classical theology, and so a certain concept of substance, into his actualistic ontology along with his adoption of Hegel's insights.

This ontology is regulated by the grammar of a basically Chalcedonian dialectic: becoming is an addition to, rather than a subtraction or alteration of essential being. In the case of Barth's theological ontology, this dialectic stands in sharp contrast to Hegel's logical trinity of spirit *an-sich*, *für-sich*, and *an-und-für-sich*. According to Barth, God-in-and-for-Godself became God-for-us without ever ceasing to be God-in-and-for-Godself.

Chapter 4

In Chapter 4, I will unpack some important implications of Barth's Christocentric revision of his speculative theology in 1936, paying close attention to his critical employment of German idealist vocabularies. This ontology, I will argue, is a corrective to both the traditional-metaphysical doctrines formulated by his predecessors in the Latin theological tradition and in the two major strands of modern theology in the German-speaking world, namely, the speculative metaphysics of nineteenth-century idealism and the historical-positivist study of theology and religion in the (neo-)Kantian school(s). The central thesis of this chapter is that the major factor leading to the Christocentric revision of Barth's doctrine of election in 1936 was the theologian's basically Anselmian mode of theological speculation.

As we saw earlier, Barth rejected the Augustinian-Anselmian understanding of the human mind as a *speculum Trinitatis*. In the early 1930s, he already began to contend that Christ alone is the speculative extension of God's essence, but

---

38. See G. W. F. Hegel, *The Encyclopaedia of Logic*, trans. T. F. Geraets, W. A. Suchting, and H. S. Harris (Indianapolis: Hackett, 1991), 125.

his actualistic doctrine of election at the time, which only allowed him to speak of God's revelation-in-act but not being-in-act, was inadequate to sustain a thoroughly Christocentric mode of speculative theologizing.

The Christocentric doctrine of election developed in 1936 allowed Barth to speak of God as being-in-act, primarily as the triune God and secondarily as the electing God. He did not wait until 1942 to identify Jesus Christ as the electing God. The speculative identity between Jesus Christ and the triune God allows us to, in Baark's words, know God by reflective after-thinking (*Nachdenken*) of God's "unsublatable subjectivity."[39]

Barth's seminal insistence upon God's unsublatable subjectivity was already explicit in the early 1920s, when his method of *Nachdenken* as a corollary thereof, later explicated in fuller detail in his famous 1931 book on Anselm, was also in place. Yet, as we shall see in Chapters 3 and 4, his methodological starting-point in the historical actuality of God's works and his reticence to speak of the incarnation as an eternal relation during the Göttingen-Münster-Bonn periods meant that he could not consistently maintain the immutability God's absolute subjectivity in-and-for-Godself in the temporal events of election and incarnation.

One major factor leading to Barth's 1936 Christocentric reorientation of his speculative theology was his attempt to steer clear of the anthropological mode of speculation of nineteenth-century German idealism. Barth's key maneuver was, to use an often quoted phrase from the late John Webster, to refocus all his theological reflections on "an almost ruthless particularity, a concentration of the imagination on one point and one point only: the name of Jesus."[40] The Christocentric revision of the doctrine of election in *Gottes Gnadenwahl*, then, constitutes a particularistic renovation of Barth's actualistic ontology to safeguard God's unsublatable subjectivity in the process of God's self-revelation in Jesus Christ. This revision also resolves some contradictions—without resolving the tensions—between the objectivist and actualistic dimensions of Barth's theology from the 1920s up to the early 1930s. The key insight that Barth develops in *Gottes Gnadenwahl*, I will argue, is that the history of the incarnation as *speculum electionis* is speculatively identical with God's eternal election, because Jesus Christ is the same subject God in both God's eternal self-determination to be *pro nobis* and the history of God's flesh-becoming.

Chapter 5

Chapter 5 focuses on one of the best known yet controversial passages of the *Church Dogmatics*, namely, II/1 (1940), §28, "The Being of God as the One who Loves in Freedom." In this chapter Barth speaks of two modes of God's being in the Hegelian language of the absolute, defined as the unity of subjectivity and objectivity in the moment of activity. God is free and absolute in the primary sense

---

39. Baark, *The Affirmations of Reason*, 256.
40. John Webster, *Karl Barth* (New York: Continuum, 2004), 62.

that as the Trinity, God is the subject, object, and act of love in-and-for-Godself. This primary absoluteness of God grounds and makes possible God's secondary absoluteness, in which God, in the person of Jesus Christ, is the subject, object, and act of God's love-in-freedom in an *ad extra interna* mode of being.

In this discourse Barth is fleshing out a characteristically post-Kantian view of freedom Christologically. This view shared among Kant and later German idealists, per Michael Rosen, contends "that freedom involves the emancipation from arbitrariness, and that 'arbitrariness' can consist in the purely contingent exercise of will ('*Willkür*') as well as in being subject to exogenous causal forces."[41] Barth insists that God is free in the primary absoluteness of God's love in that God does not need an other to determine or cause God to be God, and that God's self-determination to enter into a secondary mode of absolute being is perfectly grounded in and made possible by the absoluteness of God's triune essence. God's self-determination to be God-for-us, in other words, is not by a contingent exercise of the power of choice, but rather corresponds perfectly to God's *ad intra* essence as the one who loves in absolute freedom.

It is in this discourse from §28 that we find the most dogmatic statement of Barth's mature understanding of God's being-in-act. It is also here that we find Barth unequivocally setting forth the historic notion of the immanent Trinity as God's eternally unsublatable essence. What Hunsinger calls the "Hegelian moment" (the moment of becoming—of histories, activities, decisions, relationships, and sublations) and the "Anselmian moment" (the moment of being—of eternal essence, immutability, impassibility, and unsublatability) converge in this single paragraph in a densely dialectical manner.

The tension between these two moments in §28 is so intense, that proponents of revisionist Barth interpretation have come to claim that the Swiss theologian is simply at odds with himself in teaching the aseity of the immanent Trinity on one hand and the freedom of God in Jesus Christ on the other.[42] They deem it

---

41. Michael Rosen, *The Shadow of God: Kant, Hegel, and the Passage from Heaven to History* (Harvard: Harvard University Press, 2022), 23.

42. McCormack rejects the label of "revisionism." He argues that his interpretation of Barth is not revisionary, but rather traditional, in that it boasts of a respectable pedigree handed down from luminaries like Eberhard Jüngel in German scholarship. See Bruce McCormack, "Election and the Trinity: Theses in Response to George Hunsinger," *Scottish Journal of Theology* 63 (2010): 204. Also see Paul Nimmo, *Being in Action: The Theological Shape of Barth's Ethical Vision* (London: T&T Clark, 2007), 3–6. McCormack's argument here can be rather surprising to Anglophone readers who were introduced to Jüngel's work on Barth through John Webster, who comments: "Jüngel is insistent that 'becoming' is a function of God, not vice versa." John Webster, "Translator's Introduction," in Eberhard Jüngel, *God's Being Is in Becoming: The Trinitarian Being of God in the Theology of Karl Barth*, trans. John Webster (Grand Rapids: Eerdmans, 2001), xix. Jüngel himself is unequivocal that in Barth's theological ontology, God's triune essence *ad intra* is the ground and basis

necessary to "register a critical correction" against this "inconsistency in Barth's thought" on the basis of his own actualistic ontology.[43] Although the text itself—at least within the scope of §28—evinces no such inconsistency, an intellectual-biographical paradigm that identifies Barth as a post-Kantian thinker whose dialectical method originated from a neo-Kantian *Realdialektik* inevitably gives rise to an understanding of Barth's actualism as an ontology that is altogether at odds with the Anselmian moment governing his mature theology. This selectively post-Kantian interpretation, moreover, overlooks how Barth critically adopted the post-Kantian view of freedom as emancipation from arbitrariness.

Contra the post-Kantian reading, I will suggest in Chapter 5 that if *CD* §28 is interpreted in light of the Christocentric actualism developed in *Gottes Gnadenwahl*—as it is explicated within the interpretative framework set forth in Chapter 3—then the alleged inconsistency between Barth's doctrines of election and the Trinity easily dissipates. Jesus Christ, per *Gottes Gnadenwahl*, is not only the *speculum* of election, but also all that God is in God's *ad extra* activities, which overflow from and perfectly correspond to all that God is in-and-for-Godself. Through this actualistic correspondence, God's triune essence becomes a proper object of our *speculation*, that is, *reflection* through a mirror image, namely, the history of the incarnation.

I will demonstrate that Barth's theological speculation in §28 consists of a critical and innovative adaptation of Augustine's notion of *speculum Trinitatis*. Despite Barth's critical view that the trinitarian analogy instituted by Augustine and adopted by Anselm runs the risk of leading to the anthropological speculation represented by Descartes and Hegel, Barth in fact retained the basic *Denkform* and fundamental insights of the *speculum Trinitatis*. For both Augustine and Barth, that God is self-existent as God-in-and-for-Godself in the triune *opera ad intra* is reflected to us only by God's becoming God-for-us. The direction of the speculation—the mirror reflection—indicates that God's being-in-and-for-Godself is the *Urbild*, the original, and God's being-for-us the *Abbild*, the reflected image. Barth's key insight in §28, in other words, is that the *speculum Trinitatis* is none other than Jesus Christ.

---

of the act of election *ad extra*. Barth, per Jüngel, stresses "that God's being for us in Jesus Christ is an event. This event is called revelation and is as such God's self-interpretation. God's being-for-us does not define God's being, but rather interprets God's being in his being for us." Translation mine. Original: „ … dass Gottes Sein für uns in Jesus Christ Ereignis ist. Dieses Ereignis heisst Offenbarung und ist als solche Selbstinterpretation Gottes. Gottes Für-uns-Sein definiert nicht Gottes Sein, wohl aber interpretiert Gott in seinem Sein für uns sein Sein." Eberhard Jüngel, *Gottes sein ist im Werden* (Tübingen: Mohr Siebeck, 1986), 117.

43. Bruce McCormack, "Grace and Being: The Role of God's Gracious Election in Karl Barth's Theological Ontology," in *The Cambridge Companion to Karl Barth*, ed. John Webster (Cambridge: Cambridge University Press, 2000), 193.

Chapter 6

In the sixth chapter, I tackle the doctrine of election set forth in *CD* II/2, paying close attention to §33, where Barth describes the secondary absoluteness of God's being as the one who loves in freedom as none other than Jesus Christ who is the subject, object, and act of election. Barth's key insight is that election is not merely an act of God's will. Election in its subjectivity, objectivity, and activity *is* the secondary mode of God's being in Jesus Christ, who is at once the *speculum Trinitatis* qua electing God and *speculum electionis* as elected man. It is within this speculative context that Barth posits an identity between Jesus Christ and the electing God.

The nature of this identity is among the most intensely debated topics in recent Barth studies. McCormack and Matthias Gockel contend that the notion of this identity was yet to be developed in *Gottes Gnadenwahl*, and that once this notion was established in II/2, Barth would come to view election as the act whereby God eternally determines God's own being as God. Here McCormack and Gockel take Barth's language of divine self-determination (*Selbstbestimmung*) to denote ontological self-constitution. Accordingly, election is the act by which "God freely constitutes his own being in eternity."[44]

In Chapters 5 and 6, I will challenge this reading by resorting to (1) a re-examination of the modern history of ideas with which Barth engaged intensely and (2) an exegesis of *CD* II/2 against this intellectual-historical background. I will show that despite their commitment to a post-Kantian reading of Barth, McCormack and his peers have consistently exhibited a striking neglect of Kant's notion of transcendental freedom and how it shaped the basic trajectory for subsequent discourses on nature and freedom in German idealism.

The thrust of this trajectory is, as suggested earlier, what Rosen calls "emancipation from arbitrariness," which consists in (1) a refutation of the determinist view that all acts of the will are determined by nature and external forces, as well as (2) a rejection of the indeterminist definition of freedom as contingent exercises of the power of choice (*Willkür*).[45] Barth is emphatic that there is no arbitrariness about the freedom of God, and refutes both the determinist view that God needs an other in order to realize God's absolute freedom and the indeterminist view that election is an absolute act of God's will apart from or prior to God's essence. In his explication of God's absolute freedom in election, Barth resorts to the Hegelian language of "determination."

"Determination" (*Bestimmung*) is a term that McCormack and his peers capitalize on with a striking misinterpretation thereof. A right understanding of Barth's discourse on God's essence and freedom requires a careful exposition of the term at a very technical level. I have offered some initial analyses elsewhere,

---

44. Bruce McCormack, "Karl Barth's Christology as a Resource for a Reformed Version of Kenoticism," *International Journal of Systematic Theology* 8 (2006): 247.

45. Rosen, *Shadow of God*, 23.

and will go into much more detail in this volume (Chapter 3).[46] A preliminary explanation of how the aforementioned "identity," also a key term in Hegelian ontology, is defined in terms of "determination" would be helpful at this point.

Note that Barth chooses the term *Bestimmung*, as used by Fichte and Hegel, rather than *das Bestimmen*, the more standard terminology in (neo-)Kantianism, inherited from the Leibnizian-Wolffian school. I show in Chapter 3 that Barth uses this term within the framework of a Hegelian, rather than Fichtean, grammar. It refers to the process through which a thing enters into a state of encounter and conflict with otherness in order to know what it is and is not, so as to actualize what it has in it to become.

This is a very difficult concept, and some illustrations may be helpful at this point for readers yet unfamiliar therewith. Consider Confucius: in what sense can Confucius be described as a Chinese thinker? He lived in an era when China was not yet *determinate* as China, the modern nation-state as we know it today. Only through international conflicts such as the two Sino-British Wars and the Siege of Beijing of 1900 did China start to grapple with and eventually accept herself as a nation in the same category as, say, "America," "Great Britain," and "Japan." Without this history of conflict and *reconciliation* with *otherness*, the determination of China as China would have been impossible.

Because the China of the early twentieth-century and the sixth-century BC entity that was in the process of becoming China are the same *subject*, however, it is logically correct to say that Confucius was a Chinese philosopher. The identification of Confucius as a Chinese philosopher hinges upon the historical determination of China as China. The *identity* is, on this view, not at all immediate. It is a *speculative* identity *mediated* from the twentieth century to the ancient sage through long historical processes of conflict and reconciliation.

This example illustrates the *relationalist* and *historicist* dimensions of the Hegelian notion of determination as a process established through the historical *progress* of conflict and reconciliation with alterity. The Hegelian notion of identity differs from those of, say, Fichte and the early Schelling, precisely in that for Hegel, subject-predicate identities in synthetic predications are never *simpliciter* or immediate, but always involves some process of mediation by complex relational and historical determinations.

When Barth speaks, in the Hegelian language of God's self-determination, of an identity between Jesus Christ and the electing God in *Gottes Gnadenwahl* (pace McCormack and Gockel, Barth did not wait until 1942 to formulate this identity), an "identity" between "God's eternal counsel and our time," he is emphatic that the two are not immediately identical.[47] Rather, it is an "identity made recognisable to us" in Jesus Christ alone.[48] It is, in other words, a *speculative identity*.

---

46. See my "Barth on Actualistic Ontology." Also see my *Barth's Ontology of Sin and Grace*, 17–21.
47. *Gottes Gnadenwahl*, 45.
48. *Gottes Gnadenwahl*, 45.

The logic underlying the phrase, "Jesus Christ is the electing God," is analogous to that underlying the phrase, "Confucius was a Chinese philosopher." In its formal aspect (and in this aspect alone), it is, for the lack of a better term, what might be called a "logic of mediation." Incidentally, the Chalcedonian title of Mary as *Theostokos* can also be understood with the formal aspect of this logic.

The triune God-in-and-for-Godself determined Godself to be God-for-us in Jesus Christ without ceasing to be God-in-and-for-Godself, and so it is correct to say that Jesus Christ is, *secundum quid*, the subject of this self-determination that constitutes God's election of Godself to be the electing God and elected human in one unabridged person. Thus Barth in *Gottes Gnadenwahl*: "The eternal God and thus also the eternal Son of God is the electing God, and the electing God is none other than the eternal God and thus the eternal Son Himself in the communion with the Father and the Holy Spirit, who assumed human nature in His birth from the Virgin Mary."[49]

In Chapter 6, I will show that in *CD* II/2, Barth retains the same Hegelian grammar of identity and determination to defend an un-Hegelian ontology—a basically Chalcedonian one—in which God's primary absoluteness qua Trinity remains ever unsublated in the determination of God's secondary absoluteness that is Jesus Christ as electing, elected, and election. Election does not constitute the immanent Trinity. The free love that is the *ad intra* essence of the immanent Trinity grounds and makes possible the speculative "emanation" (*Überfluß*—a term borrowed from the speculative ontology of Platonism) of this love in the *ad extra* act of election.

Chapter 7

As Barth sees it, the modern speculative tradition beginning with Descartes and culminating in Hegel was largely responsible for providing philosophical and theological justifications for Germany's mystical nationalism. Barth's adoption of a basically Anselmian mode of speculation against the Cartesian-Hegelian tradition therefore carries profound implications against modern nationalism.

Chapter 7 offers an exegesis of a lengthy section on election and nationhood in *Gottes Gnadenwahl*. I will attend to Barth's use of Hegelian terms and concepts to demonstrate his refutation of secularistic and immanentistic reinterpretations of the Christian doctrines of election and providence under the Enlightenment principle of historical progress by modern German thinkers, most notably Hegel.

Hegel, in Barth's estimation, was largely at fault for having provided theological and philosophical justifications for the rise of Germany's mystical nationalism in the name of German Christianity. Using Hegelian language, Barth insists against Hegel that election is God's *pre*-determination (*Vorherbestimmung*) of human existence *in Christo*. Rather than negating nationhood altogether, then, Barth's repudiation of nationalism is intended to stress that nationhood

---

49. *Gottes Gnadenwahl*, 46.

is an external basis of the communion of the elect, and that the election of the community is the internal basis of nationhood.

Here Barth stands in sharp contrast to "existential"—using the term in its broader sense—responses to the immanentized eschatology of mystical nationalism from German-speaking Christian thinkers of his time. The typical response was to deny *tout court* that the human mind has any capacity to speculate on divine workings and consummate purpose in history.

The aforementioned Jewish Christian philosopher Karl Löwith, for instance, altogether rejects the "possibility" for human beings to attain knowledge of any "reasoned order" or "workings of God" in history.[50] He responded to the atrocities caused by German nationalism by renouncing the speculative program as a whole.

Rudolf Bultmann, too, deemed the Judeo-Christian view of history as linear progress culminating in the second coming of Christ responsible for the kind of historicism that featured prominently in Hegelianism and Marxism. In his celebrated 1955 Gifford Lectures, *History and Eschatology*, Bultmann dismisses both the cyclical view of history in ancient civilization and the linear view of history to which the Judeo-Christian tradition gave rise as mystical metaphysics. Demythologized reading of the New Testament, argues Bultmann, focuses kerygmatically on the Christ event that is at once timeless and immanent to the believer's present realities. For Bultmann, then, the meaning of history is not discoverable through theological speculation. Eternal meaning is existentially realized in the life of the believer only through the kerygmatic presence of the event of Christ.[51]

I will argue that Barth's approach to the question of meaning in history is best characterized as "speculative." In *Gottes Gnadenwahl*, he identifies Christ as *speculum electionis* (the mirror of election). The incarnation mirrors to us a movement within God's eternal will by which God determines Godself as God-for-us without ceasing to be God-in-and-for-Godself. History is the external basis of this eternal movement, which pre-determined human existence to be *for God*.

Under this speculative scheme, Barth identifies nationhood as one indispensable dimension of the outward basis of divine election and providence. God does not elect any earthly nation to be the priestly mediator or divine giver of right and freedom. *Recht und Freiheit* cannot be efficated by the *Einigkeit* of a modern nation-state. The *comm*-union of God's elect on earth in the form of the *ekk*-lesial community, the *una sancta ecclesia* that transcends all national boundaries, is the only appointed means by which the love and freedom of God's gracious election is imparted to the nations.

---

50. Löwith, *Meaning in History*, v.
51. See Rudolf Bultmann, *History and Eschatology: The Presence of Eternity* (Waco: Baylor University Press, 2019).

Chapter 1

SKETCHING THE BACKGROUND: THE POST-KANTIAN PARADIGM REEXAMINED

My portrayal of Barth in the present study, especially with regard to the Christocentric reorientation of his speculative theology in 1936–42, challenges the paradigm developed by Bruce McCormack, which presently dominates much of the literature on Barth. The full-fledged version of this paradigm asserts that according to what is putatively "Barth's 'rule,'" predications "about the divine modes of being antecedently in themselves cannot be different in content from those that are to be made about their reality in revelation."[1] This "entails the claim that the immanent Trinity and the economic Trinity do not differ in content."[2] This reading of Barth is supported by McCormack's intellectual-biographical assertion that Barth's Christocentric revision of the doctrine of election was not fully developed until *CD* II/2 (1942), where Barth began to describe God's activity in Jesus Christ as constitutive of God's triune essence.[3]

McCormack's 1995 masterpiece, *Barth's Critically Realistic Dialectical Theology*, has convinced the majority of Anglophone Barth scholars, myself included, that Barth first verbalized on paper the "form of 'Christocentrism' which became synonymous

---

1. Bruce McCormack, *The Humility of the Eternal Son* (Cambridge: Cambridge University Press, 2021), 2.
2. McCormack, *The Humility of the Eternal Son*, 2.
3. This exegesis of Barth on election and the Trinity in *CD* II/2 finds a full-blown expression in Tyler Frick, *Karl Barth's Ontology of Divine Grace: God's Decision Is God's Being* (Tübingen: Mohr Siebeck, 2021). Despite the kind of attention that Frick pays to Barth's text which is not always characteristic of proponents of McCormack's paradigm, his work is compromised by a number of shortcomings. First, Frick's study pays little attention to the intellectual-historical and intellectual-biographical background of Barth's theological development, and demonstrates little knowledge of how Barth's theological language was informed by the ideas of thinkers like Kant and Hegel. Second, Frick seems to take the intellectual-biographical foundations of this paradigm for granted and does not discuss it in any detail, let alone defending it against the arguments set forth by Baark and myself in our respective 2018 monographs.

with the name of Karl Barth" in his 1936 *Gottes Gnadenwahl*.[4] At the time, McCormack's take was that the Christocentric revision of the doctrine of election in 1936 immediately marked the final turning point in Barth's theological development.

In 2008, however, McCormack stated "that the picture [he] drew in" his 1995 "book, of a sudden shift in Barth's doctrine of election … needs to be revised a bit. The change was not immediate but gradual."[5] This view of a gradual change was initially proposed by Matthias Gockel in his 2002 doctoral dissertation under McCormack's supervision.[6] Central to this revision is the shared contention between McCormack and Gockel that the "identification of 'Jesus Christ' with the electing God … did not appear until *CD* II/2."[7] Accordingly, the decisive turn to Christocentrism did not take place suddenly in 1936, but over the course of 1936–42. This revision has allowed McCormack to follow through with his post-Kantian interpretation of Barth, initially set forth in *Barth's Dialectical Theology*, more consistently than before.

I have engaged with this interpretative agenda at a textual-exegetical level for years. What was lacking in the literature until around 2018 was a thorough and critical re-examination of the intellectual-historical assumptions underlying McCormack's intellectual-biographical account of Barth's development as a theologian. Sigurd Baark's 2018 monograph was a significant milestone in the literature on Barth for having filled this particular lacuna.[8] My own study from the same year followed a strikingly similar trajectory, though it did not give a thorough depiction of Barth's intellectual-historical background.[9] While both Baark and I engaged closely with McCormack's post-Kantian paradigm in our respective monographs, our primary focus was on setting forth a new intellectual-historical account of Barth.

In this chapter, I will offer a concentrated critique of McCormack's post-Kantian paradigm and expose some of its most striking weaknesses. This will serve as the basis on which I proceed to sketch out my own intellectual-historical defense of the "speculative" model of Barth interpretation in the next chapter. I begin here with a review of received models of interpretation leading up to McCormack's game-changing proposal in 1995.

---

4. Bruce McCormack, *Karl Barth's Critically Realistic Dialectical Theology* (Oxford: Clarendon, 1995), 455.

5. Bruce McCormack, "The Actuality of God: Karl Barth in Conversation with Open Theism," in *Engaging the Doctrine of God: Contemporary Protestant Perspectives*, ed. McCormack (Grand Rapids: Baker Academic, 2008), 213.

6. Matthias Gockel, *Barth and Schleiermacher on the Doctrine of Election* (Oxford: Oxford University Press, 2006), 167.

7. Bruce McCormack, "Seek God Where He May Be Found: A Response to Edwin van Driel," *Scottish Journal of Theology* 60 (2007): 64.

8. Sigurd Baark, *The Affirmations of Reason: On Karl Barth's Speculative Theology* (Cham: Palgrave Macmillan, 2018).

9. Shao Kai Tseng, *Barth's Ontology of Sin and Grace: Variations on a Theme of Augustine* (London: Routledge, 2018).

Received Models of Interpretation: A Critical Review

The Analogy Paradigm

The view advanced by the "speculative" model of Barth interpretation, that Barth adopted an Anselmian *credo ut intelligam* program in the early 1930s, has a long pedigree. It was set forth by Hans Urs von Balthasar in *Karl Barth: Darstellung und Deutung seiner Theologie* (1951), a work that gave rise to the first dominant paradigm in the field. Balthasar argues that *Anselm: Fides Quaerens Intellectum* (1931) either constitutes a radical break from Barth's previous theology, or at least it marks the beginning of a gradual turn from dialectic to analogy that was completed in *CD* II/1 (1940).[10]

This paradigm came under severe scrutiny upon the publication of McCormack's *Barth's Dialectical Theology*. McCormack contends that Barth's theology has always remained dialectical even after the so-called turn to analogy, and that *Anselm* did not give rise to any essentially new theological *Denkform* in Barth's writings.[11] Although many have opposed McCormack's post-Kantian reading of election and the Trinity and insisted upon some Anselmian principle or moment regulating Barth's mature theology as a whole, McCormack's intellectual-biographical narrative of the role of *Anselm* has dominated Barth scholarship for over two decades. Among the few who challenged his refutation of the Balthasar thesis is Stephen Wigley, who argues that "while McCormack may be right on Barth, he is wrong on von Balthasar on Barth."[12] Wigley writes: "McCormack maintains that Barth's theology remained dialectical into the *Church Dogmatics*. But von Balthasar recognises this too."[13]

Wigley's valiant attempt notwithstanding, the problem remains: in what way does Barth's theology remain "dialectical" all through his career? For Balthasar, the "dialectical" phase of Barth's theology is characterized first by a "static moment" of "Kierkegaardian dialectics" that centers on "the 'infinite qualitative difference' between God and creature," and then by a "second, *dynamic* moment ... which Hegel and German Idealism readied for our use."[14]

McCormack, on the other hand, basically marginalizes Hegelian influences in his reading of Barth, and flatly denies that Kierkegaardian dialectics had any significant bearing on the early Barth.[15] This maneuver is intended to support

---

10. See Hans Urs von Balthasar, *The Theology of Karl Barth: Exposition and Interpretation*, trans. Edward T. Oakes (San Francisco: Ignatius Press, 1992), 86–113.

11. McCormack, *Barth's Dialectical Theology*, 14–19.

12. Stephen Wigley, "The von Balthasar Thesis: A Re-Examination of von Balthasar's Study of Barth in the Light of Bruce McCormack," *Scottish Journal of Theology* 56 (2003): 345.

13. Wigley, "The von Balthasar Thesis," 350.

14. Balthasar, *The Theology of Karl Barth*, 82–3. Italics original.

15. McCormack, *Barth's Dialectical Theology*, 235–7.

McCormack's thesis that Barth's dialectical theology finds its roots in the *Realdialektik* of Marburg neo-Kantianism.

This is one of the weaker links in McCormack's otherwise dominating chain of argumentation. He does not provide any evidence to support the contention that the Barth of *Romans* II was not yet familiar with Kierkegaard's *Philosophical Fragments* or *Concluding Unscientific Postscript*. When he points to the Barth-Thurneysen letters, he does not mention the one that Barth undersigned on January 22, 1921.[16] In that letter, Barth explicitly states that he had finished reading *Philosophical Fragments* before starting on the manuscript of *Romans* II.[17] After all, it is a well-known fact that Barth himself states in the preface to *Romans* II that the work is indebted to Kierkegaard and his notion of the infinite qualitative difference between God and creatures.

The lack of evidence and argumentation in McCormack's contention that Barth's early dialectics was retrieved from Marburg neo-Kantianism rather than Kierkegaard was scrutinized by Sean Turchin's 2011 doctoral thesis at Edinburgh.[18] Cora Bartel, too, provides ample evidence to show that Barth's early dialectics was informed primarily by Kierkegaard.[19]

To be sure, McCormack does not contend that Barth's dialectical theology remained Kantian all through his career. He is clear that "Barth did not need Kant any longer once he discovered the ancient anhypostatic-enhypostatic Christology in … 1924."[20] On the other hand, however, McCormack complains that Anselmian readings of Barth offered by Balthasar and Thomas F. Torrance are guilty of construing "a Barth stripped of his dialectical origins" in Marburg neo-Kantianism.[21] However much Barth's dialectical theology transformed over the years, so believes McCormack, it started out as a neo-Kantian *Realdialektik*, and all subsequent forms of Barth's dialectical theology evolved from this origin and must be interpreted in this light.[22]

While Turchin and Bartel successfully demonstrated the influence of Kierkegaard on Barth's early dialectics, it was Baark who definitively tackled the

---

16. McCormack, *Barth's Dialectical Theology*, 235–7.

17. *Barth-Thurneysen Briefwechsel 1913–1921*, in *GA* 3, 461.

18. Sean Turchin, "Introducing Christianity into Christendom: Investigating the Affinity between Søren Kierkegaard and the Early Thought of Karl Barth" (Ph.D. Thesis, University of Edinburgh, 2011), 2–38. Also see Sean Turchin, "Kierkegaard's Echo in the Early Theology of Karl Barth," *Kierkegaard Studies Yearbook* 2012, no. 1 (2012): 323–36.

19. Cora Bartel, *Kierkegaard receptus I: Die theologiegeschichtliche Bedeutung der Kierkegaard-Rezeption Rudolf Bultmanns* (Göttingen: Vandenhoeck & Ruprecht, 2008), 141–70.

20. Bruce McCormack, "Afterword: Reflections on Van Til's Critique of Barth," in *Barth and American Evangelicalism*, ed. Bruce McCormack and Clifford Anderson (Grand Rapids: Eerdmans, 2010), 372.

21. McCormack, *Barth's Dialectical Theology*, 24.

22. McCormack, *Barth's Dialectical Theology*, 24.

question "whether Barth's theology is in fact determined by a *Realdialektik*."²³ Baark shows that "*Realdialektik*" is a rarely employed term and has no systematic usage in Barth's writings: it appears only in obscure places such as "in the context of the doctrine of the holy angels, or in a puzzled letter from Eduard Thurneysen from the early twenties, where he asks Barth if he can help him make any sense of the concept."²⁴

In a word, if the weakness of Balthasar's study on Barth is a relative lack of biographical information compared to McCormack's, then the weakness of McCormack's account is that it reconstructs an image of Barth on the basis of intellectual-biographical data without due attention to the integrity of Barth's texts and to Barth's own account of his theology.

Note here that I am not primarily interested in defending the Balthasar thesis, my apparent agreements therewith notwithstanding. One problem with Balthasar's hermeneutical strategy is that he wants to identify one single locus that governs the entirety of Barth's mature theology. For Balthasar, this regulating locus is the *analogia fidei*. George Hunsinger points out that Balthasar's own reading of Barth's actualism already implies, contra Balthasar himself, that "it is actualism, and not a doctrine of analogy, which is functioning as the relevant mode of thought."²⁵

Furthermore, Balthasar is largely unconcerned with pinpointing Barth's place on the map of modern European thought. He mentions Kierkegaard and Hegel in broad strokes without demonstrating familiarity with their writings. When he attributes Kierkegaardian and Hegelian dialectics to Barth's early theology, he does not support his view with any textual analyses, nomenclatural study, or intellectual-historical/biographical information. He demonstrates knowledge of Descartes's use of Anselm's proof and offers an insightful analysis of Barth's fundamental differences with Descartes.²⁶ Yet, he seems unfamiliar with the way Hegel and his idealist followers tried to revive Descartes's speculative metaphysics by misconstruing Anselm as a forerunner of pantheism. This nineteenth-century background, however, is crucial for understanding Barth's reinterpretation of Anselm against German idealism's dominant narrative of its own allegedly Anselmian pedigree (see Chapter 2).

The Dogmatics Paradigm

Along with the Balthasar paradigm, Thomas F. Torrance's *Karl Barth: An Introduction to His Early Theology 1910–1931* (1962), in the words of Paul Molnar, dominated "the received view of Barth in the English-speaking world until 1995 when Bruce McCormack questioned his thesis that Barth turned from dialectic

---

23. Baark, *The Affirmations of Reason*, 14.
24. Baark, *The Affirmations of Reason*, 14.
25. George Hunsinger, *How to Read Karl Barth* (Oxford: Oxford University Press, 1991), 8.
26. Balthasar, *The Theology of Karl Barth*, 148–9.

to analogy after reading Anselm."²⁷ Torrance's work is not merely a reiteration of Balthasar's thesis. While Torrance also acknowledges the turn from dialectic to analogy (as do Baark and I, for that matter), his preferred phraseology is a shift "from dialectical to dogmatic thinking."²⁸

This emphasis on dogmatics has to do with the intellectual milieu in Britain from the nineteenth century down to Torrance's student years. Molnar reports that when Barth's theology was introduced to Scotland in the 1930s, "Torrance was particularly intrigued by Barth's understanding of dogmatics as a science, by his view of the objectivity of God's self-revelation and by his trinitarian doctrine."²⁹ Torrance saw in Barth's objectivism a key to countering the subjectivism of "rationalistic liberalism" that threatened to corrupt British society and culture by the marginalization of Christianity.³⁰

In the context of nineteenth-century and early twentieth-century British Christianity, "liberalism" often refers to a specific ideology and social phenomenon that arose in early modernity to challenge the values traditionally associated with Christianity. Even today, "liberalism" continues to be used in this way in some circles to refer to an ideology opposed to the kind of British conservatism of which, say, Margaret Thatcher and Roger Scruton are representative.

The Tractarian Movement in nineteenth-century England is a classic instance of conservative Christians in Britain reacting against so-called liberalism as their archenemy. For John Henry Newman (1801–90), the essence of liberalism is what he calls "the Anti-Dogmatic Principle."³¹ Newman writes:

> Now by Liberalism I mean false liberty of thought, or the exercise of thought upon matters, in which, from the constitution of the human mind, thought cannot be brought to any successful issue, and therefore is out of place. Among such matters are *first principles* of whatever kind; and of these the most sacred and momentous are especially to be reckoned the *truths of Revelation*. Liberalism then is the mistake of *subjecting to human judgment* those revealed doctrines which are in their nature beyond and independent of it.³²

Defending the objectivity of dogmatic truths against liberal subjectivism was a burden that many British theologians from the nineteenth century to the early twentieth century shared. When Torrance began to read theology at New College, Edinburgh in 1934, he came to be acquainted with Schleiermacher's endeavors to retain the scientific status of Christian theology. Torrance turned out disappointed

---

27. Paul Molnar, *Thomas F. Torrance: Theologian of the Trinity* (London: Routledge, 2009), 5–6.
28. Thomas F. Torrance, *Karl Barth: An Introduction to His Early Theology 1910–1931* (Edinburgh: T&T Clark, 1962), 48–132.
29. Molnar, *Thomas F. Torrance*, 5.
30. Molnar, *Thomas F. Torrance*, 4.
31. John Henry Newman, *Apologia Pro Vita Sua* (New York: Norton, 1968), 216.
32. Newman, *Apologia Pro Vita Sua*, 218. Emphases mine.

by Schleiermacher, not least because, in Torrance's own words, "the propositional structure he [Schleiermacher] imposed upon the Christian consciousness lacked any realist scientific objectivity."[33]

For Torrance, the term "dogmatic" encompasses "realist," "scientific," and "objective." It is insufficient for theology to be analogical to revelation apart from dogmatic authority. *Analogia fidei* is for Torrance a function of dogmatic thinking: it holds fast to the *regula fidei*. Realist scientific objectivity cannot be established apart from dogmatic faith. Barth's theology was so valuable to Torrance, precisely because Barth showed that apart from the *regula fidei*, human thoughts about God can never enjoy realist scientific objectivity.

It is hardly surprising, then, that "the motif of greatest interest to Torrance, and the one by which the others are usually subsumed, is objectivism … Revelational objectivism so dominates Torrance's reading of Barth that the other motifs have difficulty emerging in their own right."[34] Torrance would stress the objectivist dimension of Barth's theology to such an extent that he would describe dogmatics as a science that can be as precise as physics.

This emphasis on scientific objectivism may be understood as a result of Torrance's anti-liberal impulse to liberate the natural sciences from the bondage of liberal subjectivism. This modern subjectivism, according to Torrance, is symptomatic of Kantianism's "fatal deistic disjunction between God and the world which does not allow for any real Word of God to cross the gulf between God and the creature or therefore to permit man in space and time any real knowledge of God as he is in himself."[35]

Torrance found in Barth's rendition of Anselm's *analogia fidei* the key to overcoming this disjunction. More than Barth, Torrance wanted to bring humanity's natural knowledge of creation and, therewith, the natural sciences back under the dominion of the Word of God. It was out of this concern that Torrance interpreted Barth as rejecting the "status" of

> natural theology … as a *praeambula fidei*, that is as a preamble of faith, or an independent conceptual system antecedent to actual knowledge of God, which is then used as an epistemological framework within which to interpret and formulate actual empirical knowledge of God, thereby subordinating it to distorting forms of thought … However, instead of rejecting natural theology *tout court*, Barth has transposed it into the material content of theology where in a changed form it constitutes the epistemological structure of our knowledge of God.[36]

---

33. Thomas F. Torrance, *Karl Barth, Biblical and Evangelical Theologian* (Edinburgh: T&T Clark, 1990), 121. Cit. Molnar, *Thomas F. Torrance*, 4.

34. George Hunsinger, *How to Read Karl Barth* (Oxford: Oxford University Press, 1991), 10.

35. Thomas F. Torrance, *Space, Time and Resurrection* (Edinburgh: T&T Clark, 1976), 2.

36. Torrance, *Space, Time and Resurrection*, x.

Whilst this description is, in my view, accurate and masterful, it seems to me that Torrance's fascination with Barth's Anselmian program is too deeply driven by his anti-liberal concerns in a British context, and that his narrative of Barth's appeal to Anselm is too oblivious to Barth's own Continental background. The only German idealist that Torrance discusses at length in *Barth's Early Theology* is Schleiermacher, whom Torrance deems to be a threat to the realist scientific objectivity of Christian theology.[37] Hegel only receives a few irrelevant mentions and is as good as nonexistent throughout *Barth's Early Theology*, while Fichte and Schelling are completely left out of Torrance's view in the volume.

At the end of the day, then, Torrance's book on Barth's early theology turns out to be more of a contextualized tool developed to build up Torrance's own theology—which is immensurably significant in its own right to be sure—than a high-fidelity representation of Barth as he is in his own context and writings. Torrance's portrayal does not adequately reflect Barth's concerns to overcome the idolatrous threats of modern speculative metaphysics that fostered the rise of German nationalism in the early twentieth century.

Ahistorical and Historicized Interpretations

If Torrance's objectivist model renders Barth as an empirical realist on the question of God's redemptive activity in history, then there has been an opposite tendency in both Anglophone and German (as well as Japanese) scholarship to interpret Barth as an empirical idealist in his treatment of the historicity of divine activity. This tendency is, more often than not, based on an interpretative framework that portrays the development of his theology as the unfolding of the eternity-time dialectic in his early thought. As Barth worked out this dialectic—so purport such ahistorical readings—the vertical dimension (the self-disclosure of the transcendent God from above) of his thought gradually outgrew the horizontal (God's eschatological immanence proleptically present in history). Such readings, like certain "historicized" interpretations (discussed anon), often fail to recognize the substantive discontinuities between the allegedly (neo-)Kantian and/or Kierkegaardian origins of Barth's early theology and the later stages of his intellectual development.

One representative of the ahistorical family of Barth interpretation is Wolfhart Pannenberg (1928–2014). As Pannenberg sees it, the ahistorical nature of the trinitarian form of Barth's theology in the *Church Dogmatics* was developed on the basis of the same eternity-time dialectic—a largely Kierkegaardian one in Pannenberg's view—set forth in *Romans II*.[38] In the *Church Dogmatics* the

---

37. E.g. Thomas F. Torrance, *Karl Barth: An Introduction to His Early Theology 1910–1931* (Edinburgh: T&T Clark, 1962), 56–7; 152–3.

38. See Wolfhart Pannenberg, *Systematic Theology*, vol. 3, trans. Geoffrey Bromiley (Grand Rapids: Eerdmans, 2009), 536–7. For Pannenberg's extensive treatment of Barth's intellectual biography against the background of modern German Protestant theology,

eschatological focus of the Barth's early theology fades into the background. The "eschatological mood" of the early Barth was "taken up into a Christological orientation to the unity between God and us in Jesus Christ" in the later Barth.[39] Barth's earlier view of the "dialectical turning of judgment into grace," according to Pannenberg, is retained in the *Church Dogmatics*, albeit in a much more ahistorical form.[40]

Pannenberg's ahistorical reading of the later Barth must be understood against the intellectual-historical background of German idealism. The characteristically modern interest in history that Pannenberg exhibits in his own theology first arose in the generation of idealists like Johann Gottlieb Fichte (1762–1814), Friedrich Schelling (1775–1854), and G. W. F. Hegel (1770–1831).[41] The strong process-historical incentives in Pannenberg are admittedly indebted primarily to Hegel. According to Hegel, history is the dialectical process by which spirit actualizes itself and becomes God upon the consummation of history. It is through Hegelian-historicist lenses that the characteristically modern questions of history become important in Pannenberg's eschatology.

What sets Pannenberg apart from Hegel, as well as the process ontologies of Alfred North Whitehead (1861–1947) and Charles Hartshorne (1897–2000) for that matter, is primarily his explicit reliance on Barth's understanding of history as an *ad extra* vehicle through which God is said to be self-determined in one way or another, rather than a process in which world-occurrences are in some ways filtered and taken up into God's *ad intra* essence. (Readers like Pannenberg and Moltmann would stress that for Hegel, God always remains *qualitatively*, though not *quantitatively*, transcendent to the world.)

For Pannenberg, history is the process through which God determines Godself qua God. For Barth, God determines God's own time to be time-for-us without ceasing to be God's own time in-and-for-Godself. Pannenberg, then, is opposed to Barth's insistence on divine immutability in contending that God's act is identical to God's being, even though Pannenberg is also emphatic on the ontological distinction between the history of creation and the development of God's being. Creaturely history is, for Pannenberg, the outward basis on which God acts to determine God's own essence as God.

Pannenberg is known for having adopted what he understood to be Barth's notion of the ontological determination of nature and history "from above"

---

see Wolfhart Pannenberg, *Problemsgeschichte der neueren Evangelischen Theologie in Deutschland: von Schleiermacher bis zu Barth und Tillich* (Göttingen: Vandenhoeck & Ruprecht, 1997).

39. Pannenberg, *Problemsgeschichte der neueren Evangelischen Theologie in Deutschland*, 537.

40. Pannenberg, *Problemsgeschichte der neueren Evangelischen Theologie in Deutschland*, 537.

41. See Karl Ameriks, *Kant and the Historical Turn* (Oxford: Oxford University Press, 2006).

(*von oben*), which Pannenberg calls the "vertical" dimension of historical revelation.[42] Pannenberg's complaint is that in the later, Christocentric Barth, the horizontal vector is absorbed into the vertical, a maneuver already latent in the early Barth. Pannenberg's "reconstruction of Christian eschatology" is intended to be an attempt to recover the early Barth's "focusing of primitive Christian expectation of the kingdom of God on the reality of God himself, whose immanence for us and the world means judgment as well as salvation."[43]

If Pannenberg's reading of the later Barth is characteristic of the ahistorical model of interpretation, then Pannenberg's American counterpart, Robert Jenson (1930–2017), represents a certain "historicized" rendition of Barth. Pannenberg was two years Jenson's senior and already a lecturer at the University of Heidelberg when Jenson began his doctoral studies there. As a theologian in his own right, Jenson developed a historicist approach to theology akin to that of Pannenberg.

Jenson's indebtedness to Barth is much more explicit than in the case of Pannenberg. Like Pannenberg, Jenson visited Basel to seek Barth's guidance. Jenson's first publication, *Alpha and Omega*, is a revised version of his doctoral thesis on Barth's Christological doctrine of election. It was through the publication of *God after God* (1969) that Jenson came to be celebrated as a constructive theologian in his own right.

God after God is a work that seeks to build on Barth's legacy while wrestling with him, as the subtitle clearly indicates: *the God of the Past and the God of the Future, Seen in the Work of Karl Barth*.[44] Jenson, like Pannenberg, identifies two vectors in Barth's thought—the vertical (revelation from above) and the horizontal (historical-eschatological orientation toward the future). Jenson's project is to recover the eschatological dimension of Barth's early thought that, as Jenson sees it, was watered down yet retained in Barth's later theology.

Jenson identifies the doctrine of predestination as the "heart" of Barth's theology in *Romans* II.[45] Unlike the Christocentric phase of Barth's doctrine of election, the doctrine as presented in *Romans* II is highly futuristic. Jenson explains: "The relation between the two sides of double predestination ... is but another form of the relation we have traced between time and eternity; for the meaning of time, as different from eternity, is rejection, and the meaning of eternity for time is acceptance. In time we are all rejected; in eternity we are all chosen."[46] It was with the early Barth's eschatological doctrine of double predestination that Jenson sought to reconstruct a basically historicist doctrine of the futurity of God's being.

---

42. This is a view that Pannenberg developed early on in his career. See Wolfhart Pannenberg, ed., *Revelation as History* (London: Macmillan & Co., 1969).

43. Wolfhart Pannenberg, *Systematic Theology*, vol. 3, trans. Geoffrey Bromiley (Grand Rapids: Eerdmans, 2009), 537.

44. Robert Jenson, *God after God* (Minneapolis: Fortress, 2010).

45. Jenson, *God after God*, 28.

46. Jenson, *God after God*, 28.

1. The Post-Kantian Paradigm Reexamined

What unites Jenson's historicized reading of Barth with Pannenberg's ahistorical reading is that both see in the early Barth a strongly historicist dimension expressed through the horizontal vector of divine activity. For Jenson, this horizontal vector remains the guiding principle of Barth's theology even in the later stages of his career. For Pannenberg, Barth's theology has always been dominated by the vertical vector, even though this dominance did not overwhelm the horizontal in the early Barth.

Both Jenson and Pannenberg are convinced that what they see as the dominance of the vertical vector in Barth's later theology contradicts Barth's very own historicist principle, the ontological principle that being is determined by historical activity. For Jenson, the historicist principle remains at the heart of Barth's theology in his later career, but many of his assertions about God's being contradict this central principle.

The contradiction that Pannenberg and Jenson read into Barth was in fact a charge already levelled against Barth in the late 1920s. Dietrich Bonhoeffer (1906–45) suggests in his *Habilitationsschrift*, *Act and Being* (published 1930) that Barth's notion of God's supratemporal essence in the *Münster Dogmatics* is at odds with his own principle of being-in-act.[47] Emil Brunner (1889–1966), too, asserts that Barth's actualistic principle in the *Church Dogmatics* would lead to the "extraordinary" conclusion that election constitutes the Trinity, though, fortunately in Brunner's view, "Barth does not attempt to deduce" such a conclusion.[48]

In a similar vein, but in a much more sophisticated manner, McCormack paints the picture of a "historicized" Barth by arguing that Barth's affirmation of the ontological priority of the immanent Trinity over the act of election constitutes "an inconsistency in Barth's thought."[49] McCormack proposes to "register a critical correction" of Barth on what McCormack deems to be Barth's own actualistic terms.[50]

I will demonstrate in this chapter how McCormack supports this assessment of Barth with a robust account of Barth as a post-Kantian thinker. In the next chapter, I will proceed to offer an alternative intellectual-historical portrayal of Barth that describes him as a speculative theologian. This will provide the basis on which I offer a textual-exegetical and lexical explanation of what might in a qualified sense be called Barth's "actualistic ontology" in Chapter 3.

---

47. Dietrich Bonhoeffer, *Act and Being*, ed. Hans-Richard Reuter and Wayne Whitson Floyd, trans. H. Martin (Rumscheidt Minneapolis: Fortress, 1996), 83–7.

48. Emil Brunner, *Dogmatics*, vol. 1, *The Christian Doctrine of God*, trans. Olive Wyon (Philadelphia: Westminster John Knox, 1950), 315.

49. McCormack, "Grace and Being," in *The Cambridge Companion to Karl Barth*, ed. John Webster (Cambridge: Cambridge University Press, 2000), 193.

50. McCormack, "Grace and Being," 193.

The Traditionalist Paradigm

Against both the ahistorical and historicized families of Barth interpretation, Torrance's dogmatic reading finds nuanced re-expressions in two distinguished commentators of our day, namely, George Hunsinger and Paul Molnar. "Traditionalism" has come to be the label of their paradigm in recent scholarship. The advantage of this paradigm is its commitment to faithful exegesis of Barth's texts while paying close attention to ideas permeating the intellectual air that he breathed.

Molnar, the ever-careful textual exegete, exhibits exceptional command of the history of the intellectual soil that bred the generations of Barth, Pannenberg, Karl Rahner (1904–84), and Jürgen Moltmann (born 1926). Molnar is fully capable of extended analyses of individual philosophers like Hegel when occasions arise.[51] For the most part, however, he tends to demonstrate his knowledge of the history ideas in rather subtle ways. His exposition of Rahner's notion of "absolute being," for instance, reflects firm grasp of the history of this concept in continental philosophy.[52] The way Molnar illuminates the intricate ways in which Moltmann struggles to steer clear of "Hegel's idea of God as absolute being" also reflects sound knowledge of the intellectual history behind the theological texts.[53]

When Molnar brings his knowledge of this intellectual history to bear on his interpretation of Barth, he is able to stand on par with the post-Kantian interpreters in a way that Balthasar and Torrance could not. For one thing, Molnar is fully aware of all the fine details on which McCormack's post-Kantian Barth disagrees with Hegel, and is able to demonstrate the way in which this post-Kantian Barth remains essentially committed to some neo-Hegelian conception of God.[54]

Hunsinger is a remarkable example of a Barth scholar who attaches hermeneutical primacy to the text while paying due attention to the intellectual currents in the German-speaking world passed down from the long nineteenth century to Barth's generation. Hunsinger is especially astute in recognizing Hegelian patterns in Barth's trinitarian thinking.[55] Familiarity with Hegel allows Hunsinger to notice that "Barth may indeed have liked to do a little 'Hegeling,' especially throughout *Church Dogmatics*, volume IV. But he always took special care to avoid making Hegel's mistakes. In particular he would never allow pre-temporal election or anything else to make God's triune being depend on his relationship to the world."[56]

---

51. Paul Molnar, "A Response: Beyond Hegel with Karl Barth and T. F. Torrance," *Pro Ecclesia* 23 (2014): 165–73.

52. Paul Molnar, *Divine Freedom and the Doctrine of the Trinity: In Dialogue with Karl Barth and Contemporary Theology* (London: T&T Clark, 2017), 255.

53. Molnar, *Divine Freedom*, 452.

54. Molnar, *Divine Freedom*, 127.

55. See, for example, George Hunsinger, "Mysterium Trinitatis: Karl Barth's Conception of Eternity," in *Disruptive Grace: Studies in the Theology of Karl Barth* (Grand Rapids: Eerdmans, 2000), 186–209.

56. George Hunsinger, "Election and the Trinity: Twenty-Five Theses on the Theology of Karl Barth," *Modern Theology* 24 (2008): 190.

Hunsinger is also able to properly read between the lines in Barth's text where the author is "positioning himself over against" the likes of "Feuerbach, Kant, Hegel, Schleiermacher and Ritschl."[57] His proposal to attend to the Anselmian and Hegelian moments of Barth's mature theology carries an obvious advantage over the models espoused by Balthasar and Torrance, which tend to be too one-sidedly Anselmian.

I freely admit that my own work on Barth is largely indebted to Hunsinger and Molnar. What was needed to bolster their reading of Barth was a comprehensive account of the intellectual-historical circumstances underlying the development of the Hegelian and Anselmian moments of his mature theology. This task, as already mentioned, was initially taken up by Baark, whose model is still in need of some improvement. In the next chapter, I will seek to complete Baark's intellectual-historical project by answering some key questions that remain unaddressed in his important monograph. Before then, I will offer a critical assessment of McCormack's post-Kantian paradigm.

The Post-Kantian Paradigm: A Critical Appraisal

The Post-Kantian Family of Barth Interpretation

As an initial note of explanation, the so-called post-Kantian family of Barth interpretation, as the term is used in recent scholarship, covers a range of different interpretative trajectories. In general, the term "post-Kantian," which came into use as early as the nineteenth century, describes intellectual attempts to complete Kant's philosophical project and overcome Kant's challenges by accepting the fundamental premises of his critiques. Post-Kantian interpretations of modern European thought were popularized in recent Anglophone scholarship in the 1990s with the rise of the post-Kantian school of Hegel scholarship led by Robert Pippin and Terry Pinkard.[58]

In the field of Barth studies, Simon Fischer's work from the late 1980s already pointed Anglophone readers to the influence of the Marburg school on Barth's early theology.[59] Johann Lohmann's 1995 monograph was instrumental in advancing an interpretation of Barth through the lens of Marburg neo-Kantianism.[60]

One particular line of post-Kantian Barth interpretation places primary emphasis on his putative adoption of a transcendental method as the overarching

---

57. Hunsinger, "Election and Trinity," 187.
58. See Robert Pippin, *Hegel's Idealism: The Satisfactions of Self-Consciousness* (Cambridge: Cambridge University Press, 1989); Terry Pinkard, *Hegel's Naturalism: Mind Nature, and the Final Ends of Life* (Oxford: Oxford University Press, 2012).
59. See Simon Fisher, *Revelatory Positivism? Barth's Earliest Theology and the Marburg School* (Oxford: Oxford University Press, 1988). See Qu, 56.
60. See Johann Lohman, *Karl Barth und der Neukantianismus* (Berlin: de Gruyter, 1995).

Denkform of his theology.⁶¹ Those who hold to this view have debated over whether Barth's transcendental method originated from classical Kantianism or Marburg neo-Kantianism. Clifford Anderson holds to the more balanced view that while "Barth's transcendental argument was more neo-Kantian than straightforwardly Kantian," Barth's appropriation of Kant is unique and different from any other version of Kantianism.⁶²

If the *Denkform* of Barth's mature theology is unlike any version of (neo-)Kantian transcendentalism, however, then this calls into question whether it is at all helpful to label it as "transcendental." According to Kant's transcendental idealism, spatio-temporality is a necessary form of human intuition of the appearances of external objects.⁶³ Whether the thing-in-itself and its appearance are two aspects of the same object or two separate objects is one of the oldest debates in Kant studies. Kant himself rejected two-object interpretations of his doctrine, but this line of interpretation has been perseveringly followed by both critics and proponents of his philosophy, Barth included.

The different versions of "transcendental method" developed by classical Kantians and the various schools of neo-Kantianism were largely results of different takes on Kant's transcendental idealism. Those who adopt two-object interpretations, for instance, would take transcendental idealism to be the claim "that reality is supersensible and that we can have no knowledge of it."⁶⁴ This has often given rise to a kind of transcendental method that equates being with act and denies the reality of permanent substance even as just a principle (*Prinzip*: a logical and/or ontological starting point).

---

61. For example, George Hendry, "The Transcendental Method in the Theology of Karl Barth," *Scottish Journal of Theology* 37 (1984): 213–27.

62. Clifford Anderson, "A Theology of Experience? Karl Barh and the Transcendental Argument," in *Karl Barth and American Evangelicalism*, ed. Bruce McCormack and Clifford Anderson (Grand Rapids: Eerdmans, 2011), 94.

63. I acknowledge that some Kant scholars think of transcendental idealism as a disposable aspect of Kant's thought without which his philosophical system would still stand. See Paul Guyer, *Kant and the Claims of Knowledge* (Cambridge: Cambridge University Press, 1987); Rae Langton, *Kantian Humility: Our Ignorance of Things in Themselves* (Oxford: Oxford University Press, 1998). These readings of Kant are controversial, and beyond the scope of the present work. See my *Immanuel Kant* (Phillipsburg: P&R, 2020).

64. Peter Strawson, *The Bounds of Sense: An Essay on Kant's Critique of Pure Reason* (London: Routledge, 1975), 38. Karl Ameriks comments that Kant's "transcendental idealist ontology implies a kind of immaterialism," but here "immaterialism" only refers to "an insistence on a non-spatio-temporal character for things in themselves." Karl Ameriks, *Interpreting Kant's Critiques* (Oxford: Oxford University Press, 2003), 6. Ameriks suggests that "Kant's famous Refutation of Idealism" rejects the specific form of idealism with which Berkeley is usually identified, namely, the claim "that we know inner matter 'immediately' and can 'only infer' from these to what is outer." Ameriks, *Interpreting Kant's Critiques*, 18.

Barth, as we shall see, adopted a two-object interpretation of Kant's transcendental idealism, and explicitly rejected Kant's "transcendentalism."[65] This, of course, does not constitute sufficient reason for scholars to stop trying to read into Barth a certain transcendental *Denkform*. It may be argued that Barth's rejection of a phenomenalistic version of transcendentalism does not amount to a renunciation of Kant's own empirically realistic doctrine.

The problem is that aside from *substantive* considerations of what the doctrine of transcendental idealism teaches, Barth's mature theological *Denkform* simply does not fit well with any mode of thinking that can be described as "transcendental." Phenomenalist and realist interpreters of Kant will agree that transcendental modes of cognition are by definition *a priori*, although not all *a priori* cognitions are transcendental.

In both editions of the first *Critique*, Kant provides a definition of "transcendental" early on in the introduction, when he "call[s] all cognition transcendental that is occupied not so much with objects [*Objekte*] but rather with our mode of cognition of objects insofar as this is to be possible *a priori*."[66] He explains: "transcendental" refers to the ways "we cognize *that* and *how* certain representations (intuitions or concepts) are applied entirely *a priori*, or are possible."[67] He does not ask *whether* these representations are possible. Rather, having transcendentally cognized *that* they are possible, he wants to find out *how*.

On Kant's view, God, by conceptual definition, transcends spatio-temporality, and so within the theoretical use of reason, the concept of God must be treated as a theoretical *postulate* that helps to facilitate the organization of experiences. The transcendental mode of cognition cannot be applied to God within the theoretical use of reason. Transcendental theology helps to clarify the metaphysical idea of God, but it fails to justify the claim, *God is*. It is in the practical use of reason that God becomes a constitutive principle: practical reason allows us to claim knowledge of how *God ought to be*.

Barth critically reappropriated some of Kant's insights, but, as we shall see, his actualistic ontology in its Christocentric phase does not operate on transcendental grounds. Rather, Barth takes the reality of theoretical knowledge of the triune God (theoretical reason asks, "What is," while practical reason asks, "What ought to be") in the *regula fidei* as a given, and seeks to understand this reality in the *Denkform* of a basically Anselmian mode of speculation, which presupposes a mediated identity between God-in-and-for-Godself and God-for-us. This *Denkform* bears strong resemblance to that of Hegel's absolute idealism, and yet Hegel's faith is in a different identity—the consummate identity be human consciousness and absolute Spirit.

Put another way, Barth's basically Anselmian mode of speculation pertains to what Kant calls "revealed theology," which finds its faith-seeking-understanding

---

65. *Protestant Theology*, 379.
66. Immanuel Kant, *Critique of Pure Reason*, ed. and trans. Paul Guyer and Allen Wood (Cambridge: Cambridge University Press), A11/B25. Kant distinguishes carefully between *Objekte* and *Gegenstände*.
67. Kant, *Critique of Pure Reason*, A56/B80.

point of departure in the mediated identity between God's own being and God as known to the church in the event of revelation. "Transcendental theology," by contrast, "thinks its object … merely through pure reason, by means of sheer transcendental concepts."[68] "Transcendental theology" as such belongs to "rational theology," which Kant differentiates from "revealed theology."

Any theological program properly described as "transcendental" must find its starting point in the pure, transcendental concepts built-in, as it were, to the constitution of human reason. The transcendental *Denkform*, generically understood, must posit some correlation or discursivity between thinking and that which is thought, and what transcendental theology necessarily posits is the possibility of speculative extension from *a priori* human conceptions of God to God's being itself. Transcendental theology is possible in the practical use of reason for Kant, because the *a priori* moral categories make sense to us only if God's existence is acknowledged (*an-erkennt*). In other words, the categorical imperative transcendentally dictates to practical reason, *God ought to be*.

As Barth sees it, Kant's transcendentalism is very much a form of anthropological speculation in which the imperfections of creaturely nature(s) are treated as the speculative extension(s) or mirror image(s) of God's own nature. Barth's theological *Denkform* cannot possibly be described as "transcendental" in any proper sense of the term, precisely because he refuses to treat any *a priori* concept as some speculative extension of God's being, either in the theoretical or the practical use of reason.

Barth's own *Denkform* finds its speculative starting point in the *regula fidei* given to the church through the witness of Scripture. The church dogmatically confesses on biblical grounds a speculative, mediated identity not between God's being and transcendental human concepts of divinity or categories of morality, but between God in God's *ad intra* essence and God in the *ad extra* act of revelation. Barth would vehemently reject any suggestion that human reason might reach up to God through reflective uses of transcendental concepts and/or cognitions.

In Chapter 4, I will return to the topic of Barth's rejection of the transcendental method, generically understood. I will offer close readings of passages in which he uses Kantian terms such as "regulative" and "constitutive" principles, *Denknotwendigkeit* (necessity of thought) and *Erfahrungsgegenstand* (object of experience), etc. For now, suffice it to say that the various proposals to impose on Barth a certain transcendental *Denkform* have been largely oblivious to his innovative development of a basically Anselmian mode of speculation against German idealism.

McCormack's Post-Kantian Interpretation

McCormack's version of post-Kantian interpretation is the one that the present monograph engages with primarily. It is one that truly constitutes a paradigm in the field. While McCormack's intellectual-biographical account of what Barth learned from his Marburg teachers seems to agree with, say, Lohmann's influential

---

68. Kant, *Critique of Pure Reason*, A631/B659.

narrative, it appears that McCormack is not always clear whether the primary Kantian influence on Barth was that of Kant's own philosophy or that of Marburg neo-Kantianism.

Thomas Xutong Qu rightly observes that "in contrast to Lohmann's neo-Kantian interpretation," McCormack tends to "understand Barth from the standpoint of classical Kantianism. For McCormack, Barth's realism struggles against the modern turn towards the subject, but without a return to the somewhat naïve, metaphysically based realism of classical theology."[69] In a similar vein, Baark demonstrates that "McCormack's Barth … accepts the entire framework of Kant's theoretical philosophy and views its account of the structure of human knowledge as a given."[70]

I agree with McCormack's realist interpretation of Kant's transcendental idealism.[71] McCormack rightly comments that "Kant was an empirical realist in the precise sense of holding that the content of our knowledge comes to us entirely from without."[72] Barth, per McCormack, accepted Kant's empirical realism, and so it is erroneous to impose any "phenomenalist" form of Kantianism on Barth.[73]

The problems with McCormack's reading of Kant's own empirical realism into Barth are at least twofold. First, Kant's intent to safeguard empirical realism was precisely what Marburg neo-Kantianism rejected in its highly idealistic and phenomenalistic account of empirical knowledge. This is a fact that McCormack does not seem to acknowledge when he cites Fisher to contend that the "idealism of neo-Kantianism is transcendental, not subjective."[74]

What McCormack does not seem to realize is that Fisher's description of Marburg neo-Kantianism here trades on the ambiguity of the term "transcendental." As explained earlier, the term "transcendental" can be interpreted within a two-object framework, such that transcendental idealism would be taken in a fundamentally phenomenalistic direction. The Marburg neo-Kantian version of transcendental idealism is described as "objective" only in the sense that representations (*Vorstellungen*: referring generically to everything presented to the mind) occur in the "'objective consciousness … ' from which all subjective elements have been filtered out."[75]

McCormack in fact acknowledges that for Barth's neo-Kantian teachers at Marburg, "[t]here is no thing-in-itself in Kant's sense."[76] According to Marburg neo-Kantianism, reports McCormack, "thought generates its objects."[77] Despite its

---

69. Qu, 56. Translation mine.
70. Baark, *The Affirmations of Reason*, 16.
71. *Pace* Paul Guyer, *Kant and the Claims of Knowledge* (Cambridge: Cambridge University Press, 1987).
72. McCormack, "Reflections on Van Til," 369.
73. McCormack, "Reflections on Van Til," 372.
74. McCormack, *Barth's Dialectical Theology*, 44.
75. McCormack, *Barth's Dialectical Theology*, 45.
76. McCormack, *Barth's Dialectical Theology*, 44.
77. McCormack, *Barth's Dialectical Theology*, 45.

own claim to be objectivistic, then, Marburg neo-Kantianism's phenomenalistic rendition of transcendental idealism is fundamentally at odds with Kant's own version of empirical realism, which rests upon an one-object view of appearances in relation to things-in-themselves. From the viewpoint of classical Kantianism, the Marburg version of transcendental idealism is not very far away from Berkleian subjectivism. For the Marburg neo-Kantians, empirical knowledge does not, as McCormack would have it, come to us "entirely from without."

To render transcendental idealism as a doctrine according to which empirical knowledge "comes to us entirely from without," one would have to accept what is sometimes called Kant's "discursivity thesis." To say that human cognition is "discursive" is to say that it necessarily involves an interplay between two cognitive faculties that are distinct from one another, namely, sensibility (*Sinnlichkeit*) and understanding (*Verstand*: the German rendering of the Latin *intellectio*). External objects do not conform immediately to our sensible cognition. Rather, they conform to our intellectual understanding. We do not just perceive objects with our senses and leave our sensory data in a disorganized state. We use our intellectual faculty to think these objects. Kant takes for granted that we already possess objective understanding of things. This means that there *must be* some rational order in the external world analogous to the intellectual and rational structure of our minds, in such a way that each of us can interact with other material and spiritual beings.

In other words, the fact that we can think the world means that the world must be capable of being thought. In Kant's own words, "the attempt to think them [objects of experience] … will provide a splendid touchstone of what we assume as the altered method of our way of thinking"—"for they *must be* capable of being thought."[78]

McCormack does not seem to realize that the way he and Fisher describe Marburg idealism as "transcendental" and "objective" does not square with Kant's own discursivity thesis. According to Marburg neo-Kantianism, says McCormack, "[t]hought provides not only the form of the objects known (through the categories), it also *generates* the contents of its objects."[79]

To his credit, McCormack does acknowledge that this "epistemology was … a far more radical idealism than anything envisioned by Kant."[80] Still, McCormack does not seem to realize that if this is the version of Kantianism adopted by Barth, then it would be impossible to claim that for Barth, empirical knowledge "comes to us entirely from without."

On one hand, McCormack imposes Kant's own empirically realistic doctrine of transcendental idealism on Barth. On the other hand, McCormack often slips to the side of Lohmann and Fisher to suggest that Barth's critical realism and *Realdialektik*, as well as Barth's all-important actualism, originated from Marburg neo-Kantianism. The problem is that these neo-Kantian ideas that McCormack

---

78. Kant, *Critique of Pure Reason*, Bxvii.
79. McCormack, *Barth's Dialectical Theology*, 44.
80. McCormack, *Barth's Dialectical Theology*, 44.

attributes to Barth are fundamentally incompatible with the empirical realism that McCormack imposes on Barth.

The second problem with McCormack's post-Kantian portrayal of Barth is that McCormack almost completely overlooks Barth's own interpretation of Kant, which clearly follows a phenomenalist trajectory. On Barth's reading of Kant, "empirical knowledge" is simply "constituted … by the unity of intuition and concepts."[81] Barth explains that the "object" of intuition and understanding "cannot be the 'thing-in-itself', that is a thing manifest to us in its essential nature; but is the thing as it is given and comprehended by virtue of these two forms of knowledge."[82]

Those familiar with nineteenth-century debates on Kant's transcendental idealism would recognize here that Barth has opted for a two-object interpretation. What Barth is suggesting here is that the thing-in-itself and its appearance are, according to Kant's transcendental idealism, altogether two different objects rather than two aspects of the same object. One striking feature of Barth's phenomenalist reading of Kant is that Barth completely sets aside Kant's theory of "the principle of permanent substance," discussed under the rubric of the "Analogies of Experience."[83]

The phenomenalistic, idealistic-subjectivistic, immaterialistic, basically Berkeleian, two-object (as opposed to two-aspect) interpretation of Kant dates back to his own day. As I just pointed out, Kant himself rejected it explicitly, and yet it remained influential among his followers and critics throughout the nineteenth century.[84] That Barth holds to this reading of Kant is obvious from the fact that according to Barth, "Kant's transcendentalism" is well in agreement with both Fichte's half-fledged idealism and Hegel's absolute idealism.[85]

Barth's phenomenalistic interpretation of Kant's transcendental idealism calls into question the validity of McCormack's imposition of Kant's own empirical realism on Barth's supposedly Kantian presuppositions. On McCormack's reading, reports Baark, "the importance of Kant's theoretical philosophy for Barth turns out to be its empiricism: God must become intuitable like any other object in time and space in order to be known. As the human subject encounters the object (Jesus), God imparts the knowledge that this object is God through the Holy Spirit."[86]

---

81. *Protestant Theology*, 260.
82. *Protestant Theology*, 260.
83. Kant, A183/B226. Note that Kant's treatment of the first Analogy in the second edition of the *Critique* differs from the first edition.
84. See Immanuel Kant, *Prolegomena to Any Future Metaphysics*, ed. and trans. Gary Hatfield (Cambridge: Cambridge University Press, 2004), 4: 378–9; also see the editor's introduction, xxxii–xxxiii. The two-object interpretation was popularized among Anglophone scholars in 1966 by Peter Strawson, *The Bounds of Sense: An Essay on Kant's Critique of Pure Reason* (London: Routledge, 1966).
85. *Protestant Theology*, 379.
86. Baark, *The Affirmations of Reason*, 16.

What McCormack offers, then, is (1) a reconstrual of Barth's reliance on Kant apart from Barth's own interpretation of Kant, along with (2) an imposition of this particular "post-Kantian" reading on Barth that downplays Barth's own account of his Anselmian heritage. Baark rightly observes that "a consequence of accepting [McCormack's] account of Barth's theology has been to replace Barth's own interpretation of his thinking with someone else's account of his thinking. This prioritizes a secondary reading of Barth over Barth's own texts."[87]

Barth's Use of Kant Reconsidered

There is, to be sure, some truth to McCormack's description of Barth as attempting to "overcome Kant by means of Kant; not retreating behind him and seeking to go around him."[88] Baark also concurs that "Kant's thinking provides the most basic framework of, as well as the crucial building blocks for, Barth's theology."[89] However, I will contend in the ensuing chapters that Barth was not directly reacting to Kant or Marburg neo-Kantianism. Rather, what Barth sought to overcome, as Baark has also suggested, was the phenomenalist Kant of a certain *Rezeptionsgeschichte* in nineteenth-century German idealism. Better put, it was the idealist transformation of Kant that Barth sought to overcome.

One of Barth's chief tasks in his development of Anselmian speculation in the early 1930s, I will argue, was to set himself apart from German idealism. In fact, McCormack acknowledges Barth's anti-idealist impulse, too.[90] Lacking in McCormack's interpretation is a recognition of how Barth sought to overcome idealism by means of Anselm, rather than resorting to Kant to try to overcome post-Kantian obstacles.

I share Baark's view that Barth "both critiques and develops" some of the key ideas in Hegel's system such as "freedom, reason, and self-consciousness that form the backbone of German Idealism."[91] Furthermore, "ideas are 'in the air' so to speak and exert their influence whether later actors are intimately acquainted with them or not."[92] This means that despite Barth's familiarity with Kant's texts, the Kantian ideas that Barth wrestled with "are best explained by reference to Fichte's reception of Kant," which Hegel and Schelling inherited.[93] This will be important for my demonstration of how Barth adopted an Anselmian mode of speculation in critical response to modern speculative metaphysics.

Barth's use of Kant, in any case, is not an *ad fontes* retrieval, nor does Barth rely on the positivist Kant of his Marburg teachers for the edification of his

---

87. Baark, *The Affirmations of Reason*, 17.
88. McCormack, *Barth's Dialectical Theology*, 465.
89. Baark, *The Affirmations of Reason*, 70.
90. McCormack, "Grace and Being," 100. This is acknowledged by Molnar, *Divine Freedom*, 127.
91. Baark, *The Affirmations of Reason*, 82.
92. Baark, *The Affirmations of Reason*, 72.
93. Baark, *The Affirmations of Reason*, 70.

mature theology. Rather, Barth reappropriates "the Kantian insights concerning self-consciousness" that "Hegel radicalizes" to develop "an understanding of rationality and freedom that avoids some of the pitfalls that trouble the earlier idealists."[94]

What this mean is that the conceptual building blocks that Barth eclectically and critically reappropriated are primarily from idealism's—especially Hegel's—transformation of Kant, rather than from Kant directly, or from Marburg neo-Kantianism. Only with due attention to the idealist, especially the Hegelian, background of Barth's intellectual upbringing will it be possible for us to comprehend his innovative adaptation of Anselmian speculation and the application thereof in his development of theological Christocentrism in 1936–42.

I will discuss Barth's treatment of Kant in relation to German idealism in the next chapter by turning to Barth's own writings. An accurate and precise understanding of Barth's eclectic and critical uses of Kant requires an intellectual historiography more sophisticated and larger in scope than the initial sketches that Baark has helpfully drawn. This is a task that I cannot take up fully at the present juncture. In the conclusion to this chapter, however, I will demonstrate how Barth deemed the speculative metaphysics of Hegel and Schleiermacher, rather than Kant's transcendentalism, to be the pinnacle of religious idolatry and anthropological projection in modern times that genuinely Christian theology must overcome, and how Barth did not see in Kant or neo-Kantianism any viable solution to this distinctively modern problem.

Actualistic Ontology

As suggested, one regulating concept in McCormack's interpretative framework is that of actualism. He stated his take on Barth's actualism as an ontological principle as early as 1993: "Barth understood 'nature' to be a function of decision and act."[95] McCormack's 1995 masterpiece bolstered this rendition of Barth's actualism by incorporating the ontological principle into an intellectual-biographical paradigm.

In his controversial 2000 *Cambridge Companion* essay, McCormack spells out the key implication of what he takes to be Barth's actualistic ontology:

> Barth, too, knows of an "essence" (a self-identical element) in God, but for him "essence" is given in the act of electing and is, in fact, constituted by that eternal act. It is not an independent "something" that stands behind all God's acts and relations. God's being, for Barth, is a being-in-act; first, as a being-in-act in eternity and then, corresponding to that, as a being-in-act in time.[96]

---

94. Baark, *The Affirmations of Reason*, 82.
95. Bruce McCormack, *For Us and Our Salvation: Incarnation and Atonement in the Reformed Tradition* (Princeton: Princeton Theological Seminary, 1993).
96. McCormack, "Grace and Being," 99.

Since, then, a number of leading scholars in the field have adopted McCormack's view that "there is for Barth 'no state, no mode of being or existence above and prior to this eternal act of self-determination as substantialistic thinking would lead us to believe.'"[97] They of course acknowledge that Barth himself continued to teach the doctrine of an immanent Trinity and a *Logos asarkos* that grounds and makes possible the act of election and the event of the incarnation. If Barth had followed through with his actualistic ontology more consistently, however, then Barth, they argue, would have stated that "the action of God in electing to be God for humanity in Jesus Christ is *not* the act of an already existing agent. Rather it is an act in the course of which God determines the very being of God."[98]

I will develop a different account of Barth's actualistic "ontology" in Chapter 3, explaining the motif of being-in-act as an expression of his speculative theology. At this juncture, I will offer a critical assessment of the post-Kantian narrative of Barth's intellectual biography from which McCormack's construal of Barth's actualism arose.

What needs to be said in the first instance is that this construal did not arise from any close reading of Barth's texts. In fact, as we already saw, McCormack claims that there is an inconsistency in Barth's writings between his actualistic principle and his doctrine of God, and rather than trying to offer a charitable reading of the texts, McCormack's intent is to "register a critical correction" against what Barth explicitly wrote. The ontological principle on which McCormack seeks to register this correction does not stem primarily from careful exegesis of Barth's writings either, but from the post-Kantian narrative that McCormack imposes on Barth.

McCormack claims that Barth's actualistic ontology is derived from Hermann Cohen, a Jewish philosopher of the Marburg school of neo-Kantianism.

> For Hermann Cohen ..., the human simply *is* the sum total of his or her lifetime of knowing activities. Expressed more expansively: the human is what he or she does. It was but a short step from here to reflection upon the divine nature as actualistic—a point which Barth would begin to ground christologically just two and a half years after publishing his second *Romans*.[99]

This reading of Cohen into Barth is quite a stretch. It may be true that Barth's early writings from the Marburg years reflect the influences of Wilhelm Herrmann, Hermann Cohen, and Paul Natorp.[100] However, McCormack has not provided any

---

97. Paul Nimmo, *Being in Action: The Theological Shape of Barth's Ethical Vision* (London: T&T Clark, 2007), 8. Here Nimmo cites Bruce McCormack, "The Ontological Presuppositions of Barth's Doctrine of the Atonement," in *The Glory of the Atonement*, ed. Charles Hill and Frank James III (Downers Grove: IVP, 2004), 359.

98. Nimmo, *Being in Action*, 8.

99. Bruce McCormack, *Orthodox and Modern: Studies in the Theology of Karl Barth* (Grand Rapids: Baker Academic, 2008), 12.

100. McCormack, *Barth's Dialectical Theology*, 68–77.

textual evidence—from Barth's letters or his theological writings—to demonstrate that the *Denkform* of Barth's actualism was inherited from Cohen.

The fact is that the theme of being-*as*-as (McCormack does not seem to think that there is any difference between what he calls "being-*in*-act" and the idealist understanding of being *as* act) was commonplace in German philosophy and theology in the post-Kantian era up to Barth's student years. There is little reason to believe that Cohen's idea struck Barth as anything innovative or inspirational. The same speculative theme was already found in Fichte (the immediate identity between the being and act of the thinking *Ich*) and the early Schelling (divine revelation as God's presence in self-activating beings in the creaturely realm). The later Schleiermacher developed a Christological actualism that identifies Christ as the pure activity of God's love. The distinctively post-Kantian theme of identity between being and act also featured prominently in early twentieth-century German theology down to the generation of Barth's students. Bonhoeffer's *Act and Being* is an example. As mentioned earlier, Bonhoeffer believed that Barth's view of God's supratemporal essence was in violation of the ontological principle of being-as-act.[101]

In a word, the idea of being-as-act was very much "in the air" during Barth's formative years. An intellectual-biographical account of what one of Barth's teachers at Marburg taught is far from sufficient to show that his actualistic *Denkform* was inherited from this teacher and always remained committed to what McCormack prescribes as the epistemological presuppositions of (neo-)Kantianism.

The more serious problem with McCormack's imposition of Cohen's actualism on Barth is that it is, again, incompatible with the claim that Barth adopted an empirically realistic version of Kantianism. According to McCormack himself, Cohen insisted that "there is no being which does not have its origin in thought. To 'be' is, in a word, to be known."[102] And because what is known to us is known solely in the form of spatio-temporality, we must understand being as a function of historical activity.

It is not hard to see here that Cohen's speculative identification of being with act is fundamentally incompatible with the empirical realism of classical Kantianism. Kant's affirmation of empirical realism goes hand in hand with the recognition of permanent substance as a principle (an ontological and/or logical starting point) that somehow corresponds to the thing-in-itself. Cohen emphatically denied this principle in his actualistic construal of the notion of being. And if Barth accepted Kant's empirical realism, as McCormack would have it, then Barth would have contradicted himself in accepting Cohen's actualism.

To determine the intellectual-historical roots of Barth's speculative notion of being-*in*-act (which must be strictly differentiated from the idealist notion of

---

101. Bonhoeffer's 1930 *Habilitationsschrift* is a classic instance. Dietrich Bonhoeffer, *Act and Being*, ed. Hans-Richard Reuter and Wayne Whitson Floyd, trans. H. Martin Rumscheidt (Minneapolis: Fortress, 1996).

102. McCormack, *Barth's Dialectical Theology*, 44.

being-*as*-act), a nomenclatural study of his actualistic terminology is necessary (a task that I take on in fuller detail in Chapter 3). Consider, for example, a quote from Barth that McCormack's post-Kantian model has made famous: "It [the God-human relation in Christ] is a relation in which God is *self-determined*, so that the *determination* belongs no less to him than all that he is *in and for himself*."[103]

The phrase "in and for himself" is distinctively Hegelian: it is Hegel's speculative definition of "absolute." The use of this expression in conjunction with the term "determination" (*Bestimmung*) makes it clear that Barth's use of "determination" functions within a Hegelian, rather than (neo-)Kantian or Fichtean, grammar. In fact, McCormack himself recognizes "determination" in Barth's writings as an originally Hegelian term.[104] Yet, he still tries to incorporate it into an originally neo-Kantian framework. This has created a number of difficulties in McCormack's interpretation, not least his confusion of the notion of "determination" with ontological "constitution."

In Chapter 3, I will define "determination" in light of Barth's own writings and his intellectual-historical background. I will argue that Barth critically reappropriated a distinctively Hegelian grammar to (1) reinvigorate the substance language of Anselmian speculation and (2) correct Hegel's speculative mistake of subject-predicate reversal in ontological predications about God, which prioritizes activity over essence. Barth's retainment of the classical language of essence (*Wesen*) and nature (*Natur*), I will argue, is intended to safeguard theology from falling into Hegel's error of identifying essentiality (*Wesentlichkeit*) with something consummate—something that not yet *is*. Barth's distinction between *Wesen* (essential being) and *Sein* (existential being), along with his rejection of the originally Hegelian association of *Sein* with *Schein* (appearance) and his strict differentiation "between the divine" and "the demonic" notion of the "appearance of the divine [*dem Schein-Göttlichen*]," serves to demonstrate how his actualistic ontology is tailored to a Hegelian grammar in order to overcome Hegel's idolatrous presuppositions.[105]

Barth's insistence that God is being-*in*-act serves to reject the phenomenalistic and idealistic principle of being-*as*-act. His actualistic "ontology"—if I may use the term in a very broad sense—draws a clear distinction between God's being-in-and-for-Godself and God's self-determined being-for-us. God-in-and-for-Godself is one and the same unsublatable subject as God-for-us, but the two moments of God's absolute being, the one *ad intra* and the other *ad extra*, are also abidingly distinct. The originally Hegelian language of determination serves to stress that the identity between God in God's triune essence and God in the history of revelation is a speculative (i.e., mediated through a mirror, as it were) one. Immediate identity between essence and act is, according to God's self-revelation

---

103. CD II/2, 7. Emphases added.
104. Bruce McCormack, "Election and Trinity: Theses in Response to George Hunsinger," *Scottish Journal of Theology* 63 (2010): 211n15.
105. CD II/1, 409; KD II/1, 461.

in Jesus Christ, to be found in the triune God-in-and-for-Godself alone. God is primarily being in the intra-trinitarian *opera ad intra*, and secondarily being in the act of electing to be the God of Jesus Christ, who is himself very God and very human. God's being in God's primary absoluteness grounds and makes possible God's secondary absoluteness in Jesus Christ, which in turn grounds and makes possible the objectivity of our speculative knowledge of God through God's *opera ad extra externa*.

Conclusion: Some Initial Historical-Intellectual Considerations

In the foregoing analyses, I have focused on the inconsistencies and technical mistakes of McCormack's reading of the role of (neo-)Kantian ideas in Barth's development as a theologian. I have not yet addressed the larger and more fundamental question, namely, whether Barth was primarily reacting to the challenges of (neo-)Kantianism on originally or basically (neo-)Kantian terms, or to the speculative metaphysicians of the German idealist tradition within a *Denkform* that in fact has little to do with his Marburg background.

Before proceeding to the next chapter to discuss Barth's basically Anselmian response to the idealist mode of speculative metaphysics, I will give an initial answer to this question from Barth's own account of his intellectual-historical background. In *Protestant Theology in the Nineteenth Century*, composed of written lectures from the late 1920s and early 1930s, Barth paints a very clear picture in which Hegel and Schleiermacher tower far above Kant and the various Kantian schools of thought in the fields of philosophy and theology, respectively.

Barth writes of Hegel:

> For fundamentally the astonishing thing is not that Hegel believed his philosophy to be an unsurpassable climax and culmination. It is that he was not right in thinking that after him the development was possible of a school of positivism, of pessimism and even of materialism, of Neo-Kantianism and whatever else the other modern philosophies may be called. The astonishing thing is that nineteenth-century man did not acknowledge that his concern in the realm of thought, his basic intellectual concern, had truly achieved ultimate recognition in Hegel's philosophy.[106]

It is Barth's view that in the field of philosophy, Hegel, rather than Kant or (neo-)Kantianism, represents the pinnacle of anthropological speculation that genuinely theological speculation must overcome. The passage quoted above shows that from the Münster-Bonn period (the years in which the original materials of *Protestant Theology* were composed) up to 1946 (the year in which

---

106. *Protestant Theology*, 370.

Protestant Theology was completed in the form of a book), Barth already deemed neo-Kantianism to be an unviable answer to the challenges of the speculative metaphysics of German idealism.

Pace McCormack, Barth never incorporated the "critically realistic" aspect of neo-Kantian philosophy into his own theological *Denkform*. Quite the contrary, Barth deemed critical realism useless in the face of the challenges of German idealism. He writes in the *Münster Dogmatics*:

> The question of which form of philosophy one is intentionally or unintentionally devoted to is entirely irrelevant; epistemological conversion to some critical realism would be completely meaningless in light of the matter-of-fact—that God is a hidden God precisely because He is the self-revealing God, the God before whose deity we can neither flee from transcendence into immanence nor vice versa, the God who is never so far away since He is completely near us, and near us precisely in being far from us, the One who can never be an object because He is God.[107]

In the field of theology, too, Barth deemed the neo-Kantian trajectory adopted by his Ritchlian teachers to be basically inconsequential in the face of Schleiermacher's speculative-metaphysical approach (see Chapter 2 for my explanation of how Barth saw Schleiermacher's theological program as "speculative" despite Schleiermacher's own aversion to speculative sciences). Of course, Barth's understanding of the significance of the Ritschlian school differs somewhat from the more widely accepted narrative of our own day.

In contemporary historiographies of nineteenth-century German theology, Albrecht Ristchl's (1822–89) turn to Kantian positivism in 1856 is often described as a decisive event in modern theology's break with Schleiermacher's metaphysical approach. This is a view that Barth would not quarrel with. Wilhelm Herrmann (1846–1922) and Adolf von Harnack (1851–1930), Barth's erstwhile Ritschlian teachers, are described as having taken Ritschl's anti-metaphysical Kantianism to its logical end: they "moved beyond historicism" and no longer saw history as purposively progressing toward any consummate endpoint.[108] Barth would also agree with this description of Herrmann and Harnack.

However, Barth did not see the neo-Kantian approach to theology represented by the Ritschlians as having gained dominance over the metaphysical trajectory founded by Schleiermacher. Whereas contemporary historiographers usually see Ernst Troeltsch (1865–1923) as a key figure around the turn of the twentieth century in a last-ditch battle, so to speak, to secure and revive "metaphysical"

---

107. *MD*, 291–2. Translation mine. D. Paul La Montagne is mistaken in asserting that the term "critical realism" was not readily available to Barth. See Montagne, *Barth and Rationality: Critical Realism in Theology* (Eugene: Wipf and Stock, 2012), 10.

108. See Johannes Zachhuber, "The Historical Turn," in *The Oxford Handbook of Nineteenth-Century Christian Thought*, ed. Joel Rasmussen, Judith Wolffe, and Johannes Zachhuber (Oxford: Oxford University Press, 2017), 66.

theology against the onslaught of naturalistic positivisms in German academia, Barth saw the dominance of "the band of historians led by Troeltsch" as solid evidence that Ritschlian theology had lost its ground by the 1910s.[109]

At the very beginning of his chapter on Ritschl in *Protestant Theology*, incidentally the final chapter of the book, Barth comments:

> It has been said of Ritschl that in the history of theology since Schleiermacher he is the only one who, in the true sense, has given birth to an epoch. This is not true because all the strivings proceeding from Schleiermacher, who was, despite all argument, the only one who really gave rise to an epoch, continued on their way in a very significant fashion beside Ritschl, and were even more than ever taken up again after him.[110]

In Barth's estimation, "Schleiermacher's influence was incomparably stronger in 1910 than in 1830."[111] Barth observes that during his student years, the consensus among his peers was that if theology was to break free of the bondage of philosophy, as it were, then "theology" would have to "conquer" the field "anew … under the banner of Schleiermacher, or perhaps of Hegel, and on no account under that of Ritschl."[112]

Ritschl, on Barth's account, "went back to Kant, but Kant quite definitely interpreted as an anti-metaphysical moralist."[113] While Barth took from his Ritschlian teachers a phenomenalist account of Kant (as we saw), he did not agree with their anti-metaphysical, moralistic interpretation.[114] As we shall see in the next chapter, Barth believed that Kant's "transcendentalism" was the very seed of a distinctively modern form of speculative metaphysics that culminated in Hegel.

In any case, the Ritschlian adoption of an anti-metaphysical form of Kantianism was for Barth entirely powerless against the onslaught of speculative metaphysics advanced respectively by Hegel and Schleiermacher in the fields of philosophy and theology. It would thus be a mistake to characterize Barth as attempting

---

109. *Protestant Theology*, 641.
110. *Protestant Theology*, 640.
111. *Protestant Theology*, 640.
112. *Protestant Theology*, 640.
113. *Protestant Theology*, 641.
114. Kant's treatment of metaphysics is still a subject of intense debate today. Paul Guyer has argued that Kant's transcendental idealism is a metaphysical doctrine that refutes metaphysics *in globo*. See Paul Guyer, *Kant and the Claims of Knowledge* (Cambridge: Cambridge University Press, 1987). An authoritative refutation of Guyer's view is set forth in Henry Allison, *Kant's Transcendental Idealism: An Interpretation and Defense* (New Haven: Yale University Press, 2004). Stephen Palmquist's reading of Kant in the framework of a "system of perspectives" is, to my mind, one that squares most neatly with the texts of the two editions of Kant's first *Critique*. See Stephen Palmquist, *Kant's Critical Religion: Volume Two of Kant's System of Perspectives* (London: Routledge, 2000).

to overcome Kant by means of the anti-metaphysical Kant of Barth's Ritschlian teachers (as McCormack would have it).

Kant, no matter how he is interpreted, does not represent for Barth the most significant challenges to Christian theology. (Neo-)Kantianism, moreover, does not provide Barth with any *Denkform* that promises to overcome those challenges, represented on his view by the speculative metaphysics of German idealism and romanticism.

In the next chapter, I will discuss Barth's understanding of modern speculative metaphysics that, on his account, began with Descartes and culminated in Hegel. I will show how this idealistic mode of speculation constituted for him the pinnacle of religious idolatry and anthropological projection in modern times. Then, I will demonstrate how Barth appealed to a basically Anselmian mode of speculation to develop the *Denkform* of his mature theology as the key to answering the challenges of German idealism and romanticism. It was in Anselmian speculation that Barth found his key to overturning the idolatrous renditions of self-identity and speculative extension that culminated in the subject-predicate reversal of Hegelian speculation.

One more word that can be said here, before we turn to the next chapter, is that the association between Hegel and Anselm has a long tradition dating back to the generation of Hegel's students. One mainstream view among Hegel scholars is that Hegelian speculation originated from Anselm. Howard Kainz, for instance, almost took for granted that Hegel echoes "Anselm's *credo ut intelligam* faith" as "the foundation for speculative philosophizing."[115] This view, as we shall see, was also popular in Barth's time. His reinterpretation of Anselm against this inherited view was partly aimed at highlighting the fundamental difference between the Anselmian and idealist modes of speculation, in order to overcome the idolatry of the latter.

With McCormack's narrow and often self-contradictory account of what he purports to be Barth's originally (neo-)Kantian *Denkform*, it would be quite difficult to recognize the importance of Barth's innovative adaptation of an Anselmian mode of speculative theologizing. A narrative of Barth's intellectual-historical background is necessary as an alternative to McCormack's post-Kantian paradigm. While Baark has already deployed an authoritative account of the formal and intellectual-biographical aspects of Barth's speculative theology, the intellectual-historical dimension is still in need of some significant furnishing. I will offer a more sophisticated intellectual-historical narrative in the next chapter, highlighting the themes of identity and extension or image in Barth's speculative *Denkform*. This will give us a clearer picture of the form of Barth's speculative theology, and provide us with the basis on which to make sense of his Christocentric revision of doctrine of election in 1936.

---

115. Howard Kainz, "Hegel, Providence, and the Philosophy of History," *Hegel-Jahrbuch* (1995): 184.

Chapter 2

SKETCHING THE BACKGROUND: BARTH AND THE HISTORY OF SPECULATIVE THEOLOGY

The previous chapter demonstrated the inadequacies of the post-Kantian paradigm of Barth interpretation led by Bruce McCormack. There are, as we shall further discuss in this chapter, two specific weaknesses to this interpretative approach in the intellectual-historical dimension. First, the reductionistic tendency to see the whole of nineteenth-century philosophy and scientific theology as developments of Kant's ideas is often oblivious to the richness and diversity of German thought and culture in the eighteenth and nineteenth centuries. Second, while it is true that Barth himself adopted a somewhat reductionistic approach to the history of ideas, he did not understand this history with Kant as the primary reference point, nor did he see in Kant the chief challenge that genuine theology as the science of God must overcome. It is true that Barth thought of Kant's "transcendentalism" as the source of the basic conceptual building blocks of German idealism. However, it was Hegel's formulation of speculative identity that, in Barth's view, definitively brought about an anthropological turn in modern theological speculation. Furthermore, according to Barth, while Kant's transcendentalism facilitated the culmination of idealist speculation in Hegel, the modern origin of idealist speculation is to be found in Descartes, not Kant.

Barth interpreted the intellectual-historical developments of German thought and culture as a whole through the lens of the Cartesian-Hegelian mode of speculation, rather than what he likes to call Kantian "transcendentalism." On his interpretation, the anthropocentric program of *credo ut intelligam* speculation that began with Descartes and culminated in Hegel lied at the very heart of modern philosophical idolatry, expressed not least in the notion of German Christianity as a pantheistic *Volksreligion*.

Barth's speculative theology, then, was not primarily an attempt to "overcome Kant by means of Kant; not retreating behind him and seeking to go around him."[1] Rather, it was much more of an endeavor to overcome idealism by means of Anselm. Barth adopted the conceptual and terminological apparatuses of Hegelian idealism

---

1. This was Bruce McCormack's description of Kant's role in Barth's theology. See Bruce McCormack, *Karl Barth's Critically Realistic Dialectical Theology* (Oxford: Clarendon, 1995), 465.

to express a basically Anselmian mode of theological speculation, which Barth took to be the antidote to the idolatrous theme of speculative identity between human thinking and divine being posited in the Cartesian-Hegelian program.

It is worth reiterating here that in stressing the Anselmian core of Barth's speculative theology, I seek to honor Barth's own account of himself. Barth himself reported in the preface to *CD* I/1 that after the publication of "the first volume of a *Christian Dogmatics in Outline*" in 1927, he came to realize that "the need for [his] little work on Anselm of Canterbury was so pressing," because the substantive materials of his dogmatic theology demanded a new *Denkform* that would allow him to be "saying the same thing, but in a very different way."[2]

In light of passages like this, what McCormack's proposal to replace Anselmian readings of Barth with a post-Kantian framework really amounts to is the extraordinary assertion that McCormack is right about Barth while Barth was wrong about himself. This is rather astounding, given how McCormack explicitly acknowledges on the very first page of *Barth's Dialectical Theology* Hans Urs von Balthasar's famous quotation of Barth: "The real work that documents my conversion ... from the residue of a philosophical or anthropological ... grounding of Christian doctrine ... is ... my 1931 book on Anselm of Canterbury's proofs of the existence of God."[3]

McCormack suggests that "missing from Balthasar's quotation is the larger context—which might have turned the interpretation in a very different direction from the one von Balthasar took."[4] Missing in McCormack's intellectual-biographical account, however, is even the slightest attempt to reinterpret the Barth quote above. McCormack simply dismisses what Barth says about himself in so many similar passages, and imposes a certain "larger context" on Barth, a context that McCormack reconstructed from bits and pieces of intellectual-biographical data.

The truth is that Barth's own account of the significance of *Anselm* to the *Church Dogmatics* remained consistent through to the end of his career. In the 1958 preface to the second edition of *Anselm*, he recounts:

> So far as I was concerned, after finishing this book I went straight into my *Church Dogmatics* and it kept me occupied ever since and will continue to occupy me for the rest of my days. Only a comparatively few commentators, for example Hans Urs von Balthasar, have realized that my interest in Anselm was never a side-issue for me or—assuming I am more or less correct in my historical interpretation of St Anselm—realized how much it has influenced me or been absorbed into my own line of thinking.[5]

---

2. *CD* I/1, xi.

3. See Karl Barth, "Parergon," *Evangelische Theologie* 8 (1948): 272. Quoted in Hans Urs von Balthasar, *The Theology of Karl Barth*, trans. Edward Oakes (San Francisco: Ignatius, 1992), 93. See McCormack, *Barth's Critically Realistic Dialectical Theology*, 1.

4. McCormack, *Barth's Critically Realistic Dialectical Theology*, 1.

5. *Anselm*, 11.

As if pre-empting McCormack's interpretative paradigm, Barth continues to comment here: "Most of them have completely failed to see that in this book on Anselm I am working with a vital key, if not the key, to an understanding of that whole process of thought that has impressed me more and more in my *Church Dogmatics* as the only one proper to theology."[6] Note here that the Anselmian program is for Barth not just one of many possible descriptions of his *Denkform*. It is, on his own account, "the only one proper to" his theology.

Sure enough, as we saw in the previous chapter, Balthasar's intellectual-biographical account of Barth's turn from dialectics to analogy did not pay adequate attention to what McCormack calls the "larger context" of the intellectual-historical milieu against which Barth was raised. Sigurd Baark has already offered a re-construal of that larger context by narrating the German idealist background of Barth's speculative theology.[7] With detailed and focused analyses of Kant, Fichte, and Hegel, Baark demonstrates that Barth's "being a speculative theologian is in part doing theology in light of the breakthroughs of the German Idealists; to think both with and against their fundamental ideas."[8]

As important as Baark's intellectual-historical account is to the scholarship on Barth, this aspect of the speculation model of Barth interpretation is still in need of some significant furnishing. Baark has presented an accurate picture of Kant's critical philosophy and idealist responses to Kant from Fichte and Hegel. However, some questions remain: How did Barth himself interpret Kant, Fichte, and Hegel? How was this interpretation shaped by the *Rezeptionsgeschichte* of these philosophers in the nineteenth century up to Barth's own day? And how was Barth's own speculative theology in turn shaped by his reception of this *Rezeptionsgeschichte*?

For one thing, Baark's presentation of German idealism almost leaves Barth's *Protestant Theology in the Nineteenth Century* completely out of sight. Baark offers a dense treatment of this text, the composition of which roughly coincided with *Anselm* chronologically, only on the first several pages of his fifth chapter, "The Early Dialectical Theology of Barth and Thurneysen."[9] Even there, however, Baark does not look into Barth's interpretation of the history of German idealism, and how this interpretation itself was shaped by the history that it sought to interpret.

Furthermore, in the intellectual-historical picture that Baark paints in broad strokes, some significant details have yet to be filled out. How did popular German historiographies of ideas in the nineteenth century come to regard Anselm as the founder of modern speculative philosophy? How did Anselm, Descartes, and Hegel come to be identified as representatives of the same pantheistic tradition of speculative metaphysics? Why did Barth express such a high degree of urgency to set the Anselmian mode of speculation apart from the Cartesian-Hegelian

---

6. *Anselm*, 11.
7. Sigurd Baark, *The Affirmations of Reason: On Karl Barth's Speculative Theology* (Cham: Palgrave Macmillan, 2018), 33–111.
8. Baark, *The Affirmations of Reason*, 109.
9. Baark, *The Affirmations of Reason*, 115–20.

mode? What did all this have to do with German Christianity as a mystical form of nationalism and nationalistic form of pantheism?

In this chapter I will seek to answer this array of questions. I will attempt to present Barth's own construal of the history of theological speculation, and how his account of this history was itself developed against the background of the very history that he sought to interpret. On this basis, I will demonstrate the significance of his development of a basically Anselmian mode of speculation.

For Barth's own understanding of his intellectual-historical background, I will rely primarily on *Protestant Theology in the Nineteenth Century*. Though this work was completed in Basel in 1946, the materials therein were largely comprised of "the lectures on the history of modern Protestant theology" that Barth "gave in Münster and Bonn."[10] The final "form" of these lectures "was a course that" Barth "gave in Bonn during the winter semester of 1932–3 and the summer semester of 1933."[11] His reflections on the history of modern Protestant thought in *Protestant Theology*, then, coincided chronologically with his development of a basically Anselmian *Denkform* in the late 1920s and early 1930s.

In what follows, I will interpret Barth's own account of his intellectual-historical background in light of the primary texts of the authors whom he discusses, and compare it to other accounts of the history of ideas formulated in the nineteenth and early twentieth centuries. This will help us understand the motivations and formative influences behind Barth's development of a basically Anselmian mode of speculation in a largely Hegelian form.

Speculative Theology in Classical Latin Christianity

"Speculation": A Preliminary Definition

Now, I realize that the characterization of Barth as a "speculative" theologian, initially proposed by Baark, needs to be defended, not least because of Barth's own express aversion to the term in most of the passages in which it appears. It must be understood that Barth casts this term in negative light only when referring to the rationalistic and idealistic mode of speculation that began with Descartes and culminated in Hegel in modern times. There are also instances in which Barth describes his own theology as "speculative." For example, on the concluding pages of *Anselm*, Barth explicitly uses the term "speculative" to describe the Anselmian *Denkform* that he adopted.[12]

So, what does "speculation" mean in this context in the first place? The word originated from the Latin for "mirror," *speculum*. This word carries the extended meanings of "mirror image," "imitation," and "copy," and is sometimes synonymous with *imago*. While the speculative tradition can be traced back to philosophers like

---

10. *Protestant Theology*, xi.
11. *Protestant Theology*, xi.
12. *Anselm*, 167.

Parmenides or Plato, it took on distinctively Christian presuppositions in classical Western theology. Among these is the axiom expressed most emphatically in the Reformed tradition, *finitum non capax infiniti* (the finite has no capacity for the infinite). God is incomprehensible to the creature, in that God is infinite, and the creature finite. This incomprehensibility entails God's unknowability *per essentiam* to the creature.

If the creature is to attain to any true knowledge of God's essence, this knowledge can only be *analogical* to God's self-knowledge. This means that creaturely knowledge of the transcendent God must be *mediated* to the creature by creaturely *specula*, so to speak, through which the believer may *reflect* on God's otherwise unknown essence.

John Calvin describes Scripture as the "mirror in which faith may contemplate God."[13] Thomas Aquinas states that even "Adam" in the pre-lapsarian state "did not see God through His Essence," but rather "saw God in an enigma, because he saw Him in a created effect," like the way "a man is seen through a mirror, and is seen with the mirror."[14] Thomistic speculation is *a postetriori*, not in that it finds its starting point in empirically observable objects: the redefinition of *a priori* and *a posteriori* in terms of experience did not occur until David Hume, and was not widely accepted in German philosophy until Kant's first *Critique*. Thomistic speculation is *a posteriori* in that it is a mode of speculating *from effect to cause*.

"Greater than Can Be Conceived": Anselmian Speculation

As mentioned above, Barth uses the term "speculative" as a derogative only with reference to rationalist and idealist speculation. The idealist program, which we will discuss in detail anon, finds its starting point in the assumption of the rational *conceivability* of God, which goes hand in hand with some kind of a noetic extension from the human ego to the divine being. A corollary to this speculative extension is the assumption of some identity—speculative (i.e., mirrored or mediated) or immediate—between human act and essence, thinking and being, *cogito* and *sum*, etc.

It has escaped the notice of many—if not the majority of—experts in the field that Barth explicitly uses the word "speculative" in acknowledging his adoption of a basically Anselmian *Denkform*, founded on the principle of God's *inconceivability*. This acknowledgment is found on the concluding pages of *Anselm*, in a context where Barth issues a brief critique of the rationalist mode of speculative extension that posits the *conceivability* of God: "Even if every conceivable physical and moral property were raised to the *n*th degree, that could quite well be nothing more than the sum total of the predicates of a purely conceptual being."[15]

---

13. John Calvin, *Institutes of the Christian Religion*, ed. John T. McNeill, trans. Ford Lewis Battles, vol. 1 (Philadelphia: WJK, 1960), 549.

14. Thomas Aquinas, *Summa Theologica*, trans. Fathers of the English Dominican Province, Q94A4, https://ccel.org/ccel/aquinas/summa/summa.i.html.

15. *Anselm*, 167.

Barth insists against the rationalist program that genuinely theological speculation must find its starting point not in an identity, speculative (Hegel) or immediate (Descartes and Fichte), between the essence and act of the rational human subject. The identity between act and essence is to be found in God alone, primarily in God's *opera ad intra* qua triune being as an immediate identity (which Barth calls God's primary absoluteness, God's being-in-and-for-Godself), and then between God's triune essence and God's secondary mode of absolute being qua electing God, who is at once the elected human and the very act of election, as a speculative (i.e., mirrored and mediated) identity. It is the ontic speculative extension from God's *ad intra* essence to God's revelatory mode of being *ad extra externa*, manifested through God's works *ad extra externa*, that constitutes the *speculum Trinitatis* through which the creature may contemplate God's essence.

Barth's basically Anselmian mode of speculation, then, proceeds from faith in God's revelation. More precisely, his *credo ut intelligam* program begins by believing not in any speculative identity between God's being itself and human conceptions of God, but in the mediated identity between God in God's self-revelation—"*id quod Deus est* [that which is God]"—and "God himself."[16] After-thinking (*Nachdenken*) of the matter of fact (*Tatsache*) of revelation in this way allows us to *reflect* on the immediate identity between the act and essence of God's triune being.

God's perfect nature, in other words, is not reflected through the imperfections of human nature as its *speculum*. The speculative extension, ontically speaking, is from God's inward essence to God's revelatory mode of being-in-act.

> The fact that *id quod Deus est* is synonymous with God himself makes this analogical, "speculative" understanding of his reality into true knowledge of his Nature that creates the fully efficacious, indeed over-efficacious substitute for the miss (and necessarily missing) experiential knowledge of him. This in turn compels knowledge of his Existence, the knowledge which is possible and becomes real so necessarily and so exclusively as against all other knowledge, including all denial and doubt, only in so far as it is knowledge of his Existence. God himself compels this knowledge. Whoever knows him himself cannot think, "God does not exist."[17]

Barth's exclusion of *experiential* knowledge of God is indicative of an *a priori* mode of speculation, albeit not of the kind that Kant describes as "transcendental" (see Chapter 1). The *a priori* mode of theological speculation that Barth adopts finds a classic but rather unsatisfactory definition in Anselm's *Monologion*, chapter 67:

> the mind may most fitly be said to be its own mirror wherein it contemplates, so to speak, the image of what it cannot see face to face. For, if the mind itself

---

16. *Anselm*, 167.
17. *Anselm*, 167.

alone among all created beings is capable of remembering and conceiving of and loving itself, I do not see why it should be denied that it is the true image of that being which, through its memory and intelligence and love, is united in an ineffable Trinity. Or, at any rate, it proves itself to be the more truly the image of that Being by its power of remembering, conceiving of, and loving, that Being. For, the greater and the more like that Being it is, the more truly it is recognised to be its image.[18]

Here Anselm still asserts that the human mind has the capacity to conceive of God's triune being. This *vestigium* or *speculum Trinitatis* is an Augustinian notion that Anselm never quite moved away from, and yet without significant revision, it would flatly contradict the principle of divine inconceivability stated in *Proslogion* (as we shall see anon). It has to be noted, however, that Barth is only opposed to the view that the human mind itself can be an *imago Trinitatis*. In Chapter 5, we shall see how Barth adopts the Augustinian notion of *speculum Trinitatis* in an innovative way, fleshing it out Christologically within the Augustinian-Anselmian program of *fides quaerens intellectum*.

Whatever the case, it was primarily in *Proslogion* that Barth discovered the concrete mode of speculative theologizing proper to the substance of his dogmatics. He recognizes the Anselmian *Denkform* set forth in *Proslogion* as *speculative*, rather than *deductive*. Barth comments that for Anselm, faith and understanding stand in an irreversible order: "Anselm wants 'proof' … because he wants *intelligere* and he wants *intelligere* because he believes. Any reversal of this order of compulsion is excluded by Anselm's conception of faith."[19] This is precisely why Anselm calls both *Monologion* and *Proslogion* "an example of meditation on the grounds of faith."[20]

I agree with Baark that Barth is right about Anselm. This can be demonstrated by an overview of Anselm's text. His express purpose in *Proslogion* is "to understand that thou art as we believe; and that thou art that which we believe."[21] More concretely: "we believe that thou art a being than which nothing greater can be conceived."[22] Yet, even this notion of an infinite being is not sufficiently concrete, since, on the ground of *finitum non capax infiniti* (a formula set forth by Reformed orthodox theologians to express a normative view in classical theology), the concrete existence of this being cannot be deduced from a finite creature's conception of infinity. Although the idea of an infinite being is implanted in the human mind such that even the fool cannot escape it, what we believe concretely regarding God has to be given to us through revelation.

---

18. Anselm of Canterbury, "Monologium," in *St. Anselm: Basic Writings*, trans. Sidney Norton Deane (Chicago: Open Court, 1962), 132.
19. *Anselm*, 17.
20. Anselm, *Proslogium*, in *St. Anselm: Basic Writings*, 47.
21. Anselm, *Proslogium*, 53.
22. Anselm, *Proslogium*, 53.

Anselm argues in *Proslogion*, Chapter 4, that all abstract philosophical formulations of the idea of God as infinite being can reasonably be conceived as nonexistent; only the concrete God of Scripture is the infinite being whom we cannot rationally conceive to be nonexistent.[23] This is why Anselm proceeds in the ensuing chapters to delineate God's concrete perfections in biblical terms. He is emphatic that God is self-existent as that greater than which nothing can be conceived, not as an abstract idea of infinite being, but as the triune God concretely revealed in Scripture (chapter 23).[24]

In this light, Anselmian "speculation" denotes a faith-seeking-understanding process in which the seeker after-thinks God's self-revelation in the phenomenal world as a mirror that *reflects* what God is in God's noumenal reality. When Barth adopts the language of Augustine and Calvin to speak of Christ as "*speculum electionis*" (mirror of election) in *Gottes Gnadenwahl* (1936), he is in fact exercising a basically Anselmian mode of speculation—a point of fact that proponents of McCormack's paradigm do not acknowledge.[25] In Chapters 4–6, I will explain how this identification of the history of Jesus Christ as *speculum electionis* serves to correct Anselm's view that the human mind is in itself an *imago Trinitatis*. Barth is emphatic in *CD* II/1-2 that Jesus Christ, who as the secondary mode of God's absolute being is at once the subject, object, and act of election, alone is the *speculum Trinitatis*. To treat the human mind as an image of the Trinity, in Barth's view, flatly contradicts Anselm's very own insistence on divine inconceivability.

The principle of divine inconceivability is one crucial point that sets Anselm apart from idealist modes of speculation, which Barth dismisses as anthropology in the guise of theology. It is found in chapter 15 of *Proslogion*: "Therefore, O Lord, thou art not only that than which a greater cannot be conceived, but *thou art a being greater than can be conceived*."[26] This is a statement of God's unknowability *per essentiam* that defies any attempt to reduce God to or identify God with a rational concept. There can be no speculative identity between anything within creaturely nature and the being of God.

Barth is emphatic that Anselm's God is the "inconceivable" God revealed to us in Scripture.[27] On this view, Anselmian speculation is not an attempt to demonstrate the reality of God from the starting point of a finite human conception of infinite being. Rather, it begins with faith in the *particular* God—unknowable *per essentiam*—who has concretely revealed Godself by creaturely means, and then proceeds to explicate a *general* concept of infinite being implanted in finite human reason.

The human conception of infinite being is not an extension or emanation of God's essence. It is only an *a priori* concept or category that helps to facilitate

---

23. Anselm, *Proslogium*, 55–6.
24. Anselm, *Proslogium*, 74–5.
25. *Gottes Gnadenwahl*, 49.
26. Anselm, *Proslogium*, 68. Emphasis mine.
27. *CD* II/1, 185.

our understanding of the self-revealed God whom we come to know by faith. The rational concept of infinite being in the human mind cannot extend itself noetically to God's being. Rather, knowledge of the self-revealed God through faith is necessary for us to make sense of our conception of an infinite being.

This specific mode of speculation was basically the one that Barth began to develop in the 1920s and fully adopted in the 1930s. There is no reason to think that he would be at all averse to "speculation" thus understood. However, "speculation" took on deeply idolatrous (to use a Feuerbachian expression) connotations in modern metaphysics. What Barth rejected was the anthropological, ego-centric mode of modern speculation that, on Barth's view, began with Descartes and culminated in Hegel.

Anthropological Speculation in Modern Philosophy

Cartesian Speculation and Kant's Critique

Two express purposes of Barth's *Anselm* are (1) to refute what was popularly perceived as Kant's dismissal of Anselmian speculation and (2) to distinguish between the Anselmian and Cartesian modes of speculation, rejecting the latter while critically adopting the former. We will turn to Barth's refutation of Descartes in the final section after a consideration of its intellectual-historical background.

According to the most widely accepted nineteenth-century narrative of the history of philosophy, early-modern adaptations of speculative theology find their first definitive expression in Descartes's *Meditations on First Philosophy*. I will not offer an exegesis of this text here, because what is of interest to our purpose is not an *ad fontes* study of Descartes, but rather Barth's critique of Cartesian speculation in light of Descartes's *Rezeptionsgeschichte* in nineteenth-century Germany.[28]

Descartes's metaphysics, as popularly portrayed in nineteenth-century German narratives, represents the pre-Kantian culmination of speculative metaphysics handed down from Anselm. Descartes argues that all human beings possess the idea of a perfect being. A perfect being without the attribute of existence is less perfect than an actually existent perfect being. Yet, "less perfect" is as good as "imperfect." Thus, the idea of a nonexistent perfect being is the same as that of an imperfect perfect being, which amounts to a conceptual contradiction. But because the *I* cannot doubt its own existence as a rational *ego* that *thinks* ("*cogito ergo sum*"), it must exclude all conceptual contradictions in its mind. That is, because the *I* is rational, it must affirm the existence of a perfect being that we call "God."

---

28. I am aware that this *Rezeptionsgeschichte* may well have distorted Descartes's intents, and that the Catholic dimension of his thought may in fact make his philosophy as a whole much more amenable to the Augustinian tradition than portrayed by many modern followers and critics. See Stephen Menn, *Descartes and Augustine* (Cambridge: Cambridge University Press, 1998).

Meanwhile, however, as Barth puts it, "it does not escape the notice of Descartes that in the second Meditation he had not so much proved the conclusiveness of his self-demonstration of the thinking subject as assumed it."[29] Descartes needs to prove the existence of the thinking ego, and "the idea of God serves his purpose."[30] The *Meditations* as a whole, then, constitutes little more than a large loop of circular argument: both "the self-demonstration of the thinking subject" and "the proof of God's existence" are formulated "within this circle."[31]

Descartes's speculative arguments for the existence of God and existence of the self first came under severe scrutiny in Kant's first *Critique*. A popular view that Barth inherited from Fichte and Hegel was that Kant's philosophy was responsible for the demise of speculative metaphysics and, therewith, the possibility of human knowledge of God in the realm of theoretical reason (the viability of the truth claim, "God is"). Unlike later (neo-)Kantians, Hegel and the idealist metaphysicians of his generation lamented what they saw as Kant's relegation of human knowledge of God to the realm of practical reason ("God ought to be"). On the first pages of the *Science of Logic*, Hegel complains that "metaphysics" has been "extirpated root and branch, and has vanished from the ranks of the sciences" as a result of "Kantian philosophy" that renounces all "speculative thought."[32]

Now, much of Barth's interpretation and criticism of Cartesian speculation is built on Kant and nineteenth-century receptions of and reactions to Kant. I already discussed Barth's interpretation of Kant in the previous chapter, and here I will present Kant's critique of Descartes in accordance with Kant's own texts, which serves to shed light on the intellectual-historical background of Barth's understanding of this very history itself.

In the first *Critique*, Kant sets forth two powerful arguments against Cartesian speculation as inherited by the Leibnizian-Wolffian school. The better-known argument is the one against "the illusion of [the] logical necessity" of God's existence in the rationalist version of the ontological proof.[33] As mentioned in the previous chapter, Kant's critique is strictly aimed at the *transcendental theology* that Descartes founded. The Anselmian proof pertains to the realm of what Kant calls *revealed theology*. Anselm's name is nowhere to be found in the section in which Kant refutes the kind ontological proof of God represented by Descartes and Leibniz.

The crux of Kant's refutation of what he understands to be the rationalist proof adopted is that *existence* is a *category* rather than an *attribute*, and so it does not analytically pertain to the concept of a perfect being in the same way as, say, omnibenevolence or omniscience. God is, by conceptual definition,

---

29. *CD* III/1, 351.
30. *CD* III/1, 351.
31. *CD* III/1, 359.
32. Georg Wilhelm Friedrich Hegel, *The Science of Logic*, ed. and trans. George di Giovanni (Cambridge: Cambridge University Press, 2010), 7–8.
33. Immanuel Kant, *Critique of Pure Reason*, ed. and trans. Paul Guyer and Allen Wood (Cambridge: Cambridge University Press), A594/B622.

perfect. Perfection, by definition, entails attributes such as omnibenevolence and omniscience. The concept of a perfect being without the attributes of omnibenevolence and omniscience would indeed be logically self-contradictory. However, a proposition that negates the existence of the very subject of a predication such as "God is omniscient" also negates all its predicates, so there would be no logical contradiction in the proposition, "God does not exist." Kant uses what he likes to call a "didactic" illustration to illuminate his point: "To posit a triangle and cancel its three angles is contradictory; but to cancel the triangle together with its three angles is not a contradiction."[34]

Kant's more decisive criticism of rationalist speculation is set forth in the second edition of the first *Critique*. The Cartesian starting point of rationalist speculation, according to both Kant and popular belief in the nineteenth century that Barth inherited, is the supposed indubitability of the proposition, "I think, therefore I am." Descartes takes this representation to be an *intuitio*, that is, an immediate cognition. We do not need to *reflectively* deduce the identity between the act of *cogito* and the substance of the *ego*, because this *immediate* identity is intuitively true and certain.

Kant dismantles Descartes's assumption of the identity between being and thinking by arguing that *cogito ergo sum* is either an analytic proposition in which thinking is conceptually defined in terms of being, or a synthetic proposition in which thinking and being are two different determinations. Descartes's own assumption of the *immediate* identity between being and thinking suggests that *cogito ergo sum* is an "analytic proposition," for the "I am" is taken to signify the existence of the thinking subject.[35] The proposition would then be a tautology in which the "*ergo*" is quite deceptive: a statement of immediate identity cannot possibly amount to a syllogism.

Incidentally, this was an insight that Søren Kierkegaard (1813–55) later included in *Philosophical Fragments*, which, *pace* Bruce McCormack, Barth reportedly finished reading before 1919.[36] In a way reminiscent of Kant and Kierkegaard, Barth comments in a long excursus on Descartes from *CD* III/1 that

> one cannot fail to see that although he [Descartes] maintains the existence of God according to his own presuppositions and method, he does not prove it, so that his attempt to ground all other forms of certitude fails. The circle

---

34. Kant, *Critique of Pure Reason*, A594/B622.
35. Kant, *Critique of Pure Reason*, B407.
36. See Søren Kierkegaard, *Philosophical Fragments*, ed. and trans. Edna Hong and Howard Hong (Princeton: Princeton University Press, 1985), 38–42. Contra McCormack, *Barth's Dialectical Theology*, 235–7. See *Barth-Thurneysen Briefwechsel 1913–1921*, in *GA* 3, 461. Also see Sean Turchin, "Kierkegaard's Echo in the Early Theology of Karl Barth," *Kierkegaard Studies Yearbook* 2012, no. 1 (2012): 323–36; Cora Bartel, *Kierkegaard receptus I: Die theologiegeschichtliche Bedeutung der Kierkegaard-Rezeption Rudolf Bultmanns* (Göttingen: Vandenhoeck & Ruprecht, 2008), 141–70.

of the *cogitare* is never broken through. He never penetrates to the region of the *esse*. Even the self-demonstration of the thinking subject, and the proof of mathematical truths, and supremely and finally the proof of God's existence, takes place within this circle.³⁷

As Kant sees it, however, the problems of the Cartesian *cogito* run even deeper than an argument in circle, a sophistic *ergo*. The Cartesian tradition takes the "I am" to signify a permanent substance. The concept of such a substance, however, is not analytically included within the *cogito*. Thinking and being, activity and substance, are fundamentally different determinations. To conclude from the *cogito* the existence of such a substance amounts to a leap of faith in a "synthetic proposition"—"as if" the conclusion were given "by a revelation."³⁸ Kant dismisses Descartes's "miraculous" faith in the *ego* as the "poorest representation of all."³⁹

Early Responses to Kant's Critique of Speculative Metaphysics

Kant's refutation of rationalist speculation was so powerful that his younger contemporaries, on the basis of what I consider to be misinterpretations of his writings, began to worry about its implications for the future of all speculative metaphysics.⁴⁰ Kant himself agrees that without the idea of God as the ideal of pure reason, and thus as a regulative principle in the theoretical use of reason, human knowledge would disintegrate into bits and pieces, and no *Wissenschaft* would be possible. Yet, if the regulative principle can only be an object of faith rather than knowledge (as Kant would have it)—if there cannot be a speculative science of God to regulate all other sciences—then this would mean, according to the majority view among the idealists of the post-Kantian era, that all the sciences are regulated by a principle of which we can have no rational certainty.⁴¹

In response to Kant's critical philosophy, then, a number of his younger contemporaries began to move in the direction of idealism as an attempt to ascertain the human capacity to reach something higher intellectually. Friedrich Schiller (1759–1805), for instance, engaged in a debate with Kant on aesthetic and ethical questions. In this debate, Schiller challenged Kant's conceptions of freedom and dignity (*Würde*) by arguing that dignity is not an intrinsic value that all human beings possess, but rather the actual expression of our sublime nature through the exercise of our moral freedom to overcome suffering. Dignity, in other words, is more of an act than an essential attribute. It is the scene enacted

---

37. *CD* III/1, 359.
38. Kant, *Critique of Pure Reason*, B407.
39. Kant, *Critique of Pure Reason*, B407.
40. See my *Immanuel Kant* (Phillipsburg: P&R), 40–2.
41. In fact, Kant relegates a higher degree of rational certainty to faith than to knowledge. See my *Immanuel Kant*, 81.

by a play-drive (*Spieltrieb*) in which the tragic hero or heroine embraces his or her suffering for a higher cause.[42]

This carries the aesthetic implication that the sublime (*das Erhabene*) is not an objective quality in awe-inspiring objects like mountain ranges. The feeling of the sublime, per Schiller, corresponds to something subjective within human consciousness. The feeling of the beautiful facilitates to us the objective harmony of nature, but it falls short of awakening human dignity from within. The feeling of the sublime, on the other hand, pertains to an *idealistic* realm: it uplifts consciousness above the sense-drive (*Sinntrieb*) and points us to a freedom that transcends natural limitations. This feeling is characterized by trembling sorrow and the ecstatic joy that accompanies the triumphant tragic hero. Schiller's famous *An die Freude* suggests that this joy is a "sparkle of divinity" (*Götterfunken*) within us, realized through the enactment of human dignity.

In Schiller's proto-romantic aesthetics, then, we see a strong indication of the basic trajectory of theological speculation after Kant. It is to redefine the category of being in terms of events, activities, and other spatio-temporal phenomena, so as to contend for the possibility for human beings to reflect on higher realities through their appearances in what might be described as the "elemental." Put another way, the thrust of this post-Kantian trajectory is to re-establish some kind of an identity between activity and essence as the starting point of metaphysical and/or theological reflection.

One fascinating instance of this mode of speculation is found in the classic definition of "romanticizing" (*das Romantisieren*) formulated by Novalis (1772–1801):

The world must be romanticized. So one finds the original meaning [*den ursprünglichen Sinn*] again. Romanticizing is nothing other than a qualitative empowerment [*Potenzierung*]. The lower self is identified with a better self in this operation ... By ascribing to the commonplace a higher meaning, to the ordinary a mystical esteem, to what is known the dignity of the unknown, to the finite the appearance of the infinite, I romanticize it.[43]

Among all the romantics aside from Friedrich Schleiermacher (1768–1834), Barth singles out Novalis (1772–1801) as the only one who "succeeded in exposing the meaning of Romanticism with a certain unequivocality and finality."[44] Barth's

---

42. See Bianca Weihrauch, *Friedrich Schillers Philosophisches Konzept des Erhabenen und seine Bedeutung für die Literaturtheorie* (Norderstedt: GRIN Verlag, 2016); Trinidad Pineiro Costas, *Schillers Begriff des Erhabenen in der Tradition der Stoa und Rhetorik* (Bern: Peter Lang, 2005).

43. Novalis, *Werke*, ed. Gerhard Schulz (Munich: C. H. Beck, 1987), 385. Cited in Linjing Jiang, *Carl Schmidt als Literaturkritiker: Eine metakritische Untersuchung* (Vienna: Praesens, 2016), 19. Translation mine.

44. *Protestant Theology*, 330.

summary of Novalis's poesy firmly situates the German romantic in the post-Kantian tradition of speculative extension:

> the concept of the ego or of life or, significantly, poesy, and, therefore, the concept of the neutral superior centre is, with Novalis, to be defined as the endless becoming outward of endless inwardness, or also as the endless becoming inward of endless outwardness, in the way that these processes both can and should and do in fact take place in the human act of living.[45]

Barth's description of Novalis's view of philosophy is even more indicative of the speculative nature of romanticizing.

> Philosophy is in its original form feeling. It treats of an object which cannot be learned, of no object, that is to say ... Philosophy is the *reflected* feeling, based on the *self-consciousness* of the ego, or, seen objectively, it is the proving of things by relating them with the self-consciousness of the ego, in which man perceives the absolute basis for his own existence.[46]

As Barth sees it, however, this is not yet "the most radical" development of what he takes to be Kant's phenomenalism, "which we shall come to discover in Hegel."[47] Romantic speculation is, in Barth's estimation, "in all likelihood" little more than a nuanced expression of "the philosophy of Kant."[48] (Recall from the previous chapter how Barth interprets Kant as a phenomenalist.)

Schleiermacher and Romantic Speculation

The romantic mode of speculation, according to Barth, finds its supreme expression in the "Romantic theology ... ruled and determined by Schleiermacher."[49] The early Schleiermacher seems to have accepted Kant's dismissal of speculative metaphysics. In rejecting what was popularly understood as Kant's moral approach to religion and metaphysics, Schleiermacher adopted what he took to be the Kantian position that speculative inquiries "sink back into empty mythology."[50] Thus Schleiermacher's famous line: "Praxis is an art, speculation is a science, religion is the sensibility and taste of the infinite."[51] Still, the early Schleiermacher wanted to ensure that there is some communication between the finite and the infinite. The immediacy of the association between intuition (*Anschauung*) and

---

45. *Protestant Theology*, 338.
46. *Protestant Theology*, 339. Emphases mine.
47. *Protestant Theology*, 327.
48. *Protestant Theology*, 327.
49. *Protestant Theology*, 328.
50. Friedrich Schleiermacher, *On Religion: Speeches to Its Cultured Despisers*, ed. and trans. Richard Crouter (Cambridge: Cambridge University Press, 1996), 25.
51. Schleiermacher, *On Religion*, 25.

feeling (*Gefühl*) was the early Schleiermacher's key to unlocking the access of the finite to the infinite, positing these as two poles of an identical whole.

The later Schleiermacher, on Barth's view, is unmistakably a speculative thinker in the romantic tradition, despite Schleiermacher's express "rejection of speculation."[52]

> Schleiermacher's representation of *faith* certainly rests … upon the basis of a highest knowledge of human feeling or immediate self-awareness in its *correlation* to God, upon the basis of a highest knowledge of the nature and value of faith and the diversity of ways of believing altogether. It is not the Christian religion, but certainly the type to which this phenomenon belongs, religion as a necessary *manifestation* of human intellectual life, which is for Schleiermacher an object of *speculative knowledge* of an *a priori* kind.[53]

Barth's assessment of Schleiermacher comprises an admixture of admiration and criticism. It is the Hegelian mode of speculation, and not the Schleiermacherian, that represents the greatest threat to Christian theology in modern times. Schleiermacher's "conception of speculative identity" is "more cautious" and "more restrained" than that "of Hegel."[54] "Schleiermacher did not, like Schelling, consider possible as a *proof* of Christianity a speculative theology as the science of the point of identity, nor did he, like Hegel, consider a philosophy of religion, replacing theology, as the penultimate stage at least in the dialectic of absolute mind, possible as such a *proof*."[55]

In this sense, Schleiermacher still retained, as Barth would see it, a key dimension of Anselmian speculation, namely, the *fides quaerens intellectum* program as *explication* rather than *proof* of the Christian faith. Schleiermacher stands, in Barth's view, halfway between the Cartesian and Anselmian modes of speculation. Like Descartes, Schleiermacher posited a speculative identity between the subject and object of thinking or consciousness, which the Anselm of *Proslogion* would have found appalling. Against Descartes, however, Schleiermacher insisted with Anselm that faith in God's redemptive activity, rather than in the rational ego, is the starting point of speculation, and that human reason is incapable of deductively arriving at the truth of the Christian faith.

Fichte and the Revival of Cartesian Speculation

One key figure between Kant and Hegel whom Barth only mentions in passing in *Protestant Theology in the Nineteenth Century* is Johann Gottlieb Fichte (1762–1814). It is unclear how familiar Barth was with Fichte's writings before the

---

52. *Protestant Theology*, 434.
53. *Protestant Theology*, 435. Emphases mine.
54. *Protestant Theology*, 435.
55. *Protestant Theology*, 435. Emphases mine.

late 1940s: his first and only extended discussion of Fichte did not appear until *CD* III/2 (1948).⁵⁶ Even there, Barth only demonstrates familiarity with Fichte's *Die Bestimmung des Menschen*. Despite this, however, it is still worth our while to briefly introduce Fichte's explicitly post-Kantian effort to revive Cartesian speculation, for the simple reason that the Kantian ideas that Barth wrestled with "are best explained by reference to Fichte's reception of Kant," as Baark has shown.⁵⁷

One important passage in Barth's sporadic mentions of Fichte in *Protestant Theology* is found in the chapter on Hegel. There Barth expresses the view that Fichte's program was a development of "Kant's transcendentalism," and that Hegelian speculation represented the culmination of what Barth took to be Kant's phenomenalism in the footsteps of Fichte.⁵⁸ In fact, most historians of modern German thought would agree that Fichte's response to Kant's critique of the Cartesian *ego* proved to be the most decisive one from the generation between Kant and Hegel.

Fichte, according to the intellectual-historical view suggested in Barth's chapter on Hegel in *Protestant Theology*, sought to advance, correct, and complete Kant's project by opening up the possibility of speculative metaphysics on Kantian terms. Incidentally, it was in fact Kant's own express intention for the first *Critique* to serve as the foundation for "a system of pure (speculative) reason," which Kant intended to set forth under the rubric of a "Metaphysics of Nature."⁵⁹ He attempted to carry through with this intention in the 1783 *Prolegomena to Any Future Metaphysics* and the 1786 *Metaphysical Foundations of Natural Science*. Despite these efforts, however, Kant was still taken among leading philosophers of the ensuing generation as *the* culprit for having eradicated all speculative metaphysics.

Much of this post-Kantian reception of Kant had to do with Fichte's focused attack on Kant's critique of rationalist speculation. For Fichte, the Cartesian starting point in the rational ego is the *sine qua non* of speculative metaphysics. Fichte's strategy was to revive the Cartesian *ego* in a distinctively post-Kantian way by arguing for an immediate identity between the essence and act of the thinking self, which Fichte took to be the ultimate reality, the starting point in a *credo ut intelligam* program. One of Fichte's most famous lines reads: "Consciousness is coming to be in its activity. Activity is the way in which the I realizes itself."⁶⁰

Ficthe's strategy in reviving Descartes on Kantian terms, in other words, is to argue that if the identity between the *I* and the act of thinking is immediate, then "*cogito ergo sum*" would no longer be a syllogism. It would be a simple proposition

---

56. *CD* III/2, 96–109.
57. Baark, *The Affirmations of Reason*, 70.
58. *Protestant Theology*, 379.
59. Kant, *Critique of Pure Reason*, Axx.
60. Johann Gottlieb Fichte, *The Science of Knowledge*, ed. Peter Heath and John Lachs (Cambridge: Cambridge University Press, 1982), 95. See Baark, *The Affirmations of Reason*, 72–3, for a brief yet incisive exposition of this famous phrase.

stating a self-evident truth. The *credo ut intelligam* program of Fichtean speculation, then, is fashioned after what Fichte took to be the Cartesian starting point in the *cogito*.

While Barth does not provide any extended account of Fichte's legacy to the speculative tradition of later idealism, it is clear that Barth deems this entire anthropocentric tradition to be pantheistic, which is for Barth as good as atheistic. The conclusion to Barth's 1948 excursus on Fichte's doubt-knowledge-faith triad makes this clear:

> The god in whom Fichtean man believes is himself, his own mind, the spirit of the protesting voice in which he puts his confidence and in the power of which he knows himself to be free …; a God who confronts and limits man and is thus his true determination, is for Fichte non-existent. Fichte's god is Fichte's man, and Fichte's man is Fichte's god.[61]

Hegel's Reinvention of Cartesian Speculation

While Fichte's assertion in the *Wissenschaftslehre* of an immediate and actualistic identity between the essence and act of the thinking *Ich* was the first major attempt to revive the Cartesian mode of speculation, Hegel, on Barth's view, was the one who brought about a full-scale return of speculative metaphysics in the nineteenth century. Barth calls "Hegel's philosophy … a philosophy of *self-confidence*," namely, "the self-confidence of thinking man."[62]

Hegel "takes up the inheritance of the Enlightenment," which began with Descartes, by grounding metaphysical speculation in the confidence of "the identity … between our thinking and what is thought."[63] Of course, this is not a naïve return to Descartes's program, for "Hegel affirmed Kant's transcendentalism … in the same sense that Fichte did."[64]

On the kind of "post-Kantian" interpretation of Hegel that Barth adopted (to be differentiated from the post-Kantian school of Hegel studies led by Robert Pippin and Terry Pinkard), however, Fichte was not Kantian enough for Hegel. Fichte, as we saw, attempted to restore the Cartesian mode of speculation by arguing for an immediate identity between "*cogito*" and "*sum*," so as to make "*cogito ergo sum*" an axiomatic predication rather than a deductive claim.

As Hegel sees it, this strategy is little more than a seasoned repetition of what Descartes himself already stated.[65] Kant had successfully proven that thinking and being are two different determinations, and a reiteration of the Cartesian view of

61. *CD* III/2, 109.
62. *Protestant Theology*, 377.
63. *Protestant Theology*, 377.
64. *Protestant Theology*, 379.
65. Georg Wilhelm Friedrich Hegel, *Lectures on the History of Philosophy 1825-6: Volume III: Medieval and Modern Philosophy*, ed. and trans. Robert Brown (Oxford: Oxford University Press, 2009), 109–12.

an immediate identity between act and being was powerless in the face of Kant's critique. As Hegel puts it, "Thinking and being are different determinations, so the proof of their identity must be expressly furnished, and this Descartes fails to do."[66]

Note, however, that Hegel's intent is not to jettison the kind of rationalist speculation that began with Descartes, but rather to restore its dominance in philosophy by furnishing the proof of the identity between thinking and being. Descartes's insight, per Hegel, is that "consciousness is certain of itself; with the 'I think,' being is posited. Consciousness now seeks to extend its cognitive knowledge and finds that it has within itself representations of many things"—the things that provide the materials for reflective after-thinking.[67] For Hegel, "this is on the whole the most interesting idea of modern philosophy, and Descartes was at any rate the first to formulate it."[68]

The key to restoring Cartesian speculation "is the progression from abstract unity [between thinking and being] to greater concreteness."[69] By "concretion," Hegel means the unification of the universal with the particular. As Hegel sees it, the immediate unity between being and thinking posited by Descartes and Fichte is not concrete enough.

In fact, all philosophies of sheer immediacy, in Hegel's view, result in abstraction.[70] For Hegel, the philosophy of immediate identity developed by the early post-Kantian versions of idealism, especially that of the early Schelling, threatened to dissolve all genuine particularities in a bath of abstract uniformity.

Hegel's strategy in overcoming this problem, as we shall see in the next chapter, proved to be an important source of inspiration to Barth. Hegel insisted upon a process of mediation (*Vermittlung*) necessary for the development of absolute human self-knowledge as the historical appearance (*Schein*) of Spirit. The logic of mediation includes a first moment of immediacy, a second moment of the negation of immediacy, and a consummate moment of mediation.

Hegel brings this logic to bear on his reinvention of speculative ontology in his commentary on Descartes in the *Lectures on the History of Philosophy* of 1825–6.

> When we speak of "being," therefore, we must not represent to ourselves something particular, the being of some concrete content. If we do that, then "being" means nothing but simple immediacy. Thinking is movement within self, but pure reference to self, pure identity with self. This is being too. Immediacy is being. Thinking is this same immediacy, but it is at the same time also mediation with itself—it is its self-negating mediation with itself, and therefore it is immediacy too. "Immediacy" is a one-sided determination; thinking contains

---

66. Hegel, *History of Philosophy III*, 112.
67. Hegel, *History of Philosophy III*, 112.
68. Hegel, *History of Philosophy III*, 112.
69. Hegel, *History of Philosophy III*, 112.
70. G. W. F. Hegel, *Phenomenology of Spirit*, ed. Terry Pinkard and Michael Baur, trans. Michael Baur (Cambridge: Cambridge University Press, 2018), 12.

it, but not it alone, for thinking also contains the determination of mediating itself with itself; and by virtue of the fact that the mediating is at the same time the sublation of the mediating, it is also immediacy. In thinking there is certainly being. "Being" is a much poorer determination than "thinking"; it is what is abstracted from the concrete[ness] of thinking.[71]

This logic of mediation, the formal aspect of which Barth critically reappropriated in 1936, is partly intended to avoid the pitfall of positing an abstract identity between God's being and a rational concept in the human mind. In view of Hegel's insistence on mediation, interpreters like Charles Taylor rightly insist that for Hegel, "*Geist* is not reducible to man; he is not identical with the human spirit," however much Hegel's "God ... is not a God who could exist quite independently of man."[72] Michael Rosen, in a similar vein, reminds us that "Hegel's attack on traditional oppositions between 'transcendence' and 'immanence' does not amount to ... a dissolution" of "God into His creation."[73]

Barth's reading of Hegel does not essentially contradict that of Taylor and Rosen, but Barth still believes that Hegel's theology is deeply pantheistic. As Barth sees it, despite Hegel's very Kantian critique of immediacy, Hegel still envisions God and creation as consummately and concretely, though not immediately or abstractly, identical. Barth complains that

> Hegel's brand of self-confidence is also confidence in mind which for its own part is one with God and the same with God. The characteristic thing about this, however, is that the confidence in mind or in God must also to the fullest extent and in ultimate seriousness be self-confidence, because there is likewise and in the same sense a final identity between Self and mind as there is in general between thinking and the thing thought.[74]

In other words, the consummate identity between God and the human mind, which Hegel (according to Barth) posits, ultimately reduces God to a rational concept (*Begriff*), enabling creatures to know God through the after-thinking (*Nachdenken*) of historical representations (*Vorstellungen*).

In Hegel, then, we find (on Barth's reading) a dynamic reinvention of Cartesian speculation consisting in a *fides quaerens intellectum* program. Faith is taken as an act of the intellect that intuits the immediate actualities of the world, in order to come to reflective, mediated, and comprehensive understandings of its developed actualities in light of the consummate identity between God's being and human thinking.

---

71. Hegel, *History of Philosophy III*, 112.
72. Charles Taylor, *Hegel and Modern Society* (Cambridge: Cambridge University Press, 1979), 162.
73. Michael Rosen, *Hegel's Dialectic and Its Criticism* (Cambridge: Cambridge University Press, 1982), 78.
74. *Protestant Theology*, 379.

Here we can see why Barth finds Hegel to be so much more detrimental to the Christian faith than Kant. Hegel's faith is not in the unsublatable subject God in the immutable absoluteness of the triune essence, the God who is greater than can be conceived, but rather in what human consciousness has in it to become, namely, the divine and the absolute. God and human consciousness, to be sure, will never become immediately identical for Hegel. God will never completely merge into world-occurrences, and the world will never become immediately divine. Yet, there will consummately be an essential identity between God and the world-history of human consciousness, when all phenomenal irrationalities and contingencies belong to a sublated moment of the past. The God of Hegelian speculation, in other words, is speculatively identical with a universal human concept.

Still, it is not difficult to see that the *Denkform* of Hegelian speculation is structured after Anselm in a significant way. Hegel himself suggests in his treatment of the ontological proof that he re-appropriated Anselm through Descartes.[75] Both the Anselmian and Hegelian modes of speculation are characterized by a faith-seeking-understanding program involving *Nachdenken* and *Reflexion*. This is what led commentators like Howard Kainz to believe that "Anselm's *credo ut intelligam* faith" provided Hegel with "the foundation for speculative philosophizing."[76]

Anselm and Speculative Identity in the Nationalistic Narrative of Nineteenth-Century Germany

To appreciate Barth's urge to set Anselm apart from the Cartesian philosophy of speculative identity that culminated in Hegel, we need to understand how the supposedly Anselmian pedigree of German idealism was magnified by nationalistic narratives that already began to emerge in the eighteenth century.

In fact, the association between Hegel and Anselm has a long and convoluted history that can be traced back to Hegel's own writings, though Hegel himself does not offer any extended account of his indebtedness to Anselm.[77] Hegel believes that Anselm's proof carries the "formal defect" of presupposing "the unity of thinking and being, as what is most perfect as God."[78] Yet, Hegel laments that "the whole world hasted to agree with him [Kant] that the [ontological] proof is untenable."[79] In Hegel's enthusiastic attempt to revive Cartesian speculation after Kant, then, a restoration of Anselm was also intended.

Meanwhile, the emergence of a characteristically modern form of mystical nationalism in nineteenth-century Germany also fostered the popular view that Anselm was a forerunner of pantheistic German Christianity. Heinrich Heine (1797–1856), in his *Zur Geschichte der Religion und Philosophie in Deutschland*,

---

75. Hegel, *History of Philosophy III*, 112.
76. Howard Kainz, "Hegel, Providence, and the Philosophy of History," *Hegel-Jahrbuch* (1995): 184.
77. Hegel, *History of Philosophy III*, 43–5.
78. Hegel, *History of Philosophy III*, 44.
79. Hegel, *History of Philosophy III*, 44.

ballyhooed in Germany throughout the second half of the nineteenth century, identifies pantheism as the quintessence of German nationhood.[80]

"Germany is the most fertile soil for pantheism; this is the religion of our greatest thinkers and our greatest artists," Heine asserts.[81] Modern "Germanic pantheism," however, differs from ancient Teutonic paganism, in that medieval Catholicism has "gifted" Germany's *Volksreligion* with "deeper understanding" of the inherent divinity of nature.[82] Authentic German Christianity, in other words, is a cultivated form of pantheism.

Heine, erstwhile student of Hegel, claims that the "ontological proof" of God's existence "set forth by Descartes" was in fact a baptized statement of pantheistic belief, and that the pantheistic *Denkform* of this proof was "already pronounced by Anselm of Canterbury in the form of a tranquil prayer a long time ago. Indeed, one can say that St. Augustine already set forth the ontological proof in the second book of *De libero arbitrio*."[83]

Heine faults Fichte, the later Schelling, and Hegel for having abandoned Germany's pantheistic *Volksreligion*, embedded in the enchanted worldview of medieval Catholicism, to complete Kant's very Protestant project of *Naturphilosophie*, the philosophy that, in a nutshell, identifies nature as a manifestation rather than emanation of the divine. However, Heine's identification of Anselm as a proto-pantheist, who sees something within human nature as essentially divine, would eventually come to be conjoined with the more popular view of German idealism as metaphysical pantheism rather than panentheism.

Before discussing this more popular view, we can briefly observe here that Barth's take on Fichte, Schelling, and Hegel as followers of Kant was a widespread one inherited from the nineteenth century. Barth's assessment of Hegel's superiority to Kant in terms of influence as well as intellectual sophistication and consistency can also be traced back to the generation of Hegel's students. Heine describes "the great Hegel" as the "greatest philosopher Germany has produced since Leibniz. There is no question that he towers far above Kant and Fichte."[84]

The difference between the view that Heine represents and the one that Barth adopted lies in their respective categorizations of Kant and the major German idealist philosophers. Hegel as the culmination of this philosophical tradition, according to Heine, represents the pinnacle of the panentheistic *Naturphilosophie* that ensued from the apostasy of the Protestant Reformation. From Barth's Protestant perspective, by contrast, *Naturphilosophie* is essentially pantheistic. What he calls Kant's "transcendentalism" provided the conditions for a distinctively

---

80. For Henrich Heine's influence on the interpretation of German idealism and romanticism, see Terry Pinkard, "How to Move from Romanticism to Post-Romanticism: Schelling, Hegel, and Heine," *European Romantic Review* 21 (2010): 391–407.

81. Heinrich Heine, *Zur Geschichte der Religion und Philosophie in Deutschland*, Zweites Buch, http://www.zeno.org/nid/20005029740. Translation mine.

82. Heine, Drittes Buch.

83. Heine, Drittes Buch.

84. Heine, Drittes Buch.

modern form of pantheism, and Hegel represents the most sophisticated and consistent expression of post-Kantian pantheism.

The view held by Barth turned out to be the more popular one by the early twentieth century. The reception of this popular view in Barth's generation is clearly seen in the intellectual-historical account offered by Barth's long-time rival, Paul Tillich (1886–1965). In a way akin to Barth's appeal to Strauss and Feuerbach to disclose the materialistic and atheistic essence of German idealism, Tillich attaches the label of "naturalism" to Kantian and neo-Kantian positivism, and asserts that the *Naturphilosophie* of romanticism and idealism was essentially naturalistic as well. Tillich comments that "idealism and naturalism differ very little in their starting point when they develop theological concepts."[85] Tillich, however, is against the view represented by Heine that *Naturphilosophie* from Kant to Hegel constitutes an abandonment of pantheism. For Tillich, *Naturaphilosophie* is at once pantheistic and naturalistic.

Very much like Barth, Tillich asserts that both naturalism and idealism are essentially pantheistic in that they both operate on the central theme of speculative identity between cognitive subject and object. "Both are dependent on a point of identity between the experiencing subject and the ultimate which appears in religious experience or in the experience of the world as 'religious.' The theological concepts of both idealists and naturalists are rooted in a 'mystical a priori,' an awareness of something that transcends the cleavage between subject and object."[86] For Tillich, both are forms of "monism," and "in terms of philosophy of religion, both forms of monism are called 'pantheistic.'"[87]

Unlike Barth, of course, Tillich tends to be more sympathetic toward the pantheistic element in naturalism and idealism, even though he rejects pantheism as a doctrine. Tillich acknowledges that in his generation, especially after the Second World War, "'Pantheist' has become a heresy label of the worst kind."[88] Needless to say, Barth was the leading voice against pantheism in Tillich's time.

Still, Tillich, in a way reminiscent of Heine, suggests that there is a pantheistic element to the classical doctrine of God which is indispensable for Christian theology. "Pantheism," Tillich explains,

> is the doctrine that God is the substance or essence of all things, not the meaningless assertion that God is the totality of things. The pantheistic element in the classical doctrine that God is *ipsum esse*, being-itself, is as necessary for a Christian doctrine of God as the mystical element of the divine presence. The danger connected with these elements of mysticism and pantheism is overcome by exclusive monotheism and its philosophical analogues.

---

85. Paul Tillich, *Systematic Theology: Volume One* (Chicago: University of Chicago Press, 1951), 9.
86. Tillich, *Systematic Theology*, 9.
87. Tillich, *Systematic Theology*, 233.
88. Tillich, *Systematic Theology*, 233.

It is of course unclear whether Barth and Tillich were familiar with Heine. My reference to Heine only serves the purpose of demonstrating the ideas that were "in the air" in the nineteenth century after the first generation of idealist philosophers like Hegel and Schelling. In fact, it has been well established in the secondary literature that as early as his student years, Barth, under the influence of Aldolf von Harnack (1851–1930), already began to interpret the history of German literature in the eighteenth and nineteenth centuries through the lens of pantheism's opposition to deism.[89] There is no question that Heine's view of pantheism as a necessary element integral to the classical Christian doctrine of God taught by Augustine and Anselm remained popular up to the generation of Barth's teachers, and continued to be held by his contemporaries like Tillich. Barth was not only averse to Tillich's critical sympathies toward pantheism. As we shall see anon, Barth was at pains to claim Anselm as an ally against the speculative themes of divine conceivability and divine-human identity underlying modern pantheism.

Barth's Appeal to Anselmian Speculation

Anselm's speculative conviction that God is greater than can be conceived was Barth's antidote to the idealist philosophy of speculative identity that, on his view, began with Descartes and culminated in Hegel. At the beginning of *CD* II/1, Barth states that his treatment of "the problem of the knowledge of God" was developed "at the feet of Anselm of Canterbury, and in particular from his proofs of God set out in *Prosl.* 2-4."[90] Barth stresses later in the same half-volume that for Anselm, God is *inconceivable*: "God is He than whom no greater can be conceived. But an inconceivable is, as such, conceivable. If it were not identical with God, then it would be a greater than God. Therefore, since no greater than He can be conceived, God is Himself the inconceivable (*Prosl.* 15)."[91]

Insistence on the inconceivability of God is what sets Anselm fundamentally apart from the idealist mode of speculation. The principle of divine inconceivability—which is basically another expression of the axiom of God's unknowability *per essentiam*—means that there can be no speculative extension from human conceptions of God to God's being itself. Furthermore, there can be no identity, immediate or not, between act and essence in the creature: creaturely identities are determined by the Creator and cannot be self-determined.

In the Anselmian program, the identity between act and essence resides in God alone: it is the immediate identity between God's triune *opera ad intra* and God's unsublatable subjectivity in relation to Godself as the object of the *opera*. This *ad*

---

89. Thomas Xutong Qu, *Barth und Goethe: Die Goethe-Rezeption Karl Barths 1906–1921* (Neukirchen-Vluyn: Neukirchener, 2014), 29–35; 96–7.
90. *CD* II/1, 4.
91. *CD* II/1, 185.

intra identity is ontically revealed to us through a speculative extension from the subject God to a secondary, revelatory mode of absolute being. In other words, the speculative identity that enables human knowledge of God is the mediated identity between God in God's essential being and God's being in the actuality of revelation. Barth explains in *Anselm*: "He is the God in whom *intelligentia* and *veritas* are identical, the God whose Word to us is nothing other than the *integra veritas paternae substantiae*."[92]

Of course, it would be quite a stretch to assert that *Anselm* is a treatise against Hegel, for the obvious reason that Hegel is nowhere mentioned in the volume. However, it is safe to say that Barth wanted to refute a received view of Anselm in the German-speaking world passed down from the post-Kantian era as a result of Kant's refutation of the so-called ontological proof.

Barth states in the preface to the first edition of *Anselm* that Kant's "denial of that very aspect of Anselm's theology which is to be our special concern here" was out of a gross "misunderstanding" of Anselm on Kant's part.[93] In the very concluding sentence of the volume, Barth reiterates:

> That Anselm's Proof of the Existence of God has repeatedly been called the "Ontological" Proof of God, that commentators have refused to see that it is in a different book altogether from the well-known teaching of Descartes and Leibniz, that anyone could seriously think that it is even remotely affected by what Kant put forward against these doctrines—all that is so much nonsense on which no more words ought to be wasted.[94]

Here is an instance where Barth is tackling an inherited view of Anselm in relation to an inherited view of Kant, rather than trying to engage directly with Kant's own refutation of the so-called ontological proof (which we discussed earlier). The fact is that even in the first edition of the first *Critique* (1781), where the 1786 policy forbidding philosophers to publish critiques of Christian theology was not yet in effect, Kant makes no mention of Anselm at all in the passages refuting the ontological family of theistic proofs.[95] Kant's refutation, as we saw earlier, is specifically directed toward the Cartesian version, which the Wolffian school inherited.

Yet, as we saw, the popular view from the nineteenth century up to Barth's time was that Kant did away with Anselm and Descartes altogether, while Hegel revived them in a distinctively modern way. Hegel's own narrative is partly responsible for popularizing this view.[96] It was the Kant of this popular view espoused by nineteenth-century German idealism that Barth was tackling, and not the Kant of the first *Critique*.

---

92. *Anselm*, 18–19.
93. *Anselm*, 8.
94. *Anselm*, 171.
95. See Kant, *Critique of Pure Reason*, A592/B620–A602/B630.
96. Hegel, *History of Philosophy III*, 44.

Barth not only intended to discredit what was popularly perceived in the German-speaking world as Kant's refutation of Anselm. He was all the more at pains to set Anselm apart from the Cartesian mode of speculation. "Anselm is not Descartes," Barth urges.

> [If] the Existence of God is to be proved then it must be proved that he cannot be conceived as not existing. But Anselm has no intention of relating this to any analogous statement about his own existence, let alone of setting it in a relation of dependence on such a statement … There is no analogous statement (Anselm is not Descartes) concerning man's own existence.[97]

Balthasar offers a splendid exposition of this passage in light of "Barth's extensive treatment of Descartes' *Meditations*" in *CD* III/1 to show how, on Barth's view, Anselm and Descartes fundamentally differ.[98] Descartes's proof

> resembles Anselm's except for one crucial feature: Descartes presupposes the revelation, not of divine, but of finite and contingent existence. The clearest, truest and most distinct of all the ideas in the mind proves to be *Descartes'* idea. And it is this idea that God has stamped as a seal on the finite spirit as the signature of his work of creation.[99]

Barth stresses in *CD* II/1 that in the Anselmian mode of speculation, "the inconceivability of God is imputed to His positive greatness and not deduced from a human deficiency."[100] Contrast this to Barth's critique of Cartesian speculation in *CD* III/1:

> The [divinity of the] God of Descartes … has nothing to do with the fact that He has revealed Himself and is therefore to be believed. This idea of divinity is innate in man … It is made up of a series of preeminent attributes which are relatively and primarily attributes of the human mind, and in which the latter sees its own characteristics—temporality, finitude, limited knowledge and ability and creative power—transcended in the absolute, contemplating itself in the mirror of its possible infinitude, and yet remaining all the time within itself even though allowing its prospect of itself to be infinitely expanded by this speculative extension and deepening.[101]

It is not difficult to see how Barth's critique of Descartes here makes use of recognizably Feuerbachian and Straussian patterns. Ludwig Feuerbach

---

97. *Anselm*, 139.
98. Balthasar, *The Theology of Karl Barth*, 147.
99. Balthasar, *The Theology of Karl Barth*, 147.
100. *CD* II/1, 185.
101. *CD* III/1, 360.

(1804–72), we may recall, famously drew on the theme of speculative identity between human consciousness and divine essentiality in Hegel, his erstwhile teacher, to argue that the essence of religion is idolatry, the essence of theology anthropology. "In the consciousness of the infinite, the conscious [human] subject has for his object the infinity of his own nature."[102] The idealist rendition of speculative identity means for Feuerbach that "the divine being is nothing else than the human being, or rather, the human nature purified, freed from the limits of the individual man, made objective—i.e., contemplated and revered as another ... All attributes of the divine nature are ... attributes of the human nature."[103] In a similar vein, David Strauss (1808–74) drew on idealist motifs in Hegel and Schleiermacher to contend that "humanity is the union of the two natures—God become man, the infinite manifesting itself in the finite, and the finite spirit remembering its infinitude."[104]

As Barth sees it, Descartes's speculative theology falls right into "the difficulties disclosed by Strauss and Feuerbach" in much the same way as Hegel's.[105] Descartes's method of speculative extension is but an anthropological self-projection unto a pseudo-object that is no more than an idol made in human image. Descartes "only needs to produce the idea of God from the treasury or deficiency of his mind and at once it stands at his disposal with no less but no greater power than the idea of a triangle."[106] "The God of Descartes," declares Barth, "is hopelessly enchained in the mind of man."[107]

Against Descartes, Barth adopts a basically Anselmian mode of speculation as the *Denkform* of his own theology:

> The validity of any proof of God's existence depends on its basis in the power of God's self-demonstration; on the fact that it gives this scope; on the fact that the description given of God and of the role ascribed to Him, not merely do not conceal but reveal the divine character to the extent that the proof attempted by man ascribes existence to God because it is prescribed that he should do so and he is obedient to this command ... In *Prosl.* 2-4 Anselm showed that the God who is revealed and believed in the Christian Church, cannot not exist, or even be thought of as not existing, because by His self-revelation as the being *quo maius cogitari non potest*, by His self-revelation as the Creator, He forbids man his creature to entertain such a thought, making it logically and morally impossible for him to think it ... The man who knows God by God himself,

---

102. Ludwig Feuerbach, *The Essence of Christianity*, trans. George Elliot (New York: Prometheus, 1989), 2–3.
103. Feuerbach, *The Essence of Christianity*, 14.
104. David Strauss, *The Life of Jesus Critically Examined*, 3 volumes, trans. George Eliot (London: Continuum, 2005), 3:435–6.
105. *Protestant Theology*, 554.
106. *CD* III/1, 359.
107. *CD* III/1, 360.

on the basis of His revelation and by faith in it, is necessarily aware of God's existence, so that there can be no question of His non-existence ... The God of Descartes does not bear this divine character.[108]

Barth explains that the Cartesian God's "divinity has nothing to do with the fact that He has revealed Himself and is therefore to be believed. This idea of divinity is innate in man. Man can produce it at will from the treasury or deficiency of his mind."[109]

In this light, what sets Barth's basically Anselmian mode of speculation apart from modern speculative philosophy beginning with Descartes and culminating in Hegel is the starting point of reflective after-thinking. Descartes's Enlightenment *fides*, on Barth's inherited view, is in the certainty of human *cogito*, the immediate identity between thinking and being, and in the speculative identity between God's being and *my* rational conception of God. Descartes's ontological proof of a perfect deity is but a noetic extension or speculation on the basis of this faith in human self-identity and rationality. Hegel's speculative philosophy constitutes an explicit effort to revive this Cartesian mode of metaphysical speculation.

In *Protestant Theology*, as we saw, Barth recognizes the Enlightenment heritage of Hegel's faith in the identity between thinking and being. According to Hegel and the major idealists of his generation, God is noetically accessible to the reflective speculations of human consciousness only through processes in which the divine subject, in one way or another, sublates Godself in order to determine Godself as God.

The starting point of Barth's theological reflection is diametrically opposed to this idealist mode of speculation. Faith in the self-revelation of the God who never ceases to be God even in historical actuality is the Anselmian—rather than Cartesian—starting point of Barth's speculative theology. Barth's Anselmian conviction that "God is that above which nothing greater can be conceived," Baark astutely observes, can be restated in German idealist terms: "God's unsublatable subjectivity is identical with God's essence as the one who loves in freedom."[110]

Barth rejects the idealist position that human thinking can extend itself from the deficiencies of human nature to the perfections of divine nature. This includes both the hidden pantheistic core of Descartes's *Meditations*, as well as Hegel's explicit view of speculative identity between the divine and the human, which goes hand in hand with the view that Spirit becomes absolute and divine through a process of sublatory self-determination—that God needs to become God-for-us in order to determine Godself as God qua absolute being (i.e., being-in-and-for-itself).

What Baark describes as Barth's insistence on God's unsublatable subjectivity is in fact a more sophisticated way of expressing the Anselmian principle of God's

---

108. *CD* III/1, 361.
109. *CD* III/1, 361.
110. Baark, *The Affirmations of Reason*, 256.

inconceivability. In the process of revelation, God is always the subject. Even in becoming God *pro nobis*, the same subject God does not cease to be absolute *a se*. The speculative (i.e., mediated) identity between God-in-and-for-Godself and God-for-us (rather than Spirit's being-for-itself) is the starting point of genuinely theological reflection, given to us through the gift of faith to the church.

How Barth sustains the notion of God's unsublatable subjectivity in terms of the Trinity and election will be explained in the ensuing chapters. Suffice it to say here that Baark is right in pointing out that Barth's seminal insistence upon God's unsublatable subjectivity, stated early on in his career, goes hand in hand with the speculative *Denkform* formulated in *Anselm*: the ground of rational certainty in human knowledge of God is the unsublatable subjectivity of the triune God even in God's self-revelation at Golgotha.

Conclusion

It is hardly an exaggeration to say that Barth adopted a basically Anselmian mode of speculation as the *Denkform* that undergirds the *Church Dogmatics* as a whole. We have already seen how Barth explicitly acknowledges his indebtedness to Anselm in the preface to *CD* I/1, and how he states at the beginning of II/1 that his doctrine of God was developed "at the feet of Anselm." In §40, "Faith in God the Creator," the opening paragraph of III/1, Barth states that his doctrine of creation is formulated in the same Anselmian *Denkform*.

> In all our previous deliberations we have presupposed that we do not have an unknown but a known quantity in Jesus Christ as the revelation and fulfilment of the eternal decree of God ... It is with the help of this known quantity that we have proved what had to be proved ... We have presupposed that He is actually this known quantity for us as His own, as members of His body, as adherents of His Church. And in the light of this known quantity we have perceived and understood the truth and necessity of the statement that God created heaven and earth. But this being the case, it obviously follows that this perception and understanding are those of faith. Our first task was to show that here, too, it is the case: *Credo ut intelligam*. In the present instance this means: I believe in Jesus Christ, God's Son our Lord, in order to perceive and to understand that God the Almighty, the Father, is the Creator of heaven and earth. If I did not believe the former, I could not perceive and understand the latter.[111]

One recognizable difference between the specific formulation of Anselmian speculation stated in this passage and that found in *Anselm* lies in the sharp Christocentrism characterizing the former. In Chapters 4–6, I will paint a portrait of Barth's Christocentric reorientation of his speculative theology in 1936–42. The

---

111. *CD* III/1, 28.

present chapter has only sketched the intellectual-historical background of Barth's adoption of a basically Anselmian mode of speculation.

I have not provided an intellectual-biographical account of Barth's early theology, because Baark has already done an impeccable job in this area, and his work is not in need of any furnishing. While Baark acknowledges that Barth's Christocentric revision of the "doctrine of election" in 1936 marked "the culmination of Barth's development as a theologian," however, he has yet to take up the task of interpreting this revision in light of Barth's speculative theology, his brief treatments of *CD* II/1-2 notwithstanding.[112] Before I discuss this subject in Chapters 4–6, I will first proceed in the next chapter to delineate the basic shape of Barth's speculative theology in the Christocentric phase of his career, with particular focus on the theme of actualism.

---

112. Baark, *The Affirmations of Reason*, 4.

Chapter 3

SKETCHING THE CONTOURS: ACTUALISTIC ONTOLOGY AND SPECULATIVE THEOLOGY

This chapter introduces a key motif underlying Barth's speculative theology, namely, the overarching notion of "being-in-act" (*Sein in der Tat*). In the secondary literature, this has come to be called Barth's "actualism" or "actualistic ontology." It is an "ontology" according to which being and act are equally basic and mutually determinative.

Despite the prominence of the topic of actualism in the literature on Barth, it has escaped the notice of the majority of scholars that it was within the framework of a basically Anselmian mode of speculation that he developed the mature rendition of the notion of being-in-act. This is the case even with Sigurd Baark, who, in a footnote, identifies actualism as one of Bruce McCormack's "central explanatory terms" in the exposition of Barth's theology.[1]

In Chapter 1, I demonstrated the inadequacies and inconsistencies of McCormack's post-Kantian interpretation of Barth's actualism. The purpose of the present chapter is to offer a reinterpretation of Barth's central motif of being-in-act in light of his speculative theology, and to explicate his speculative theology with a right understanding of his actualistic ontology.

The idealist mode of speculation, as we saw in Chapter 2, posits an *identity* (immediate or speculative) between the being and act of the human person, and treats the human person as some being-*as*-act in one way or another. Faith in this identity serves as the starting point of noetic speculative extension from humanity to divinity. In this speculative program, divine nature is no more than the projected perfection of human nature from its deficiencies.

This chapter is an expansion and reworking of my essay, "Barth on Actualistic Ontology," in *The Wiley-Blackwell Companion to Karl Barth*, ed. George Hunsinger and Keith Johnson (Oxford: Wiley-Blackwell, 2020), 739–51. Also published in German: Shao Kai Tseng, "Karl Barths aktualistische Ontologie: Ihre Substanzgrammatik des Seins und Prozessgrammatik des Werdens," *Neue Zeitschrift für Systematische Theologie und Religionsphilosophie* 60 (2019): 32–50.

1. Sigurd Baark, *The Affirmations of Reason: On Karl Barth's Speculative Theology* (Cham: Palgrave Macmillan, 2018), 17n25.

Barth insists against this idealist mode of speculation that identity between being and act is to be found in God alone, primarily in God's triune being-in-and-for-Godself as an immediate identity (i.e., the unmediated identity between God's triune essence and God's *opera ad intra*), and secondarily between God-in-and-for-Godself and God-for-us as a speculative identity. God is unsublatably the subject of speculative extension, which takes place in the reality of God's secondary absoluteness in Jesus Christ. In *CD* II/1-2, as we shall see in Chapters 5–6, Barth boldly describes this extension in the Platonist language of emanation (*Überfluss*).

There is for Barth no human self-identity: there is no identity, immediate or speculative, between being and act in the human person *per se* or *a se*. Human activity does not ontologically determine the human being. The human essence is ontologically determined by God's gracious activity in Jesus Christ, who is the speculative extension, the *speculum* or *imago*, of God's absolute essence as the one who loves in freedom.

"Actualistic Ontology" Clarified

Against Post-Kantian Interpretations

Before proceeding, I should say a brief word about the term "actualistic ontology," which I realize may cause unease among some of my peers, especially those who share my convictions about Barth's innovative adaptation of Anselmian speculation. In recent scholarship, this term has for the most part been associated with the revisionist view that "the action of God in electing to be God for humanity in Jesus Christ is *not* the act of an already existing agent. Rather it is an act in the course of which God determines the very being of God."[2] This interpretation draws heavily on the contention that "there is for Barth 'no state, no mode of being or existence above and prior to this eternal act of self-determination as substantialistic thinking would lead us to believe.'"[3]

This view, as we saw in Chapter 1, stems from Bruce McCormack's post-Kantian intellectual-biographical account of Barth, which makes the claim that Barth's actualistic view of being is derived from Hermann Cohen, a Jewish philosopher of the Marburg school of neo-Kantianism.

> For Hermann Cohen …, the human simply *is* the sum total of his or her lifetime of knowing activities. Expressed more expansively: the human is what he or she

---

2. Paul Nimmo, *Being in Action: The Theological Shape of Barth's Ethical Vision* (London: T&T Clark, 2007), 8.

3. Nimmo, *Being in Action*, 8. Here Nimmo cites Bruce McCormack, "The Ontological Presuppositions of Barth's Doctrine of the Atonement," in *The Glory of the Atonement*, ed. Charles Hill and Frank James III (Downers Grove: IVP, 2004), 359.

does. It was but a short step from here to reflection upon the divine nature as actualistic—a point which Barth would begin to ground christologically just two and a half years after publishing his second *Romans*.[4]

No serious reader of Barth can deny that the post-Kantian paradigm of Barth interpretation is immensely valuable in a number of ways. For one thing, the appearance of this paradigm in 1995 pointed Anglophone scholars to a hitherto neglected history and biography that shaped Barth's thoughts in decisive ways. As already pointed out in Chapter 1, however, this interpretative trajectory carries some serious flaws and inconsistencies.

In particular, the kind of "actualistic ontology" that proponents of McCormack's paradigm read into Barth reflects precisely the idealist mode of speculation that Barth firmly rejected. On their reading, what Barth posits is an immediate identity between God's act of election and God's triune essence: they claim that what God *is* qua Trinity is constituted by the act of election. That is, God *is* God's *act* in relation to humanity, even though this humanity is said to be the very humanity of God in Jesus Christ. This rendition of God as being-*as*-act is, as we shall see, little more than a sophisticated and seasoned repetition of the Cartesian-Hegelian mode of speculation.

In this chapter, I will reconstrue Barth's actualistic ontology and its underlying grammars by a close examination of key terms like "determination," "nature," "essence," and "being." I will argue that in and through formal Chalcedonian patterns, Barth's actualistic ontology dialectically operates on both a "substantialist" (for the lack of a better term) grammar of being retrieved from Augustine and Anselm and an idealist grammar of becoming retrieved from Hegel, while remaining ever critical of the "metaphysical" systems that Barth sees as the underpinnings of both these grammars. In this way, Barth maintains that Jesus Christ as the subject God *pro nobis* is the sole *speculum* the triune God-in-and-for-Godself. There is no identity between being and act within human nature as some *imago Dei* or *vestigium Trinitatis*. Speculative human knowledge of God is possible—it is indeed a given reality in the church—only because God-in-and-for-Godself, in God's unsublatable subjectivity, became God-for-us without ceasing to be God-in-and-for-Godself.

"Ontology" Clarified

In speaking of Barth's actualistic "ontology," I am mindful of George Hunsinger's caveat that the Swiss theologian rejects ontology in the stricter sense of the term as a branch of metaphysics that might offer a prior framework within which to unfold Christian theology. "Metaphysics" in the historical context in which Barth was situated carried some very specific connotations from the nineteenth century.

---

4. Bruce McCormack, *Orthodox and Modern: Studies in the Theology of Karl Barth* (Grand Rapids: Baker Academic, 2008), 12.

What it denoted for Barth was the kind of philosophical speculation that, in modern times, began with Descartes and culminated in Hegel (see Chapter 2).

In this historical context, "metaphysics" generally refers to the basically idealist enterprise that, positing intrinsic connections between the human mind and supposedly intelligible realities above and behind the sensible world, seeks to uncover the first principles or ultimate truths of the universe, so as to speculatively explain them. Barth's dismissal of "metaphysics," and "speculation" therewith, has to be understood against this backdrop. This also explains his antagonism toward natural theology. He saw in the Thomist notion of *analogia entis* a prototype of the central theme of speculative identity in idealist metaphysics.

The point that I am trying to make here is that Barth is not "anti-metaphysical" in the same way as Kant supposedly was according to, say, Hegel or Ritschl (see Chapters 1 and 2). The anti-metaphysical Kant of popular nineteenth-century narratives rejected the metaphysics of early-modern rationalism handed down Descartes to Wolff on the basis of an *epistemological* critique of human reason. Barth, by contrast, rejected the particular mode of metaphysical speculation characteristic of German idealism on the basis of a *theological* faith in divine revelation as speculative extension from God-in-and-for-Godself to God-for-us.

Now, it is an express intent of the post-Kantian school of Barth interpretation to offer a "strictly 'anti-metaphysical'" reading of Barth.[5] It seems to me that proponents of this interpretation are often oblivious to the ways the term "metaphysics" was usually understood in Barth's intellectual-historical context. They tend to describe Barth as being opposed to the kind of rational metaphysics of the early modern period that Kant deemed unviable in the *Critique of Pure Reason*. That is, they tend to interpret Barth's anti-metaphysical impulse as basically *epistemological* rather than *theological*.

The truth is that Barth was concerned more about theology than epistemology. He rejected the speculative metaphysics of German idealism because of its theological error of positing an immediate (e.g., the early Schelling) or speculative (e.g., Hegel) identity between human activity and essentiality. For Barth, immediate identity between act and essence resides in God's triune being alone, and the triune God is unsublatably the subject of speculative extension from *ad intra* essence to *ad extra* revelation. Only in this sense may we speak of Barth's "ontology" with all the speculative underpinnings of the term.

Furthermore, as Hunsinger points out, proponents of the post-Kantian agenda often "seem to trade on the ambiguity" of the term "ontology" by "slipping into" the distinctively modern kind of idealist metaphysics to which Barth was averse.[6] Already in the McCormack quote on Cohen and Barth above, we can see that Barth is described as having adopted a prior concept of "being," defined in terms of

---

5. Bruce McCormack, *Karl Barth's Critically Realistic Dialectical Theology* (Oxford: Clarendon, 1995), 246.

6. George Hunsinger, *Reading Barth with Charity: A Hermeneutical Proposal* (Grand Rapids: Baker Academic, 2015), 2.

some immediate or speculative identity between activity and essence, to be filled with Christological content.

This, according to Barth, was precisely the mistake of the idealist mode of speculation. Hegelian speculation, in particular, finds its *credo ut intelligam* starting point in the mediated identity between act and being, in order to contend for the determinability of the rational concept (*Begriff*) of God qua absolute Spirit. For Barth, the unsublatable subjectivity of the triune God as revealed in Jesus Christ is always the starting point from which human understanding can make sense of general concepts such as "being" and "the absolute." Barth refuses to find his speculative point of departure in a general notion of being: God—the God self-revealed in Jesus Christ—is being, but being it not God.

The foregoing discussion serves to clarify my use of the term "ontology" in presenting Barth's theology. In a more general sense, when I speak of Barth's "ontology," I shall heed Hunsinger's reminder and use the word in the extended meaning of the term (which Hunsinger accepts) to refer to any "general area of action, inquiry, or interest" that addresses the notion of being.[7] In a more particular sense, I use the term "ontology" to refer to the speculative *Denkform* of Barth's basically Anselmian program, while being mindful that Barth refused to describe Anselm's proof of God's existence as "ontological" because of the idealist connotations of the term (see Chapter 2).

"Substantialism" and Barth's Anselmian Grammar

"Substantialism" Defined

In addition to "ontology," "substantialism" is another explanatory term that I use with some hesitation in view of its connotations. It gained a considerable degree of importance in the secondary literature on Barth's actualistic ontology from the post-Kantian quarter. Paul Nimmo offers a succinct summary of what he calls "substantialist ontology," which he and others have argued to be diametrically opposed to what they call Barth's "actualism": Nimmo defines it as the basic metaphysical tenet according to which "what a person 'is' is something complete in and for herself, apart from and prior to the decisions, acts and relations which make up her lived existence."[8]

Opposed to this "substantialist ontology," so contends post-Kantian revisionism, is Barth's "actualistic ontology" that describes *being* as *determined* by *act* and *history*. This broad definition is correct, as long as "determination" is not confused with "constitution." Understood more simply, central to Barth's actualistic ontology is the notion of "being-in-act."

I shall argue, however, that Barth's actualistic ontology is significantly different from but not diametrically opposed to what has been labelled as "substantialism"

---

7. Hunsinger, *Barth with Charity*, 2.
8. Nimmo, *Being in Action*, 10n40.

from the post-Kantian quarter. Without acknowledging Barth's continuities with the so-called substantialist tradition, his actualism could easily be misconstrued as some variant of Hegel's panlogistic speculation.[9]

While the basic meaning of "substantialism" has generally been clear in the secondary literature on Barth, what Paul Jones calls "the connotative richness of substance terminology" in classical theology has only been mentioned in passing and rarely explained in any adequate detail.[10] Even the very term "substantialism" is seldom given any explicit elaboration in the revisionist oeuvre developed under the post-Kantian paradigm.

It has escaped the attention of many that the way "substantialism" is used in recent Barth studies originated from the tradition of process philosophy of which Hegel is often considered the direct or indirect patriarch.[11] It refers to what Hegel famously dubbed the "tendency towards substance" in the history of Western metaphysics.[12] Substantialism as understood from a process-philosophical perspective may be defined in his words as the view that the substance(s) constituting reality is an "abstract universality [*abstrakte Allgemeinheit*]" characterized by bare "simplicity [*Einfachheit*]"—it is "undifferentiated, unmoved substantiality [*ununterschiedne, unbewegte Substantialität*]."[13]

Against substantialism, Hegel insists that "everything depends on grasping and expressing the True [*das Wahre*] not only as Substance, but also as Subject."[14] By redefining substance in terms of subjectivity, Hegel effectively posits a speculative identity between what the subject *is* or what it has in it to *become* (i.e., its essentiality) and what it *does* (i.e., its activity) to actualize itself. This means that the truth of reality lies in "the becoming of its own self, the circle that sets forth its end as its purpose and has its end as its beginning, and is actual [*wirklich*] only through its execution and its end."[15]

Upon a (traditional or revised) metaphysical reading of Hegel, the difference between substance and process approaches to metaphysics can be understood as follows. Substance metaphysics envisions the essential nature of reality statically. "Nature" is the potentiality of a thing that dictates what it is to become in actuality: being determines becoming. Hegel, by contrast, contends that what a thing *is*

---

9. See Paul Molnar, *Divine Freedom and the Doctrine of the Immanent Trinity: In Dialogue with Karl Barth and Contemporary Theology* (London: T&T Clark, 2017), 112n74.

10. Paul Jones, *The Humanity of Christ: Christology in Karl Barth's Church Dogmatics* (London: T&T Clark, 2008), 32–3.

11. There are two broad versions of process philosophy, the one dialectical, the other more organic. The one is represented by Hegel, the other by Whitehead and Hartshorne.

12. See Johanna Seibt, "Particulars," in *Theory and Applications of Ontology: Philosophical Perspectives*, ed. Johanna Seibt and Roberto Poli (New York: Springer, 2010), 28.

13. G. W. F. Hegel, *Phänomenologie des Geistes* (Hamburg: Meiner, 2011), 14–15. Translation mine henceforth.

14. Hegel, *Phänomenologie des Geistes*, 14.

15. Hegel, *Phänomenologie des Geistes*, 14.

is determined by what it has in it to *become*: becoming determines being. This metaphysical priority of becoming over being leads to what Joel Rasmussen aptly describes as a radical "reconceptualisation of God as dynamic Spirit in, with, and under the world, rather than as the perfect unchanging being fully transcendent to the world," which "signalled a radical modern alternative to classical theism."[16] This way of understanding "being" is also characteristic of process metaphysics, from which the term "substantialism" originated.

Instead of using the term "process," of course, proponents of the post-Kantian interpretation oppose substantialism to what they call Barth's "actualism." This opposition fits well with a certain twentieth-century reception of Adolf von Harnack's (1851–1930) famous Hellenization thesis. Jürgen Moltmann (born 1926) represents a classic instance of this reception. He makes almost no distinction between the classical theology of Augustine and Anselm and the classical theism of Hellenistic philosophy.[17]

In a similar vein, post-Kantian interpreters of Barth think of substantialist thinking as fundamentally Hellenistic. They see not only Augustine and Anselm, but also the Niceno-Constantinopolitan and Chalcedonian Creeds as predicated upon a metaphysical framework of Greek substantialism.[18] Because Barth rejects substantialism as a product of Greek metaphysics, they contend, it is problematic to describe his theology as "basically Chalcedonian."[19]

This contention does not square with the fact that the Nicene Fathers already found the substance language of Greek metaphysics, largely delimited by the Peripatetic school, to be inadequate for the expression of the biblical truth of the triune Godhead.[20] In the Patristic period, Greek philosophers generally used the terms "*hypostasis*" and "*ousia*" synonymously to denote "substance." Simply understood, a substance is an *actual* thing that *is*. For Platonism, the substance of a thing is purely intelligible, while its sensible properties are merely shadows of

---

16. Joel Rasmussen, "The Transformation of Metaphysics," in *Oxford Handbook of Nineteenth-Century Christian Thought*, ed. Joel Rasmussen, Judith Wolffe, and Johannes Zachhuber (Oxford: Oxford University Press, 2017), 16.

17. See, for example, Jürgen Moltmann, "The Crucified God and the Apathetic Man," in *The Experiment Hope*, ed. and trans. Douglas Meeks (Philadelphia: Fortress, 1975), 73–5; Jürgen Moltmann, *The Trinity and the Kingdom: The Doctrine of God* (Minneapolis: Fortress Press, 1993), 21–5; Jürgen Moltmann, *Der lebendige Gott und die Fülle des Lebens: Auch ein Beitrag zur gegenwärtigen Atheismusdebatte* (Gütersloh: Gütersloher, 2014), 47–9.

18. E.g. Jones, *Humanity of Christ*, 31.

19. For a debate on the Chalcedonian character of Barth's Christology, see George Hunsinger, "Karl Barth's Christology: Its Basically Chalcedonian Character," in *Disruptive Grace: Studies in the Theology of Karl Barth* (Grand Rapids: Eerdmans, 2000); Bruce McCormack, "Karl Barth's Historicized Christology: Just How 'Chalcedonian' Is It?," in *Orthodox and Modern*; Paul Nimmo, "Karl Barth and the *Concursus Dei*—A Chalcedonianism Too Far?," *International Journal of Systematic Theology* 9 (2007): 58–72.

20. See John Zizoulas, "Human Capacity and Human Incapacity: A Theological Exploration of Personhood," *Scottish Journal of Theology* 28 (1975): 409.

the real thing. Ideas in the human intellect are, according to Platonism, *specula* of substantial realities. Aristotelianism, on the other hand, teaches the hylomorphic view that a substance must consist of both form and matter. Noetically, the mind must speculatively extend itself from particulars as primary substances to universals as secondary substances, even though ontically speaking, universals are primary and particulars secondary. In any case, different schools of philosophy held to different theories of the general concept of substance, and yet no Greek philosophical concept was readily available to serve as a generic term for the Father, the Son, and the Holy Spirit in the biblical doctrine of the Trinity.

When the Nicene Fathers distinguished between *ousia* and *hypostasis*, they gave rise to an ontology that was inconceivable for the Greeks. For one thing, "hypostasis" in classical Greek metaphysics does not denote the kind of personal subjectivity or agency that Christianity ascribes to the term. To confess that God is one *ousia* in three *hypostaseis* is to set forth the ontology of a dynamic and relational substance that is *a se* by virtue of, rather than in denial of, its inherent subjectivity, objectivity, and activity (i.e., eternal generation and procession).

The Latin adaptation of the Niceno-Constantinopolitan view of the triune *ousia* makes the further emphasis that God's substance is *free*. It is free, not only in that it is *a se* in its inherent subjectivity, objectivity, and activity. It is free in the secondary sense that this inward absoluteness—if we may borrow Hegel's terminology here—grounds and makes possible *ad extra* activities that are completely contingent upon the one will (and not three wills) of the Godhead, which nevertheless correspond perfectly to the *ad intra* essence of the Trinity. In other words, God is free to become what God *is not*, without ceasing to be what God immutably *is*. This is really salient point of Augustine's *De Trinitate*, 4.2: the suffering and death of God the Son is a free and perfect expression, rather than sublation, of God's immutable essence (see Chapter 5).

No Greek ontology of substance comes anywhere near such a view of free, dynamic, and relational *ousia*, not even Aristotle's notion of pure actuality or Plotinus's theory of emanation. The ontology of substance in classical theology, on this view, may quite properly be described as "actualistic." It is not actualistic in a Hegelian sense, nor is it the actualism of Hermann Cohen: it does not hold to the speculative ontology of being-*as*-act. It holds to a view of God's substance and being as eternally determinate in-and-for-Godself, and thus immutable, but at the same time it describes this determinacy in terms of God's eternal *opera ad intra* that grounds and makes possible God's free act of speculative extension *ad extra*.

This, I will argue, is precisely the prototype of Barth's notion of being-*in*-act. Barth, of course, repudiates both Augustine and Anselm for their view that the human mind is a *speculum Trinitatis*. For Barth, the *imago Dei* as a *speculum* of the triune subject is none other than Jesus Christ who is the very unsublatable subject God. Still, in both Barth and the classical theology of the Latin tradition, we can discern both a substantialist dimension (make no mistake: a distinctively Christian substantialism that sees God's substance as immutable and dynamic, necessary and free at once) and an actualistic one (again: a distinctively Christian, rather than idealist, actualism that affirms immutability and the necessity of being).

Now, Hegelian actualism—the assertion of a speculative identity between activity and essentiality within God's being realized through a process of sublative self-determination—appears to be what proponents of the post-Kantian paradigm tend to read into Barth, sometimes in the name of Cohen. On this reading, substantialism and actualism are not only distinguished. They are diametrically opposed to one another. Immutability and the necessity of being are altogether rejected as Hellenistic concepts. Substance, so they claim, must make way for activity in Christian theology.

My intention, again, is not to question the value of the contribution of post-Kantian scholarship to contemporary Barth studies. It goes without saying that the works of the post-Kantian interpreters have drawn our attention to previous neglected issues that are of fundamental import to the field. My own work builds on their insights in significant ways. I shall contend, however, that Barth's actualistic ontology is more complex than what they have depicted: Barth adopts the speculative grammars of both classical theology and idealist philosophy, in eclectic and dialectical ways, while remaining ever critical of their underlying metaphysics taken as a system.

Barth and Classical Theology: The Substance Language of Natur *and* Wesen

One confusion in recent Barth studies with regard to the theologian's extensive use of substance nomenclature is reflected in Paul Jones's contention that "*Natur* and *Wesen* take up no meaningful role" in Barth's later theology.[21] He, following the revisionist line of post-Kantian reading, falls short of recognizing Barth's grammatical use of *Natur/Wesen* as a means of distinguishing between the *ontological constitution* and *historical determination* of the human being.

Of course, revisionist scholars are not entirely wrong in distinguishing between what McCormack calls "substantialist ontology" and Barth's "actualistic ontology."[22] Barth is indeed against the physiocratic view that the human being's actual mode of existence is inescapably predetermined by its inherent nature—if this is what McCormack means by "substantialism." However, it is a mistake to suppose that Barth simply supplants one metaphysical view with another.

The assertion of post-Kantian revisionism that Barth "understood 'nature' to be a function of decision and act" begs some serious interpretative questions.[23] True enough, Barth sees the terms *Natur* and *Wesen*, which indeed have their origins in Greek substantialism, as in need of revision, but he does not simply "historicize" them by positing an immediate identity between act and being apart from or prior to God's triune essence. What he seeks to avoid is the basically idealist (be it that of the substantialist idealism of the Greek philosophers or the

---

21. Jones, *The Humanity of Christ*, 33.
22. Bruce McCormack, *For Us and Our Salvation: Incarnation and Atonement in the Reformed Tradition* (Princeton: Princeton Theological Seminary, 1993), 21.
23. McCormack, *For Us and Our Salvation*, 21.

historicist idealism of the modern philosophers) attempt to define human nature in the prior framework of a general anthropology, and divine nature from the starting point of some general notion of divinity. That is, Barth refuses to find his speculative starting point in general human conceptions. The particular person and work of Jesus Christ, who is the very speculative image of the triune God and the very ontological determination of human nature, is always the starting point of Barth's *fides quaerens intellectum* program—this is sometimes called Barth's "particularism."

Despite his aversion to rational metaphysics, however, Barth retains the traditional metaphysical definition of *nature* as the formal-causal aspect of different *kinds* of substances. Even in IV/2 Barth adopts the substantialist grammar of Greek metaphysics to state that "'human nature' means quite simply that which makes a man a man as distinct from God, angel or animal …, his *humanitas*."[24]

It is seldom noted that Barth's employment of substance vocabularies is generally in line with their more or less standard grammatical delimitations in the Latin tradition. Barth notes that in Western theology, "the essence [*das Wesen*] of God is the being [*Sein*] of God as divine being."[25]

In Latin theology, "*essentia*" primarily denotes "being." An *essentia* can also be called a *natura* in the sense that a real thing is "intelligible" only through a definite *essentia* in and through which a thing "has existence [*esse*]."[26] In the stricter senses of the terms, however, *essentia* is already actual and is the subject of its existence, while *natura* is a potentiality that becomes and is actual only in and through *essentia* as its agent.

Note that even the originally substantialist vocabulary of classical Latin theology is not aimed at conveying an ontology that can be described as substantialist in any simplistic sense. It is true that Barth sees in classical theology vestiges of Greek substantialism that need to be corrected, not least the problematic doctrine of the *imago Dei* in human nature as a speculative extension of God's inner essence. However, his intention is to follow through with the *speculative* principles of classical theology in the adaptation of substance terminology from Greek philosophy.

Already in Augustine, whom we discussed briefly earlier, we have a significant renovation of substance vocabulary in which the notions of "activity" and "relationship" are incorporated into the category of "substance," "being," and "essence." When Augustine (baptized 387) expounded on the Trinitarian doctrine established at Nicaea (325) and Constantinople (381), he rendered *ousia* interchangeably as *essentia* and *substantia*. Ronald Teske comments that although Augustine's use of "'*substantia*' and '*essentia*' in speaking of God … would seem to indicate that he means to say that God is an Aristotelian substance," this would

---

24. *CD* IV/2, 25.
25. *CD* I/1, 349; *KD* I/1, 369.
26. Thomas Aquinas, *On Being and Essence (De ente et essentia)*, trans. Robert Miller (1997), at [http://sourcebooks.fordham.edu/halsall/basis/aquinas-esse.asp], accessed August 23, 2021.

be "an Aristotelian substance unlike any other."[27] Bradley Green takes his cue from Teske's observation that Augustine's preference for *"essentia"* over *"substantia"* is an "un-Aristotelian move," and comments that "Augustine may be influenced by Aristotelian tendencies, but shapes these influences such that he uses them for his own ends."[28] Green quotes Augustine's *De Trinitate*: "God is a substance (*substantia*), or perhaps a better word would be being (*essentia*); at any rate what the Greeks call *ousia* ... We have the word 'being' (*essentia*) from 'be' (*esse*)."[29]

Augustine's preference for *essentia* as a rendering of the Nicene term *ousia* has much to do with his understanding of God's immutable and simple substance as a being in perpetual *opera ad intra*. It is insufficient to understand God only as "Being Itself" (*ipsum esse*) in light of Exodus 3:14 (which Augustine does in *Confessions* 7.10.16). God's aseity must be understood in light of 1 John 4:16: "God *is* love." Augustine explains: "love is of some one that loves, and with love something is loved. Behold, then, there are three things: he that loves, and that which is loved, and love."[30] God does not need an *ad extra* object to determine Godself as love. God *is* love *a se* as the unsublatable *ousia* of the subject, object, and act of love, in-and-for-Godself, expressed in the *opera ad intra* of eternal generation and procession.

Later Latin theology made *substantia* the standard translation of *ousia* in order to emphasize the immutability and simplicity of the Godhead, which, according to Augustine, is "simple and manifold," but the trinitarian connation of Augustine's use of *essentia* is preserved.[31] This is especially evident in the classical doctrine of God's unknowability *per essentiam*, which refers not to what God *is* in a static sense, but rather to God dynamic and relational being qua Trinity.

It is true that Barth is critical of Augustine's notion of *speculum* or *imago Trinitatis* (see Chapter 5). This speculative theology runs the danger of leading to an *analogia entis* in which "anthropology ... disguised itself as cosmology and theology."[32] In it, the philosophy of "Plato and Plotinus ... was deepened and illuminated" in a way analogous to "what Thomas made of [Aristotle]."[33]

Barth appreciates how Augustine (as well as Anselm) stresses that God cannot be reduced to a rational concept, and that no human concept can serve as a speculative image of God's essence. Yet, Barth is worried that their analogical notion of *speculum Trinitatis* can easily lead to a Platonist understanding of speculative image of the divine within the human intellect.

---

27. Ronald Teske, "Augustine's Use of '*Substantia*' in Speaking about God," *Modern Schoolmen* 62 (1985): 149.

28. Bradley Green, *Colin Gunton and the Failure of Augustine* (Eugene: Pickwick, 2011), 163–4.

29. Green, *Colin Gunton and the Failure of Augustine*, 148.

30. Augustine, *On the Holy Trinity*, ed. Philip Schaff, trans. Arthur Haddan (Edinburgh: T&T Clark, 1887), 124.

31. Augustine, *On the Trinity*, 101.

32. *CD* III/2, 21.

33. *CD* III/2, 10.

Instead of rejecting *tout court* Augustine's *speculum Trinitatis*, however, we shall see in Chapter 5 that Barth adopted it in an innovative way and incorporated it into his basically Anselmian mode of speculation. In fact, as we shall see, Barth acknowledges Augustine for having developed the *speculum Trinitatis* within a *fides quaerens intellectum* program that remained faithful to the *regula fidei*, even though the way Augustine tried to establish the *how* of God's *opera ad intra* from an anthropomorphic starting point contradicted the principle of his own *analogia fidei*.

In any case, contemporary scholars unfamiliar with the history of Latin theology are prone to make the mistake of drawing false dichotomies between what they call "substantialism" and what they deem to be modern modes of ontological thinking such as actualism, historicism, and relationalism. Millard Erickson, for instance, erroneously describes Barth's relational view of the *imago Dei* as "antisubstantialist" by setting up a false opposition between substantialism and relationalism.[34] This account is doubly incorrect in that it fails to see the relationalist character of what may be called Augustine's "substantialist" view of *imago Trinitatis*, and what may be called a "substantialist" dimension to Barth's notion of the *analogia relationis*.[35] Many mistakes committed by post-Kantian interpreters of Barth stem from precisely this kind of false opposition between what they call "substantialism" and "actualism."

That Barth indeed retains what may in some sense be called a "substantialist" dimension in his mature ontological thinking is evinced by his adoption of the vocabulary and grammar of classical Latin theology. He uses *Wesen* and *Natur* as the direct German renderings of *essentia* and *natura*, respectively. The common usage of *Wesen*, like *essentia*, can sometimes denote "essence" in the sense of "nature," but *Natur* is the direct equivalent of *natura*.[36] As we shall see anon, Barth speaks of divine and human *Wesen* and *Natur* in the framework of a basically Anselmian mode of speculation inherited from Augustine. Failure to acknowledge Barth's basically Anselmian *Denkform* has resulted in a lack of ability to make sense of his substance vocabulary on the part of post-Kantian revisionism.

On this note, Jones's assertion that the Greek substantialist "concept of *physis*" is "translated both as *Natur* and *Wesen*" in Barth's writings reflects a technical misperception typical of post-Kantian scholarship.[37] Jones claims that "*Natur* and *Wesen*" are "basically interchangeable" for Barth.[38] As we have seen, however, Barth's terminological framework is derived from the Latin tradition,

---

34. Millard Erickson, *Christian Theology* (Grand Rapids: Baker Academic, 2013), 520–30.
35. See my *Barth's Ontology of Sin and Grace*, 57–9.
36. This is well reflected in the Torrance-Bromiley edition. "*Gottes innerem, ewigem Wesen*" (*KD* II/2, 102), for example, is translated as "inward and eternal being of God" (*CD* II/2, 95). The same word is translated as "nature" in *CD* I/2, 53.
37. Jones, *The Humanity of Christ*, 31.
38. Jones, *The Humanity of Christ*, 18n9.

and not directly from the Greek. *Natur* and *Wesen*, just as *natura* and *essentia*, are *sometimes* interchangeable, but not *basically* so. Without appreciating the Augustinian-Anselmian heritage of Barth's theological vocabulary, it would be difficult to appreciate the speculative shape of his *Denkform*. The converse is also true. As we shall see, the lexical construct of Barth's theology makes sense only if we come to understand how it serves to support his speculative *Denkform*.

Two Conceptions of "Being": Wesen *and* Sein

The concept of being lies at the heart of speculative ontology. All speculative thinking—in Western philosophical and theological traditions at least—must posit some identity or interconnectedness between a being and its actions in order to make any predication about the being in relation to objects to which it ontically extends itself through its actions. This is reflected by the most basic onto-hermeneutical rule of the grammar of Western languages: there must be some speculative identity or ontological interconnectedness between the subject and the verb of a proposition such that the subject may extend itself to objects either other than or identical to itself.

Barth's generation was among the first to witness what Hans Lenk, in his preface to an edited volume on Chinese epistemology, calls an "on-going demise of the epistemological imperialism of Cartesian dualism" as a result of intellectual attempts to move away from "the overstated philosophical relevance of the grammatical subject-object separation."[39] This was part and parcel of a general distaste for speculative modes of philosophizing and theologizing among thinkers of Barth's generation.

To describe Barth as a speculative theologian is a way to stress that he wanted to retain a certain dimension of the traditional concept of "being" in relation to activity and objectivity. When referring to this concept, he sometimes uses "*Wesen*" and "*Sein*" synonymously.[40] However, the onto-grammatical connotations are quite different. *Wesen* is a direct equivalent of the originally "substantialist" term *essentia*, while *Sein* is reflective of an idealist grammar.

Barth's distinction between *Wesen* and *Sein*, uncharacteristic of traditional metaphysics, may initially seem reminiscent of Hegel. In Hegel's vocabulary, *Wesen* designates the *conceptual* underpinning of a thing: it is the *determination* (see definitions below) of the thing as it really is (i.e., what it has in it to ultimately become), behind the veil of *appearance* (*Schein*). *Sein*, by contrast, is the essence of a thing *as it appears*, disclosed phenomenally through the veil of contingencies and irrationalities.[41] In other words, *Schein* is the phenomenal veil through which an essence appears (*scheint*), and the subject determined by the verbal predicate

---

39. Hans Lenk, "Introduction," in *Epistemological Issues in Classical Chinese Philosophy*, ed. Hans Lenk and Gregor Paul (Albany: SUNY Press, 1993), 4.
40. E.g. *KD* II/1, 300.
41. See Michael Inwood, *A Hegel Dictionary* (Oxford: Blackwell, 1992), 39.

scheinen is "being" (*Sein*): being is determined by the act of appearing. (The phonetic similarity between *Sein* and *Schein* is a pure coincidence: there is no etymological connection here.)

It serves well to note here that Hegel uses the word "*Schein*" in a very different conceptual framework than that of (neo-)Kantianism. In (neo-)Kantian vocabulary, the "appearance" of a thing, distinct from the thing-in-itself (*das Ding an sich*), is designated as "*Erscheinung*," which Hegel uses to refer to the act or event of appearing. "*Schein*," by contrast, is often used synonymously with "*Illusion*."

According to (neo-)Kantianism, the belief that we have determinate knowledge of the objects to which metaphysical ideas such as God supposedly refer is merely an illusion: this is an important part of the (neo-)Kantian doctrine that McCormack likes to describe as "critical realism." According to this doctrine, we innately possess metaphysical ideas such as God, and the illusion of cognizing real objects to which these ideas refer arises from the very constitution of our intellectual and rational faculties. Kant compares the unavoidability of this kind of illusion to the way that, to our eyes, "the sea appears higher at the middle than at the shores."[42] The difficult and much debated Kantian doctrine of transcendental idealism, which advocates a "transcendental" mode of cognition that transcends cognition itself in order to cognize *that* and *how* we cognize reality, is partly aimed at critically recognizing such illusions in order for human cognition to correspond more closely to empirical reality itself. The Marburg neo-Kantians insisted that even the thing-in-itself as something metaphysical must also be treated as an illusion.

As it turns out, Barth did not incorporate the language of (neo-)Kantian transcendental idealism into the grammatical construct of his own theology. Barth's usage of *Sein* in formulating the notion of being-in-act (*Sein in der Tat*) is found within the structure of a basically Hegelian grammar. The weak association that McCormack tries to establish between Barth's actualism and the actualism of Hermann Cohen (see Chapter 1) pays little attention to the fact that Barth's nomenclature does not fit well with Cohen's neo-Kantian vocabulary at all.

The grammatical similarity between Barth's and Hegel's respective usages of *Sein* notwithstanding, there is a fundamental difference. Unlike Hegel, Barth does not grammatically associate God's *Sein* with *Schein*. In Hegel, appearances of the divine are imperfect *specula* of God's rational essence in the realm of creation. Barth rejects this understanding of speculative extension. For Barth, there is no *speculum* of God in creatures aside from Jesus Christ.

Between God's *ad intra* and *ad extra* modes of being—God's primary absoluteness qua Trinity and secondary absoluteness in Jesus Christ who is the very *imago Dei* as *speculum Trinitatis*—Barth draws a clear distinction. Even the incarnation as the flesh-becoming of the *I am* must not be thought of as a

---

42. Immanuel Kant, *Critique of Pure Reason*, ed. and trans. Paul Guyer and Allen Wood (Cambridge: Cambridge University Press), A297/B353-A298/B354. Henceforth abbreviated as *CPR*.

phenomenal appearance of God's essence. Appearance involves historical process, and God's "immutable" essence would never "appear" in any Hegelian sense of the term.[43] The man Jesus is not an imperfect appearance of God's essence. Rather, as the *speculum* or "emanation" (*Überfluss*) of God's essential being, Christ is truly and fully the subject God, whose subjectivity is unsublatable in both the primary and secondary modes of absolute being.

Barth firmly rejects Hegel's speculative logic according to which Spirit evolves through the moments of being and nothingness into the moment of the absolute, characterized by the actuality (*Wirklichkeit*) of becoming. Hunsinger rightly points out that Barth follows Thomas Aquinas in referring to the triune being-in-act as *actus purus* in order to retain the "classical theist" view that God does not need to actualize Godself as God by an exercise of the divine will.[44]

Barth agrees with Hegel that the historic tendency to understand "substance" and "nature" in terms of static universals or formal causes that set different kinds of things apart from one another was largely the result of Plato's influence. Hegel thinks that while Aristotle advanced Plato's substance ontology, Aristotle also introduced a proto-process way of attributing subjectivity to substance. Gilbert Gérard explains that according to Hegel, although both classical philosophers

> recognize the idea as universal in itself, determined and concrete, for Plato, this universality remains strictly "objective" and thus "inert", lacking "the activity of realization (*die Tätligkeit der Verwirklichung*)" whereas in the Aristotelian notion of the idea appears the "principle of vitality, of subjectivity," or the intrinsically active characteristic of the idea, which Hegel calls its "efficacy (*Wirklichkeit*)".[45]

The word *Wirklichkeit* is another key term in Barth's actualism. Again, it is borrowed from Hegel. In Anglophone Barth studies it is usually translated as "actuality." Hegel uses *Wirklichkeit* to denote the fully developed form (*Gestalt*) of a subject, and equates the actual with the positively rational. On this view the contingent and the irrational are merely appearances that are in one sense without actuality. However, the contingencies in the appearance of a concept are also described as *immediate actualities*. Only through the stage of appearances can immediate actualities become *developed actualities*. Hegel equates the truly actual—the rational and the absolute in its fully developed moment in which all contingencies have been expelled—with God.

Barth resolutely rejects the Hegelian view that God needs to actualize Godself in relation to an other that is not God, and that in this process of self-actualization God somehow "appears" through the veil of historical contingencies and irrationalities. In distinctively Hegelian language, Barth unequivocally denies, contra Hegel,

---

43. *CD* II/1, 496.
44. Hunsinger, *Reading Barth with Charity*, 168–9.
45. Gilbert Gérard, "Hegel, lecteur de la métaphysique d'Aristote. La substance en tant que sujet," *Revue de Métaphysique et de Morale* 74 (2012): 201.

that God's "being [*Sein*], speaking and acting are only an appearance [*Schein*]" of God's eternally immutable essence.[46] There is a fundamental difference "between the divine and the appearance of the divine [*dem Schein-Göttlichen*]": because Christ who is very God and fully God as a secondary mode of God's very own absolute being has come to be known in the church by faith, phenomena positing themselves as appearances of the divine must be regarded as "the demonic."[47]

As far as creatures are concerned, of course, Barth would agree with Hegel that a being (*Sein*) can either manifest or contradict its own essence (*Wesen*) in historical appearance.[48] There is no ontological identity, speculative or immediate, between creaturely being and activity *a se*. Such self-identity *a se* is found in God alone. This is why Barth consistently uses *Sein* instead of *Wesen* to describe the human "being" as radically and totally sinful in the "state of corruption."[49] The sinful activity that overwhelms the human being has no power to determine humanity's essence.

As explained earlier, in Barth's theological grammar, the originally "substantialist" term *Wesen* denotes substance defined by its inherent nature, i.e., that by which a thing is what it is. It comprises something complete in itself that no activity from below can ever alter. His usage of *Wesen*, then, differs significantly from Hegel's.

Hegel defines the essence or essentiality (*Wesentlichkeit*) of a thing as what it has in it to become in the consummate stage or moment of its evolution. By contrast, Barth's usage of *Wesen* critically and eclectically incorporates both a "substantialist" dimension and a Hegelian one. In the *perfect tense* of the one and inseparable triune economy *pro nobis* (which perfectly corresponds to but remains abidingly distinct from the immanent Trinity), our essence is a God-given covenantal nature in Jesus Christ that cannot be altered. That is to say, human identity or essence is determined not by human activity, but by God's gracious activity in Christ. In the *present* and *future tenses* (which are distinct and ontically necessary aspects of one and the same triune economy) of the historical re-enactment of God's work by the Holy Spirit *in nobis*, our essence is what we are to ultimately become in Christ, which is distinct, albeit inseparable, from what we already *are* in him.

And because our essence is determined by our being in Jesus Christ, sin and nothingness have no power over our essence. Sin for Barth pertains to the category of *act*, not *essence/nature*. The subject of the act of sin is the existential human *Sein*, not ontological *Wesen*.[50] Sin, in other words, is an ontological impossibility.

---

46. *CD* II/1, 496; *KD* II/1, 558. Translation revised.
47. *CD* II/1, 409; *KD* II/1, 461.
48. E.g. *CD* IV/1, 90–1; *KD* IV/1, 96.
49. *CD* IV/1, 492.
50. See Wolf Krötke, *Sin and Nothingness in the Theology of Karl Barth*, ed. and trans. Philip Ziegler and Christina-Maria Bammel (Princeton: Princeton Theological Seminary, 2005), 73.

The Speculative Grammar of "Determination" (Bestimmung)

Hegelian Origin of the Term

Another keyword closely associated with Barth's notion of "being" is "determination" (*Bestimmung*), which he critically borrows from Hegel. This difficult term can be understood as a speculative notion with which Hegel seeks to reinvigorate classical conceptions of *Natur/Wesen*. Lexical study of this term reveals two striking weaknesses in revisionism's post-Kantian reading of Barth, which capitalizes on his language of "divine self-determination" to contend that election is "a constitutive or necessary aspect of God's being."[51]

First, this reading does not pay due respect to the Hegelian origin of the term, explained below. Second, the confusion between "determination" and "constitution" is a rare instance in which revisionism falls short of relying on the strength of its own post-Kantian paradigm, which carries an obvious advantage in its knowledge of (neo-)Kantian philosophy.

"Determination" and "constitution" are two different concepts in Kantian terminology that are only distantly related to one another in the same framework. "*Beschaffenheit*" and "*Konstitution*" are rendered as "constitution" in English to denote the structure and properties that make a thing what it is, with "*Konstitution*" carrying more deeply ontological connotations (e.g., as in the case of "constitutive principles"—"*konstitutive Prinzipien*"). ("*Verfassung*," another concept also translated as "constitution," is not within the scope of our discussion here.) One central intent of Kant's first *Critique* is to answer the question, "What is the constitution [*Beschaffenheit*] of a thing that thinks?"[52]

Kant's answer to this question constitutes a sharp critique of the immediate identity between *sum* and *cogito* posited in the Platonic-Cartesian tradition. Kant dissolves the identity between the substance and activity of the thing that thinks, in much the same way as he distances things-in-themselves from their appearances that make up the objects of our thinking. Kant is emphatic that our empirical cognition has no ability to "conform to the *constitution* of the objects" of sense.[53] We must hold to the hypothesis that "the object (as an object of the senses) conforms to the *constitution* of our faculty of intuition."[54]

In the third *Critique*, Kant writes: "given the *constitution* of the faculty of our reason, we could not even make comprehensible the kind of purposiveness related to the moral law and its object that exists in this final end without an author and

---

51. Matthias Gockel, "How to Read Karl Barth with Charity: A Critical Reply to George Hunsinger," *Modern Theology* 32 (2016): 260.
52. Kant, *Critique of Pure Reason*, A398.
53. Kant, *Critique of Pure Reason*, Bxvii.
54. Kant, *Critique of Pure Reason*, Bxvii.

rule of the world who is at the same time a moral legislator."⁵⁵ Still, Kant wants to ascertain that the faculty of the power of judgment is capable of attaining to some *Beschaffenheit* of the subjective principle for seeking laws.⁵⁶

Kant also developed a concept of "determination" that (neo-)Kantianism adopted, and this concept is only remotely related to "constitution." In Kant, the preferred grammar is the nominal infinitive, "*das Bestimmen*," and not "*Bestimmung*," which Barth uses. "Determination" is a key term in Kant's vocabulary, and plays a crucial role in the doctrine of transcendental idealism. A famous passage from the first edition of the first *Critique* defines transcendental idealism as the doctrine that appearances "are all together to be regarded as mere representations and not as things in themselves, and accordingly that space and time are only sensible forms of our intuition, but not *determinations* given for themselves or conditions of objects as things in themselves."⁵⁷

The Kantian term *das Bestimmen* refers to the reasons underlying the actuality of a factual possible and the reasons underlying the exclusion of its counterfactual possible. This definition of *das Bestimmen* is inherited from Christian Wolff (1679–1750), whose dogmatistic rendition of Leibnizian thought dominated philosophy departments across German universities during Kant's student years. Wolf developed philosophy as a "science of possibles" that builds on the originally Molinist notions of factuals and counterfactuals, which G. W. Leibniz (1646–1716) adopted from Francisco Suárez (1548–1617). The existence of the world, according to this philosophy, is a factual possible; it is also possible, though counterfactual, that the world never came into being. That the world exists is not only possible and factual, but also becomes "determinate" in view of the *sufficient reasons* explaining not only how and why this is so, but also how and why the contradictory possible is excluded.

Kant takes this Wolffian definition further by proposing the notion of a *complete determination*: something is completely determinate when the sum total of all its possible predicates is considered in relation to the contradictory opposite of each predicate. Kant retains the rationalist view that reality is ultimately rational and not contingent. This means that there must be ultimate reasons why some possibles are factual and why others are not.

One key question that Kant seeks to answer in the first *Critique* is: what objects are we capable of determining in the theoretical use of reason? A transcendental critique of our cognitive faculties reveals that appearances are not determinations in themselves, and that we are incapable of determining the thing-in-itself. Furthermore, metaphysical ideas such as God, the world, and the soul cannot be determined within the theoretical use of reason.

---

55. Immanuel Kant, *Critique of the Power of Judgment*, ed. Paul Guyer, trans. Paul Guyer and Eric Matthews (Cambridge: Cambridge University Press, 2000), 320. Henceforth abbreviated as *CPJ*.

56. Kant, *Critique of the Power of Judgment*, 65.

57. Kant, *Critique of Pure Reason*, A369. Emphasis mine.

This brings us back to Kant's critique of Descartes's ontological proof, which we discussed in the previous chapter. Recall that for Kant, Descartes failed to recognize that existence is a *category* rather than an *attribute*. The proposition, "God is omnibenevolent," is true by conceptual necessity, because omnibenevolence is by conceptual definition an attribute of God as perfect being. Existence, however, is an *a priori* concept, a category, that does not pertain analytically to the idea of God.

Kant identifies the idea of God as the "ideal" of pure reason, that is, "the representation of an individual being as adequate to an idea."[58] In the idea of God, then, no attribute can be contingent. All predications about God must all be analytical. Analytical propositions are true by conceptual necessity, but they cannot be existential predications. All existential predications are synthetic. That is, the theoretical proposition, "God is," is one that synthesizes two distinct concepts, namely, the metaphysical idea of God and the *a priori* concept of existence. No synthetic proposition can be true by logical necessity: "this privilege pertains only in the analytic propositions, as resting on its very character."[59]

Analytic propositions about the idea of God, however, cannot *determine* God as a real being, for determination necessarily involves synthetic judgments. In the theoretical use of reason, an idea can become determinate to us only when it is measured against another object. Because the idea of God is that of the original and highest being, there is no other object against which God's being can be determined. If God is indeed the only true ideal of pure reason—an idea of the highest rank—then it can never satisfy the criterion of determinacy (being affirmed or negated on the ground of an other).

Descartes, on Kant's view, thought that he could affirm God's existence by asserting an immediate identity between *cogito* and *sum* to reflect on the necessity of God's existence. This speculative program became disillusioned after Kant. The *cogito*—sheer speculative thinking—is incapable of determining the synthetic proposition, "God is." The very "illusion" of the Cartesian proof consists precisely "in the confusion of a logical predicate with a real one (i.e., the determination of a thing)."[60]

Hegel, as we saw in the previous chapter, dedicated himself to reviving the Cartesian mode of theological speculation after Kant. Hegel identifies absolute Spirit as the concrete universal in much the same way as how Kant speaks of God as the ideal of pure reason. One of Hegel's most important objectives in his speculative program is to establish a way for human reason to speak of the determinacy of absolute Spirit.

As Hegel sees it, one key reason why Kant thought that the idea of God cannot be determined in the theoretical use of reason is that the Wolffian-Kantian notion of *das Bestimmen* is all too architectonic. This notion of determination is basically

---

58. Kant, *Critique of the Power of Judgment*, 117.
59. Kant, *Critique of Pure Reason*, A589/B626.
60. Kant, *Critique of Pure Reason*, A589/B626.

an attempt to sort out the world-plan in which the Leibnizian principle of sufficient reason can be applied to all factuals and counterfactuals.

Hegel's grammatical transformation of the nominal infinitive to *Bestimmung* is aimed at expressing an organic, rather than architectonic, notion of determination, such that truth and reality are no longer characterized by being and nonbeing (*is* and *is not*), but rather by the dialectical process of alienation and mediation.[61] The truth of reason, the essential rationality of reality as a whole, is the process through which Spirit *determines* itself as the absolute, that is, the divine.

By "determination," Hegel means the definition of a subject through a history of conflict and reconciliation with otherness. A thing is *determinate* (*bestimmt*) only in relation to an other in the dialectical process of sublation (the negation of a negative moment of logic for the purpose of uplifting the logical subject to the moment of the absolute). Stephen Houlgate describes "determination" in relationalist terms as "the specific quality or character that something manifests or asserts in its relation to an other."[62] A more historicist nuance is expressed in Terje Sparby's explanation of the notion as "the uncovering of the essential nature of something" through the dialectical process of history.[63] In the introduction to the present volume, we illustrated the relationalist and historicist dimensions of the Hegelian notion of *Bestimmung* with the example of Confucius as a Chinese philosopher.

Hegel speaks of self-determination (*Selbstbetimmung*), and means thereby the autonomous disclosure of something's own essence by negating its present form and lifting itself up to a higher form of appearance. In other words, in Hegel's usage, self-determination involves self-sublation. History as a whole is the external basis through which Spirit determines itself as absolute Spirit by alienating itself from itself and reconciling itself to itself in an other.

The determinacy of God qua absolute Spirit is not *immediately* accessible to our knowledge. Through the speculative identity (which, to be sure, will always remain speculative for the later Hegel) between Spirit and human consciousness, however, we can *reflect* on the consummate determinacy of God through *after-thinking* the logical history of Spirit's self-determination.

Barth rejects Hegel's view that God needs the world in order to actualize Godself as God, but he critically adopts the Hegelian grammar of *Bestimmung*

---

61. Fichte also developed the notion of determination in an idealist direction after Kant by replacing the nominal infinitive, "*das Bestimmen*," with "*die Bestimmung*"—but Fichte never quite reached Hegel's idealist rendition of the notion. The Fichtean use of the term *die Bestimmung* is largely non-technical, and never gave rise to a systematic grammar in later philosophy. See Johann Gottlieb Fichte, *The Vocation of Man*, trans. Peter Preuss (Indianapolis: Hackett, 1987). Barth treats this work at length in an excursus: CD III/2, 96–109.

62. Stephen Houlgate, *The Opening of Hegel's Logic: From Being to Infinity* (West Lafayette: Purdue University Press, 2006), 348.

63. Terje Sparby, *Hegel's Conception of the Determinate Negation* (Leiden: Brill, 2015), 200.

as an overarching notion supporting the construct of his actualistic ontology and speculative theology. A determination qualifies but does not constitute an entity's nature or essence.

It is a technical mistake on revisionism's part to confuse "determination" with "constitution." Barth says that God determines Godself as the electing God who is identical with Jesus Christ. It is precisely this language of determination that makes the identity a mediated one: the elected man "is" the electing God in the same logical sense that Mary "is" *Theotokos*.

When Barth first adopted the Hegelian language of God's self-determination to speak of an identity between Jesus Christ and the electing God in 1936 (contra McCormack and Gockel, Barth did not wait until 1942 to formulate this identity: Barth's ground-breaking insight in 1942 is that Jesus Christ as electing, elected, and election is the secondary mode of God's absolute being), he was emphatic that the two are not *immediately* identical. Immediate identity between act and being, again, resides within God's triune essence alone.

As the elected human, Christ was "determined" to suffer at Golgotha: "It is the highest justice of this God—and Jesus Christ is Himself God's Son—to be in our place as reprobated man and to bear our punishment Himself."[64] The relationship between the electing God and Jesus Christ—"the relationship between God's eternal counsel and our time"—"is a relationship of identity, but this is the identity made recognizable to us in revelation," that is, in the history of the incarnation.[65]

The logic underlying the phrase, "Jesus Christ is the electing God," on this view, is analogous to that underlying the phrase, "Confucius was a Chinese philosopher." In its formal (but not its substantive) aspect, it is, for the lack of a better term, what might be called a "logic of mediation" reminiscent of Hegel. The triune God-in-and-for-Godself determined Godself to be God-for-us without ceasing to be God-in-and-for-Godself, and so it is correct to say that Jesus Christ is mediately the electing God, just as we must affirm with Chalcedon the title of Jesus's mother as *Theotokos*. Thus the Barth of 1936: "The eternal God and thus also the eternal Son of God is the electing God, and the electing God is none other than the eternal God and thus the eternal Son Himself in the communion with the Father and the Holy Spirit, who assumed human nature in His birth from the Virgin Mary."[66]

Twofold Determinations of the Human Being

In the case of "human nature," Barth actualizes this vocabulary by speaking of it as a determination *from above* (*von oben*) by the covenantal history of God and humankind in Christ. It is a determination in the sense that it is an essence enacted by the history of the covenant toward its ultimate fulfilment on the external basis of creation.

---

64. *Gottes Gnadenwahl*, 21. *Pace* Bruce McCormack, "Seek God Where He May Be Found: A Response to Edwin Van Driel," *Scottish Journal of Theology* 60 (2007): 64.
65. *Gottes Gnadenwahl*, 45.
66. *Gottes Gnadenwahl*, 46.

In line with the substance vocabulary of the Latin theological tradition, "nature" is grammatically associated with creation. Barth moves beyond the tradition by identifying creation as the external ground of the covenant, thus overcoming what he perceives to be the nature-grace dualism characteristic of Augustinian and Anselmian ontology. Contra Augustine and Anselm, Barth contends that nature as a product of creation was never ontologically antecedent to and thus independent of reconciliatory grace in Christ. The gracious history of the covenant is what determines the nature of the external ground on which it is enacted.[67]

With this redefinition of *Natur*, the connotations of *Wesen* are also actualized. Barth retains the grammatical relations between *natura* and *essentia* in classical Latin theology. But since *Natur* now refers to God's determination of the human essence by the history of the covenant, *Wesen* is no longer understood as merely the agent of Platonic forms. Rather, the human *Wesen* is determined by the active and concrete history of Jesus Christ to correspond to that gracious history.

At this juncture, Barth makes a significant and subtle move. He insists that human *Natur* remains good after the fall and consistently avoids using *Wesen* to describe the human being-in-sin. He thereby posits more (but not less) than the traditional understanding of the inherent goodness of creation. In the ontological framework of the broad Augustinian-Anselmian tradition, to say that human *nature* is in itself sinful is tantamount to saying that sin is either created by God, or else uncreated and self-existent as some kind of a second deity. Barth accepts this traditional grammar but argues that sin is a foreign intrusion that is not proper to good human nature.

As Barth carries through with this Augustinian insight, he registers a critical correction against Augustine's meontological understanding of a *corrupted* nature. Barth deems this understanding "quite untenable" because "the Bible accuses man as a sinner from head to foot, but it does not dispute to man his *full and unchanged humanity*, his *nature as God created it good*."[68] Whereas mainstream theologians of the Augustinian tradition claim that only what remains of human nature is still good in the state of corruption, Barth contends that humankind "has not lost— even in part—the good nature which was created by God."[69]

Barth holds to the premise that only God has the power to alter human nature.[70] If human nature were somehow corrupted, then even if what remained of it was still good, it would nonetheless have been altered. This outcome would imply either that God authored the *corruptio*, or else that sin possessed quasi-divine powers to alter the nature of God's creatures. These were precisely the implications that Manichaeism could not avoid, and Barth rejects them with Augustine. For this reason, too, he insists against Augustine upon the full integrity of human *nature* after the fall.

---

67. See Krötke, *Sin and Nothingness in the Theology of Karl Barth*, 73.
68. *CD* IV/1, 492, italics added.
69. *CD* IV/1, 492.
70. *CD* IV/2, 421.

To be sure, Barth stresses that in the "state of corruption" the human "being [*Dasein*]" is totally and radically sinful.⁷¹ On one hand the human *being* is determined "from above" by the "powerful and superior reality of God and man" in Christ—this determination is what human *nature* signifies.⁷² On the other hand, "*from below* it [the human being] is also continually determined by the falsehood of man in a sinister but very palpable manner."⁷³

This determination "from below" by sinful human activities is foreign and contradictory to human *nature* as determined "from above," and yet both determinations are *total* with respect to the human *Sein*. This actualistic rendition of anthropological ontology allows Barth to say that the human being is totally and radically sinful while also maintaining that human *nature* remains totally good and uncorrupted under the sway of nothingness.

It is true that Barth sometimes speaks loosely about the corruption or distortion of human nature. In such passages, however, he would often clarify that strictly speaking, sin is "un-nature [*Unnatur*]" foreign and contradictory to human "nature."⁷⁴

At this juncture it might help to clarify that the unaltered goodness of human nature does not mean for Barth the tenability of the Cartesian-Hegelian mode of speculation, which, as he sees it, asserts that what remains of original human nature still enables fallen humans to reason their way up to God apart from Christ. Against this view, Barth contends emphatically that the human being is *totally* corrupted by sin, such that human beings are utterly incapable of *actual* knowledge of God. Furthermore, because human nature is the determination of the human being by the history of God's perfect and thus unrepeatable work of reconciliation in Christ, the actualization of human knowledge of God in the speculative form of *Nachdenken* completely hinges upon the present-tense re-enactment or actualization of Christ's grace *extra nos* by the renewing work of the Holy Spirit *in nobis*. More simply, what Christ accomplished in his finished and perfect work of salvation there and then, the Holy Spirit actualizes in us here and now in a secondary and dependent form.

Analogia Relationis: *An Actualistic* Speculum

Up to this point we have only discussed Barth's view of God's *works*, the *opera ad extra externa*, as the ontological grounding of human nature. We would fail to do Barth justice if we stop here, for he is not afraid to follow the Augustinian-Anselmian tradition in rooting his speculative anthropology in the doctrine of God's *being*. On the other hand, we must also stress that his trinitarian account of the *imago Dei* is a significantly revised version of the *speculum Trinitatis* espoused by Augustine and Anselm.

71. *CD* IV/1, 492.
72. *CD* IV/3, 477.
73. *CD* IV/3, 477.
74. *CD* IV/2, 26; *KD* IV/2, 26.

Augustine and Anselm ascribe the *vestigium* or *imago Trinitatis* to the human intellect and memory as some *speculum* of God's triune essence. This, for Barth, flatly contradicts the very Anselmian principle of God's inconceivability. Nimmo rightly cautions that although "the relationship between God and the true human revealed in Jesus Christ is analogous to the prior intra-trinitarian relationship of God the Father to God the Son," this analogy does not consist in "any correspondence or similarity of being, an *analogia entis*, but in terms of what Barth calls 'an *analogia relationis*.'"[75]

Barth introduces the crucial concept of an "analogy of relations" in *CD* III/2 as an actualistic repudiation of what he sees as an analogy of being between God and humankind instituted by Augustine's theology of image and adopted by Anselm in *Monologion*.[76] The analogy of being posits some kind of an identity between essence and act within human nature resembling the pure actuality of God's being. Augustine's emendatory use of the originally Platonist language of *imago* carries the implication that there is a speculative correspondence (though not consubstantiality) between the human being and the being of the triune God that allowed him to speak of God analogically.

This Augustinian formulation, as Barth sees it, fails to identify Christ as the *imago Dei* that determines the essence of all humankind. In *CD* II/1-2, Barth insists against Augustine that the *imago Trinitatis* is none other than Jesus Christ who is the very subject God in God's secondary mode of absolute being as the electing, elected, and election (see Chapter 5). This version of the *speculum Trinitatis* is further developed in III/2, where Barth, again identifying Jesus Christ as the *imago Dei apropos*, clarifies that by "the term 'image'" he means "a correspondence and similarity between the two relationships," namely, "the relationship within the being of God on the one side" and "between the being of God and that of man on the other."[77] This is "not … an *analogia entis*," but an "*analogia relationis*" that "consists in the fact that the freedom in which God posits" Godself as the triune God "is the same freedom as that in which he is the Creator of man, in which man may be his creature, and in which the Creator-creature relationship is established by the Creator."[78] In both the primary (qua Trinity) and the secondary (as the electing God, the Creator, and lord of the covenant) modes of existence, the subjectivity of God remains unsublated in the abiding absoluteness of God's being as the one who loves in freedom.

The particular Creator-creature relationship that serves as a "copy" of the "divine original" (the intra-trinitarian relationship) *is* none other than Jesus Christ who is very God and very human.[79] Christ *is* the true *imago Dei* not just by virtue of his

---

75. Nimmo, "Karl Barth and the *Concursus Dei*—A Chalcedonianism Too Far?," 89.
76. See Archie Spencer, *The Analogy of Faith: The Quest for God's Speakability* (Downers Grove: IVP Academic, 2015), 22.
77. *CD* III/2, 220.
78. *CD* III/2, 220.
79. *CD* III/2, 221.

consubstantiality with the Father (as Augustine and Anselm would have it), but also by virtue of the speculative extension from the intra-trinitarian relationship within God's eternal essence to the divine-human relationship in Christ's incarnate person, by which he is at once consubstantial with God and consubstantial with us. "In this [covenantal] relationship *ad extra*, God *repeats* a relationship proper to himself in his inner divine essence."[80] It is only in this sense that the human essence, determined by the very name Jesus Christ, can be described as having been made in God's image. As Father, Son, and Holy Spirit are *for* one another, and as the one triune God is *for us*, "it is the essence of this man [created by God], to be for God."[81]

God's Self-Determination: Election and the Trinity Revisited

The foregoing discussion suggested that writers following the revisionist line in thinking of election as *constitutive* of God's triune essence do not seem to have fully grasped the grammar underlying the term *Bestimmung* in Barth's usage. They have consistently exhibited a tendency to confuse "determination" with the essential "constitution" of a being. This is a mistake on revisionism's part that Hunsinger pointed out early on in the Trinity-election debate.[82] Yet proponents of the revisionist agenda persist in committing the same mistake rather consistently, trading on Barth's language of "divine self-determination" to contend that election is "a constitutive or necessary aspect of God's being."[83]

Against this reading, the case of Barth's anthropological ontology shows that "nature" as the constitution of a being and its "determination" are grammatically distinct concepts in his speculative vocabulary. The determination of the human being (*Sein*) "from above" *constitutes* human essence (*Wesen*); the determination "from below," by contrast, is by no means constitutive of the human being. It is thus not only a hermeneutical mistake at an intellectual-historical level, but also an exegetical one at a textual level to treat "determination" as a synonym of "constitution."

It is true that Barth sees the covenantal grace of election as in some way "necessary" to God's being: "it is almost integral to [God's] very nature and essence to be our Saviour."[84] He stresses that this "inner necessity with which Jesus is at one and the same time both for God and for man" reveals to us that "there is freedom in God, but no caprice."[85]

The contrast between freedom and caprice here is a reference to Barth's actualistic construal of the Trinity and election in II/1-2, which we will discuss in

---

80. *CD* III/2, 218. Italics added.
81. *CD* III/2, 71.
82. George Hunsinger, "Election and the Trinity: Twenty-Five Theses on the Theology of Karl Barth," *Modern Theology* 24 (2008): 181.
83. Gockel, 260.
84. *CD* III/2, 218.
85. *CD* III/2, 218–19.

Chapters 5 and 6 in fuller detail. It occurs in the context of the overarching theme of God's being as the one who loves in freedom, first set forth in §28. On one hand, God is love, and God loves necessarily. On the other hand, God is free, and God loves in complete freedom. Barth explicates these predications, which might seem contradictory, with a critical adaptation of Augustine's *speculum Trinitatis*, fleshing out a post-Kantian view of freedom as emancipation from arbitrariness with a Christocentric doctrine of election (see Chapters 5 and 7).

Borrowing Augustine's notion of God as the subject, object, and act of love, Barth posits a kind of "primary objectivity" in God's eternal triune essence, critically using the Hegelian notion of absolute freedom (the perfect communion of the subjective and the objective in a moment of fully developed actuality) to describe God's mode of being qua Trinity as God's "primary absoluteness." "We have seen that the freedom of God, as his freedom in himself, his primary absoluteness, has its truth and reality in the inner trinitarian life of the Father with the Son by the Holy Spirit."[86] The primary absoluteness of the freedom of God's love that is the being of God entails that "even if there were no such relationship [between God and the creature], *even if there were no other outside of him, he would still be love*."[87] God *is* the pure actuality of love in God's inner subjectivity and objectivity. Within the triune God there is an immediate identity between what God *is* and what God *does*, and God does not need to *act* upon an *ad extra* object to determine God's being.

Eberhard Jüngel (whom followers of McCormack's model like Nimmo and Tyler Frick purport to follow) comments that for Barth, "God can be the God of humanity without being defined as God by his relation to humanity … God's being-for-us does not define God's being."[88] As Barth himself puts it, God "is the same even in himself, even before and after and over his works, and without them … They are nothing without him. But he is who he is without them."[89] God is love *a se* (in-and-for-Godself), and the primary absoluteness of God as the one who loves in freedom entails the aseity of God's loving essence. As Father, Son, and Holy Spirit, God is abidingly absolute before any *ad extra* act of self-determination.

Yet, the primary mode of God's absolute being would have been unknowable to us without covenantal condescension. To talk about divine *aseity* apart from the concrete history of *promeity* would be to commit what Barth considers to be the idolatry of idealist speculation.

---

86. *CD* II/1, 317.
87. *CD* II/2, 6. Italics added.
88. Eberhard Jüngel, *God's Being Is in Becoming: The Trinitarian Being of God in the Theology of Karl Barth*, trans. John Webster (Grand Rapids: Eerdmans, 2001), 119–20. *Pace* Bruce McCormack, "Election and the Trinity: Theses in Response to George Hunsinger," *Scottish Journal of Theology* 63 (2010): 204; Nimmo, "Karl Barth and the *Concursus Dei*—A Chalcedonianism Too Far?," 3–6; Tyler Frick, *Karl Barth's Ontology of Divine Grace* (Tübingen: Mohr Siebeck, 2021), 17–31.
89. *CD* II/1, 260.

Covenantal promeity is precisely the secondary mode in which God is absolutely free as the very subject, object, and act of the love that is the being of God. In addition to (but not in place of) Barth's own description of the primary absoluteness of God's freedom as aseity and unconditionedness, he states that God's love is free in the secondary sense that God freely binds Godself to covenant with the creature without altering God's essence. In this secondary mode of being the subject God remains abidingly absolute in the secondary objectivity of divine loving. Jesus Christ who is the very subject God is also the object and act of election that is the "emanation" (*Überfluss*: see Chapters 5–6) of the essential love of the triune God. Jesus Christ is as such the secondary absoluteness of God's being, and not just a *decretum Dei* as an absolute something detached from God's essence.

In this secondary absoluteness, Christ the electing God *is* also the object of election, albeit not *as* the Creator but as a creature, in the same way that Christ who died at Golgotha *is* God and yet did not die *as* God. The covenantal relationship between Creator and creature in Jesus Christ is the *speculum* of the inner relationship of the triune God. God remains absolutely free in God's *ad extra* self-binding in a way that corresponds perfectly to God's essence *ad intra*. Jüngel explains that "God's being for itself ... grounds and makes possible God's being-for-us."[90]

With Kant, Barth insists that true freedom is at once emancipation from coercion of the will and from contingent exercise of the power of choice (*Willkür*), and that genuine freedom consists in the *perfect correspondence* between inner essence and *ad extra* activities. With Hegel, Barth stresses that *actual* freedom consists in active communion between subjectivity and objectivity. Barth, however, rejects Hegel's idea that God's freedom becomes absolute only through a history of reconciliation between the subjective and the objective. The triune being of God as the one who loves in absolute freedom remains absolutely free in God's self-determination as the electing God. Subjectivity, objectivity, and activity are equally basic to the being of God, in such a way that God's being is not self-determined by any act ontologically or logically prior to God's absolute essence qua Trinity.

Barth's speculative actualism differs from the speculative metaphysics of Hegel's absolute idealism precisely in that the former speaks of God as being-*in*-act rather than being-*as*-act.[91] For Hegel, the process of reconciliation (*Versöhnung*) must involve a historical stage in which God becomes God-for-us (*für uns*), which is the same as God-for-Godself (*für sich*), and thus no longer God-in-Godself (*an sich*). To call Hegel's God-for-us "God" is logically analogous to calling Confucius a Chinese philosopher: the subject that was to become China was not yet determined as China in Confucius's time. There is no objectivity and thus no activity within

---

90. Jüngel, *God's Being Is in Becoming*, 121.
91. Although on the odd occasion Barth refers to God *as* act or event, he does not in those places depart from his basic conception of God as being-in-act. The context shows that what he means to emphasize there is simply that God is the living God. See CD II/1, 263, 264; CD IV/3, 47.

Hegel's God-in-Godself, which is why Hegel's notion of reconciliation must involve logical moments in which God is, strictly speaking, not yet God.

Barth's insistence on God's primary absoluteness as the basis of the absoluteness of God's secondary mode of being is intended to ascertain that God is unsublatably the subject God in the process of reconciliation. Unceasing objectivity and activity eternally abide within the essence of God, and so God's becoming an object of God's love in the form of a creature is not a contradiction to, but rather an "emanation" or speculative extension of, God's essence (see Chapters 5–6 for explanations of Barth's rather daring use of this Platonist term in II/1-2). God can become God-for-us without ceasing to be God-in-and-for-Godself. Even suffering and death on the cross *pro nobis* correspond perfectly to God's impassibility and immortality *a se*.

Already in Augustine's *De Trinitate*, 4.2, in fact, we have an expression of this understanding of the work of the atonement as an expression of the inner essence of God. There is objectivity and activity, and thus love and compassion, within God's triune essence. Therefore, God can suffer without ceasing to be impassible; God can die without ceasing to be immortal. Suffering and death are manifestations of God's impassibility and immortality. It is the Augustinian-Anselmian moment of Barth's speculative theology that allows him to affirm God's impassibility and immutability (explanations to ensue in Chapter 6).[92]

In a word, whereas Hegel would say that what God-in-the-making, so to speak, has in Godself to become grounds and makes possible God's present being-for-us, Barth insists, in light of Jesus Christ and his work of reconciliation, that it is God's being-in-and-for-Godself that grounds and makes possible God's being-for-us. God's aseity in God's primary absoluteness *ad intra* is the very basis of God's promeity in God's secondary absoluteness *ad extra interna*.

The Self-Determined God: Barth's Basically Anselmian Speculation

The covenantal relationship between God and humankind "is a relation *ad extra*, undoubtedly; for both the man and the people represented in him [Christ] are creatures and not God."[93] However, "it is a relation which is irrevocable, so that once God has willed to enter into it, and has in fact entered into it, *he could not be God without it*. It is a relation in which God is self-determined, so that the determination belongs no less to him than all that he is *in and for himself*."[94] "*In and for himself*"—that is: all that God is in God's primary absoluteness.

Proponents of revisionism, as we have seen, have capitalized on the phraseology of God's self-determination to assert that in Barth's actualistic ontology, God's acts and decisions are ontologically constitutive of God's being. This metaphysical

---

92. See George Hunsinger, *Evangelical, Catholic, and Reformed: Essays on Barth and Other Themes* (Grand Rapids: Eerdmans, 2015), 168n32.
93. *CD* II/2, 7.
94. *CD* II/2, 7. Emphasis mine.

3. Actualistic Ontology and Speculative Theology

misreading overlooks the difference between the Hegelian background of Barth's grammar and his un-Hegelian and anti-metaphysical ontology.

To be sure, revisionist scholars are for the most part careful to set Barth apart from Hegel. Jones, for instance, argues that Barth's notion of "*Geschichte* signals a deft riposte to the charge of Hegelianism, easily levelled against Barth given his intensive utilization of the motif of *Aufhebung* throughout the *Dogmatics*."[95] As acknowledged by Paul Molnar, McCormack has also "carefully and rightly" distinguished

> Barth's position from Hegel's insisting that for Barth, in opposition to Hegel, the incarnation is God's free act; that Barth sharply distinguished the creator/creature relation; that Barth insisted that God preexisted creation; and that God's eternal actions could not be collapsed into history. Hence, "The immanent Trinity is complete, for Barth, before anything that has been made was made (including time itself)."[96]

"Still," comments Molnar, "McCormack wishes to argue that both the incarnation and outpouring of the Holy Spirit are in some sense 'constitutive' of God's eternal being, by way of anticipation."[97] It is the misinterpretation of Barth's language of God's "self-determination" as some ontological "constitution" that makes it difficult for the revisionist Barth to avoid a basically Hegelian mode of theological speculation.

We have already discussed Barth's critical use of the Hegelian language of determination at some length. It would be helpful to add here that in Hegel's usage, per Michael Inwood, this term refers to the process of "making a concept [*Begriff*] or a thing more determinate by adding features to it, or the feature(s) so added."[98] Self-determination is "the autonomous DEVELOPMENT or operation of something ... in contrast to its determination by external forces."[99] In other words, self-determination is the process by which a being is determined by its own essence, defined in Hegel as what a thing has in it to ultimately become.

As we have seen, Barth's definition of *Wesen*, unlike Hegel's, comprises a strongly "substantialist" dimension to convey the quality of something that is complete in and of itself. When he adopts the Hegelian grammar of *Bestimmung* to describe God, then, he has in mind an un-Hegelian notion of God's essence that is perfect in itself, and whatever features added to this essence in the process

---

95. Jones, *The Humanity of Christ*, 198.
96. Molnar, *Divine Freedom*, 127. See Bruce McCormack, "Grace and Being: The Role of God's Gracious Election in Karl Barth's Theological Ontology," in *The Cambridge Companion to Karl Barth*, ed. John Webster (Cambridge: Cambridge University Press, 2000), 100.
97. Molnar, *Divine Freedom*, 127.
98. Inwood, *A Hegel Dictionary*, 77.
99. Inwood, *A Hegel Dictionary*, 77.

of *Selbstbestimmung* do not alter God's being ontologically.[100] What God self-determines is God's *Sein*—God's being-for-us *ad extra*—not God's triune *Wesen*.

God's act of entering into covenantal relationship with humankind is perfectly free on God's part, but God's freedom is not the caprice of a tyrant. God's will corresponds perfectly to God's essence, which is according to Barth "entirely self-sufficient" as the intra-trinitarian act of love.[101]

Precisely because election corresponds perfectly to God's triune essence *ad intra*, it is a decision that the immutably faithful God does not revoke. In this sense God "could not be God without" the loving relationship into which God has freely decided to enter.[102] We must bear in mind that whenever Barth speaks of the necessity of God's acts *ad extra*, he is honoring the "necessity of his actual manifest will, his *potentia ordinata* [ordained power]."[103] Far from denying the aseity of the immanent Trinity, his language of necessity is intended to affirm the immutability of God's will as a perfect expression of God's immutable essence.

Barth is emphatic in his 1936 revision of the doctrine of election that God's essence is eternally determinate in-and-for-Godself qua Trinity, which admits of no act of (self-)determination apart from the triune *opera ad intra*. This insistence on the unsublatable subjectivity, the "*actus purus*" as Barth later puts it in *CD* II/1, of God's triune essence is part and parcel of Barth's basically Anselmian mode of speculation underlying the Christocentric doctrine of 1936.[104] Barth writes in *Gottes Gnadenwahl*:

> The essence and act of God cannot be determined from one attribute, be it love or glory. What does God's glory mean, and what does God's love mean …? If we think through our human conceptions and try to understand God as the epitome of such a human conception, then we have not come to know God, but rather we have erected an idol. We can only confess of God: God is the Father and the Son and the Holy Spirit. And all that we can say about His omnipotence, love, glory, and wisdom can only be an explication of what it means to say that God is Father, Son, and Holy Spirit, that is, God as revealed to us in Jesus Christ.[105]

That is, our conceptions of love and glory, which arise out of our own creaturely nature, are not speculative extensions of God's essence. God is love, but love is not God. We must never proceed to understand God's love and glory with a starting point in human conceptions of love and glory, positing by faith a speculative correspondence between our conceptions and God's essence. The correspondence is between God's essential love qua Trinity and God's love *pro nobis* in Jesus Christ.

---

100. So rightly Hunsinger, *Reading Barth with Charity*, 139–42; cf. 127–36.
101. *CD* II/2, 10.
102. *CD* II/2, 7.
103. *CD* I/2, 41.
104. *CD* II/1, 264–5.
105. *Gottes Gnadenwahl*, 47.

By faith in Christ as the *speculum* of God's eternal essence and will, we come to understand our conceptions of love and glory.

In *CD* II/1, Barth formulates this speculative program by first setting forth the notion of primary absoluteness within the Godhead.[106] Recall that the originally Hegelian notion of "absoluteness" entails the concrete unity of subjectivity, objectivity, and activity. As we just saw, God's primary absoluteness means for Barth that God's triune essence is already determinate in-and-for-itself (*an und für sich*), and thus unsublatable (its subject cannot *become* absolute, for it has always been and never ceases to be absolute in eternally active communion with the object).[107] When Barth speaks of God's self-determination, then, he means thereby God's determination of Godself as God-for-us, which is grounded in and made possible by God's unsublatable subjectivity as God-in-and-for-Godself qua Trinity.[108] God's being-for-us is the *speculum* of God's being-in-and-for-Godself; the *speculum Trinitatis* is none other than Jesus Christ.

Barth is very clear in *CD* II/2 that the identity between God the Son and the elected human, just as the identity between Jesus Christ and the electing God, is *speculative* (i.e., indirect and mediated): "As the Son of the Father He has no need of any special election."[109] God the Son is immediately the electing God with the Father and the Holy Spirit, and mediately the elected human. By the same token, Jesus Christ *is* the electing God only by virtue of the speculative identity between God's time and ours.

Faith in this mediated identity in Jesus Christ allows creatures living in our time to know, in Baark's words, "that God is who God reveals God to be."[110] In Jesus Christ the unsublatable subjectivity of the triune God is revealed to us as the freedom of God's love.

Because God qua unsublatable subject is that greater than which nothing can be conceived—and indeed greater than can be conceived—our rational conception of God as such cannot be identical to God-in-and-for-Godself or even to God's self-knowledge. It can only be an after-thinking, an understanding proceeding from faith, that corresponds indirectly to God's immutable being and immediate self-knowledge. This is why the revelation of the mediated and mediatory identity between Jesus Christ and the electing God in historical actuality must carry a noetic "twofold indirectness" (to use a phrase from *CD* I/1).[111] The specific form of speculative reasoning characterizing Barth's theology, then, constitutes an attempt to steer clear of any idealist tendency to reduce God to a rational concept or to elevate human consciousness to any divine status.

---

106. *CD* II/1, 317.
107. *CD* II/2, 6. Italics added.
108. See Jüngel, *God's Being Is in Becoming*, 121. *Pace* Bruce McCormack, "Election and Trinity: Theses in Response to George Hunsinger," *Scottish Journal of Theology* 63 (2010): 204.
109. *CD* II/2, 103.
110. Baark, *The Affirmations of Reason*, 257.
111. *CD* I/1, 68.

Conclusion: A Chalcedonian Dialectic

This chapter has sorted out the grammatical relations between some key terms of Barth's actualistic ontology by means of a lexical approach to his texts and intellectual-historical background. We may conclude here with the observation that his emendation of the Hegelian correlations between these terms has to do with a rudimentary problem that he sees in Hegel, one that often resurfaces in revisionist portrayals of Barth's actualistic ontology.

Hegel's grammatical association of *Wesen* and *Sein* with *Bestimmung* and *Schein* signals a subject-predicate reversal typical of his idealist objection to what later came to be called "substantialism." The all-encompassing notion of "the absolute" (*das Absolute*), for instance, is an adjectival noun (German) or nominal adjective (English) reflecting an especially interesting grammatical manipulation on Hegel's part.

Theologians of the Western tradition are accustomed to the predication, "God is absolute." When the adjective here becomes the subject and vice versa, an interesting reversal arises: "the absolute is God." Because "absolute" is originally an adjective, it is void of actual existence without corresponding subjects that it predicates. Indeed, Hegel frequently uses "absolute" as an adjective to describe subjects such as Spirit, which evolves into "absolute Spirit" through the process of a subjective-objective-absolute triad. The absolute, in other words, is God fully developed as God in the consummate moment of actuality.

While Barth saw Hegel's philosophical-terminological system as a supreme expression of this onto-grammatical reversal, we must also understand that he saw this reversal as symptomatic of all idealistic systems that "affirmed Kant's transcendentalism."[112] Cohen's notion of being-*as*-act very much falls into this category. As we saw in Chapter 1, Cohen only paid lip service to Kant's empirical realism when he reconstructed the doctrine of transcendental idealism on fundamentally phenomenalistic terms. Barth's rejection of Hegel's onto-grammatical reversal of the subject and the predicate should clearly indicate a renunciation of Cohen's actualism.

The problem with attributing ontological priority to the predicate, as Barth sees it, is that in order to avoid abstraction, the kind of idealism of which Hegel is representative must assert an identity, immediate or consummate, between the adjectival noun and all the subjects it predicates. Reality then becomes one living substance or subject. What Kierkegaard would later call the infinite qualitative difference between God and creation would then be ultimately wiped out in idealist metaphysics.

This is why Barth insists that subject-predicate relations must never be reversed in predications involving "God." Baark's insight that the notion of God's "unsublatable subjectivity" undergirds Barth's "speculative theology" as a whole proves most valuable at this juncture. Even the predication "God is being" requires

---

112. *Protestant Theology*, 379.

3. Actualistic Ontology and Speculative Theology

us to bear in mind the strictly unsublatable subjectivity of God. Thus Barth: "it is not being in an ascribed simplicity and pure actuality which is God, but God who is being. We do not believe in and pray to being, but to God who is being."[113]

To make the predicate ontologically prior to the subject—which is to make "becoming" the essential constitution of "being"—would be to repeat the error of Hegel and German idealisms, taken in a broad sense to include the "idealistic" (in a quasi-Berkeleian sense) reorientation of Kant in the Marburg school. This, on Barth's view, is essentially the same error committed by the *alte Metaphysik* of natural theology. Barth unequivocally declares with a nod to Feuerbach that "Hegel's living God ... is actually the living man."[114]

Barth is in partial agreement with Hegel against Hellenistic substantialism, and to a certain extent Latin Christian adaptations thereof, that God is a *living* subject rather than abstract substance. His usage of the term *Sein* is reflective of this agreement. His retainment of the substance grammar of the Latin tradition, however, shows that he has dialectically incorporated classical theology, and so a certain concept of substance, into his actualistic ontology.

It is not hard to see that this ontology is regulated by the grammar of a basically Chalcedonian dialectic: *becoming* is an *addition* to, rather than a *subtraction* or *alteration* of *essential being*. In the case of Barth's theological ontology, this dialectic stands in sharp contrast to Hegel's logical trinity of Spirit *an-sich, für-sich,* and *an-und-für-sich*. In Barth's case, God-in-and-for-Godself became God-for-us without ever ceasing to be God-in-and-for-Godself. For Barth, God was free to enter into the world in Christ, and so to become immanent to the world, without entering into self-contradiction as the transcendent God, without surrendering the complete perfection of his eternal trinitarian essence, and without becoming actual and concrete only by entering into process with the created world.

---

113. *CD* II/1, 564.
114. *Protestant Theology*, 405.

Chapter 4

PAINTING THE PORTRAIT: JESUS CHRIST AS *SPECULUM ELECTIONIS* (1936)

Introduction

Aims and Objectives of the Chapter

In the previous chapter we delineated the basic contours of Barth's speculative theology. In his *credo ut intelligam* program, he begins with faith in the speculative (i.e., mediated, mirrored, reflected) identity between God-for-us (*Deus revelatus*) and God-in-and-for-Godself (*Deus absconditus*), and proceeds to explicate our human predications of God in anthropomorphic and analogical terms such as love and glory. Anthropomorphic speech of God is inevitable, because God is unknowable *per essentiam*. However, if we find our speculative starting point in anthropological concepts, then the god of our putatively theological speech would unavoidably be idolatrous projections of human attributes unto a pseudo-divine object. This problem, astutely disclosed by Feuerbach, results from philosophical assumptions of human self-identity, that is, immediate or speculative identity between the human subject and predicate, essence and act, being and thinking, *sum* and *cogito*, etc. Jesus Christ as God-for-us reveals to us a self-identity in God, primarily as an immediate identity between the Godhead and the triune *opera ad intra*, and secondarily a speculative identity between Jesus Christ and all that God is in-and-for Godself.

This speculative *Denkform*, which Barth developed in the late 1920s and early 1930s, begged a series of questions that were yet to be answered. Given that Jesus Christ is the *speculum* of God's essence, are we to understand him primarily as a divine-human *hypostasis* in what is often called a "substantialist" sense, or are we to understand him primarily as a historical act of God, an event of divine appearance (*Schein*) in a Hegelian sense?

If Jesus Christ is understood as a speculative image of God in a "substantialist" sense, then this would mean that we can only know of everything that Jesus was and did in his human nature, while his divine nature would transcend everything that he could be and do in his human agency, and thus everything of which we are capable of knowing. God's transcendent essence would then remain unmediated to us. Christ as the *speculum* of God's essence would then fail to reflect to us what it was intended to reflect.

On the other hand, if Christ is merely a historical act of God, then how does Christ differ from any other divine *opera ad extra externa*, such as creation? If Christ is merely a historical appearance of the divine rather than very God and wholly God, then how does Christ differ from other events of theophany? But if Christ is very God and wholly God as an event and act rather than a *hypostasis* of God's *ousia*, then this would mean that God is not an essential being-in-act, but a rather a being-as-act without any immutable substance. This act, moreover, is taken as a historical act. This would then mean that there is no God except a God who is bound to temporal transience. The distinction between God's eternal essence and temporal acts thus erased, God would be reduced to sheer activity, process, and historicity. Barth's intention, as we saw in the previous chapters, was precisely to avoid this error committed by Hegel and other nineteenth-century German idealists.

In *Gottes Gnadenwahl*, Barth ties together these loose ends by conjoining his Christology with the doctrine of election, identifying Jesus Christ as *speculum electionis*, the mirror or image of election: the temporal history of the elected man Jesus Christ is the outward basis of his own eternal history of as the electing God. This all-important understanding of speculative identity between Jesus Christ and the electing God came to be fully developed in *CD* II/2, where Barth describes Jesus Christ as the secondary mode of God's absolute being. That is to say, election is not merely a *decretum absolutum*, an arbitrary act of God's will. Jesus Christ who *is* God is the full actuality of election in its subjectivity, objectivity, and activity, and election as such is an *ad extra interna* mode of God's absolute being.

This entails that the identity between Jesus Christ as elected human and as electing God is *speculative*, that is, *mediated* through the *act* of election in the pattern of archetype-ectype analogy. In *Gottes Gnadenwahl*, Barth describes the man Jesus as *speculum electionis*. Election is the free act of God's love *ad extra*, not merely as an act of God's will, but as a secondary mode of God's being. As *speculum electionis*, the man Jesus who is also the electing God reflects to us the subject, object, and act of eternal election. Election as such is revealed to be the speculative extension, the "emanation" (*Überfluss*: see Chapters 5–6) as it were, of the *ad intra* love that God eternally and immutably is. In other words, election is first and foremost God's self-determination to be God-for-us without ceasing to be God-in-and-for-Godself.

The language of divine self-determination, as we shall see, indicates that the identity between Jesus Christ and the electing God is *speculative* and *mediated*, rather than immediate. The electing God is immediately identical with Godself as the subject, object, and act of God's *ad intra* essence. The man Jesus Christ, by contrast, is identical with the electing God in the same way Mary is identified as the *Theotokos*. This identity, because it was established by a divine act of self-determination, must be understood in terms of a logic of mediation. In the birth, death, and resurrection of Jesus Christ, the self-giving love of God is speculatively revealed to us, and this love is in turn the speculative image of the essential love that God eternally and unsublatably is. The immutability of God's being in the eternal act of love is revealed to us through the flesh-*becoming* of Christ.

Historical Background

My interpretation of *Gottes Gnadenwahl* in the framework of Barth's speculative theology challenges, *inter alia*, the revisionist agenda initially proposed by Bruce McCormack. At the same time, however, this interpretation is significantly indebted to McCormack in many positive ways.

One of the many valuable contributions of McCormack's *Karl Barth's Critically Realistic Dialectical Theology: Its Genesis and Development 1909–1936*, with which the present study has already engaged at some depth, is its highlight of Barth's turn to Christocentrism in 1936.[1] McCormack's volume led to the generally accepted view in Anglophone Barth studies that the Helvetic theologian's Christocentric doctrine of election developed in the 1936 *Gottes Gnadenwahl* marks, in one way or another, the beginning of the mature phase of Barth's theology.

As McCormack puts it, it was in this small booklet that Barth first set forth the "form of 'christocentrism' which became synonymous with the name of Karl Barth."[2] Sigurd Baark also states that he remains "a student of McCormack and follow[s] his lead" in accepting the view that the Christocentric reorientation of "the doctrine of election was the culmination of Barth's development as a theologian."[3]

Gottes Gnadenwahl was published in November 1936 in the *Theologische Existenz heute* series edited by Barth and Eduard Thurneysen. The main body of the booklet consists of lecture manuscripts on the doctrine of election that Barth delivered in Debrecen, Hungary, and Cluj-Napoca, Romania, in September and October of the same year. Appended at the end of the booklet is an edited compilation of answers to a selection of questions raised in Debrecen and Cluj, as well as Sárospatak and Oradea, which Barth visited on the same trip.

One important catalyst leading to Barth's Christocentric reorientation of the doctrine of election was his audition of a lecture by Pierre Maury on Calvin's doctrine of predestination at the *Congrès international de théologie calviniste* in Geneva in 1936.[4] It was again McCormack who drew scholarly attention to the influence of Maury's lecture on Barth's thought. Even though McCormack would later come to concur with Matthias Gockel's corrective that "Maury never quite reached the point of equating divine reprobation with the reprobation of Jesus Christ" and that "the identification of 'Jesus Christ' with the electing God is also Barth's invention,"[5] both of them still retain the view that Barth "owed to his good friend

---

1. Bruce McCormack, *Karl Barth's Critically Realistic Dialectical Theology* (Oxford: Clarendon Press, 1995), 453–63.

2. McCormack, *Barth's Dialectical Theology*, 455.

3. Sigurd Baark, *The Affirmations of Reason: On Karl Barth's Speculative Theology* (Cham: Palgrave Macmillan, 2018), 4.

4. See Simon Hattrell, ed., *Election, Barth, and the French Connection: How Pierre Maury Gave a "Decisive Impetus" to Karl Barth's Doctrine of Election* (Eugene: Wipf and Stock, 2016).

5. Bruce McCormack, "Seek God Where He May Be Found: A Response to Edwin Van Driel," *Scottish Journal of Theology* 60 (2007): 64.

Pierre Maury" the core insight of *Gottes Gnadenwahl*, namely, "the correlation of election and reprobation with the crucifixion of Jesus."[6]

In *CD* II/2, Barth credits Maury for being the one who brought out "the Christological meaning and basis of the doctrine of election ... in our own time."[7] Barth recounts that "this service has been rendered by Pierre Maury in the fine lecture which he gave ... in Geneva, 1936."[8] Maury stated in his lecture a thesis that Barth found to be of central significance not only to the doctrine of election, but to the Anselmian tradition of speculative theology as a whole:

> Outside of Christ, we know neither of the electing God, nor of His elect, nor of the act of election ... One cannot speak of damnation as a decision of God otherwise than on the basis of the cross on Golgotha, but on this basis one must speak of it ... The cross on which Christ was damned, does not damn us. It makes us children of God.[9]

One important intellectual-biographical question regarding Barth's adoption of Maury's thesis is: why would Barth be so impressed by Maury's lecture, if Barth's own theology, with all its basic convictions, was not already developing in a direction and at such a point of maturity that would demand him to embrace the inspiration he found in Maury's Christological rendition of predestination? As McCormack rightly suggested, during the composition of *CD* I/2, "already there were strong indications that [Barth] would like to revise this ontology [of his Christology]."[10]

The immediate context of Barth's excursus in *CD* II/2 quoted above, in which Barth gives Maury his due credit, provides us some hints to the motivations behind his revisionary adaptation of Maury's thesis: "Historically there are to hand all kinds of important materials which should encourage and even necessitate an adoption of this thesis [that Jesus Christ is the central mystery of election and reprobation]."[11]

The "important materials" that Barth identifies here include John Knox's Scots Confession of 1560, Athanasius, Augustine, Coccejus, the Lapsarian Controversy in seventeenth-century Reformed orthodoxy, and the "general Reformation assertion that Christ is the *speculum electionis* [mirror of election]."[12] This suggests

---

6. Matthias Gockel, *Barth and Schleiermacher on the Doctrine of Election* (Oxford: Oxford University Press, 2006), 202.
7. *CD* II/2, 154.
8. *CD* II/2, 154.
9. Pierre Maury, "Erwählung und Glaube," in *Theologische Studien*, vol. 8 (Zurich: Evangelischer Verlag Zürich, 1940), 7–12. Quoted in McCormack, *Barth's Dialectical Theology*, 457.
10. Bruce McCormack, "Karl Barth's Historicized Christology," in *Orthodox and Modern: Studies in the Theology of Karl Barth* (Grand Rapids: Baker, 2008), 207.
11. *CD* II/2, 155.
12. *CD* II/2, 154–5.

that before encountering Maury's thesis in 1936, Barth was already wrestling with a host of historical materials that he felt to have demanded a Christocentric revision of the doctrine of election.

Rhetorically, the last named is often the most important. Barth found in the classical Reformed assertion that Christ is the *speculum electionis* an important key to tying the loose ends of his basically Anselmian mode of speculative theology. As he sees it, this is "an assertion which obviously stands in need of more profound and comprehensive treatment."[13] Maury's lecture provided Barth with an important clue for the right treatment, but this lecture was more of a catalyst rather than the primary motivation of Barth's Christocentric reorientation of the doctrine of election. Barth's ever deepening and broadening engagement with historical theology—not least the basically Anselmian mode of speculation developed in the early 1930s—was what prompted him to move in the direction of a Christocentric doctrine of election.

One important impetus that Barth attained from these historical materials was his struggles with the problem of the actuality of sin upon the supposition of the freedom of God's love and sovereignty of God's grace.[14] In the excursus in which he credits Maury for advocating a Christocentric rendition of election, he begins not with Maury's lecture, but by commending Knox's Scots Confession for pointing in the direction of a Christological doctrine of predestination.

Barth stresses that Knox was driven by his struggles with the problem of sin to seek the marriage of Christology and predestination: "It can hardly be denied that in the *Conf. Scotica* the specific conception of sin is intimately connected with the peculiar Christological conception of predestination."[15] Additionally, Barth states in the same excursus that "we can appeal in support of our" Christocentric rendition of double predestination "to the inevitability of such a solution in the light of the Supralapsarian controversy," a seventeenth-century debate on the logical relations between double predestination and God's decrees to create humankind and permit Adam's fall.[16]

The epistemic gulf, the great Kantian distance as it were, between God and humankind, as Barth sees it, is not only a result of an ontological divide between the Creator and creatures. Surely he holds to tenet central to the *extra Calvinisticum*: "*finitum non capax infiniti*" (the finite has no capacity for the infinite), as he puts it in *CD* I/1 (1932).[17] However, the "much more incisive principle" is "*homo peccator non capax verbi divini*" (fallen humanity has no capacity for God's Word).[18] In

---

13. *CD* II/2, 155.
14. This impetus would continue into the latest phases of Barth's dogmatic cycle. See my *Karl Barth's Ontology of Sin and Grace: Variations on a Theme of Augustine* (London: Routledge, 2019).
15. *CD* II/2, 154.
16. *CD* II/2, 155.
17. *CD* I/1, 407.
18. *CD* I/1, 407.

a letter from the Göttingen-Münster period, he calls this the "great Calvinist distance between heaven and earth."[19]

If we may sum up the solution that Barth offers in *Gottes Gnadenwahl* by borrowing the famous creation-covenant dialectic developed in the third volume of the *Church Dogmatics*, it can be spelled out as follows: Golgotha is the outward basis of election, while election is the inward basis of the crucifixion. That is to say, the very history of Jesus Christ is a speculative image of God's eternal act of election: Christ is *speculum electionis*. How Barth sustains this thesis is in large part what the rest of the present chapter seeks to explain. Before I offer an exegesis of the text, however, a brief outline of the volume would be helpful, not least because of its unfamiliarity to Anglophone readers.

A Brief Outline of Gottes Gnadenwahl

The small but all-important booklet from 1936 comprises four chapters and a relatively lengthy *Fragebeantwortung* (questions and answers). In Chapter 1, Barth defines the concept of grace and explains what it means to say that predestination is God's grace. He emphasizes that predestination should never become a self-standing doctrine concerned with an abstract idea of divine freedom and sovereignty. Rather, the doctrine of predestination is sound biblical doctrine only insofar as it is an explication of the concrete grace of God once-for-all accomplished in Jesus Christ and enacted in us again and again by the Holy Spirit. The freedom of God's grace seen in this light is one that overcomes the sin of humankind, not for the sake of denying human freedom, but for the sake of actualizing true human freedom as freedom determined by grace in Jesus Christ. Thus Barth concludes the chapter on the high note: "In this freedom [of God], grace is wholly and unconditionally placed in the hands and bosom of man, such that man is wholly directed and bound to the giver of grace."[20]

Chapter 2 focuses on methodological considerations, identifying predestination as "truth of revelation," which is "truth in Jesus Christ."[21] This entails, in Kantian language, that it is neither a "necessity of thought" (*Denknotwendigkeit*) nor an "object of experience" (*Erfahrungsgegenstand*).[22] Any deductive or inductive attempt to formulate the doctrine by resorting to conceptual analyses or empirical syntheses as sources of knowledge would lead to the idolatry of idealist speculation.

Chapter 3 begins with biblical testimonies to the selectivity of election (*Auswahl*). In this chapter, double predestination is presented as a process of sublation (*Aufhebung*). Reprobation, which Christ suffered vicariously in place of sinful humankind, is God's negation of humanity's sin that negates God's grace,

---

19. Thomas F. Torrance, *Karl Barth: An Introduction to His Early Theology, 1910–1931* (Edinburgh: T&T Clark, 1962), 49.
20. *Gottes Gnadenwahl*, 10.
21. *Gottes Gnadenwahl*, 13.
22. *Gottes Gnadenwahl*, 13.

and this negation of negation is for the purpose of God's gracious election of all humankind in Christ.

In Chapter 4, Barth revisits the doctrine of double predestination, this time setting forth the thesis that the elect and the reprobate are not two classes of people inflexibly separated by a *decretum absolutum Dei* (absolute decree of God) from eternity. Rather, all humans are elected in and with Christ who was vicariously reprobated for all. This rendition of double predestination is intended to ensure that

> we ... know God's gracious election not through the moment of the spectator's question about whether we or other men are elect or reprobate, but rather (1) for the ever pertinent and pressing insight that God is with us on the way, that we are in His hands, that His decision as it has been made once for all in Jesus Christ is the pre-determination of our life; (2) for the confidence that leads to the goal of what He has ordained and will ordain over us in Jesus Christ; and (3) for the obedience necessary for our confirmation of this insight and confidence.[23]

Speculative Formulation of the Doctrine of Election

Against Post-Kantian Interpretations

Barth begins chapter 1 of *Gottes Gnadenwahl* with exegetical considerations of Romans 9:11-13, contending that in all biblical passages where "we encounter this notion [predestination] expressly or *en substance*," the doctrine of predestination appears "as salt in the food, so to say, and not as the food itself."[24] This metaphor conveys the understanding that the doctrine "must stand at the beginning and behind all Christian thinking, but it is not the first link in the description of how man comes into communion with God."[25] In Kantian language: "the doctrine of predestination is not a *constitutive principle*, but rather a *regulative* one."[26]

The Kantian term "principle" (*Prinzip*) refers to a logical or ontological starting point. A principle is either *regulative* or *constitutive*. A "regulative principle" (*regulatives Prinzip*) is a theoretical-rational principle whereby the existence of a thing is postulated for the purpose of facilitating the organization and interpretation of actual experiences. In the theoretical use of reason (which deals with the question, "What is") metaphysical ideas such as God must be treated as regulative principles that do not admit of any rational proof—not even proofs *reductio ad absurdum*. A regulative principle, then, is an object of rational faith, rather than knowledge.

A "constitutive principle," by contrast, is a postulate that we can ascertain by reason, so long as this postulate provides a "certain determinate condition" that

---

23. *Gottes Gnadenwahl*, 26-7.
24. *Gottes Gnadenwahl*, 4.
25. *Gottes Gnadenwahl*, 35.
26. *Gottes Gnadenwahl*, 35. Emphases mine.

is "absolutely necessary" for what we know to be true and real: this is the basic thought-form of Kant's transcendental arguments.[27] Kant claims in the second *Critique* that metaphysical ideas such as freedom, immortality, and God, which are transcendent and regulative in the theoretical use of reason, become "immanent and constitutive" within the "practical capacity" of "pure reason."[28] The practical use of reason (which asks, "What ought to be" or "What ought we affirm to be") provides a ground for the extension of theoretical reason to objects that are otherwise transcendent and unknowable.

What Barth means to say by using this Kantian language is that God's eternal act of predestination is not directly intuitable to human beings in this world. Double predestination as speculatively (i.e., as in a mirror image) revealed to us through the history of Christ's death and resurrection is an all-encompassing truth to be accepted by faith in the believer's quest for understanding of God's works. The doctrine, then, is a reflective after-thinking (*Nachdenken*) of the actual fact (*Tatsache*) of God's concrete grace, accomplished in Jesus Christ once for all and re-enacted in us again and again by the Holy Spirit.

This *Nachdenken* is a basically Anselmian form of speculation, rather than a (neo-)Kantian sort of transcendental argument that finds its starting point in some theoretical or practical *Postulat*: the doctrine of predestination is neither a regulative nor a constitutive principle in any (neo-)Kantian sense. To be sure, predestination is indeed what Kant would call a "transcendent" reality—the reality of God's immutable being in the eternal act of election—but this principle that regulates our theological reflection is not a Kantian or neo-Kantian postulate. Barth insists that the doctrine of predestination pertains to the doctrine of God, and "has no proper place in the economy of salvation."[29] And because our reason must recognize God as that greater than which nothing can be conceived, and indeed greater than can be conceived, "the immutability of God cannot be questioned whatsoever."[30]

This differs markedly from Kant's transcendental idealism or what McCormack calls the "critical realism" of Marburg neo-Kantianism. For Kant as well the Marburg school of neo-Kantianism, God as a postulate within the theoretical use of reason is an object of faith rather than knowledge. Faith differs from opinion in that faith is based on a considerable degree of rational certainty. Yet, the validity of objects of faith is always open to rational critique—it can always be questioned—for it lacks the kind of epistemic justification necessary to be universally communicated as knowledge.

Barth rejects this (neo-)Kantian distinction between faith and knowledge. In line with the Anselmian tradition, Barth insists that knowledge consists in both faith and understanding: *fides* in the immutable God is the very starting point of an *intellectum* that, as stated in the quote above, "cannot be questioned whatsoever."

---

27. Immanuel Kant, *Critique of Pure Reason*, ed. and trans. Paul Guyer and Allen Wood (Cambridge: Cambridge University Press), A632/B660.

28. Immanuel Kant, *Critique of Practical Reason*, ed. and trans. Mary Gregor (Cambridge: Cambridge University Press, 1997), 141.

29. *Gottes Gnadenwahl*, 35.

30. *Gottes Gnadenwahl*, 47.

To be sure, Barth is emphatic that humans within fallen spatio-temporality cannot possess immediate knowledge of God. We can only come to reflect upon God's immutability speculatively through human mutability, hence the revelation of God's eternal being in the flesh-becoming of Christ.[31] The doctrine of predestination, then, is a speculative *Nachdenken* of God's immutability in light of Christ, carried out by faith as the initial moment of knowledge.

In line with this program of *Nachdenken*, Barth emphasizes that predestination should never be treated as an *abstract* postulate of divine immutability, omnipotence, or freedom: he fundamentally disagrees with Kant's transcendental method that relies on abstract postulations. To grasp the core of the doctrine of predestination is to understand it as the *concrete* grace that underlies all God's works attested to in Scripture. It must not be treated as an abstract first principle apart from the revealed actuality of grace, be it "a self-standing predication about the sovereignty and immutability of God, or about the meaning and content of the divine world-plan, or about the different essences and fates of human individuals."[32]

Barth stresses that predestination must be understood as an *explicatio* (as he would say in *Anselm*) of *actual* grace to which Scripture attests: "that is the all-encompassing and fundamental meaning of the doctrine of predestination."[33] Grace is "the free, Fatherly benevolence in which God adopts us and treats us as His children *in time and for eternity*."[34] Grace, in other words, is the perfect correspondence between God's freely loving and lovingly free decision from eternity and God's execution of that decision in time. Concrete grace as such allows us to gain concrete knowledge of God's immutable being in the eternal act of predestination.

God's "eternal *decretum*" as seen in the light of concrete grace is historically actualized in three distinct but inseparable modes of temporal expression: the perfect, the present, and the future tenses.[35] The temporal actuality of grace indirectly reveals to us what God is from all eternity. "We cannot rush our way up to a *Deus absconditus*," that is, "we do not reach eternity itself."[36] However, "we must and we may hold on to the *Deus revelatus*," and because we know by faith with certainty that the hidden and revealed God is one and the same unsublatable subject, we may indeed know of God's eternal will and being by knowing what God has done and does for us in time.[37] "The relationship between God's eternal counsel and our time is a relationship of identity," an "identity made recognizable to us" only in Jesus Christ who is very God and very human.[38] (We shall discuss Barth's speculative language of identity in a later section.)

---

31. *Gottes Gnadenwahl*, 48.
32. *Gottes Gnadenwahl*, 5.
33. *Gottes Gnadenwahl*, 6.
34. *Gottes Gnadenwahl*, 6. Emphases mine.
35. *Gottes Gnadenwahl*, 45.
36. *Gottes Gnadenwahl*, 45.
37. *Gottes Gnadenwahl*, 45. See Baark, *Affirmations of Reason*, 189–228.
38. *Gottes Gnadenwahl*, 45.

Designation of the Term "Conceptual Necessity"

What all this entails, says Barth, is that "God's gracious election ... is not a necessity of thought [*Denknotwendigkeit*], and it is not an object of experience [*Erfahrungsgegenstand*]."[39] Here his use of the term *Denknotwendigkeit* is not intended to deny the conceptual necessity of God's unsublatable subjectivity. Rather, the (neo-)Kantian term refers specifically to analytic judgments in which the predicate is contained in the subject (e.g. "all boys are male"). Such judgments, though necessarily true, are tautological and do not provide any new knowledge.

The conceptual necessity of God's unsublatable subjectivity does not conceptually necessitate God's gracious election. That is to say, the triune God is not immediately identical with the electing God. Immediate identity between essence and act is to be found in God's *ad intra* being qua Trinity alone. The electing God is mediately and speculatively identical with the triune God, for the act of election is a determination that is not essential to God's self-sufficient being.

In other words, election is contingent upon God's will. It is a speculative extension, an "emanation" (*Überfluss*) as Barth calls it in *CD* II/1-2, of all that God is and does in-and-for-Godself. It is not a necessary or constitutive aspect of God's being. Precisely because God's unsublatable subjectivity is a conceptual necessity—not as the conclusion but as the starting-point of theological speculation—God's gracious election as a sublatory act (which we shall explain in a later section) is not and cannot be. The doctrine of gracious election, therefore, cannot be a deductive or even reductive (as in the reductive *Denkform* of transcendental arguments) consequence of any conceptual necessity.

Note in passing that this reading of the text precludes the view that according to Barth's "actualistic ontology ..., the action of God in electing to be God for humanity in Jesus Christ is *not* the act of an already existing agent. It is rather an act in the course of which God determines the very being of God."[40] This view draws heavily on McCormack's contention that "there is for Barth 'no state, no mode of being or existence above and prior to this eternal act of self-determination as substantialistic thinking would lead us to believe.'"[41] This post-Kantian interpretation, which reads Hermann Cohen's actualism into Barth (see Chapter 1), disallows the reader to speak of God's eternal and immutable essence with any epistemic certainty. It dictates that only if God's essence is constituted by God's act-for-us can this essence become noetically accessible to us.

As we have seen, however, the basically Anselmian starting point of Barth's actualistic ontology is fundamentally at odds with the transcendental argument

---

39. *Gottes Gnadenwahl*, 11.

40. Paul Nimmo, *Being in Action: The Theological Shape of Barth's Ethical Vision* (London: T&T Clark, 2007), 8.

41. Nimmo, *Being in Action,* 8. Here Nimmo cites Bruce McCormack, "The Ontological Presuppositions of Barth's Doctrine of the Atonement," in *The Glory of the Atonement*, ed. Charles Hill and Frank James III (Downers Grove: IVP, 2004), 359.

of Marburg neo-Kantianism. We shall see that although Barth is indeed opposed to what he sees as vestiges of the substantialism of Greek metaphysics in the classical formulations of the doctrine of election, his notion of God as "being-in-act" is not to be misconstrued as "being-as-act," characteristic of idealist speculation, that renders election as necessary to and constitutive of God's being.

Christocentric Actualism

"*Erfahrungsgegenstand*" (object of experience), another keyword in the quote above, is yet another term that Barth critically borrows from Kant. It refers to external objects of sense that give rise to *a posteriori* propositions attained through empirical judgments. Judgments of this kind, though providing new information, are only contingently true. Only synthetic *a priori* judgments can provide necessarily true knowledge of what is previously unknown. Such judgments, per Kant, are impossible in rational metaphysics, including rational theology.

Barth does not take what he sees as Kant's moral alternative to metaphysics framed within a transcendental idealism to be a viable path to true knowledge of God, but he basically agrees with Kant on the unviability of traditional metaphysics. This does not mean that Barth (or Kant, for that matter) intends "to abrogate or negate experience" or reason.[42] As human beings, we must "possess experience as something necessary."[43]

Both reason and experience are necessary *tools* of knowing, but by no means should they be "seen as a second source of our knowledge. There is only one source of knowledge—Holy Scripture."[44] Scripture alone is the form of God's Word that carries normative authority over the church's proclamation of God's self-revelation in Jesus Christ. The Christ of Scripture is not only the sole source of our knowledge, but also its only proper object.[45]

As Barth sees it, the various classical forms of the doctrine of predestination have, to various extents, unduly shifted their attention away from the proper source and object of knowledge to the tools of knowing. He is of course deeply appreciative of the tradition(s) before him. He considers himself especially a "pupil" of Calvin in the "'authentically' Reformed" tradition.[46] However, "the old Reformed theologians decidedly did not do well in seeing the reconciliation and revelation accomplished in Jesus Christ as only the means and not also the ground of election. They wanted to reduce eternal election to a divine decree prior to the *actuality* of the cross and the resurrection."[47] Barth, appealing to Kant's critique of traditional metaphysics, cautions that this runs the danger of opening

42. *Gottes Gnadenwahl*, 34.
43. *Gottes Gnadenwahl*, 34.
44. *Gottes Gnadenwahl*, 34.
45. *Gottes Gnadenwahl*, 34.
46. *Gottes Gnadenwahl*, 34.
47. *Gottes Gnadenwahl*, 17. Emphasis added.

up an avenue "for the interpretation of predestination as a necessity of thought [*Denknotwendigkeit*] or object of experience [*Erfahrungsgegenstand*]."[48]

To avoid such traditional-metaphysical renditions of predestination, Barth cites Calvin to refer to Christ as the "mirror of election" (*speculum electionis*).[49] Here is a decisive reference to his basically Anselmian mode of speculation. In fact, Barth already adopted this expression in *The Göttingen Dogmatics* (henceforth GD).[50] There he insisted that "we must stand by revelation in Christ and thus start with what predestination is in the first instance, that is, election."[51] But because he could not explain reprobation as anything other than the Holy Spirit's withholding or withdrawal of the gift of faith from human individuals, his understanding of double predestination was delimited by the notion of a pneumatological-actualistic revelation-in-act.

In *Gottes Gnadenwahl*, he makes a Copernican shift, so to speak, in his understanding of predestination from a center in pneumatology (the present tense of salvation), in which election and reprobation are still defined in terms of existential faith and unbelief, to a center in Jesus Christ (who is the same subject God in God's eternal and temporal modes of existence). "God's gracious election is the truth of revelation. More concretely: it is the truth of Scripture. With complete concreteness: it is truth in Jesus Christ. Knowledge of it will thus be able to be nothing—really nothing—other than a specific form of the knowledge of Jesus Christ."[52]

This carries direct implications for the doctrine of *double* predestination— and herein lies the key to Barth's Copernican revolution. The mistake he made in the Göttingen-Münster-Bonn years, as he now sees it in *Gottes Gnadenwahl*, is essentially the same as that handed down from Calvin. Calvin's "great mistake" was that in rightly identifying Christ as the "*speculum praedestinationis*" (mirror of predestination), he fell short of considering *reprobation* in light of Christ.[53] Calvin rightly sees in Christ the "*causa et materia*" (cause and matter) of election, but he ascribes the "*causa et materia*" of reprobation to sinful creatures and insists that the divine cause of reprobation remains a "*causa absconditus*" (hidden cause) to us.[54]

Against Calvin's "arbitrary construction" of rational-metaphysical speculation and empirical induction, Barth contends: "if the doctrine of predestination is based on a Christological foundation, then one can and may rest assured in saying that election and reprobation are both grounded in the eternal counsel of God, so firmly such that election is superordinate to reprobation, and yet so firmly such that they are both actual in Christ as well."[55]

48. *Gottes Gnadenwahl*, 17.
49. *Gottes Gnadenwahl*, 13.
50. GD, 471.
51. GD, 474.
52. GD, 474.
53. *Gottes Gnadenwahl*, 49.
54. *Gottes Gnadenwahl*, 49.
55. *Gottes Gnadenwahl*, 49.

In other words, if predestination can only be understood Christologically, then reprobation, just as election, must be considered in light of the *actuality* of Jesus Christ that is at once eternal and temporal. This means that double predestination cannot be a metaphysical proposition based on any necessity of thought or object of experience. It can only be based on the Christ of Scripture who is the *speculum* mediating to us knowledge of God's immutable essence and will through the mutability of Christ's flesh.

At the same time, double predestination is not a (neo-)Kantian postulate that Barth employs to explain the actuality of Jesus Christ. Double predestination *is* fully actual in Christ who is at once eternal and temporal, and so those who gaze upon him gaze upon the truly eternal actuality of election and reprobation. "It is in Jesus Christ and in Him alone, and thus not in a logically derived thought-image [*Denkbild*] or in the images of our experience, that we are to recognize what we call election and thus reprobation."[56]

Here, then, we have a decisive turn to Christocentrism in Barth's speculative program. Between God's transcendent reality and the immanent realities of God's creation is an ontological divide and a gulf of sin. No creature has any direct epistemic access to the other side of the gulf. We can only see a reflected image of what is on the other side, and Jesus Christ is the mirror through which God's transcendent reality on the other side is reflected to us. Christ, whose history is truly and fully immanent, is also the subject and object of God's eternal election as a mode of being *ad extra interna*, by which God determined Godself to be God-for-us, which corresponds perfectly to what God is in-and-for-Godself.

Immediacy and Identity: Incarnation as the Actuality of God's Time-for-Us

Election as God's Activity Extra Nos

The question remains, however: how can double predestination be understood in light of the actuality of Jesus Christ? Here we must probe into Barth's use of the speculative language of identity and immediacy, borrowed as it were from German idealism, in his novel reinterpretation of the doctrine of election in light of the incarnation.

Inspired by Maury's 1936 lecture, Barth writes in *Gottes Gnadenwahl*: "'Elected in Jesus Christ'—we must first go back to the central mystery of the Christian message, namely, the incarnation, to understand this."[57] What this implies is, first, that the central locus of the event of election is *extra nos*: "God began with Himself and therefore, from the human point of view, from *what is outside of us*: it was by virtue of the decision and act of the eternal Son and Word that this man ..., when He began to be human, began to be the Son and Word of God. This is election!"[58]

---

56. *Gottes Gnadenwahl*, 15.
57. *Gottes Gnadenwahl*, 15.
58. *Gottes Gnadenwahl*, 15. Emphasis mine.

The starting point of speculation cannot be the self-identity of the human ego. The human being has no capacity to make itself determinate. Ontically, speculative extension begins with God, and the speculative identity between the original and the mirror image, as it were, that allows for our knowledge of God is not within us. It is outside of us.

Barth's identification of election with the incarnation *extra nos* carries the profound implication that he no longer sees predestination as primarily an *indirect* work of God *in nobis* in the here-and-now. It is an eternal act of God *ad extra* that is immediately identical with the historical event of the incarnation: "[Incarnation] is election! And this is completely directly and immediately [*ganz direkt und unmittelbar*] what our election is."[59]

The present tense of election actualized by the Holy Spirit *in nobis* is no more and no less than a re-enactment of Christ's perfectly accomplished work *extra nos*. Christ's birth in history as a temporal act of God is *directly and immediately* identical to God's eternal election (but not to God's *ad intra* essence). The man Jesus is not just an appearance [*Schein*] of the divine in some idealist sense. He who died at Golgotha *is* very God, even though he did not die *as* God. The person who suffered there is directly and immediately the impassible Son who is the electing God. Election and Golgotha, in other words, are not two separate actualities, but rather two distinct aspects of one inseparable reality.

Barth's doctrine of election, then, undergoes a Copernican shift from a center in our own time to a center in God's time-for-us, a shift that is proper to the *Denkform* of his speculative theology. In the previous dogmatic phase, Barth still thought that "the incarnation is not an eternal relation."[60] The Barth of *Gottes Gnadenwahl*, however, asserts that the birth of Christ is where "eternity" as "God's time and ... as such the true and real time" meets history as the time of the fallen creature.[61] Thus, Barth can now say that the incarnation is "completely directly and immediately" our eternal election.

Divine Knowability and the Idealist Problems of Immediacy and Identity

Barth's language of directness and immediacy, borrowed from German idealism, is especially noteworthy. Reacting to what has often been dubbed a "critique of immediacy" in Kant's transcendental idealism, figures like Fichte, the early Schelling, and the early Schleiermacher resorted to various notions of immediacy or direct identity between the essence and act of the (self-)conscious *Ich*, the divine and the human, the infinite and the finite, and what not, to contend for the knowability of what they might call "God." By 1807, Hegel had found this philosophy of immediacy deeply troubling, and famously mocked the early Schelling's identity metaphysics as "the night in which ... all cows are black."[62]

---

59. *Gottes Gnadenwahl*, 15.
60. *GD*, 155.
61. *Gottes Gnadenwahl*, 45.
62. G. W. F. Hegel, *Phenomenology of Spirit*, ed. Terry Pinkard and Michael Baur, trans. Michael Baur (Cambridge: Cambridge University Press, 2018), 12.

4. Jesus Christ as Speculum Electionis (1936)

To overcome the problem of immediacy, as we saw in Chapter 2, Hegel insisted upon a process of mediation necessary for the development of absolute human self-knowledge as Spirit. Even so, however, Hegel still envisions God and creation as consummately and speculatively, though never immediately, identical. This speculative identity reduces God to a rational concept (*Begriff*), enabling creatures to know God through some neo-Cartesian kind of rational speculation that Barth firmly rejected.

In asserting a direct and immediate identity between the eternal and historical aspects of the actuality of election in Christ, Barth has packed a robust theological ontology into a short statement. First of all, we have seen that his use of the language of directness and immediacy is applied not to the relationship between God and creaturely reality, but rather to God's act of election in its different dimensions, actualized in different modes by the Son and the Holy Spirit, as a single, unabridged reality. This is a modern reassertion of the classical trinitarian doctrine that the Trinity has one will rather than three.

The same description of immediacy and directness does not apply to Creator-creature relations. With Hegel, Barth asserts that there is an identity between God's time and ours, and that this identity has to be speculative (i.e., mediated and analogical). Against Hegel, however, Barth insists that this identity is not consummate. That is, God does not *become* determinate as God by becoming identical with us.

There is for Barth indeed an "identity" between "God's eternal counsel and our time."[63] The two, however, are not *simpliciter* identical. This identity, as we have seen, is an "identity made recognizable to us" in Jesus Christ alone.[64] Surely this man is God, but he is God by virtue of the hypostatic union in which his humanity remains abidingly distinct from his deity. By the same token, the *Logos asarkos* is Jesus Christ who is *Logos ensarkos*, but the two are *secundum quid* identical, in a way akin to how Confucius was a Chinese philosopher, or how Joseph Ratzinger "is" Pope Benedict XVI. Ratzinger's *being* Benedict XVI is his being-in-becoming. God the Son *is* Jesus Christ also in his being-in-becoming, and this, as we saw in the previous chapter, is grounded in and made possible by God's immutable triune essence.

Barth's language of identity and immediacy has to be understood in light of classical trinitarian doctrine, which is always careful to avoid both Sabellianism and Nestorianism. On one hand, we must affirm that he who died on the cross *is* immediately identical with God: he is very God not as one-third but rather the fullness of the Godhead. Thus we affirm that the death of Christ is the death of God. On the other hand we must distinguish between Christ's two natures, as well as the persons of the Godhead. First, then, Christ who *is* God did not die *as* God. Second, the Son is neither the Father nor the Holy Spirit, and so neither the Father nor the Holy Spirit died personally on the cross. Against Nestorianism, we must affirm the immediate identity between Christ and God. Against Sabellianism, however, we

---

63. *Gottes Gnadenwahl*, 45.
64. *Gottes Gnadenwahl*, 45.

must stress that the identity between the crucified man and the impassible God is mediated through the hypostatic union.

Against Nestorian modes of understanding, Barth asserts a direct and immediate identity between election and the history of the incarnation. Against Sabellian modes of understanding, however, he stresses in *Gottes Gnadenwahl* that the identity between the electing God and Jesus Christ is mediated. "The eternal God and thus also the eternal Son of God is the electing God, and the electing God is none other than the eternal God and thus the eternal Son Himself in the communion with the Father and the Holy Spirit, who assumed human nature in His birth from the Virgin Mary."[65]

Here we can see that Barth has already identified the God-man "who assumed human nature" with "the electing God" in the same way he identifies "God's eternal counsel" with "our time." This is highly pertinent to my contention for the continuity between *Gottes Gnadenwahl* and II/2. As mentioned in Chapter 1 of the present volume, McCormack and Gockel have asserted that the Christocentric reorientation of Barth's doctrine of election was not complete until the 1942 half-volume. One of their key arguments is that Barth's "identification of 'Jesus Christ' with the electing God ... did not appear until *CD* II/2."[66]

McCormack and Gockel, under a post-Kantian framework of interpretation, take this identity to be direct and immediate (although, to my knowledge, they have not used these exact words). Jesus Christ, on their reading of II/2, is *simpliciter* identical with the electing God. This means that apart from the act of electing to be God-for-us in Christ, the Son is not determinate *qua* Son. It is, in other words, the act of election that determined and constituted the Son as the Son, and, by the same token, the Trinity as Father, Son, and Holy Spirit.

It is true that in II/2 the identity between Jesus Christ and the electing God becomes more unequivocal and occupies a more prominent place than in *Gottes Gnadenwahl*. At the very outset of the half-volume Barth states: "Jesus Christ ... is both the electing God and elected man in One."[67] However, there is no textual evidence whatsoever suggesting that Barth's view of the identity has changed since 1936.

I have previously argued that the *abiding distinction* between Christ's deity and humanity, concomitant with the infinite qualitative difference between God and creatures, is everywhere presupposed in Barth's mature theology.[68] This also applies to Barth's identification of Jesus Christ as the subject of election: Jesus Christ is not *simpliciter*, but rather *secundum quid*, the electing God, in the pattern of *communicatio idiomatum* in its *genus idiomaticum*. The doctrine dictates that on the basis of the unity of Christ's person, whatever predicates that may be

---

65. *Gottes Gnadenwahl*, 46.
66. McCormack, "Seek God Where He May Be Found," 64.
67. *CD* II/2, 3.
68. Shao Kai Tseng, *Karl Barth's Infralapsarian Theology* (Downers Grove: IVP Academic, 2016), 278.

attached to the one nature may *secundum quid* be applied to his whole person—to the whole Christ but not the whole *of* Christ. This, as we just saw, is a view that Barth already developed in *Gottes Gnadenwahl*: the identity between Jesus Christ and the electing God is *mediated* rather than *immediate*.

Neither McCormack nor Gockel has provided any decisive textual evidence to suggest that Barth's view of the identity between Jesus Christ and the electing God changed from an indirect and mediated one in 1936 to a direct and immediate one in 1942. Barth in fact makes very clear in II/2 that the identity remains indirect and mediate: "As the Son of the Father He has no need of any special election."[69] When Barth says that God the Son *is* the elected human, the word "is" refers to God's being-in-becoming. God the Son is *simpliciter*—directly and immediately—the electing God with the Father and the Holy Spirit, and *secundum quid* the elected human. By the same token, Jesus Christ is *secundum quid* the electing God by virtue of the indirect and mediated identity of God's eternal counsel with our time.

This indirect and mediated identity allows creatures living in our time to know, in Baark's words, "that God is who God reveals God to be."[70] In Jesus Christ the unsublatable subjectivity of the triune God is revealed to us as God's love in absolute freedom.

Because God qua unsublatable subject is that greater than which nothing can be conceived, and indeed greater than can be conceived, our rational conception of God as such cannot be identical with God-in-Godself or God's self-knowledge, but only a human conception that corresponds speculatively to God's immutable being and self-knowledge in an Anselmian framework of *analogia fidei*. This is why the revelation of the aforementioned identity in historical actuality must carry a noetic "twofold indirectness" (to use a phrase from I/1).[71] The specific form of "speculative" reasoning characterizing Barth's theology, then, constitutes an attempt to steer clear of any idealist tendency to reduce God to a rational concept or to elevate human consciousness to any divine status.

The Determinacy of the Incarnation through Golgotha

Actuality and Consummation

As suggested earlier, McCormack, Gockel, and others have capitalized on Barth's language of God's "self-determination" to reconstruct an "ontology" according to which God's activity in relation to human otherness constitutes God's essence. In this section I will challenge this reading by clarifying Barth's use of the Hegelian notion of determination/determinacy (*Bestimmung/Bestimmtheit*) in *Gottes Gnadenwahl*, and show that this employment of Hegelian grammar is retained in *CD* II/2.

---

69. *CD* II/2, 103.
70. Baark, *Affirmations of Reason*, 257.
71. *CD* I/1, 68.

I begin here with a consideration of how he applies the Hegelian terms "actuality" and "consummation" to double predestination in *Gottes Gnadenwahl*. Barth critically takes his cue from Hegel's metaphysics of becoming to contend that what Christ *became* and *is* as God incarnate is determined by what he *has done* and *does* for us, and we have no noetic access to Christ's person apart from his works.

It is therefore not enough to stop at the point of understanding election in light of the incarnation. Augustine and Calvin already resorted to the incarnation in one way or another in their respective formulations of the notion of election, and to that extent Barth is admittedly following them in *Gottes Gnadenwahl*.[72] Yet, as mentioned earlier, Barth thinks that they fell short of understanding *reprobation* in light of Christ.

To understand predestination as *double* predestination, the identification of election with the incarnation is only necessary but insufficient. The second implication of our having been "elected in Christ," says Barth, is that "this points us to the knowledge of election from the resurrection of Jesus Christ."[73] At this point Barth finds himself in untrodden territory in the history of Christian dogmatics.[74]

So, how does Christ's resurrection shed light on *double* predestination, especially the dreaded doctrine of reprobation? Barth answers this question with two Hegelian terms: "the proof of the full and unlimited *actuality* [*Wirklichkeit*] of the *consummation* [*Vollendung*] and, as it were, the last word of the incarnation is the suffering and death of Jesus Christ."[75]

In Hegel, actuality (sometimes translated as "efficacy") is the fully developed form (*Gestalt*) of a subject.[76] He equates the actual with the rational, and so the contingent and the irrational are merely appearances (*Erscheinungen*) that are in one sense without actuality. However, the contingencies in the appearance of a concept are also described as *immediate actualities*. Only through the stage of appearances can immediate actualities become *determinate* (*bestimmt*) as *developed actualities*. Hegel equates the *truly actual*—the positively rational and the absolute—with God. This moment of the truly actual is the stage of *consummation* (*Vollendung*): it is the moment in which the rationality and essentiality of Spirit become fully developed and manifest.

Barth of course rejects the kind of logical evolution that Hegelian philosophy ascribes to God, but he is not afraid to use Hegelian vocabulary to construe his own theological ontology. What Barth means to say in the quote above is that Golgotha is the rationality and essentiality of the flesh-becoming of God the Son. Golgotha is, to use a Hegelian term that occurs frequently in *Gottes Gnadenwahl*, what makes the incarnation *determinate*.

---

72. *Gottes Gnadenwahl*, 15.
73. *Gottes Gnadenwahl*, 16.
74. *Gottes Gnadenwahl*, 16.
75. *Gottes Gnadenwahl*, 16.
76. See my *G. W. F. Hegel* (Phillipsburg: P&R, 2018), 48–50.

Determination, Determinacy, and God's Self-Determination

Barth's critical use of the term determination/determinacy is a subject that I treated in detail in the previous chapter. Let it suffice here to note that he critically borrows the Hegelian understanding that a thing is *determinate* only in relation to another in the dialectical process of sublation. Hegel speaks of self-determination and means thereby the autonomous disclosure of something's own essentiality by negating its present form and lifting itself up to a higher form.

The primary absoluteness within the Godhead means for Barth that God's triune essence is already determinate in-and-for-itself (*an und für sich*), and thus unsublatable (it cannot *become* absolute, for it has always been and never ceases to be absolute). When Barth speaks of God's self-determination, he means thereby God's determination of Godself as God-for-us, which is grounded in and made possible by God's unsublatable subjectivity as God in-and-for-Godself qua Trinity. "God's being for itself," explains Eberhard Jüngel, "grounds and makes possible God's being-for-us."[77]

When Barth says in *Gottes Gnadenwahl* that "the suffering and death of Jesus Christ" is the "full and unlimited actuality" and "consummation" of the incarnation, what he means is that Jesus Christ became and is determinate as God-for-us (distinct but inseparable from God-in-and-for-Godself) not just through an act of union of two natures, but, consummately, through suffering on the cross. That is to say, the flesh that the Logos assumed was what it was by virtue of what it had in it to become and what it actually became—the crucified man at Golgotha. As Barth would later put it in II/2:

> "The Word became flesh" (Jn. I^{14}). This formulation of the message of Christmas already includes within itself the message of Good Friday. For "all flesh is as grass." The election of the man Jesus means, then, that a wrath is kindled, a sentence pronounced and finally executed, a rejection actualized ... From all eternity judgment has been foreseen—even in the overflowing of God's inner glory.[78]

Yet, because the glory of Christ qua Son is hidden on the cross, the question remains as to how Golgotha reveals to us God's gracious election, and not merely reprobation.[79] To answer this question, Barth's newly developed identification of election with the incarnation in *Gottes Gnadenwahl* is crucial:

---

77. Eberhard Jüngel, *God's Being Is in Becoming: The Trinitarian Being of God in the Theology of Karl Barth*, trans. John Webster (Grand Rapids: Eerdmans, 2001), 121. Pace Bruce McCormack, "Election and Trinity: Theses in Response to George Hunsinger," *Scottish Journal of Theology* 63 (2010): 204.

78. *CD* II/2, 122.

79. *Gottes Gnadenwahl*, 16.

It is in all seriousness that God made Himself one with sinful and mortal man in Christ, and took upon Himself the sin and death of this man. But God's oneness with Himself, the unity of the Father with the Son, cannot be rent asunder, nor can his glory be destroyed, not even by virtue of the fact that the Son, who is truly God, is now truly human.[80]

Note here that the necessity of the incarnation is not predicated upon any aspect of God's inward essence that is immutable in its unsublatable subjectivity—"God's oneness with Himself ... cannot be rent asunder." We must bear in mind that whenever Barth speaks of the necessity of God's acts *ad extra*, it is not a necessity with respect to the *constitution* of God's being. Rather, as he puts it in I/2, he is honoring the "necessity of his [God's] actual manifest will, his *potentia ordinata*."[81] Here *potentia ordinata* (ordained power) is a scholastic term referring to God's power as bound and limited by God's own ordinances with regard to creaturely reality. In *Gottes Gnadenwahl*, this means that Christ "has to" become incarnate, "because He wills to"—indeed he "executes His own will as God" (note incidentally that this is yet another implicit reference to the indirectness and mediacy of the speculative identity between Jesus Christ and the electing God).[82]

Barth retains this view in 1942: he explains in II/2 that the divine-human relationship into which God has elected to enter "is a relation *ad extra*, undoubtedly; for both the man [Christ] and the people represented in him are creatures and not God."[83] However, "it is a relation which is irrevocable, so that once God has willed to enter into it, and has in fact entered into it, *he could not be God without it*. It is a relation in which God is *self-determined*, so that the *determination* belongs no less to him than all that he is *in and for himself*."[84]

This "determination" refers to God's self-determination as God-for-us. Barth's use of the Hegelian term "in and for himself" (which Hegel equates with the essence of the absolute) here indicates that he, unlike Hegel, insists that the sublatory self-determination of God in Jesus Christ is an addition to, rather than an alteration or constitution of, God's immutable essence. It was by Christ's very own decision as electing God that he "had to" bear humanity's sin and death, and this decision is grounded in and made possible by the unsublatable subjectivity of God. The same subject God who is necessarily absolute qua Trinity remains abidingly absolute and thus unsublated in God's secondary mode of being *ad extra*.

The determinacy of the incarnation through Golgotha, as Barth tells us in *Gottes Gnadenwahl*, is precisely what Christ's resurrection reveals: "This is Easter, the resurrection of Jesus Christ: the revealed and reconciling glory of the crucified Son of God, His glory for us and unto us as those who are born again in His birth.

---

80. *Gottes Gnadenwahl*, 16.
81. *CD* I/2, 41.
82. *Gottes Gnadenwahl*, 16.
83. *CD* II/2, 7. Emphases added.
84. *CD* II/2, 7. Emphasis added.

Our sin and death, carried by Him, are defeated and carried away."[85] Golgotha is the outward basis of reprobation and election, and Easter is a manifestation of this accomplished actuality. "What took place on Golgotha for us and unto us, *which became manifest on Easter*—although it took place in time—*is* our *eternal* election."[86]

The historicity and eternality of double predestination are two aspects of the same actuality in the pattern of the *concursus Dei*. They are not two constituent parts of that actuality, but rather two modes of existence in each of which the same actuality is totally manifest and present, just as the same person of Christ is fully God and fully human, albeit with abiding distinction.

Election as the Sublation of Reprobation

Barth's Rejection of the Decretum Absolutum

On the basis of his formulation of Easter in relation to Golgotha, Barth proceeds to explicate the notions of election and reprobation. He stresses that according to what Scripture "indubitably" attests to us, "there is no election, where there is not also non-election, omission, and reprobation. The doctrine of predestination must thus be the doctrine of double predestination."[87]

Reprobation as such, Barth urges, must not be treated as a "logical postulate" that goes hand in hand with election, as if predestination had to be twofold because "there can be no Yes without a No, no day without night."[88] He is troubled by "the tidiness of the symmetry in which election and reprobation are spoken of" in the historic doctrine of the *decretum absolutum* (absolute decree of God inflexibly dividing humankind into elects and reprobates from and to all eternity) taught by Calvin, Beza, and later Reformed theologians.[89] As Barth sees it, this "all too architectonic symmetry of election and rejection" is the result of a conceptual necessity (*Denknotwendigkeit*) combined with the empirical observation that individuals who live by faith and obedience rank among the few: in this way the biblical doctrine of double predestination is inevitably "interpreted arbitrarily through reason and experience."[90]

In rejecting this classical-metaphysical doctrine of a *decretum absolutum*, Barth appeals to Maury's thesis to develop a Christocentric paradigm for understanding double predestination: "If election were not election in Christ, there would have

---

85. *Gottes Gnadenwahl*, 16.
86. *Gottes Gnadenwahl*, 17. Emphases added.
87. *Gottes Gnadenwahl*, 18.
88. *Gottes Gnadenwahl*, 18.
89. *Gottes Gnadenwahl*, 19.
90. *Gottes Gnadenwahl*, 20.

been no double predestination ... One can speak of a reprobation predetermined by God only in view of Golgotha; but here one must speak of it."[91]

Barth then sets forth two statements of his own in dialectical fashion as a corollary to Maury's thesis. On one hand, "we cannot recognise our election in Jesus Christ without recognising first and foremost our reprobation in Him."[92] On the other hand, "we must know about ... our election in Jesus Christ, in order to really know about our reprobation."[93] This dialectic finds its basis in Barth's view that election and reprobation are not architectonic *parts* of the whole, but rather different moments of the same divine movement and actuality in Jesus Christ: "There is no architecture here; here a path is traversed."[94]

The Organicist Language of Sublation

Implicit in this statement, evidently inspired by German-idealist organicism, is Barth's criticism of what he sees as vestiges of the substantialism of Greek metaphysics in classical Western theology.[95] Substantialism, as we saw in the previous chapter, tends to view reality architectonically and statically as consisting in different parts held together by what Hegel calls "abstract universality" and "bare uniformity," rather than seeing the whole process concretely as a subject undergoing organic growth.[96]

To say that double predestination is a "path" rather than an "architecture" is to view it as an *organic process*. "The relationship between election and reprobation cannot be seen as a rigid coexistence."[97] It is, rather, a "pathway from death to life. The person who has traversed this pathway is still the same person, and yet fundamentally a different person. What has happened to him is the transition from one hand of God to the other."[98] This process that takes place *in nobis* here and now is the Holy Spirit's re-enactment of what has taken place once for all at Golgotha *in Christo* and thus *extra nos*.[99]

To stress that the whole Christ—and we in and with him—underwent every moment of the process, Barth adopts the Hegelian language of "sublation." What is

---

91. *Gottes Gnadenwahl*, 20. Here Barth is paraphrasing Pierre Maury, "Election et Foi," *Foi et Vie* 27 (1936): 221. English translation: Ed. Simon Hatrell, *Election, Barth, and the French Connection: How Pierre Maury Gave a "Decisive Impetus" to Karl Barth's Doctrine of Election* (Eugene: Wipf and Stock, 2016), 40.
92. *Gottes Gnadenwahl*, 20.
93. *Gottes Gnadenwahl*, 23.
94. *Gottes Gnadenwahl*, 23.
95. For a detailed discussion of Barth and substantialism, see my "Barth and Actualistic Ontology."
96. Hegel, *Phenomenology*, 13.
97. *Gottes Gnadenwahl*, 51.
98. *Gottes Gnadenwahl*. 51.
99. Cf. G. W. F. Hegel, *Lectures on the Philosophy of Religion*, vol. 3, ed. Peter Hodgson (Oxford: Oxford University Press, 2007), 327–30.

"ordained and executed" at Golgotha is "really not injustice, but the highest justice of God."[100] Precisely "because God's justice is ordained and executed, because our reprobation is revealed and surely revealed in its righteousness, because the Elect of God affirmed it by faith and took it upon Himself, it is *sublated* as our reprobation."[101]

There is, again, much to unpack in Barth's use of Hegelian vocabulary here. Barth, as we have seen, rejects Hegel's idealist mode of speculation according to which human consciousness is sublated to become divine and absolute in the moment of consummation. The process of human life determined by double predestination, insists Barth, "is not about consummation [*Vollendung*]; it is about the resurrection of the flesh. It is about resurrection from death."[102]

When Barth adopts the Hegelian language of *Aufhebung*, then, he is really using it to convey a process that "the New Testament describes."[103] It is that process aptly construed by the dialectic of Luther's theology of the cross: God conceals Godself on the cross in order to reveal Godself. The glory of the resurrection shines forth only through Golgotha.[104]

Yet, just as Christ died in order to conquer death, reprobation must be understood as God's No that serves the purpose of the Yes. Even the crucified Christ was reprobated as God's elect. "Make no mistake: even on the cross, Jesus Christ is the Elect of God."[105] The determination (*Bestimmung*)—predetermination (*Vorherbestimmung*) indeed—of Christ as the elect is the essentiality that determined the whole sublatory process of double predestination.

Christ as God's elect was chosen to be reprobated in the place of sinful humankind, and he was reprobated for the sake of his own election and the election of all humankind in him. In other words, reprobation is God's eternal negation of humanity's sin that negates God's grace, and this double negation is sublated in the moment of election. "Only where we see [reprobation] as having been sublated do we see it truly."[106]

Election of All in Christ: *Particularist Reorientation of Barth's Actualistic Ontology*

Particularity and Universality in Classical Predestinarianism and Schleiermacher

Barth's formulation of double predestination as the sublation of reprobation in election, along with his emphasis on the election of *all* in Christ, has led many readers to believe that his doctrine inevitably implies some form of soteriological

---

100. *Gottes Gnadenwahl*, 22.
101. *Gottes Gnadenwahl*, 22.
102. *Gottes Gnadenwahl*, 41.
103. *Gottes Gnadenwahl*, 51.
104. *Gottes Gnadenwahl*, 16.
105. *Gottes Gnadenwahl*, 21.
106. *Gottes Gnadenwahl*, 23.

universalism.[107] How he treats the problem of universal salvation in the later volumes of the *Church Dogmatics* is a topic I have addressed elsewhere.[108] Suffice it here to say that in *Gottes Gnadenwahl*, Barth's *particularistic* and *actualistic* discourse on the election of all in Christ leaves "no room for the speculation of an eternal apocatastasis."[109]

It is worth noting that both Barth's particularism and actualism rely critically on some of Schleiermacher's insights, and we shall discuss these in turn. The problem of particularity and universality is one of the oldest themes in the history of speculative philosophy. Traditionally, particulars are usually considered to be concrete, and universals are considered intelligible by the method of abstraction. Concrete particulars are taken as *specula* of abstract universals.

Barth follows Hegel in contending that God's truth is to be sought *concretely* rather than *abstractly*. Whereas Hegel proposes to speculatively comprehend the whole of reality through the lens of what he calls the "concrete universal" (*das konkrete Allgemeine*), however, Barth follows Schleiermacher in insisting upon a theological starting point that focuses relentlessly on *particularity*.

As we saw in Chapter 2, the early Schleiermacher, in his speculative program, already asserted that the infinity of the universe is to be found in the "smallest part of the particular," for "the realm of intuition is so infinite precisely because of this independent particularity."[110] In his *magnum opus*, *The Christian Faith*, the particularity of his theological starting-point is narrowed down to "no other individual life than that of the Redeemer."[111]

The problem with Schleiermacher, as Barth sees it in *Gottes Gnadenwahl*, is that the Prussian pastor-theologian frames the particularity of Christ in a "systematics of human history that can certainly not be described as anything other than a speculative worldview."[112] The idealist term "worldview" (*Weltanschauung*) is perhaps better translated as "world-intuition." For Schleiermacher, every intuition is associated with a feeling (*Gefühl*), and this (as Barth understands him) serves as the basis of speculative extension from the human side to God's side through Christ. Consequently, the particularity that Schleiermacher fought so hard to maintain is inevitably dissolved in "statements

---

107. Notable examples in recent years include Tom Greggs, "'Jesus Is Victor': Passing the Impasse of Barth on Universalism," *Scottish Journal of Theology* 60 (2007): 196–212; David Congdon, "*Apokatastasis* and Apostolicity: A Response to Oliver Crisp on the Question of Barth's Universalism," *Scottish Journal of Theology* 67 (2014): 464–80.

108. See my "Condemnation and Universal Salvation: Karl Barth's 'Reverent Agnosticism' Revisited," *Scottish Journal of Theology* 71 (2018): 324–38.

109. *Gottes Gnadenwahl*, 27.

110. Friedrich Schleiermacher, *On Religion: Speeches to Its Cultured Despisers*, ed. and trans. Richard Crouter (Cambridge: Cambridge University Press, 1996), 27.

111. Friedrich Schleiermacher, *The Christian Faith*, trans. H. Macintosh and J. Stewart (London: T&T Clark, 1999), 525.

112. *Gottes Gnadenwahl*, 25.

about an ultimate and general overcoming of judgment by grace, about a gradual and finally triumphant restoration of all things."[113]

Schleiermacher's universalistic rendition of election of course stands in contradiction to historic Reformed theology. However, Barth thinks that "here Schleiermacher has" merely "drawn the undesired consequences" that the metaphysical tendency toward abstract universality in classical theology ultimately leads to.[114]

Barth agrees with the "the representatives of the classical doctrine of predestination" that "we are not authorised to declare who the elect and who the reprobate is."[115] However, this does not sufficiently ward off the temptation of speculative universalization or abstraction. He insists that "we must go even further: we are not authorised to make the general declaration that there are the elect and the reprobate as two separate classes of men."[116]

Christ and Adam: Election as the Sublation of Abstract Universality

It is true that in this context Barth immediately proceeds to speak of the election of *all* in Christ. However, it would be a grave mistake to interpret this as a *universalistic* statement. Quite the contrary, this is a *particularistic* statement: all are elected *in Christ*. Without emphasizing the reprobation that *Christ* suffered particularly in our stead, any doctrine asserting the election of *all* would be dissolved into the generalization of abstract universals.

Abstract universality belongs not to Christ, but to Adam: "When we speak of Adam's sin, we speak of the sin of us all. The name Adam tells what the actuality of us all is."[117] Abstract universality can only describe the prison of disobedience into which God has concluded us all. "The name Christ," however, "does not speak of 'all' in this sense."[118]

The name Christ spells particularity. "Already in the name lies the particularity: this man, the Anointed, Christ! It is concerned with the selectivity of election [*Auswahl*] here."[119] God did not elect us all immediately. God elected this one man out of the mass of perdition, and, mediately, us *in* and *with* him.

"Election refers to the call out of the *universality* of *all*, and so it refers to movement and event," namely, the movement and event whereby the pathway from crucifixion to resurrection is traversed.[120] The notion of a *simpliciter* election of *all* is tantamount to an apocatastasis in which particularity is dissolved.

---

113. *Gottes Gnadenwahl*, 25.
114. *Gottes Gnadenwahl*, 25.
115. *Gottes Gnadenwahl*, 26.
116. *Gottes Gnadenwahl*, 26.
117. *Gottes Gnadenwahl*, 45.
118. *Gottes Gnadenwahl*, 45.
119. *Gottes Gnadenwahl*, 45–6.
120. *Gottes Gnadenwahl*, 46. Emphasis added.

The election of *all* (universality) in *Christ* (particularity), by contrast, is a process in which the particularity of Christ as God's elect sublates the universality of the prison of disobedience. This leaves no room for any universalistic understanding of election: "'God has shut up all under disobedience, whereupon He might have mercy upon all' (Rom. 11:32). All: that is to say without the shadow of a doubt from the meaning and the context: all, upon whom He wills to and shall have mercy in Jesus Christ—thus there is no room for the speculation of an eternal apocatastasis."[121]

Being-in-Act: Self-Revelation of the Unsublatable Subject God

Barth's Rejection of the Apocatastasis

But if Christ was reprobated in the stead of all humankind, is the election of all *in Christ* still, in the final analysis, not an election of *all*? In the last resort, does Barth's Christocentric doctrine of election not lead to soteriological universalism, in spite of his commitment to the particularity of election? It is tempting to answer this question in the affirmative, if one neglects the *actualistic* character of Barth's Christocentric particularism, a theme to which we now turn in this section.[122]

Let us first note that as far as *Gottes Gnadenwahl* is concerned, it is textually perspicuous that Barth unequivocally affirms the prospect of an eschatological separation of the elect from the reprobate: "There certainly is a predestinedhood of man corresponding to the *praedestinatio* of God. But the separation of men into believers and unbelievers by this concept will become visible—it will become actual—in the last judgment ... We are heading towards this actuality."[123]

What Barth intends to say with his rejection of the *decretum absolutum* is that "we should not make a *present* separation out of this future separation. Rather, we should accept in obedience our situation between Christ's ascension and His return as the situation in which we walk by faith and not by sight."[124]

From GD to CD II/2: Overcoming Hegel and Schleiermacher

Underlying this openness to the future of election and reprobation is the actualistic character of Barth's Christological particularism. This is again an insight that he critically retrieved from Schleiermacher in 1936. In the confines of Kant's critique

---

121. *Gottes Gnadenwahl*, 27.
122. As I suggest in "Condemnation and Universal Salvation," Tom Greggs's analysis of universal salvation and particularism in Barth is strikingly oblivious to the Swiss theologian's actualism. See Tom Greggs, *Barth, Origen, and Universal Salvation: Restoring Particularity* (Oxford: Oxford University Press, 2009).
123. *Gottes Gnadenwahl*, 48.
124. *Gottes Gnadenwahl*, 48. Emphasis added.

4. Jesus Christ as Speculum Electionis (1936) 143

of speculative metaphysics, as we saw in Chapter 2, idealists of Schleiermacher's generation shied away from speaking of the incarnation in terms of *being* and *nature*. Humans within the temporal world cannot know what God *is*. Our knowledge is confined to events and activities—to *becoming*. The Schelling of 1809, for instance, identified God's existence as activity and asserted that human activity is an expression of God's life, claiming that "God can only reveal himself in creatures who resemble him, in free, self-activating beings."[125] It was against this intellectual milieu that the later Schleiermacher developed his Christological actualism, which claims that we can know Christ as God incarnate only insofar as Christ is understood as the *pure activity* of God's love.[126]

Barth is inspired by the German idealist insight that God is knowable to us only through historical activity and process. As early as the Göttingen years, Barth had grown fond of speaking of God's self-revelation in the person of the Holy Spirit as "the pure act of the Spirit" in admittedly "Hegelian terms."[127] The Barth of *GD*, however, was hesitant to speak of the incarnate Son in actualistic terms for the fear of following Schleiermacher in slipping "willy-nilly into the neutral sphere where the I and Thou merge into one another."[128]

Meanwhile, Barth's fierce insistence upon God's absolute and immutable subjectivity in *GD* is also an attempt to steer clear of the "intolerable situation" in which Hegel's subject-object-act trinity is found.[129] The subject of the Hegelian trinity is sublated by the object to be elevated unto the moment of activity or developed actuality. Barth, by contrast, adamantly affirms the Christian doctrine of the Trinity as an expression of, in Baark's words, "God's unsublatable subjectivity, which is revealed in Jesus Christ."[130]

This seminal insistence on God's unsublatable subjectivity in abiding absoluteness is what Barth came to describe famously in *CD* II/1 as the primary sense of the loving "freedom of God ..., his primary absoluteness," which "has its truth and reality in the inner trinitarian life of the Father with the Son by the Holy Spirit."[131] God's freedom in this primary absoluteness, Jüngel observes, is precisely the ground whereupon "God can be the God of humanity without being defined as God by his relation to humanity ... God's being-for-us does not define God's being."[132]

It was also on the basis of the very same insistence that Barth revised his own actualism in 1936. The Barth of *Gottes Gnadenwahl* was ready to

---

125. Friedrich Schelling, *Philosophical Inquiries into the Nature of Human Freedom*, trans. James Gutmann (Chicago: Open Court, 2003), 19.
126. See Keven Hector, "Actualism and Incarnation: The High Christology of Friedrich Schleiermacher," *International Journal of Systematic Theology* 8 (2006): 307–22.
127. *GD*, 127.
128. *GD*, 62.
129. *GD*, 107.
130. Baark, *Affirmations of Reason*, 255.
131. *CD* II/1, 317.
132. Jüngel, *God's Being Is in Becoming*, 119–20.

re-appropriation from Schleiermacher a Christological form of actualism. Yet, Barth was also severely critical of "how Schleiermacher has in fact formulated the relationship" between creation and reconciliation in his Christocentric doctrine of predestination, which amounts to a "monistic speculation … in which reconciliation becomes merely an arena for the enactment of creation."[133] Schleiermacher's doctrine, on Barth's view, inevitably amounts to a dynamic Christomonism in which creation becomes speculatively identical with Christ who is the pure activity of God's love.

The Notion of "Being-in-Act" in Gottes Gnadenwahl

Actualism is a theological motif that Barth strenuously grappled with in his early career, not least because he did not want to repeat the errors of Schleiermacher, Hegel, and other German idealists in identifying God with sheer activity or historical process in one way or another. Barth's actualism during the Göttingen-Münster-Bonn phase is formulated in terms of God's "revelation-in-act."[134] One purpose, as we just saw, was to ascertain that the subject God does not become sublated in the process of revelation. This, of course, created serious problems for his speculative *Denkform*, problems that we identified at the outset of this chapter.

In *Gottes Gnadenwahl*, he begins to construe God's act in Christ as speculatively extending God's essential being to us. He has not yet found the precise vocabulary to convey this newly developed version of his actualism, and the all-important term "being-in-act" is not yet in place. However, he has begun to speak of "the essence and act of God" in such a way that we can and do indeed come to know God's immutable essence indirectly through God's act.[135]

In our "human mutability" we can only cognize God's "act" in historical actuality: "we have to gaze upon God's immutability in human mutability."[136] We do, however, know by faith that Jesus Christ *is* the electing God, and so by faith and "only by faith can we speak about God's immutability and faithfulness and identity," the speculative identity between *Deus absconditus* and *Deus revelatus*.[137]

Echoing his own distinction between *ratio fidei* and *ratio veritatis* set forth in *Anselm*, Barth qualifies here that "we must recognise that what we know of God's act is not God Himself, but God in our understanding of His revelation, in the broken rays of light that we are not allowed to see directly."[138] We can only know of God's immutable being as revealed through God's being in the act of becoming

---

133. *Gottes Gnadenwahl*, 43.
134. See George Hunsinger, "Karl Barth's The Göttingen Dogmatics," *Scottish Journal of Theology* 46 (1993): 374.
135. *Gottes Gnadenwahl*, 46.
136. *Gottes Gnadenwahl*, 48.
137. *Gottes Gnadenwahl*, 48.
138. *Gottes Gnadenwahl*, 48.

(i.e., the incarnation).[139] This means that "if we speak of God's eternal counsel, we can only speak of it as God has revealed Himself to us in our time."[140]

When we speak of God's eternity—"God's time ... as ... the true and real time"—from the perspective of creaturely time and history, we must understand it in three distinct modes of temporality.[141] The simple simultaneity—immediate identity—of past, present, and future pertains to God alone. We cannot recognize God's eternal predestination from God's perspective; we can only know it as it has been revealed to us in our time. "In light of His revelation, we can put into words the eternal *decretum* of God: He has decided; He will decide; He decides."[142]

Note that the present and future tenses of predestination are both anchored in the perfect tense.[143] God's gracious election is revealed to us once for all in the death and resurrection of Christ, so that it can be revealed again and again through the ongoing work of the Holy Spirit in ever new forms.

Because the revelation of God's eternal predestination is an ongoing process as much as it is an accomplished reality, we are not permitted to speculate about an eschatological apocatastasis or separation of the elect from the reprobate. All that we may know and say about God's eternal predestination is what has *actually* been revealed to us in the death and resurrection of Jesus Christ.[144]

The truth of double predestination as such, according to Barth, is definitively expressed in Romans 11:32, which speaks of God's "conclusion" of "all" in the prison of disobedience in order to have mercy upon "all."[145] Double predestination as seen in this light is not about the separation of humankind into two different classes, nor is it about the final salvation of all by the annihilation of reprobation. Rather, the *present* situation of humankind under God's double predestination is such that *all* are at once placed under the threat of reprobation and the promise of election: "the notion that there might be elects who are not threatened with reprobation or reprobates who are not promised with election is firmly excluded."[146]

The actual condition of humankind at present is that we are all determined by acts of disobedience. "This disobedience is of our own being and act, but it is the divine reprobation that God transfers and leaves to us that shuts us up in

---

139. *Gottes Gnadenwahl*, 45.
140. *Gottes Gnadenwahl*, 45.
141. *Gottes Gnadenwahl*, 45.
142. *Gottes Gnadenwahl*, 45.
143. In *Gottes Gnadenwahl*, Barth has not yet developed the understanding that our present situation is determined by both the perfect and future tenses of God's work in Christ—this two-way determination would not be clearly spelled out until *CD* IV/3. See my "Condemnation and Universal Salvation."
144. *Gottes Gnadenwahl*, 26.
145. *Gottes Gnadenwahl*, 26.
146. *Gottes Gnadenwahl*, 27.

the prison ... without grace and in opposition to grace."¹⁴⁷ Barth makes it clear that the sublation of reprobation is not an elimination: "'Whereupon He might have mercy upon all': that is the promise. This promise *does not eliminate* the threat."¹⁴⁸

From the perspective of Christ's accomplished work at Golgotha, however, we may be assured of our deliverance from the threat. Barth speaks of this deliverance in the perfect tense: "'God has shut up all under disobedience': that is the threat from which we *have been delivered* through the promise freely given to us in Jesus Christ."¹⁴⁹ This *already* must not be affirmed at the expense of the *not yet*. Christ's accomplished work not only assures us of the promise, but also proclaims to us that we are still prisoners of disobedience.¹⁵⁰

It must be stressed again that the threat and the promise do not stand in a symmetrical relationship. The promise *sublates* the threat. This language of *Aufhebung* suggests that the same subject that traverses the path is transformed rather than annihilated. The promise is the purpose of the threat, and thus the threat as a moment in this journey is *determined* by the promise. God's promise in the crucified and risen Lord is precisely where the threat receives its force and validity as a threat that presently looms over us.

"Now, sublated in the promise and veiled in it, the threat will certainly remain in its place, retaining, nay, receiving its seriousness as a call to humility, to repentance, to faith."¹⁵¹ This threat is a call presently issued to human beings again and again by the Holy Spirit who also assures us of our hope moment by moment. This is the double predestination that the history of Jesus Christ as *speculum electionis* mirrors to us.

Conclusion

Some concluding observations are now in order with regard to the significance of *Gottes Gnadenwahl* to the development of Barth's speculative theology. Prior to the Christocentric reorientation of his speculative theology, as we saw, he refused to claim any knowledge of an *eternal* predestination of God except an eternity-in-time intuitable to human beings in historical actuality.¹⁵² The history of Christ's death and resurrection mirrors a movement in God's will from reprobation

---

147. *Gottes Gnadenwahl*, 27. This is an especially rich statement that awaits unpacking in *CD* IV/1–2. See my "*Non potest non peccare*: Karl Barth on Original Sin and the Bondage of the Will," *Neue Zeitschrift für Sytematische Theologie und Religionsphilosophie* 60 (2018): 185–207.
148. *Gottes Gnadenwahl*, 27. Emphasis added.
149. *Gottes Gnadenwahl*, 27. Emphasis added.
150. *Gottes Gnadenwahl*, 27.
151. *Gottes Gnadenwahl*, 28.
152. See *GD*, 454.

to election, but there is no assurance that anyone is eternally elected in Christ, because to claim such an assurance would be to probe into an eternal will of God above and behind God's revelation-in-act.

This premature version of Barth's actualism, which lies at the heart of his earlier speculative theology, carries two possible implications. First, it could imply that the electing God is indeed a subject that eternally posits itself as unsublated subject, but human beings can only come to know of God's *act* of revelation in time. This would have amounted to the postulation of the existence of an unknowable absolute apart from God's essence mirrored through revelation. As Barth sees it, this is precisely the metaphysical error committed by the classical representatives of the doctrine of predestination, an error symptomatic of the rationalist mode of speculation.

The second possible implication would be that there is no God except the God whose eternity is bound to temporal actualities. In this case God's subjectivity would have been sublated in creaturely objectivity through historical activity. God's being-for-us would have determined God's essence as God-in-and-for-Godself. This would have erased the distinction between God's eternal essence and temporal acts, and reduced God to sheer activity, process, and historicity. Barth's intention, as we have seen, was precisely to avoid this error committed by Hegel, Schleiermacher, and other nineteenth-century German idealists.

This dilemma in Barth's early theology up to 1936 was resolved by his Christocentric revision of the doctrine of election set forth in *Gottes Gnadenwahl*, where he developed the notion—though not yet the precise terminology and all the implications—of God's being-in-act for the first time in his career. In *Gottes Gnadenwahl*, predestination no longer consists in merely temporal actualities. What is still lacking in *Gottes Gnadenwahl* is a clear articulation of election as not merely an act of God's will, but a secondary mode of God's absolute being as the subject, object, and act of love-in-freedom. However, Barth has begun to describe election as an eternal act by which a secondary mode of God's being is determined, an *ad extra* mode of being that allows us to gaze upon God's immutable eternality through mutable temporality.

Election as an eternal reality, furthermore, is manifested in three distinct but inseparable tenses. This eternity is not merely eternity-in-time. It is true eternity as God's time that has entered into ours to become God's time-for-us in which God's own time remains unsublated: it is at once an eternity in, with, and above creaturely time. Election, in other words, is an eternal act of God's eternal being, transcendent to time, entering into time in Christ without ever ceasing to be transcendent—without sublating God's subjectivity in any way.

On this view, the Christocentric reorientation of Barth's actualistic ontology in 1936, while to some degree contingent upon his audition of Maury's lecture in that year, was primarily the result of his resolution to follow through with his seminal insistence upon God's unsublatable subjectivity even in the historical event of revelation. Without this revision of his actualistic ontology, his basically Anselmian mode of speculation would have remained under the shadow of anthropological projection symptomatic of idealist speculation.

Barth, as we have seen, retained this insistence on God's unsublatable subjectivity in *CD* II/2. This implies that the development of his theological ontology from 1936 to 1942 was not as radical as McCormack and Gockel have depicted. Barth was never moving in the direction of an "ontology" in which God's being-for-us constitutes God's being-in-and-for-Godself. Quite the contrary, this was precisely the idealist sort of speculative ontology that he sought to avoid in the Christocentric reorientation of his actualism and speculative theology in 1936–42.

In *Gottes Gnadenwahl* Barth is able to maintain consistently that God is made knowable and indeed known to humans through God's works in creaturely history without ceasing to be God. Thereby he is also able to proclaim that double predestination "is a path that God traverses with" us, without reducing God to sheer activity or process in such a way that we may have no assurance of our eternal election in Christ.[153]

This highly sophisticated version of his speculative theology allows Barth to affirm with his predecessors—Augustine, Luther, Calvin, and others—that we are indeed in possession of God (a notion he consistently rejected from *Romans II* up to early 1936) by faith in Jesus Christ, and thereby a speculative assurance of salvation. This assurance is no self-confidence, for it is not built on the classical-metaphysical quicksand of *Denknotwendigkeit* or *Erfahrungsgegenstand*, or any sort of Cartesian-Hegelian mode of speculation that finds its starting point in the presumptuous certainty of human self-identity. Rather, it consists in the believer's confidence in the speculative identity between Jesus Christ and the electing God. This speculative identity is the self-revelation of the graciously electing God greater than whom nothing can be conceived—and indeed greater than can be conceived.

God's objectivity in the event of our speculative possession-by-faith is grounded in and made possible by God's unsublatable subjectivity whereby God possesses us by grace. "We possess the assurance of our election if we possess God who is the object and origin of faith; but we are indeed in possession of Him, for He is in possession of us. That He is in possession of us is what we have to say and always continue to say about Him through His promise."[154]

---

153. *Gottes Gnadenwahl*, 51.
154. *Gottes Gnadenwahl*, 30.

Chapter 5

PAINTING THE PORTRAIT: JESUS CHRIST AS *SPECULUM TRINITATIS* (1940)

Introduction

On Barth's own account, the doctrine of God set forth in *CD* II/1 (published 1940) was formulated "at the feet of Anselm of Canterbury, and in particular from his proofs of God set out in *Prosl.* 2-4."[1] Barth's development of a basically Anselmian mode of theological speculation, as we saw in the preceding chapters, found its first decisive statement in the "1931 book on Anselm of Canterbury's proofs of the existence of God," which Barth describes as the "real work that documents" his "conversion ... from the residue of a philosophical or anthropological ... grounding of Christian doctrine."[2] On his own account from the 1932 preface to *CD* I/1, his "little work on Anselm" effectively prevented him from "continuing on the level and in the strain of the initial volume of 1927" on the "Doctrine of the Word of God" in the "Christian Dogmatics in Outline."[3]

In *CD* I/1 Barth works out the dogmatic implications of the speculative *Denkform* retrieved from Anselm, and in 1936 Barth began to flesh out his speculative theology Christologically (see Chapter 4). Most of the materials in I/2 had been written by the time of the delivery of Barth's lectures on the doctrine of election in September and October of 1936 and the publication of *Gottes Gnadenwahl* in November. When Barth completed the final revisions to I/2 in the summer of 1937, he had already begun to write up II/1 as a continuation of the Christocentric project that he began in 1936. The summer of 1939 saw the completion of II/1. This half-volume, published in 1940, marks the first dogmatic statement of Barth's Christocentric reorientation of his speculative theology in his career.

As we saw in Chapter 2, one of the graver challenges that Barth had to overcome in adopting an Anselmian mode of speculation in the late 1920s and early 1930s was the intellectualist tendencies in Anselm's writings. Cartesian speculation, according to Barth's narrative of the history of ideas, re-emerged in a pantheistic mode in the post-Kantian era precisely because of its intellectualist core handed

---

1. *CD* II/1, 4.
2. Karl Barth, "Parergon," *Evangelische Theologie* 8 (1948): 272.
3. *CD* I/1, xi.

down from classical theology: Descartes treated human intellect as a mirror image of God's mind, and finite attributes of human nature as *specula* of God's infinite perfections. Feuerbach, on Barth's view, rightly disclosed the anthropological essence of speculative theology formulated in this way. In the speculative tradition founded by Descartes and culminating in Hegel, theology is little more than the projection of human nature unto a pseudo-object given the name of God.

Barth, as we saw, appealed to Anselm to repudiate what Barth understood to be the incipient pantheism underlying Descartes's intellectualist speculation, later transposed into a distinctively post-Kantian mode by nineteenth-century German idealism and romanticism. Anselm's insistence on the inconceivability of God in *Proslogion* was central to the speculative *Denkform* that Barth developed around 1930.

Descartes posited an immediate identity or analytic unity between the *cogito* and the *sum*, knowing that these are in fact two separate determinations, the synthesis of which had to be proved through a series of meditations. Anselm, on the other hand, accepted by faith that immediate self-identity, *ipsum esse*, is to be found in God alone. This immediately self-identical essence of God *a se* is unknowable to finite creatures. Knowledge of God's essence can only be mediated to human reason through revelation given in creaturely form. In *Proslogion*, then, Anselm does not posit any speculative identity between divine and human intellects. The speculative identity is between God's *ad intra* essence and *ad extra* acts actualized through God's works in the creaturely realm.

The problem is: how do creaturely images mirror God's *triune* essence? Anselm, of course, takes the doctrine of the Trinity as revealed doctrine. He accepts it by faith, and takes faith in the triune Creator and Redeemer to be his concrete starting point in making sense of an otherwise abstract idea, innate to the human intellect, of God as infinite being. But in light of the triune God revealed to us in Jesus Christ, can we not also make sense of things in the sensible world that, in one way or another, serve as mirror images of God's triune essence?

In other words, is there not indeed a *speculum, imago,* or *vestigium Trinitatis* within creation? This Anselm affirms in *Monologion*, as we saw in Chapter 2. There he contends that the human "mind may most fitly be said to be its own mirror wherein it contemplates, so to speak, the image of what it cannot see face to face," for "the mind itself alone among all created beings is capable of remembering and conceiving of and loving itself ... through its memory and intelligence and love ... united in an ineffable Trinity."[4]

Here Anselm is in line with a longstanding tradition founded by Augustine, whose notion of human love and self-knowledge as *speculum Trinitatis* has dominated much of the analogical tradition in Western theology. In *Summa Theologiae* 1.45.7, for instance, Thomas Aquinas cites and defends Augustine's *De Trinitate* and *De Natura Boni* to assert in a moderately intellectualist way that some *vestigium Trinitatis* is necessarily manifested in creatures.[5]

---

4. Anselm of Canterbury, *Monologium*, in *St. Anselm: Basic Writings,* trans. Sidney Norton Deane (Chicago: Open Court, 1962), 132.

5. Thomas Aquinas, *Summa Theologiae: Latin-English Edition, Prima Pars, Q1-64* (Scotts Valley: NovAntiqua, 2008), 548–9.

5. Jesus Christ as Speculum Trinitatis (1940)

Anselm, like Augustine, affirms God's unknowability *per essentiam* and the ineffability of God's triune essence. The intellectualist elements in the notion of *speculum Trinitatis* formulated by both Augustine and Anselm, however, seem to suggest rather strongly that the human intellect is in some way an emanation of God's triune essence. If pushed to its logical extreme, Augustine and Anselm may be forced to agree with Meister Eckhart's neo-Platonist assertion that the memory of God in the human mind is uncreated.

Barth was sharply wary of the pantheistic implications that can be drawn from the *speculum Trinitatis* tradition handed down from Augustine. In *CD* III/2, Barth complains in Feuerbachian terms that in Augustine's idea, "anthropology ... disguised itself as cosmology and theology."[6] The intellectualistic pantheism of "Plato and Plotinus ... was deepened and illuminated in the thought of Augustine."[7]

In fact, as early as the *Göttingen Dogmatics* §15, "The Knowability of God," Barth began to blame Augustine's idea of the *imago Trinitatis* as the intellectual-historical root of the neo-pietist "breach of the subject-object relation" between God and creatures, a "breach" that found its idealist counterpart in Hegel.[8] "Hegel discovered the trinity of the subjective, objective, and absolute Spirit, in itself, for itself, and in and for itself. This was simply a variation on Augustine's ancient insight."[9] For both Hegel and German neo-pietism, "the divine subject would cease to be an object confronting us, and the knowledge with which God knows himself ... would be identical with our own knowledge."[10]

As we saw in Chapter 2, the attribution of the root of this anthropomorphic speculation on the basis of divine-human identity to Augustine was not Barth's invention. Heinrich Heine's influential *Zur Geschichte der Religion und Philosophie in Deutschland*, which represented a mainstream view in the latter decades of the long nineteenth century, also made the same assertion. Augustine was at any rate responsible for having introduced to Western theology an analogical mode of speech that originated from Platonism. While Augustine's predecessors like Victorinus and Ambrose already tried to Christianize the Platonist concept of image, Archie Spencer is right that "it was Augustine ... who first formally instituted analogical ways of theological speech" typical of the Latin West in subsequent traditions.[11]

Barth found the Platonist origins of Augustine's theology of image troubling, not least because it led to what Barth saw as the pantheistic mode of speculation that dominated much of nineteenth-century German theology and philosophy.

---

6. *CD* III/2, 21.
7. *CD* III/2, 10.
8. *GD*, 335–6.
9. *GD*, 104.
10. *GD*, 335–6.
11. Archie Spencer, *The Analogy of Faith: The Quest for God's Speakability* (Downders Grove: IVP Academic, 2015), 22. Also see Gerald Boersma, *Augustine's Early Theology of Image: A Study in the Development of Pro-Nicene Theology* (Oxford: Oxford University Press, 2016).

Instead of rejecting Augustinian speculation wholesale, however, Barth found it worthwhile and even necessary to adopt and purify it.

In the early 1920s, Barth already came to acknowledge that Augustine's *speculum Trinitatis* "was only as a kind of retrospective reference that he wanted people to understand," while "the famous auxiliary construction which Hegel changed into its opposite" falls into what Barth considers an "intolerable situation."[12] That is, Augustine, like Anselm who followed him, honored the unsublatable subjectivity of God by proceeding from faith in the speculative identity between God's *ad intra* essence and *ad extra* revelation, while Hegel posited a consummate identity between the essentialities of the human and the divine. The triune essence of the God of Augustine and Anselm is abidingly absolute. Hegel's Spirit becomes absolute only by positing itself in human otherness and sublating this otherness in the process of self-determination.

In *CD* I/1, Barth distinguishes Augustine's formulation of the "*imago trinitatis*" from Thomas's intellectualistic expansion thereof.[13] Incidentally, this is the context from which Bruce McCormack retrieves what he takes to be "Barth's 'rule,'" discussed anon.[14] Especially worth noting in this context is Barth's critical acceptance of Augustine's trinitarian speculation. "Augustine, unlike Thomas, did not fail to point out that the light which is thrown on the question by the *imago trinitatis* which we ourselves are, is always opposed by the *infirmitas* which our *iniquitas* has caused and only God can heal."[15] In *CD* I/1, Barth everywhere presupposes the theological principles underlying historic Reformed theology: "*finitum non capax infiniti*" and "*homo peccator non capax verbi divini*."[16] He is thus appreciative of the way Augustine kept human *infirmitas* in view in formulating the *imago Trinitatis*. Still, says Barth, "we for our part were unable to accept the entire theory of the *imago trinitatis*."[17]

What irritates Barth is the way Augustine tries to "establish the How of … the divine modes of being," that is, to deduce *how* the Son is born of the Father and *how* the Holy Spirit proceeds from the Father and the Son by speculative analogies between God's *opera ad intra* and the interactions between the distinct faculties of the human mind.[18] Barth insists that "in our thinking we are not to go beyond revelation."[19]

This does not mean, as McCormack would have it, that "statements about the divine modes of being antecedently in themselves cannot be different in content from those that are to be made about their reality in revelation."[20] Contra

---

12. *GD*, 107–8.
13. *CD* I/1, 479.
14. Bruce McCormack, *The Humility of the Eternal Son* (Cambridge: Cambridge University Press, 2021), 2.
15. *CD* I/1, 479.
16. *CD* I/1, 407.
17. *CD* I/1, 479.
18. *CD* I/1, 479.
19. *CD* I/1, 479.
20. McCormack, *The Humility of the Eternal Son*, 2.

5. Jesus Christ as Speculum Trinitatis (1940)

McCormack, Barth states very clearly in this context that from the content of revelation, "we must accept the fact that these three [Father, Son, and Holy Spirit] who delimit themselves from one another are antecedently a reality in God Himself."[21] More: "We can state the fact of the divine ... modes of being," even though "all our attempts to state the How of this delimitation will prove to be impossible."[22]

The question that remains to be answered here is: given that we can make sense of some *imago Trinitatis* in our human nature in light of the antecedent reality of God's triune essence given through revelation in Jesus Christ, what exactly is the analogy between this essence and its speculative image *in nobis*? Without probing into the *how* of eternal generation and procession in God's *ad intra* essence, we should at least be able to explain *how* the *speculum* permits us to speak analogically of God as Father, Son, and Holy Spirit. This Barth does not explain in *CD* I/1-2.

With the Christocentric reorientation of his basically Anselmian mode of speculation in place by 1936, Barth finally sets out to revise Augustine's trinitarian theology of image. The fruit is a paragraph published in *CD* II/1, titled "the Being of God as the One who Loves in Freedom" (§28). Hans Urs von Balthasar famously contended that this specific paragraph along with the rest of the half-volume marks the completion of Barth's turn from dialectic to analogy.[23]

The importance that Balthasar attaches to both *Anselm* and *CD* II/1 is what Bruce McCormack sets out to refute on the very first page of the monumental *Karl Barth's Critically Realistic Dialectical Theology*.[24] In this work, as we saw in Chapter 1, McCormack contends that Barth's mature theology is demarcated by the completion of the Christocentric reorientation of the doctrine of election in *Gottes Gnadenwahl* (1936). McCormack, under the influence of Matthias Gockel, later came to revise this thesis, claiming that *Gottes Gnadenwahl* was only the beginning of Barth's Christocentric revolution, the completion of which did not occur until the identification of Jesus Christ with the electing God in *CD* II/2 (1942). This means that Barth's Christocentric ontology was not yet fully spelled out in II/1.

McCormack's immense contribution to the scholarship on Barth is of course undeniable. Both Sigurd Baark and I agree with McCormack that the Christological revision of "the doctrine of election was the culmination of Barth's development as a theologian."[25] *CD* II/1, then, is not of the same revolutionary nature as *Gottes Gnadenwahl*. In other words, McCormack is right that II/1 does not mark the full maturation of Barth's theology.

---

21. *CD* I/1, 479.
22. *CD* I/1, 479.
23. See Hans Urs von Balthasar, *The Theology of Karl Barth: Exposition and Interpretation*, trans. Edward T. Oakes (San Francisco: Ignatius Press, 1992), 86–113.
24. Bruce McCormack, *Karl Barth's Critically Realistic Dialectical Theology* (Oxford: Clarendon Press, 1995), 1.
25. Sigurd Baark, *The Affirmations of Reason: On Karl Barth's Speculative Theology* (Cham: Palgrave Macmillan, 2018), 4.

However, McCormack is incorrect in thinking that Barth's identification of Jesus Christ with the electing God in II/2 indicates a denial of the assertion in II/1 that the primary absoluteness of the immanent Trinity grounds and makes possible God's *ad extra* mode of absolute being in Jesus Christ. McCormack is not right in thinking that II/2 is of a revolutionary nature. Barth does not say anything essentially different from before in II/2. He is only exploring some of the most important implications of the Christocentric reorientation of his basically Anselmian mode of speculation.

What makes *CD* II/1-2 more authoritative than *Gottes Gnadenwahl* is that in the latter Barth is only theologizing in didactic form, while in II/1-2 he sets forth his theology dogmatically. But as far as the development of Barth's theology is concerned, both II/1 and II/2, however innovative and ground-breaking they may be, are dogmatic expansions on *Gottes Gnadenwahl* that do not present any revolutionary idea against his previous theology.

One significance of II/1 to the development of Barth's speculative theology is his Christocentric revision of the *speculum Trinitatis* tradition handed down from Augustine through Anselm. Barth's ground-breaking idea is that Jesus Christ is the *imago Trinitatis apropos*. God's *ad intra* absoluteness qua subject, object, and act of love-in-freedom in God's triune essence is repeated in a secondary absoluteness in which God self-determines to be the free subject, object, and act of love in the man Jesus Christ who is very God and fully God.

In this chapter I will discuss the intellectual-historical and intellectual-biographical backgrounds of Barth's innovative incorporation of Augustine's insight into a basically Anselmian mode of theological speculation. I will give an exegesis of II/1 while referencing II/2 at key junctures to show that Barth's identification of Jesus Christ with the electing God in II/2 is based on the trinitarian ontology set forth in II/1. This serves to demonstrate how Barth reacts against the pantheistic mode of speculation typical of nineteenth-century German theology and philosophy by insisting with Augustine and Anselm the inconceivability and unsublatable subjectivity of God's abiding absoluteness. In particular, I will discuss how Barth appeals to Augustine and Anselm to address the distinctively post-Kantian problem of nature and freedom.

Brief Intellectual-Historical and Intellectual-Biographical Review

Hellenization Thesis and Revisionism's Rejection of Classical Theology

In the previous chapters we discussed how Barth's generation saw a group of theologians who reacted strongly against the influence of German idealism on Christian theology. Many of them blamed idealism for having given rise to the idolatry of Germany's mystical nationalism.

The influence of German idealism in general and Hegelianism in particular on Christian theology, however, took on a distinctively twentieth-century form after Barth's generation. Karl Rahner (1904–84) took his cue from Hegel and idealism to insist that there is no difference or distinction between the immanent Trinity and God's triune economy. Jürgen Moltmann (born 1926) and Wolfhart Pannenberg (1928–2014) appealed to German idealism, most notably Hegelianism, to develop historicist and eschatological understandings of divine presence. Whereas earlier twentieth-century Protestant theologians like Barth and Herman Bavinck (1854–1921) resorted to Feuerbach's insight to disclose the idolatrous nature of German idealism, Moltmann adopted a more recent interpretation of writers like Hegel and Hölderlin as having retained a strong notion of God's "qualitative transcendence" to creation in contrast to Feuerbach and Marx who reduced it to a mere "quantitative transcendence."[26]

One feature that sets twentieth-century theologians like Moltmann and Pannenberg apart from Protestant theologians born in the nineteenth century is their unique understanding of the classical theology of the Latin West. We saw in Chapter 2 that metaphysical theologians of the nineteenth century, idealist or not, widely accepted the view that the speculative *Denkform* of Augustine and Anselm was the seed of modern pantheism. Twentieth-century theologians like Moltmann, however, came under the influence of Adolf von Harnack's (1851–1930) famous Hellenization thesis. Instead of recognizing the continuities between Augustinian and Anselmian speculation with modern thought, they tend to think of the classical theology represented by the former as a product of the classical theism of the Hellenistic period.

Moltmann is well representative of a large cohort of twentieth-century theologians like Kazoh Kitamori (北森 嘉蔵, 1916–98) and Paul Fiddes (born 1947) in rejecting the doctrine of divine impassibility or *Apathie* as a Hellenistic idea that runs contrary to the biblical witness to Jesus Christ as the crucified God.[27] In one of his latest works, Moltmann commends Hegel and Hölderlin for having developed what Moltmann sees as a truly Christian doctrine of God who lives, evolves, and suffers in and with the world.[28]

It is in a very similar vein that revisionist Barth scholars oppose Barth's actualism to what they like to call substantialism, a term that, as we saw in Chapter 3, originated in the Whiteheadian tradition of process philosophy. In revisionism, the classical theology of Augustine and Anselm is often wrongly deemed to be a kind of substantialism that has its roots in the classical theism of Hellenistic philosophy. When revisionists impose their version of "actualistic ontology" (the thrust of which is a misleading conflation between being and act) on Barth, they exhibit a strong tendency to deny what George Hunsinger aptly calls the "Anselmian moment" of Barth's theology. They also tend to deny that Barth's mature theology can be described as "basically Chalcedonian," because they think that Chalcedon

---

26. Jürgen Moltmann, *Der lebendige Gott und die Fülle des Lebens: Auch ein Beitrag zur gegenwärtigen Atheismusdebatte* (Gütersloh: Gütersloher, 2014), 27 and 42.

27. E.g. Jürgen Moltmann, *The Trinity and the Kingdom: The Doctrine of God* (Minneapolis: Fortress Press, 1993), 21–5.

28. Moltmann, *Lebendiger Gott*, 42–3.

presupposes the substantialist ontology of Hellenistic theism, which is in their view entirely opposed to what they like to call Barth's actualistic ontology.

Platonism and Classical Theism: Barth's New Vantagepoint in CD II/1

It is true that Barth was also influenced to some extent by his Ritschlian teacher's Hellenization thesis, but there is very little textual evidence to suggest that in his earlier career up to the early 1930s, he had come to any formed opinion about the influences of Hellenistic theism on classical Western theologians like Augustine or Anselm. Barth's association of Augustine with Platonism is better explained by major developments of Augustine scholarship in the early 1930s.

In 1933 and 1934, respectively, Willy Theiler and Paul Henry published important findings on the influence of Platonism on Patristic theology in general and Augustine in particular.[29] There is no evidence of Barth's familiarity with Theiler or Henry, but "Christian Platonist" models of Augustine interpretation quickly ensued from their works, and reading the Doctor of Grace in light of Plato, Plotinus, and Porphyry became a popular trend in academic theology in the late 1930s. Perhaps more significantly than Harnack's Hellenization thesis, then, these new studies on Augustine and Platonism gave to Barth a fresh perspective on the Hellenistic background of Augustine's theology.

This may serve to explain why in *CD* I/1-2, there is no mention of Plotinus at all, let alone associations of Augustine with Platonism. In Barth's works from the 1920s up to *CD* I/2, his criticisms of Augustine characteristically focused on the ways later thinkers like Thomas Aquinas and Hegel drew on Augustine's ideas to develop theological ontology in an intellectualist and subsequently pantheistic direction.

By the time Barth began to pen *CD* II/1 in 1937, however, he had come to be sharply critical of Platonist elements in Patristic thought as a whole and Augustine's theology in particular. In his discussion of patristic formulations of divine "ἀκαταληψία" or "*incomprehensibilitas*, the incomprehensibility of God," for instance, he probes into the "linguistic problem how far they were clear about the fact that … they were saying anything basically different from what Plato and Plotinus could also say."[30] In this discussion Barth cites a passage from Augustine to suggest that Augustine's linguistic formulation did not satisfactorily break free of Platonist overtones.[31]

Barth then immediately proceeds to quote Anselm and commend him as the first thinker to have developed a distinctively Christian formulation of speculative theology free of Platonist implications:

---

29. Willy Theiler, *Porphyrios und Augustin* (Halle: Niemeyer, 1933); Paul Henry, *Plotin et l'Occident* (Louvain: Spicilegium Sacrum Lovaniense, 1934).

30. *CD* II/1, 183.

31. "De Deo loquimur, quid mirum, si non comprehendis? Si enim comprehendis, non est Deus. (Augustine, Sermo 117, 3, 5)." *CD* II/1, 183.

> Ergo Domine, non solum es, quo maius cogitari nequit, sed es quiddam maius quanm cogitari possit [Therefore, Lord, you are not only one greater than which nothing can be conceived, but you are greater than can be conceived], writes Anselm of Canterbury. And he proves his statement in this way God is He than whom no greater can be conceived. But an inconceivable is, as such, conceivable. If it were not identical with God, then it would be a greater than God. Therefore, since no greater than He can be conceived, God is Himself the inconceivable (Prosl. 15). (We may notice continually in this construction that the inconceivability of God is imputed to His positive greatness and not deduced from a human deficiency). So far as I know, it was Anselm who first used the formula—paradoxical but very important and suitable for the whole problem—that the task of theology is rationabiliter comprehendere (Deum) incomprehensibile esse [to rationally understand (God) to be incomprehensible]. (Monol. 64)[32]

Contra revisionism, Barth is not diametrically opposed to the misleadingly so-called substantialist theology represented by Augustine and Anselm. Better put, Barth never deemed the theological ontologies of Augustine or Anselm to be simply "substantialist" in a Hellenized way.

What Barth sees in Anselm is a possibility for Augustine's linguistic construction of trinitarian speculation in originally Platonist terms to be purged of remaining vestiges of Platonist implications. Anselm, as we saw, retained Augustine's *speculum Trinitatis* in *Monologion*. Barth, too, never proposed to reject it *tout court*. He just did not have sufficient intellectual tools to reconstruct it in line with his basically Anselmian *Denkform* before 1936. With his Christocentric doctrine of election in place, he was now ready to incorporate the *imago Trinitatis* into his basically Anselmian mode of speculation. In fact, the Christocentric reorientation of his speculative theology in the late 1930s emboldened him to such an extent that he would even use the Platonist language of emanation or overflow (*Überfluss*) to describe the actualistic correspondence (*Entsprechung*) between God's *ad intra* and *ad extra* modes of absolute being in CD II/1.[33]

Imago Trinitatis: *Augustine on Divine Incomprehensibility and Speakability*

The core insight that Barth retrieved from Augustine can be summed up in a brief statement: "'God is' means 'God loves.'"[34] Barth expounds on this statement in the Platonist language of emanation as well the Hegelian language of determination:

---

32. CD II/1, 184.
33. E.g. CD II/1, 280. The same language is retained in 1942. E.g. CD II/2, 10; KD II/2, 9.
34. CD II/1, 280.

This, then, is the particular actuality of the being of God ... This is the nature of God disclosed in the revelation of His name. God loves. He loves as only He can love. His loving is itself the blessing which as the One who loves He communicates to the loved. His loving is itself the ground of His loving ... His loving in the turning of the One who loves to a loved different from Himself is an emanation [*Überfluß*] of the loving with which God is blessed in Himself ... And this loving is God's being in time and eternity ... Whatever else we may have to know [*erkennen*] and confess [*bekennen*] in relation to the divine being, it will always have to be a determination [*Bestimmung*] of this being of His as the One who loves.[35]

Before proceeding to an exposition of this modern adaptation of Augustine's trinitarian speculation, it would help to offer an analysis of Augustine's own formulation here. The first thing to be noted is that the development of Augustine's thought as a whole after his conversion to Christianity was centered on the axiom of divine transcendence, delimited by the doctrine of *creatio ex nihilo*. As Janice Soskice puts it, "ultimately it is not Greek philosophy but the biblical doctrine of *creatio ex nihilo* that serves the foundation for Augustine's metaphysics of being."[36] God transcends the world not merely in a quantitative way, like heaven above the earth.[37] God is transcendent to everything that is not God, in that God alone is self-existent as the timeless Creator, while everything else came into being out of nothing, not by themselves or by some cosmic force, but by God's act of creation.[38]

Augustine's understanding of transcendence as such differs fundamentally from Platonist doctrine. For Platonism, God, variously called "the Good" or "the One," alone is transcendent, and this transcendence entails an absolute unity and simplicity that leaves no room for any sort of inward differentiation. This would mean that the Good or the One cannot even be described as being. It cannot *be* anything. It cannot even be itself, for self-being or self-identity would require self-differentiation as subject and predicate. The simple God of Platonism admits of no predication and is thus absolutely ineffable.

Augustine was opposed to radical apophaticism and sought to establish the legitimacy of cataphatic theology: he wanted to positively proclaim, "God is." He described God as *ipsum esse* or "being itself." This is primarily a philosophical exegesis of the name of God in Exodus 3:14: "I am *I AM*" (see *Confessions* 7.10.16). Some commentators deny that in identifying God as *ipsum esse* Augustine is

---

35. *CD* II/1, 280; *KD* II/1, 319. Translation revised.
36. Janet Soskice, "Augustine on Knowing God and Knowing the Self," in *Faithful Reading: New Essays in Theology in Honour of Fergus Kerr, O.P.*, ed. K. Kilby, T. O' Loughlin, and S. Oliver (London: T&T Clark, 2012), 20. Also see Yonghua Ge, "The Role of *creatio ex nihilo* in Augustine's *Confessions*," *Sino-Christian Studies* 22 (2016): 54.
37. Augustine, *Confessions*, trans. Henry Chadwick (Oxford: Oxford University Press, 1991), 124.
38. Augustine, *Confessions*, 124.

making use of an Aristotelian concept.[39] I tend to agree with Ronald Teske and Bradley Green, however, that Augustine did indeed make critical use of Aristotle.[40] In the case of Augustine's identification of God as *ipsum esse*, my view is that he would agree with Thomas Aquinas's description of God as *actus purus*—but I will refrain from digressing to defend this thesis here.

When Augustine calls God *ipsum esse*, what is implied is God's pure actuality and immediate self-identity: God does not need an other outside of God's own being in order to actualize Godself as God. This move is deeply anti-Platonist, because it posits a subject-object or subject-predicate distinction in God: it makes the predication, *God is*.

Augustine, then, was confronted with a profound challenge from the Platonist side. Accepting the doctrine of divine transcendence and simplicity, he was burdened with the task to explain how he could speak of God as being and attach to the subject God manifold predicates that stand in a relation of simplicity.

Note that Augustine's formulation of divine transcendence was much more radical than that of Plotinus or Porphyry. For one thing, even though Plotinus taught the generation of time and the timelessness of Intellect, he could never have thought that time was created *ex nihilo*. There is for Plotinus an ontological continuity between the eternal and the temporal. Augustine's doctrine of *creatio ex nihilo* entails a denial of this ontological continuity. It constitutes a resolute rejection of the Platonist notion of emanation as well as that of the pre-existence of chaotic matter. There is no substantial or essential emanation from God to creatures in Augustine's theology, and there is for him nothing that pre-exists alongside God.

This formulation of divine transcendence gives rise to a serious challenge to Augustine's ontology: how can the God of Augustine be spoken of in terms of being, if this God is so radically more transcendent and thus ineffable than the God of Platonism? In his later theology, Augustine appealed to the trinitarian dogma set forth at Nicaea to overcome this Platonist challenge.

In order to understand and express the church's confessions of faith in the biblical witness to the one transcendent God as Father, Son, and Holy Spirit, the ante-Nicene Fathers already began to adopt and revise the language of Greek philosophy made normative by the Peripatetics. In Peripatetic terminology, ὑπόστασις and οὐσία were often used as synonyms to denote "substance." Plotinus adopted this terminology and described the One, Intellect, and Soul as three principal *hypostaseis*. In Aristotelian language, although these three *hypostaseis* are ontologically connected through substantial emanations, they do not constitute a specific (adjective for "species") unity, much less a numeric one. Furthermore,

---

39. E.g. Stephen Menn, *Descartes and Augustine* (Cambridge: Cambridge University Press, 1998), 169.

40. Ronald Teske, "Augustine's Use of '*Substantia*' in Speaking about God," *Modern Schoolmen* 62 (1985): 149. Bradley Green, *Colin Gunton and the Failure of Augustine* (Eugene: Pickwick, 2011), 163–4.

as Eyjólfur Emilsson points out, in Greek philosophy in general and the writings of Plotinus in particular, ὑπόστασις "lacks all the personal characteristics" that Nicene Christianity attributes to the term.[41]

When the Nicene Fathers tried to express the biblical doctrine of the one God as Father, Son, and Holy Spirit in philosophical language, they redefined ὑπόστασις and οὐσία: God is three ὑποστάσεις in one οὐσία.[42] The *homoousion* or consubstantiality of the Father, Son, and Holy Spirit differs from Christ's consubstantiality with us in that Christ and the rest of humankind constitute a specific but not a numeric unity, while the triune *ousia* is both specifically and numerically one.

Furthermore, the fullness of the Godhead dwells in each of the three divine persons. They are not three parts of God. Rather, each person is the fullness of the Godhead. This is why Chalcedon would later speak of Mary as "mother of God" rather than merely "mother of the Son." To assert that Mary was only the mother of Christ and not the mother of God the Son would be to treat Christ and the Son as two persons; to assert that Mary was only the mother of the Son and yet not the mother of God would amount to the heretical claim that the Son is merely a part of God and not the fullness of the Godhead. Mary, of course, never became the mother of the Father or the Holy Spirit—this would be a heresy of a Sabellian sort— for the Son is neither the Father nor the Holy Spirit. But the Son *is* the fullness of God, and so Mary was rightly proclaimed by the church to be the mother of God.

Now, the triune God is a living God in everlasting relationship and activity. Theologians of the early church attempted to find analogies of the *opera ad intra* of eternal generation and procession in creaturely phenomena, which was for Barth a grave mistake. Yet, Barth appreciated the fact that patristic theology described the triune God as being-in-act who is at once immutable and dynamic.[43] In short, the Nicene Fathers confessed God as a transcendent, immutable, and simple subject in whom there is both abiding objectivity and endless activity. The God of Nicaea is thus the impassible God who could suffer without ceasing to be impassible: in becoming an object *ad extra* to Godself, God does not cease to be the subject that God is in-and-for-Godself.[44]

When Augustine was baptized in 387 A.D., the ecumenical council of 381 at Constantinople had just reaffirmed and clarified the trinitarian dogma set forth at Nicaea 325. He began to write *De Trinitate* around 400 and completed it at a much later date (possibly around 417). By the time, he had already come to a mature solution to the exegetical problem of the *tohuw* and *bohuw* in Genesis 1:2.[45] The

---

41. Eyjólfur Emilsson, *Plotinus on Intellect* (Oxford: Oxford University Press, 2007), 5.

42. See John Zizioulas, "Human Capacity and Human Incapacity: A Theological Exploration of Personhood," *Scottish Journal of Theology* 28 (1975): 409.

43. *CD* I/1, 477–9.

44. This is the salient point of Paul Gavrilyuk, *The Suffering of the Impassible God: The Dialectics of Patristic Thought* (Oxford: Oxford University Press, 2004).

45. Augustine, *Confessions*, 249.

5. Jesus Christ as Speculum Trinitatis (1940)

Creator-creature distinction was solidified by a mature formulation of *creatio ex nihilo*, and Augustine was now ready to set forth the speakability of the ineffable God by appealing to Nicene trinitarianism.

Book 2 of *De Trinitate* makes the claim that God's transcendent *substantia* is invisible and incomprehensible: God is unknowable *per essentiam*. In Book 4, Augustine stresses that the immutable *essentia* of the triune God can be known to us only speculatively through the incarnation. He sets forth a theology that would have been unimaginable upon the essentialist or substantialist presuppositions of Greek philosophy: God is "a substance both simple and manifold."[46]

What is most ground-breaking about Augustine's appeal to Nicaea, in Barth's estimation, is the way Augustine establishes God's speakability by an affirmation of God's objectivity and activity *a se*. This Augustine does by considering the biblical predication, "God is love" (1 Jn. 4:16).

In *De Trinitate*, Book 8, Augustine describes human love as *speculum Trinitatis*. "Love," explains Augustine, "is of some one that loves, and with love something is loved. Behold, then, there are three things: he that loves, and that which is loved, and love."[47] Book 9 is a continuation of this argument, beginning with exegetical comments on 1 John 4:16.[48] God is love *a se*. God does not need an other outside of God in order to actualize Godself as love. As Father, Son, and Holy Spirit, the subjectivity, objectivity, and activity of love are eternally actual in God's immutable essence. When God's *ad intra* love overflows in God's *opera ad extra*, God created Adam and Eve in correspondence with God's image (*ad imago Dei*), so that human beings are capable of self-love and love of others.

In this way, Augustine was able to speak of God on the supposition of *ad intra* acts and self-relations. Because there are abiding subjectivity, objectivity, and activity in God's self-existent essence, God as subject can admit of predicates without being sublated by the predicates. God can be spoken of as *ipsum esse* because God is being-in-act. This, as Barth sees it, is one of the most important ideas in the history of Christian doctrine and must be incorporated into his speculative theology.

In *CD* II/1, Barth credits Augustine for having laid the foundations of an actualistic ontology that is distinctively Christian. In fact, Barth's trinitarian formulation of being-in-act at this stage is admittedly retrieved from Augustine, and not Schleiermacher, Hegel, or Hermann Cohen.

> Augustine had already adduced the differentiation that in so far as it has as its object something other than God, the divine loving is not to be described passively like ours ..., but actively ... But God's act is His loving. It is His

---

46. Augustine, *On the Holy Trinity*, ed. Philip Schaff, trans. Arthur Haddan (Edinburgh: T&T Clark, 1887), 101.
47. Augustine, *On the Trinity*, 124.
48. Augustine, *On the Trinity*, 126.

blessedness in so far as it is His essence even apart from us. But He wills to have this same essence, not merely for Himself alone, but also, having it for Himself, in fellowship with us. He does not need us and yet He finds no enjoyment in His self-enjoyment. He does not suffer any want and yet He turns to [*zuwendet*] us in the emanation [*Überfluß*] of the perfection of His essence and therefore of His loving, and shares with us, in and with His love, its blessedness. This blessedness of the love of God is founded on the fact that He is Father, Son and Holy Spirit and as such loves us: as our Creator, Mediator and Redeemer, as love itself, the One who loves eternally.[49]

What must be added here is that Augustine's trinitarian speculation explicitly takes on the *Denkform* of *fide quaerens intellectum*. He is unequivocal that the truth of the Trinity is a truth of revelation to be accepted by faith and then understood by reason. Knowledge of the Trinity is knowledge only insofar as it is understanding grounded in faith. As such it differs from knowledge *apropos*, that is, God's immediate self-knowledge and knowledge of all creation.

Book 9 of *De Trinitate* begins with a reference to 1 Corinthians 8:2-3: "And the apostle: 'If any man,' he says, 'think that he knows anything, he knows nothing yet as he ought to know. But if any man love God, the same is known of Him.'"[50] Augustine stresses: "He [the apostle] has not said, has known Him, which is dangerous presumption, but 'is known of Him.'"[51] Strictly speaking, believers are known of God, and only in a secondary and analogical sense can believers be said to know God. "So also in another place, when he [the apostle] had said, 'But now after that you have known God': immediately correcting himself, he says, or rather are known of God."[52]

What Augustine is trying to say here is that human knowledge of God can never be univocal with God's self-knowledge. God's knowledge is immediate. Human knowledge is necessarily mediated and speculative before the attainment of beatific vision. That is, pre-beatifical human *scientia* necessarily begins with faith. "For a certain faith is in some way the starting-point of knowledge; but a certain knowledge will not be made perfect, except after this life, when we shall see face to face."[53]

More concretely, faith in the Trinity as revealed in the incarnation is the starting point of the believer's quest for understanding the Trinity.

> As regards this question, then, let us believe that the Father, and the Son, and the Holy Spirit is one God, the Creator and Ruler of the whole creature; and that the Father is not the Son, nor the Holy Spirit either the Father or the Son, but

---

49. *CD* II/1, 280; *KD* II/1, 319. Translation revised.
50. Augustine, *On the Trinity*, 125.
51. Augustine, *On the Trinity*, 125.
52. Augustine, *On the Trinity*, 125.
53. Augustine, *On the Trinity*, 125.

a trinity of persons mutually interrelated, and a unity of an equal essence. And let us seek to understand this, praying for help from Himself, whom we wish to understand.[54]

In other words, Augustine's *speculum Trinitatis* is not a deductive attempt at proving the truth of the Trinity from the matter-of-fact of human love. It is not even a *reductio ad absurdum*. Rather, Augustine takes as his starting point faith in the God self-revealed in Jesus Christ to be immediately self-identical as *ipsum esse* in God's triune being-in-act, and seeks to understand this starting point by an after-thinking (*Nachdenken*) of the phenomenon of human love.

It is true, as nineteenth-century historiographers of ideas like Heine would have it, that Augustinian speculation provided a prototype for Descartes and Hegel. However, Augustine's God is immediately and immutably what God is in God's triune being-in-act, and speculatively identical with what God self-determined to become in Jesus Christ. Nothing other than God can be self-determined, immediately or not. God alone "is," in the proper sense of the word as *ipsum esse*. Everything else "is" only in the sense of being-in-becoming. God, even in God's flesh-becoming, never ceased to be *ipsum esse*.

Augustine's intention, in this light, was to avoid all the monistic and pantheistic implications of Platonist speculation. And with this intention, he also precluded what Barth deemed as the incipient pantheism of Cartesian speculation and the explicit pantheism of nineteenth-century *Identitätstheologie*.

Although Barth remains critical of certain Platonist elements in Augustine's trinitarian speculation, Barth unequivocally acknowledges Augustine for reminding

> us of the mystery of the divine love which transcends all thought, of its divinity which is different from all other love and eternally surpasses all other love, and of the fact that as we have to do with God's being in God's revelation, we have to do with the one true love to which all other love can only bear witness, not of itself, not by an indwelling power of witness, but only because our creaturely loving is confronted in God's revelation with this one true love, and that we, who love as creatures, are claimed in God's revelation as the objects of this divine, this one, true loving.[55]

We can see here that by *CD* II/1, Barth has come to be appreciative not only of Augustine's trinitarian idea of God as being-in-act, but also of the speculative *Denkform* by which Augustine contemplates the Trinity as being-in-act. Barth's criticism of Augustine, as we saw, is primarily concerned with the way the Doctor of Grace tried to identify analogies between the *how* of God's *opera ad intra* and the constitution of the human mind, thus identifying the human mind as the

---

54. Augustine, *On the Trinity*, 125.
55. *CD* II/1, 280.

imago Trinitatis. Barth retains the *Denkform* of Augustine's *speculum Trinitatis* and fleshes it out Christologically by identifying Jesus Christ as the image of the Trinity *apropos*, bringing it to bear on distinctively modern problems.

Love and Freedom (§28): An Actualistic Speculum Trinitatis

Intellectual-Historical Background: Freedom and Nature in Post-Kantian Thought

Especially remarkable about Barth's critical adaptation of Augustine's trinitarian speculation is how Barth brings the *speculum Trinitatis* to bear on distinctively post-Kantian formulations of the notion of freedom in relation to nature. Because of their significance to Barth's intellectual-historical as well as socio-political context, I will take a longer detour at this juncture to introduce the history of these ideas.

I begin here with Kant's notoriously difficult notion of transcendental freedom. Michael Rosen's recent work demonstrates that this Kantian notion is central to later idealist formulations of freedom.[56] The basic definition of the notion itself is quite simple. Derk Pereboom provides a neat summary thereof: "Transcendental freedom consists in the power of agents to produce actions without being causally determined by antecedent conditions, nor by their natures, in exercising this power."[57]

The difficulties associated with this ostensibly simple notion arise from the context in which it is set forth, where Kant tackles the antinomy between determinism and indeterminism. Spinoza's identification of God with nature is representative of a deterministic metaphysics according to which there is no genuine contingency in the universe. All events are predetermined by prior causes governed by the laws of nature.

Kant, of course, rejected this view. In the theoretical use of reason, however, he deemed it impossible to offer any satisfactory proof for transcendental freedom. In the theoretical use of reason, transcendental freedom can be as easily refuted as physiocracy (i.e., the rule of nature).[58] The antinomy of pure reason concerning nature and freedom is such that

> nature and transcendental freedom are as different as lawfulness and lawlessness; the former burdens the understanding with the difficulty of seeking the ancestry of occurrences ever higher in the series of causes, because the causality in them is at every time conditioned, but it promises in compensation a thoroughgoing and lawful unity of experience, while the mirage of freedom, on the contrary,

---

56. Michael Rosen, *The Shadow of God: Kant, Hegel, and the Passage from Heaven to History* (Cambridge: Harvard University Press, 2022), 67–102.

57. Derk Pereboom, "Kant on Transcendental Freedom," *Philosophy and Phenomenological Research* 73 (2006): 537.

58. Immanuel Kant, *Critique of Pure Reason,* ed. and trans. Paul Guyer and Allen Wood (Cambridge: Cambridge University Press), A447/B475. Henceforth abbreviated as *CPR*.

5. Jesus Christ as Speculum Trinitatis (1940)   165

though of course offering rest to the inquiring understanding in the chain of causes by leading it to an unconditioned causality that begins to act from itself, since it is itself blind, breaks away from the guidance of those rules by which alone a thoroughly connected experience is possible.[59]

Despite the antinomy, however, Kant insists that transcendental freedom must be accepted by faith as a regulative principle in the theoretical use of reason (what is), and that it becomes immanent and constitutive in the practical use of reason (what ought to be). He is clear that "the abolition of transcendental freedom would also simultaneously eliminate all practical freedom."[60]

In the practical use of reason, freedom is revealed to be something quite other than lawlessness. Non-coercion of the power of choice (*Willkür*) is only a negative presupposition of what can properly be called freedom, namely, autonomy. In the *Groundwork to the Metaphysics of Morals*, Kant defines and discusses autonomy under the rubric of his all-famous notion of the categorical imperative.

Autonomy is the third formula of the categorical imperative: it is "the idea of the will of every rational being as a universally legislating will."[61] Human beings are autonomous in that "every rational being, as an end in itself, must be able to view itself as at the same time universally legislating with regard to any law whatsoever to which it may be subject, because it is just this fittingness of its maxims for universal legislation that marks it out as an end in itself."[62] In the second *Critique*, Kant identifies human moral agents as the "lawgiving members of a kingdom of morals."[63]

This does not amount to a denial that God is the supreme moral legislator. In the third *Critique* Kant clarifies that God is not only the supreme determining ground of our moral will, but also "the highest morally legislative author."[64] Human beings are derivatively legislative in the sense that "*given* the constitution of the faculty of our reason, we could not even make comprehensible the kind of purposiveness related to the moral law and its object that exists in this final end without an author and ruler of the world who is at the same time a moral legislator."[65]

On this ground he distinguishes between a "juridically civil society" and an "ethically civil" one in *Religion within the Bounds of Bare Reason*.[66] An ethically

---

59. Kant, *Critique of Pure Reason*, A447/B475.
60. Kant, *Critique of Pure Reason*, A534/B562.
61. Immanuel Kant, *Groundwork of the Metaphysics of Morals*, ed. and trans. Mary Gregor and Christine Korsgaard (Cambridge: Cambridge University Press, 2012), 43.
62. Kant, *Groundwork*, 49.
63. Immanuel Kant, *Critique of Practical Reason*, ed. and trans. Mary Gregor (Cambridge: Cambridge University Press, 1997), 68.
64. Immanuel Kant, *Critique of the Power of Judgment*, ed. Paul Guyer, trans. Paul Guyer and Eric Matthews (Cambridge: Cambridge University Press, 2000), 320.
65. Kant, *Critique of the Power of Judgment*, 320.
66. Immanuel Kant, *Religion within the Bounds of Bare Reason*, trans. Werner Pluhar (Indianapolis: Hackett, 2009), 103.

civil society, in contrast to a juridically civil society, is one in which "the people itself cannot be legislative": "God as the moral ruler of the world" becomes the ruler of human society when an ethically civil society, having now left the state of nature to enter into a social contract, becomes the "people of God" by making laws "according to the laws of virtue" universally discoverable by pure practical reason.[67]

According to this Kantian paradigm, the rule of law presupposes transcendental freedom. Michael Rosen rightly argues that transcendental freedom "is an ingenious and complicated attempt to make use of the broader doctrines of transcendental idealism to reconcile free human agency with the claims of physics and the natural sciences. Without such a defense, Kant's idea of human life as being given value by freedom would be untenable and divine punishment of human beings for their misdeed obviously unjust."[68]

There are of course many difficulties with Kant's notion of transcendental freedom as something noumenal. How can something that is *an sich* be known to human beings whose cognition is conditioned by spatio-temporality? That, as suggested in Chapter 2, was a question that later German idealists sought to answer.

Hegel, for one, agreed with Kant that something merely *an sich* is unknowable. We can only know of that which is *für sich*, something that has entered into a history of relatedness with otherness conditioned by spatio-temporality. But through what is *für sich*, we can after-think that which was *an sich* and reflectively speculate on that which is in the course of becoming *an und für sich*, namely, the absolute.

In this light, then, there is some truth to the description of German idealists like Hegel as "post-Kantian." It is true that they developed ideas of freedom that differed vastly from Kant's vision. However, there is something about Kant's notion of transcendental freedom that was bequeathed to subsequent German philosophy, especially the idealist tradition.

The salient feature of Kant's conception of freedom is "that freedom involves the emancipation from arbitrariness, and that 'arbitrariness' can consist in the purely contingent exercise of will ('*Willkür*') as well as in being subject to exogenous causal forces. This Kantian idea," Rosen demonstrates, "runs through the later German Idealists—Fichte, Schelling, Hegel—and constitutes an interpretive key to their very un-Kantian seeming philosophical projects."[69]

I will discuss Hegel's alternative to Kant in more detail and explore its social implications in Chapter 7, but it is worth our while to introduce Hegel's idea of freedom briefly at this juncture. The first thing to be noted for our purpose is that if Kant's discourse on freedom focuses on the human side, then Hegel's is much more emphatically theological. Hegel, in short, envisions human freedom

---

67. Kant, *Religion*, 108–9.
68. Rosen, *The Shadow of God*, 22–3.
69. Rosen, *The Shadow of God*, 23.

as the "self-actualization" (*Selbstverwirklichung*) of Spirit's absoluteness in human consciousness and society: "freedom is precisely ... to be at home with oneself in one's other, to be dependent upon oneself, to be the determining factor for oneself."[70] This freedom that is "at home with oneself in one's other" is freedom *an und für sich*, that is, absolute freedom. Absolute freedom is attained through three stages or moments: the subjective, the objective, and the absolute.

Subjective freedom is the moment in which Spirit is merely *an sich*. In this stage Spirit is indeterminate. This can be likened to an unmarried person who lives by herself or himself. The person may seem to enjoy the ostensible freedom of singleness. Without the fulfilment of personhood through an intimate relationship, however, this person remains indeterminate in the relative arbitrariness of her or his will and desires.

When I was single, dining out by myself meant choosing any restaurant and ordering any menu item to my liking. These choices can be arbitrary in two contradictory ways: they may be determined by my instinctual or habitual preference for proteins, fats, and carbohydrates (determinism), or they may be contingent upon the randomness of my desires (indeterminism).

Becoming a married person meant that dining out would come to involve making choices together with my beloved. Initially, my choices would often conflict with my wife's. She would, for instance, choose salad as a side when I did not expect our deep-fried fish to come with anything other than chips at a very local restaurant in England.

Entering into relationship with an other is what Hegel calls the objective moment of freedom. The objective often stands in conflict with the subjective. Yet, without this "dialectical" moment of contradiction, my ego in itself would remain indeterminate and arbitrary. Without being related to an other outside of myself, I have no identity, and without an identity, I am not genuinely free, for genuine freedom is actualized through expressions of who I am: freedom is emancipation from arbitrariness.

Absolute freedom is the reconciliation of the subjective and the objective. At some point in my marriage, my wife and I became at home with ourselves in one another in matters such as choosing between salad and chips as well as much more important issues in which we were already at one accord when we first met. There is hardly any more conflict between the subjective and the objective in our married life now.

This moment of reconciliation may sound quite appealing as far as marriages are concerned, but when applied to society, it would entail an absolute and totalitarian power that abolishes genuine individuality. I will discuss this *Lebenstotalität* in more detail in Chapter 7.

---

70. G. W. F. Hegel, *Encyclopedia of the Philosophical Sciences in Basic Outline, Part 1: Logic*, ed. and trans. Klaus Brinkmann and Daniel Dahlstrom (Cambridge: Cambridge University Press, 2010), 60.

In this chapter I will focus on the theological dimension of Hegel's notion of absolute freedom, which is problematic not only from a socio-political perspective. It carries theological implications profoundly challenging to classical Christian understandings of God's freedom grounded in the doctrine of divine aseity. According to classical theology, God does not need an other outside of God to actualize Godself as God, and this is the primary sense in which God is said to be free. It is expressed in terms of God's *potentia absoluta*.

Hegel, in contrast to classical theology, projects the moments of human freedom unto a pseudo-object given the name of God. He presents an anthropomorphic picture according to which God's essentiality is unactualized and indeterminate in itself. Spirit *an sich* is not yet actualized as God. Without the world, God is indeterminate and therefore unfree.

God's freedom, according to Hegel, has to be realized in and with the world. Spirit enters into objective freedom to encounter creatures in a historical progress fraught with irrationalities manifested through conflicts and contradictions. Only by being reconciled to the world does Spirit attain absolute freedom and become truly free as God.

Barth may not be entirely accurate about Kant, but Barth's assessment of Hegel in relation to Kant in *CD* II/1 is quite on the mark:

> Kant speaks forcefully of God. But when he defines God as the necessary postulate of the limit and goal of pure reason, and the equally necessary presupposition of the law-giver and guarantor of practical reason, what else does he do (without adding substantially to his anthropology) but powerfully to speak again and strictly about man (about the depth of the nature of his rational capacity)? Again, Hegel speaks forcefully of God. But when he describes Him as the process of absolute spirit, which exists eternally in itself, eternally proceeds from itself, and existing in itself and outside itself is eternally the same, this is indeed a forceful and profound description of the movement of nature and spirit which proceeds from ourselves and returns to ourselves. But it is not a description of God, whose movement is infinitely more than our self-movement even when the latter is hypostatised, i.e., projected into eternity, and by whose movement this hypostatisation and projection is necessarily forbidden and prevented.[71]

To address the post-Kantian problem of freedom, Barth adopts Augustine's *speculum Trinitatis*. George Hunsinger helpfully points out that Barth's purpose in aligning himself with the "classical theists" in affirming the pure actuality of "God's triune being" is to ensure that in his theological discourse, "both absolute being and a contingent will" is ascribed to the God who is absolutely free prior to and apart from any *ad extra* decision or relationship.[72]

---

71. *CD* II/1, 267.
72. George Hunsinger, *Reading Barth with Charity: A Hermeneutical Proposal* (Grand Rapids: Baker Academic, 2015), 168–9.

Being of God as the One who Loves in Freedom

The thrust of Barth's trinitarian response to the post-Kantian problem of freedom is found in *CD* II/1, §28, "the Being of God as the One who loves in freedom." Agreeing with the key insight that German idealists like Hegel inherited from Kant, Barth stresses, in Kantian terms, that "there is no caprice [*Willkür*] about the freedom of God."[73] Barth, in line with the Augustinian as well as the post-Kantian heritage, is at pains to emphasize that freedom—divine or human freedom—is not arbitrariness.

Barth's refusal to define freedom in terms of *Willkür* is strikingly neglected in the revisionist oeuvre. According to McCormack, "the freedom of God is a freedom for self-determination … It is God's Lordship over all things, including his own being."[74] This implies that "God's freedom is finally the freedom to exist—or not to exist. The opposite of the determination to be God in the covenant of grace is not a determination to be God in some other way; it is rather the absence of such a determination, which would mean choosing not to exist."[75]

Citing Frederick Beiser's introductory work on Hegel, McCormack acknowledges that "determination" is "a word which has its provenance in German idealism."[76] Yet, McCormack does not demonstrate adequate familiarity with Hegel. McCormack does not seem to realize that in using this Hegelian term, Barth's intention is precisely to express partial agreement with Hegel, that an indeterminate subject is unfree. On Hegel's view, a subject becomes free only when it begins to become determinate in relation to an object, and absolutely free when reconciled to the object.

For Hegel, as for Barth, the subjective freedom to exist or not to exist cannot be freedom in any "final" sense. God's freedom, for both Hegel and Barth, is finally freedom in-and-for-Godself, in the fully determinate subjectivity, objectivity, and activity of God's absolute being. With Hegel, then, Barth asserts that genuine freedom is freedom in actual relationship. Without objectivity and activity, there is no actual freedom.

Yet, Barth maintains against Hegel that God does not need the world to actualize absolute freedom. God is absolutely free both in-and-for-Godself and in relation to an other outside of God's being. Even God's absolute freedom outside of Godself, in God's secondary objectivity, is for Barth the ground rather than the result of God's decision to enter into loving fellowship with an other outside of Godself.

---

73. *CD* II/1, 318; *KD* II/1, 358.

74. Bruce McCormack, "Election and the Trinity, Theses in Response to George Hunsinger," *Scottish Journal of Theology* 63 (2010): 222.

75. McCormack, "Election and the Trinity," 223.

76. McCormack, "Election and the Trinity," 211. Citing Frederick Beiser, *Hegel* (London: Routledge, 2005), 60, 74–5.

Barth thus introduces the notion of God's primary and secondary absoluteness with an appeal to Augustine's trinitarian speculation, which Barth fleshes out with the Christocentric ontology developed in 1936 (see Chapter 4).

> We have seen that the freedom of God, as His freedom in Himself, His *primary absoluteness*, has its truth and reality in the inner Trinitarian life of the Father with the Son by the Holy Spirit. It is here, and especially in the divine mode as the Son who is the "image of the invisible God" (Col. 1^{15}), in God Himself, that the divine freedom in its aspect of communion with the other, i.e., the *secondary absoluteness* of God, has its original truth … God Himself becomes Another in the person of His Son. The existence of the world is not needed in order that there should be otherness for Him. Before all worlds, in His Son He has otherness in Himself from eternity to eternity.[77]

In other words, God is absolute (that is, fully determinate as being-in-and-for-Godself) in the primary sense that as Father, Son, and Holy Spirit, love is fully actual in God's eternal essence. There is an endless communion of subjectivity, objectivity, and activity in the God who is love. God as such is absolutely free prior to and apart from election and creation.

Barth's exposition of God's freedom in terms of primary absoluteness is first intended as a refutation of metaphysical determinism. He is basically in agreement with the Kantian view that freedom is what Rosen calls "emancipation from arbitrariness," which can "consist … in being subject to exogenous causal forces" (as we saw earlier).

God's primary absoluteness and freedom means that "He is the same even in Himself, even before and after and over His works, and without them. They are bound to Him, but He is not bound to them. They are nothing without Him. But He is who He is without them."[78] God does not need to determine Godself as God by acting toward an other outside of God's essence.

This is a position that Barth emphatically and explicitly retains in *CD* II/2, where he draws out the implications of his identification of Jesus Christ as the subject and object of election from *Gottes Gnadenwahl* (see Chapter 4): "God is love. But He is also perfect freedom. Even if there were no such relationship [between God and humankind in Christ], even if there were no other outside of Him, He would still be love."[79]

The question is: how can we know *that* (without trying to know *how*) God *is* love qua Father, Son, and Holy Spirit? Even Augustine, as we saw, acknowledges that what Barth calls God's primary absoluteness is not immediately knowable to creatures.

God's primary absoluteness is for Barth speculatively mediated to us only through God's secondary absoluteness, introduced in the block quote above.

---

77. *CD* II/1, 317. Emphases mine.
78. *CD* II/1, 260.
79. *CD* II/2, 6.

5. Jesus Christ as Speculum Trinitatis (1940)

"Absoluteness," a term borrowed from Hegel as we have seen, refers to the communion of subjectivity and objectivity through activity. God becomes absolute in a secondary mode in that God becomes a creaturely other in the one unabridged subject of the Son who is very God and very human. In Jesus Christ the *ad intra* objectivity of God's love overflowed into an *ad extra* other in election.

Even prior to creation, then, God was absolute not only in-and-for-Godself, but also in relation to the *ad extra* object that God self-determined to become in Jesus Christ. God's secondary absoluteness, in other words, is the covenantal basis of God's relationship to the world. God does not need to be reconciled to the world in order to become absolutely free in relation to the world. Contra Hegel, reconciliation is grounded in God's absoluteness, in both its primary and secondary modes, and not the other way around.

God's election to be God-for-us has its eternal objectivity in none other than Jesus Christ. Even in its secondary reality, God's love-in-freedom is already absolute before the creation of the world, while the history of reconciliation of the world to God is no more and no less than the external basis of God's secondary mode of absolute being.

Barth's discourse on God's freedom in this secondary mode of absolute being is in line with the Kantian opposition to indeterminism, which defines freedom as arbitrariness in contingent exercises of the power of choice. Barth insists that God's decision to enter into the secondary mode of absoluteness is grounded in and corresponds perfectly to God's primary absoluteness. This decision is therefore not a contingent exercise of the power of choice. To be sure, the choices that God makes are entirely contingent upon God's will, but God's will is not an abstract entity detached from or prior to God's absolute essence as the one who loves in freedom. Barth explains in II/1:

> As and before God seeks and creates fellowship with us, He wills and completes this fellowship in Himself. In Himself He does not will to exist for Himself, to exist alone. On the contrary, He is Father, Son and Holy Spirit and therefore alive in His unique being with and for and in another. The unbroken unity of His being, knowledge and will is at the same time an act of deliberation, decision and intercourse. He does not exist in solitude but in fellowship. Therefore what He seeks and creates between Himself and us is in fact nothing else but what He wills and completes and therefore is in Himself.[80]

God's secondary freedom, in other words, does not sublate, determine, or complete God's primary freedom, which is eternally complete in-and-for-Godself. Rather, the freedom of God's love *pro nobis* is an *ad extra* repetition of the freedom of God's love *a se*.

The speculative identity between God's primary and secondary modes of love-in-freedom is what allows us to know the immutability of the triune God through

---

80. *CD* II/1, 275.

the human mutability that Christ has entered into. "In the light of what He is in His works it is no longer an open question what He is in Himself. In Himself He cannot, perhaps, be someone or something quite other, or perhaps nothing at all. But in His works He is Himself revealed as the One He is."[81]

This discourse on God's primary and secondary modes of being entails, *inter alia*, that God is necessarily the Trinity and contingently the electing God. This contingency, however, is not indeterminate arbitrariness. God became the electing God by a choice that corresponds perfectly to what God necessarily is in-and-for-Godself.

> God's loving is necessary, for it is the being, the essence and the nature of God. But for this very reason it is also free from every necessity in respect of its object. God loves us, and loves the world, in accordance with His revelation. But He loves us and the world as He who would still be One who loves without us and without the world; as He, therefore, who needs no other to form the prior ground of His existence as the One who loves and as God. Certainly He is who He is wholly in His revelation, in His loving-kindness, and therefore in His love for us.[82]

In this passage Barth is doing a very subtle bit of un-Hegelian Hegeling. Hegel in fact maintained a qualitative sense of divine transcendence in his system, such that Spirit and world history never entirely merge into one another. For this reason, world history is full of appearances of the divine, but nothing in God's revelation is for Hegel wholly God.

When Barth says that God "is who He is wholly in His revelation," he is denying that God's "being, speaking and acting" in Jesus Christ are only an "appearance [*Schein*]" of God's transcendent essence.[83] In the man Jesus Christ is the fullness of the triune Godhead, and because Christ has come, everything purported in any Hegelian sense to be "the appearance of the divine [*dem Schein-Göttlichen*]" must be repudiated as "the demonic."[84]

But when Barth says that God "is who He is wholly in His revelation," he is also drawing on Hegel's insight. The insight is that a subject is identical with itself in different moments of the process of its (self-)determination. Her Late Majesty Queen Elizabeth II was the same person from 1952 to 2022. The Platinum Jubilee did not make her a different person. It only added to her the new feature or determination of being a monarch with a seventy-year reign. It is this logic of mediation which allows Barth to say that the *Logos ensarkos* is wholly identical with the *Logos asarkos*. The identity between God in God's eternal "essence and nature" and God "in His revelation" is established in the sense of this logic of mediation.

---

81. *CD* II/1, 260.
82. *CD* II/1, 280.
83. *CD* II/1, 496; *KD* II/1, 558.
84. *CD* II/1, 409; *KD* II/1, 461.

5. Jesus Christ as Speculum Trinitatis (1940)

Faith in the mediated identity between the same subject God in the mode of aseity and that of promeity is what allows for speculative human knowledge of God's immediate self-identity within the God's triune essence. This is exactly what Barth says in II/2, where he fleshes out the content of the statement that Jesus Christ "is" the electing God: "To be truly Christian, the doctrine of God must ... [make] the Subject known as One which in virtue of its innermost being, willing and nature does not stand outside all relationships, but stands in a definite relationship *ad extra* to another."[85] Barth stresses here: "It is not as though the object of this relationship ... constitutes a part of the reality of God outside of God ... It is not as though God is forced into this relationship ... It is not as though He is in any way constrained or compelled by this other."[86]

This is completely in line with what Barth states in II/1:

Before all worlds, in His Son He has otherness in Himself from eternity to eternity. But because this is so, the creation and preservation of the world, and relationship and fellowship with it, realised as they are in perfect freedom, without compulsion or necessity, do not signify an alien or contradictory expression of God's being, but a natural, the natural expression of it *ad extra*.[87]

In other words, creation is a *free* act of God not in the sense that it was out of a whimsical choice, but rather in that it perfectly corresponds to God's eternal essence. More concretely, creation is the external basis on which the history of Jesus Christ who is the very subject God in a secondary mode of absolute being is enacted.

The world is, because and as the Son of God is ... When we now learn that, over and beyond all this, it is said of the same Son of God: σὰρξ ἐγένετο (Jn. 1¹⁴), that therefore, besides being Creator, He became creature, it is clear that in this singular and supreme relationship and fellowship between God and the world realised in the incarnation we have the quintessence of all possible relationship and fellowship generally and as such, and that in the transcendent freedom of God thus expressed we see the archetype and the norm of all the possible ways in which He expresses His freedom in this relationship and fellowship.[88]

Correspondingly, genuine human freedom is the activation and repetition of this freedom of love in a relationship and fellowship already determined in Jesus Christ once for all. What this means concretely and how Barth responds to Kantian and Hegelian views of freedom therewith will be discussed in Chapter 7. Suffice it to say here that the *imago Trinitatis* means for Barth that God's archetypal

---

85. *CD* II/2, 5–6.
86. *CD* II/2, 5–6.
87. *CD* II/1, 317.
88. *CD* II/1, 317.

love-in-freedom is re-enacted among creatures in an analogical and ectypal manner, determined first and foremost in Jesus Christ.

Jesus Christ is as such, strictly speaking, the image of the Trinity *apropos*. Barth expands on this in *CD* III under the rubric of the doctrine of creation, where he identifies Jesus Christ as the very *imago Dei*. "[T]he term 'image'" refers to "a correspondence and similarity between the two relationships," namely, "the relationship within the being of God on the one side" and "between the being of God and that of man on the other."[89] The human essence is determined from above by the God-human relationship in Jesus Christ who is the image of God. Christ the electing God is for himself (*für sich*) as the elected human, and he as the elected human is for himself as electing God. Human beings created in his image as such are ontologically determined to be for God, as God is *pro nobis* in Jesus Christ.

Furthermore, human nature is determined in Christ, and so "the characteristic and essential mode of man's being, is in its root fellow-humanity."[90] Human love and freedom in fellowship correspond to the love and freedom of the triune God manifested in Jesus Christ. The image of the "God who is no *Deus solitarius* but *Deus triunus*" cannot be "mirrored in a *homo solitarius*."[91]

The originally Augustinian language of *speculum Trinitatis* is clear in this passage. What Barth wants to say is that human love in the freedom of fellowship is a mirror of God's love and freedom in Jesus Christ. It is impossible for us to deduce the triune mode of God's being from a starting point in the phenomenon of human relationships. Faith in Jesus Christ as *imago Trinitatis apropos* is the starting point by which we can after-think this phenomenon and reflect on the immutable love and freedom of the triune God.

It may be worthwhile to point out here that for Barth, the *imago Dei* is expressed "primarily and supremely," though not exclusively, "in marriage," in which "God manifests Himself in His unity as Creator-God and God of the covenant, who as such is the God of free, electing grace."[92] This is a powerful statement against dominant nineteenth-century views of absolute freedom to which German idealists like Hegel and Schelling gave rise. According to these views, absolute freedom is realized supremely not through the institution of marriage, but through the modern state. From a Christian viewpoint, lacking in the modern state is the kind of covenantal love and self-sacrifice of God revealed in the person and history of Jesus Christ. There is no genuine freedom of reconciliation in the absolute state.

Marriage, by contrast, best reflects God's loving freedom in election and covenant, which "gives unconditional and compelling character to the requirement of monogamy": the "choice of love" between husband and wife corresponds to God's "free and gracious election, and … the bond of marriage the faithfulness of

---

89. *CD* III/2, 220.
90. *CD* III/4, 117.
91. *CD* III/4, 117.
92. *CD* III/4, 197.

his covenant, so that it is true to say: 'God created man in his own image, in the image of God created he him; male and female created he them'" (Gen. 1:27).[93]

This understanding of creation and fellowship finds its basis in Barth's Christocentric reorientation of Augustine's *speculum Trinitatis* in II/1, §28. "Creation itself ... is already a seeking and creating of fellowship. This seeking and creating is heightened in the work of revelation itself, which is not so much a continuation of creation as its supersession, and is identical with the reconciliation of sinful man in the incarnation, death and resurrection of the Son of God."[94]

In this passage Barth again engages intensely with Hegelian ideas. Hegel, too, asserts that creation is Spirit's act of seeking and creating relationship with otherness. Creation as such is Spirit's act of revealing itself, manifesting itself in an other by veiling itself in historical contingencies and irrationalities. When Barth says that revelation "is not so much a continuation of creation," he is acknowledging that while creation is revelatory in some sense, it does not consist of appearances of the divine subject. Creation is revelatory in a speculative sense in that it is determined by the history of the covenant in Jesus Christ and serves as the external basis of this history. Creation as such is not immediately identical to revelation.

The person and history of Jesus Christ alone is revelation in the most proper sense of the term, in that the man Jesus Christ is himself the very unsublatable subject God in a secondary mode of absolute being. In Barth's own words from the passage above, revelation is "identical with the reconciliation of sinful man in the incarnation, death and resurrection of the Son of God." As such revelation is the "supersession" of creation.

Barth's word choice is especially noteworthy here. He uses the adjective *überbietend*, from the verb *überbieten*. It means "to surpass," and carries the connotation of "to eliminate" in the sense of elimination in a competition or tournament. This unusual word choice may reflect Barth's reluctance to use the Hegelian term *Aufhebung* in this context. Revelation does not sublate creation because revelation does not negate creation. Creation is the external basis of revelation; revelation is the purpose of creation. Revelation is God's becoming a creature without ceasing to be God, and revelation as such is surpassingly superior to creation.

This surpassing (*überbietend*) superiority means, *inter alia*, that God does not need creation as an object of love to determine Godself as God. Revelation as the history of God's covenant with us in Jesus Christ (grace) makes creation (nature) determinate. That is to say, grace does not just perfect nature. Surely it does. But what is more important is that grace "supersedes" nature and determines nature "from above" (*von oben*).

93. *CD* III/4, 198.
94. *CD* II/1, 274; *KD* II/1, 307. The translation is somewhat problematic. The original reads: "Es potenziert sich aber dieses Suchen und Schaffen in dem die Schöpfung nicht sowohl fortsetzenden als überbietenden Werk der Offenbarung selber: identisch mit der Versöhnung des sündigen Menschen in der Fleischwerdung, im Tode und in der Auferstehung des Sohnes Gottes."

In *CD* II/2, Barth, on the basis of his innovative adaption of Augustine's *speculum Trinitatis*, daringly describes the grace that determines nature in Platonist language as an "emanation" or "overflow" (*Überfluss*) of the essential love of the triune God, a term that he already started to use in II/1 (as we saw).

> The fact that God makes this movement, the institution of the covenant, the primal decision 'in Jesus Christ,' which is the basis and goal of all His works—that is grace. Speaking generally, it is the demonstration, the emanation [*Überfluß*] of the love which is the being of God, that He who is entirely self-sufficient, who even within Himself cannot know isolation, willed even in all His divine glory to share His life with another, and to have that other as the witness of His glory.[95]

The speculative *Denkform* of Augustine's *speculum Trinitatis*, now fleshed out Christologically, is neatly summed up in this passage. The being of God in the primary mode of existence is the pure actuality of love in the fellowship of Father, Son, and Holy Spirit: God "within Himself cannot know isolation." God's gracious election—God's "primal decision 'in Jesus Christ'"—is not immediately identical with the *ad intra* "love that is the being of God." Election as the "institution of the covenant" is a "demonstration" and "emanation" of God's freely loving essence.

It is not an ontological emanation of some Platonist, Hegelian, or other pantheist or panentheist sort. It is an *ad extra* mode of God's absoluteness that corresponds perfectly to God's triune essence *ad intra*. The subject God enters into a secondary mode of being-in-act without ceasing to be the same unsublatable subject.

Because God *is* love in God's primary absoluteness qua triune being-in-and-for-Godself, God can become God-for-us in a secondary, self-determined absoluteness without sublating God's subjectivity. That is to say, God can freely become an object of God's love outside of God's being without altering all that God is in-and-for-Godself, because within God's immutable being is an endless fellowship of the subject, object, and act of love. In this sense and only in this sense is God's love *pro nobis* a "demonstration" and "emanation" of God's love *a se*: it is, again, an emanation of the unsublatable subject God in an *ad extra* mode of relationality, that is, objectivity and activity. It is an *analogia relationis* rather than *analogia entis*.

Conclusion

The foregoing analysis shows, *inter alia*, that the *Denkform* of Barth's actualistic and Christocentric revision of Augustine's *speculum Trinitatis* is not what McCormack would have liked to describe as a "quasi-transcendental" argument. There is no "must be" or "ought to be" in Barth's *Denkform* here.

---

95. *CD* II/2, 10; *KD* II/2, 9. Translation revised.

Barth is not saying, "Jesus loves me, therefore God ought to be triune," as it were—this argument would have been a quasi-transcendental deduction. What McCormack fails to see is that Barth's argument is not deductive or even reductive— it is not even what Karl Ameriks might call a "regressive" deduction.[96] Even as *disputatio*, dogmatic theology is for Barth primarily *explicatio*: it is the *expositio* of what the church confesses by faith. Barth has no interest in any transcendental or even quasi-transcendental sort of deductive reasoning, not even by a *reductio ad absurdum*.

Barth begins with faith in revelation: that is, faith in the speculative identity between God's primary and secondary absoluteness. He finds his starting point in the church's confession of faith that Jesus is God, and that God is Father, Son, and Holy Spirit. This confession means that God's love in Christ is a demonstration of God's essential being in the act of love, and Barth seeks to explicate this demonstration. In this explication he comes to understand *that* (but not *how*) God is immediately self-identical as *ipsum esse* qua Father, Son, and Holy Spirit. He also comes to understand *that* and *how* "God so loved the world" (Jn. 3:16), as well as *that* and *how* we are commanded to and actually do "love one another" as "God so loved us" (1 Jn. 4:11). In light of God's love *a se* and *pro nobis*, Barth comes to understand the sense in which God is free in-and-for-Godself and free in relation to us. He then tries to explicate the sense in which all humans are said to be endowed by their Creator with a freedom that is essential and inalienable.

This *credo ut intelligam* program is the speculative *Denkform* of an Augustinian and Anselmian mode. It is not some transcendental or quasi-transcendental argument with (neo-)Kantian origins. As we shall see in the ensuing chapters, this carries profound theoretical as well as practical implications. The speculative character of Barth's Christocentric actualism is crucial for ensuring the genuinely theological, as opposed to anthropological, essence of Christian theology. It ensures that nothing in God's good creation is idolized as some *Schein-Göttlichen* or *Götterfunken*. Barth's insistence that Christ alone is the *imago Trinitatis apropos* constitutes a powerful criticism of all forms of idolatry, not least the mystical nationalism that culminated in the Third Reich, which posited itself as a *Schein-Göttlichen* that Barth denounced as "the demonic."

---

96. Karl Ameriks, *Interpreting Kant's Critiques* (Oxford: Oxford University Press, 2005), 25.

Chapter 6

PAINTING THE PORTRAIT: JESUS CHRIST AS ELECTING, ELECTED, AND ELECTION (1942)

Introduction

In the previous chapter we saw how in *CD* II/1, written between the summers of 1937 and 1939, Barth applied the Christocentric ontology developed in 1936 to the classical doctrine of *speculum Trinitatis*, making this originally Augustinian analogy the core of his speculative theology. The thrust of Barth's adaptation of the *speculum Trinitatis* is that God's primary absoluteness, the essential being of God as love-in-freedom, is mirrored through God's secondary absoluteness, the *ad extra* mode of God's being as love-in-freedom in the person and history of Jesus Christ. "Absoluteness" in this context, as we saw, is a term retrieved from Hegel's innovative adaptation of Augustine's construal of God as the subject, object, and act of love—God as being-in-and-for-Godself. Barth contends against Hegel that God as the one who loves in freedom in both the primary and secondary modes of God's being remains unceasingly absolute. That is, the subjectivity of God's absoluteness is unsublatable both in God's eternal triune essence and in relation to God's covenant-partner in Jesus Christ.

The second volume of the *Church Dogmatics* was written almost in one breath from the summer of 1937 to the winter of 1941. The seminars and lectures Barth delivered during the academic semesters did not seem to slow down his progress, and his project remained uninterrupted even by military duties. When *CD* II/2 was due for the press in the spring of 1942, Barth, on his own account, read part of the proofs while serving in the military, "correcting them late at night in a federal guardroom."[1]

In this half-volume, as we saw briefly in the previous chapter, Barth retains the *speculum Trinitatis* developed in II/1. In that regard, he does not say anything different from what he already said in the 1940 half-volume. In 1942, he continues to speak of God's secondary absoluteness as an emanation (*Überfluss*) of God's primary absoluteness—an emanation of relationality and activity of the same unsublatable subject God.

---

1. Eberhard Busch, *Karl Barth: His Life from Letters and Autobiographical Texts*, trans. John Bowden (London: SCM, 1975), 315.

Barth does, however, describe this analogy in a much clearer and concretely Christological manner in II/2 than in II/1. The most important idea in II/2, so I shall contend in this chapter, is not the identification of Jesus Christ with the electing God, as Bruce McCormack and Matthias Gockel would have it (discussed below). The most important idea in II/2 is that Christ is the subject, object, and act of election, and is as such the absolute being of God in God's secondary mode of existence. This idea is already latent in *Gottes Gnadewahl* and II/1, but it is in II/2 that Barth gives to it a full-fledged dogmatic articulation.

This idea is ground-breaking in the history of Christian dogmatics in that Barth no longer speaks of election merely as an *ad extra* act of God's will, as classical theologians from the Middle Ages up to the post-Reformation period did. Surely election pertains to the "*opera Dei ad extra*," but as Reformed theologians in the period of high orthodoxy already pointed out, election differs from "*opera Dei ad extra externa*" such as creation and providence, which are called the works of God.[2] Election as an act outside of God's *ad intra* essence and yet within God's eternal will is to be ranked among God's "*opera ad extra interna*."[3]

Thus far Barth is in agreement with classical Reformed theologians, but he takes issues with the way they defined election as an "*interna voluntatis divinae actio*."[4] In Barth's view, this ascription of election solely to the will of God falls short of understanding election as an absolute mode of God's being *ad extra* that corresponds perfectly to God's primary absoluteness qua Father, Son, and Holy Spirit.

Ascribing election to the will of God and detaching it from God's being, the Reformed orthodox spoke of election and reprobation as *decretum Dei absolutum*, the notion that God unconditionally elected some out of a *massa perditionis* upon God's sheer good pleasure, rendering God as an "absolute world-ruler" who arbitrarily divided humankind into the elect and the reprobate.[5] In this classical doctrine, the will of God is, in Barth's view, elevated to the status of an absolute apart from God's loving essence.

Having purged the *speculum Trinitatis* of its intellectualistic vestiges in II/1, Barth now sets out in II/2 to purify the classical Reformed doctrine of election by rejecting its voluntaristic assumptions. When carried to their logical ends, both intellectualism and voluntarism, just as determinism and indeterminism, are for Barth erroneous ways, for both, no matter how unintendedly, elevate something that is not God to the status of an absolute something.

The ground-breaking insight in II/2 is that the *ad extra interna* absoluteness of God is not an act of God's will detached as it were from the being of God, but rather the very being of God in Jesus Christ as subject, object, and act of election. Election as such is an emanation of God's primary love-in-freedom as Father,

2. *CD* II/2, 80.
3. *CD* II/2, 80.
4. *CD* II/2, 80.
5. *CD* II/2, 50.

Son, and Holy Spirit. Jesus Christ as the electing, the elected, and election *is* God's secondary absoluteness, the *speculum Trinitatis*. Rejecting all forms of "arbitrary speculation concerning an arbitrarily conceived absolute," then, Barth sets out to understand the absoluteness of election in terms of "the One whom Jesus Christ called His Father, and who called Jesus Christ His Son."[6]

The "decisive point in" Barth's "amendment of the doctrine of predestination," in the current analysis, is "the substitution of the election of Jesus Christ for the *decretum absolutum*."[7] This is a statement of Barth's thoroughgoing Christological revision of his speculative theology in the form of *speculum Trinitatis*, and not only of the classical doctrine of predestination.

This Christocentric reorientation of the doctrine of predestination means that election is not only an act of God's will that determines the essences of all creatures. Election is first and foremost God's self-determination in a secondary mode of being that corresponds perfectly to God's triune essence in-and-for-Godself. In election as the secondary mode of God's absolute being as the one who loves in freedom, God's primary absoluteness qua triune God is speculatively "reflected [*spiegelt*]" to us.[8] The following passage sums up Barth's Christocentric reorientation of his speculative theology by the doctrine of election in II/2, and the rest of this chapter as a whole will be an attempt to interpret this passage.

> God in His love elects another to fellowship with Himself. First and foremost this means that God makes a self-election in favour of this other. He gives to Himself the determination that He should not be entirely self-sufficient, although He could remain self-sufficient in Himself. He gives to Himself the determination of that emanation [*Bestimmung jenes Überströmens*], that gift of love [*Zuwendung*], that condescension. He makes Himself a gift [*Wohltat*]. And in so doing He elects another as the object [*Gegenstand*] of His love. He draws it upwards to Himself, so as never again to be without it, but to be who He is in covenant with it. In this concept of election there is mirrored [*spiegelt*] more clearly, of course, the other element in the essence of God: the freedom in which He is the One who eternally loves.[9]

Jesus Christ the Electing God According to Revisionism

The passage above speaks of God's self-determination as the electing God. As we saw in Chapter 3, revisionism has capitalized on this language of divine self-determination to contend that according to Barth's mature theological

---

6. *CD* II/2, 25.
7. *CD* II/2, 162.
8. *CD* II/2, 11; *KD* II/2, 11.
9. *CD* II/2, 11; *KD* II/2, 11. Emphases mine. Translation revised.

ontology, election constitutes the Trinity. McCormack suggested as early as 1993 that according to Barth's actualism, what a thing *is* is entirely identical to and constituted by what it *decides* and *does*.[10] The monumental *Karl Barth's Critically Realistic Dialectical Theology* (1995), as we saw in Chapter 1, offers an intellectual-biographical narrative that serves to support this ontology of being-as-act. Then in the ballyhooed 2000 *Cambridge Companion* piece, McCormack set forth the controversial statement that for Barth, election constitutes God's triune essence.

This contention is of course difficult to square with what Barth explicitly states in *CD* II/1 (see Chapter 5), which Hans Urs von Balthasar takes to be the culmination of Barth's Anselmian turn from dialectics to analogy (see Chapters 1 and 2). The trinitarian analogy set forth so forcefully in II/1 would mean that if Barth did in fact teach that election constitutes the Trinity at some point of his career, it would have to be in a work written later than II/1. Accordingly, the 1936 *Gottes Gnadenwahl* could not have represented the completion of Barth's Christocentric reorientation of the doctrine of election.

This picture would contradict McCormack's thesis in *Barth's Dialectical Theology* with regard to the role of *Gottes Gnadenwahl* in Barth's development as a theologian. Gockel's doctoral work at Princeton Theological Seminary under McCormack's supervision lent McCormack the key to resolving this difficulty. In his 2002 doctoral dissertation, Gockel suggested that Barth's Christocentric revision of the doctrine of election remained incomplete until II/2, where Barth posits an identity between Jesus Christ and the electing God.[11] Election as such, according Gockel, constitutes "God's self-determination to be God in a covenant with humankind."[12] On Gockel's account, this revolutionary idea was not yet in place in 1936, when Barth only set forth the thesis that Christ is the subject and object of election.

Taking his cue from Gockel, McCormack eventually came to revise his own intellectual-biographical account of Barth. McCormack's mature view is "that the picture [he] drew in [his] book [*Barth's Dialectical Theology*], of a sudden shift in Barth's doctrine of election which was alleged to have taken place immediately after hearing Pierre Maury's lecture on Calvin's doctrine of predestination at the International Calvin Congress of 1936, needs to be revised a bit. The change was not immediate but gradual."[13] In a well-known 2007 article titled "Seek God Where He May Be Found," McCormack expresses

---

10. Bruce McCormack, *For Us and Our Salvation: Incarnation and Atonement in the Reformed Tradition* (Princeton: Princeton Theological Seminary, 1993).

11. Matthias Gockel, *Barth and Schleiermacher on the Doctrine of Election: A Systematic-Theological Comparison* (Oxford: Oxford University Press, 2006), 166.

12. Gockel, *Barth and Schleiermacher on the Doctrine of Election*, 167.

13. Bruce McCormack, "The Actuality of God: Karl Barth in Conversation with Open Theism," in *Engaging the Doctrine of God: Contemporary Protestant Perspectives*, ed. McCormack (Grand Rapids: Baker Academic, 2008), 213.

full agreement with Gockel that Barth's "identification of 'Jesus Christ' with the electing God ... did not appear until *CD* II/2."[14]

The revisionist claim set forth by McCormack and Gockel is that in *CD* II/2, Barth began to assert that Jesus Christ as *Logos incarnandus*, "the Logos as he appears in the eternal plan, or *consilium* of God," rather than as *Logos asarkos* apart from and priori to God's decision to become incarnate, is the electing God.[15] The history of Jesus Christ as *Logos incarnatus* (the Word actually incarnate) reveals to us the eternally electing God as *Logos incarnandus* (the Word eternally determined to become incarnate), and we are forbidden to probe beyond this revelation to speculate about an immanent Trinity and a *Logos asarkos* prior to and apart from the act of election.[16] Election, in other words, is "a constitutive or necessary aspect of God's being."[17]

Baark has already pointed out that this reading is highly problematic on an epistemological level:

> McCormack is in fact arguing that we can conceive something, some state of affairs, beyond the form in which God is known, that is, the Trinity. We can conceive of a logical moment in which God is not identical with the one whom God reveals God to be in God's revelation. We can occupy a position from which we can call into question the unsublatable subjectivity of God.[18]

What may be added here is that revisionism's noetic separation of an indeterminate moment of the subject God, in which God is not yet existent as God, from God's triune essence is symptomatic of a radically voluntaristic and indeterministic ontology that renders the *act* of election as an absolute something that constitutes and is necessary to God's being. This voluntaristic elevation of God's will to the status of an absolute something is precisely the mistake that Barth sees (rightly or wrongly) in the classical Reformed doctrine of *decretum absolutum*. Kevin Hector once tried to provide a resolution to the election-Trinity debate by qualifying that election is necessary to God's being only in the sense that it is "volitionally necessary."[19] This, however, does not

---

14. Bruce McCormack, "Seek God Where He May Be Found: A Response to Edwin van Driel," *Scottish Journal of Theology* 60 (2007): 64.

15. Bruce McCormack, "Grace and Being: The Role of God's Gracious Election in Karl Barth's Theological Ontology," in *The Cambridge Companion to Karl Barth*, ed. John Webster (Cambridge: Cambridge University Press, 2000), 92.

16. See McCormack, "Seek God Where He May Be Found," 64.

17. Matthias Gockel, "How to Read Karl Barth with Charity: A Critical Reply to George Hunsinger," *Modern Theology* 32 (2016): 260.

18. Sigurd Baark, *The Affirmations of Reason: On Karl Barth's Speculative Theology* (Cham: Palgrave Macmillan, 2018), 258.

19. Kevin Hector, "Immutability, Necessity and Triunity: Towards a Resolution of the Trinity and Election Controversy," *Scottish Journal of Theology* 65 (2012): 71.

provide a viable remedy, because it still renders the will of God as an arbitrary absolute prior to God's essential being.

It is within the pre-established metaphysical framework of voluntaristic indeterminism that McCormack and his peers capitalize on Barth's language of divine self-determination (*Selbstbestimmung*). McCormack takes Barth's notion of God's "act of self-determination" to denote "a freely willed act of self-constitution."[20] Recognizing that Barth borrowed the notion of divine "self-determination" from Hegel, McCormack seems oblivious to the role it plays in the post-Kantian discourse on freedom in German idealism (see Chapter 5).[21]

Self-determination as a free act of God's will, per McCormack, is not grounded in any essence within the subject God. Barth "makes the eternal act of self-determination that is election to be a determination of *the divine essence*," and in so doing, "he has committed himself to the view that election *makes essential* to God that which is its content."[22] In other words, God's triune essence as the one who loves in freedom does not ground and make possible God's act of self-determination as God-for-us. On the contrary, election is the ontological ground of God's essential mode of existence as the Trinity: "God's freedom is finally the freedom to exist—or not to exist."[23]

We already saw in Chapter 3 that revisionism's appeal to Barth's use of the originally Hegelian term *Bestimmung* involves serious misinterpretations and distortions. In the previous chapter, we saw how Barth adopted this term from Hegel to express basic agreement with a view of freedom that German idealism inherited from Kant, namely, the view "that freedom involves the emancipation from arbitrariness, and that 'arbitrariness' can consist in the purely contingent exercise of will ('*Willkür*') as well as in being subject to exogenous causal forces."[24]

Barth is emphatic in *CD* II/1 that God is free precisely in that (1) God is who God is in utter aseity and that (2) "there is no caprice [*Willkür*] about the freedom of God."[25] In II/2, he describes the notion of an absolute will of God apart from and prior to God's essence as the "caprice of a tyrant."[26] Jesus Christ as the electing, the elected, and election *is* the secondary mode of God's absolute being. Election is not an absolute act of God's will prior to God's essence. God's absolute freedom is not the absoluteness of an arbitrary will, but rather the absoluteness of God's being in the eternally voluntary and essential act of love, both in the primary objectivity of God's *opera ad intra* and in the secondary objectivity of God's *opera ad extra interna*.

---

20. Bruce McCormack, "Election and the Trinity: Theses in Response to George Hunsinger," *Scottish Journal of Theology* 63 (2010): 211.
21. McCormack, "Election and the Trinity," 211.
22. McCormack, "Election and the Trinity," 211. Emphases original.
23. McCormack, "Election and the Trinity," 223.
24. Michael Rosen, *The Shadow of God: Kant, Hegel, and the Passage from Heaven to History* (Harvard: Harvard University Press, 2022), 23.
25. *CD* II/1, 318; *KD* II/1, 358.
26. *CD* II/2, 43; *KD* II/2, 45.

Jesus Christ as Electing, Elected, and Election (CD II/2, §33): A Basically Chalcedonian Formulation

Election as the Secondary Mode of God's Absolute Being

Barth's key insight in *CD* II/2, that Jesus Christ is the subject, object, and act of election, is primarily set forth in §33, "The Election of Jesus Christ." Leading up to this paragraph and standing at the outset of the half-volume is §32, "The Problem of a Correct Doctrine of the Election of Grace." This paragraph and the entire half-volume begin with the following statement.

> The doctrine of election is the sum of the Gospel because of all words that can be said or heard it is the best: that God elects man; that God is for man too the One who loves in freedom. It is grounded in the knowledge of Jesus Christ because He is both the electing God and elected man in One. It is part of the doctrine of God because originally God's election of man is a predestination not merely of man but of Himself.[27]

This statement helps to demonstrate my contention that the doctrine of election in *CD* II/2 is an exposition and expansion of the trinitarian speculation set forth in II/1, §28, "the Being of God as the One Who Loves in Freedom," discussed in the previous chapter. God is in-and-for-Godself the one who loves in freedom qua triune God. But "God is for man too the one who loves in freedom." God is absolute *pro nobis* as God is absolute *a se*. Speculative knowledge of God's primary absoluteness is mediated to us through the man Jesus Christ who is abidingly absolute in relation to us: knowledge of the unsublatable subjectivity of God qua Trinity "is grounded in the knowledge of Jesus Christ." The perfect correspondence between divine aseity (God's primary absoluteness) and promeity (secondary absoluteness) is established by the truth, given to and confessed by the church through the gift of faith, that "He is both the electing God and elected man in One."

The doctrine of election as such is not only about the *will* of God. Surely it is about the will of God, but not an arbitrary will detached as it were from God's being. The doctrine of election is about God's self-determination in an *ad extra* mode of God's being as the unsublatable subject who loves in freedom. As such the doctrine of election "is part of the doctrine of God because originally God's election of man is a predestination not merely of man but of Himself."

Jesus Christ as Election

The prolegomenal considerations offered in §32 have been discussed in the previous chapter of the present work, where I delineated the implications of §28 for the doctrine of election formulated in §33. In the two sections that make up

---

27. *CD* II/2, 4.

§33, respectively titled "1. Jesus Christ, Electing and Elected" and "2. The Eternal Will of God in the Election of Jesus Christ," Barth sets forth the all-important insight that Jesus Christ is the subject, object, and act of election.

At the beginning of §33 Barth states that the doctrine of election is an exposition of the church's confession of Jesus Christ as God incarnate: "Between God and man there stands the person of Jesus Christ, Himself God and Himself man, and so mediating between the two."[28] While the first section of §33 is on Christ as the *subject* and *object* of election—as "Electing as Elected," Barth begins his discussion by identifying Jesus Christ as the fully developed actuality of election. "He is the election of God before which and without which and beside which God cannot make any other choices. Before Him and without Him and beside Him God does not, then, elect or will anything."[29] This is the thrust of Barth's replacement of the classical doctrine of *decretum absolutum* with Jesus Christ as the very and full reality of election: "He is the decree of God behind and above which there can be no earlier or higher decree and beside which there can be no other, since all others serve only the fulfilment of this decree."[30]

Christ is absolute not merely as a decree, but also as the subject and object of this decree. A decree of God in itself, apart from the subjectivity and objectivity of God's being, cannot be absolute. God is absolute as the subject, object, and act of God's love-in-freedom, in both the primary and secondary modes of God's existence. There is no *decretum absolutum* apart from Jesus Christ who is electing, elected, and election in an inseparable unity with abiding distinction.

Note here that Barth's understanding of Jesus Christ as electing, elected, and election is regulated by the anhypostatic-enhypostatic principle of Chalcedonian Christology. This principle dictates that Christ's human nature is an addition to rather than subtraction from or alteration of the fullness of the Godhead in the person of the Son. God's flesh-becoming is at once an *ad extra* event in relation to God's triune essence and an event that added to God a second mode of being in which God does not cease to be all that God is in God's *ad intra* essence.

God-in-and-for-Godself became God-for-us without ceasing to be God-in-and-for-Godself. God's secondary absoluteness does not subtract from, abolish, alter, or sublate God's primary absoluteness. Rather, the secondary mode of God's absolute being corresponds perfectly to the primary, and in both modes, the subject of God's love-in-freedom remains the same. "He, Jesus Christ, is the free grace of God, provided that this not only remains identical with the inner and eternal essence of God, but is active in the ways and works of God *ad extra*."[31]

---

28. *CD* II/2, 94.
29. *CD* II/2, 94.
30. *CD* II/2, 94.
31. *KD* II/2, 102. "Er, Jesus Christus, ist die freie Gnade Gottes, sofern diese nicht nur mit Gottes innerem, ewigem Wesen identisch bleibt, sondern in Gottes Wegen und Werken nach außen kräftig ist." Original translation is problematic: *CD* II/2, 95.

This identity rests on the biblical truth confessed by the church, that God became human without ceasing to be God. The Nestorian notion of a historical Jesus detached from the second person of the Trinity cannot be the subject of election. Barth is emphatic that Christ, "with the Father and the Holy Spirit, is the electing God."[32]

Put another way, the unsublatable subjectivity of God means that even in God's secondary mode of being, God does not cease to be absolute, that is, to be a perfect communion of the subject, object, and act of love-in-freedom. The electing God, therefore, is not Jesus Christ abstracted from the concrete life of the Trinity. "The Subject of this decision [election] is the triune God—the Son of God no less than the Father and the Holy Spirit. And the specific object of it is the Son of God in His determination as the Son of Man, the God-Man, Jesus Christ, who is as such the eternal basis of the whole divine election."[33]

Because Jesus Christ is consubstantial with the Father in his deity, and because in the one unabridged person of Christ dwells the fullness of the Godhead, this man is from and to all eternity the electing God. That the man named Jesus Christ is called the electing God whom no name can describe and that Mary is rightly called the mother of God (and not merely the mother of Christ or mother of the Son) share the same theo-logical ground, namely, the hypostatic union and the unity of the triune Godhead. God in Jesus Christ, in God's *ad extra* mode of being-in-becoming, is identical with God the Son who is the fullness of God's love-in-freedom with the Father and the Holy Spirit.

The Unsublatable Subjectivity of God in Jesus Christ as Electing and Elected

Jesus Christ is election. This means that he is the full actuality of election as the inseparable union of the subject and object of God's love-in-freedom. As such Jesus Christ is the secondary mode of the absolute being of God, who does not cease to be all that God is in God's primary absoluteness even in entering into and assuming this secondary absoluteness. This line of thought, of course, can sound like a dangerously Hegelian idea.

Chalcedonian Christology is Barth's key to avoiding Hegel's error when describing election in terms of the Hegelian triad of subjectivity, objectivity, and activity. Hegel treats the actuality of God (i.e., the absolute) as the consummation of the process in which the subjective freedom of some God-in-the-making, so to speak, is sublated by an objective freedom of the same subject. Against Hegel, Barth insists that election cannot be a process by which God makes Godself determinate through a sublation of God's subjectivity in the object of election: Barth is emphatic that God became human without ceasing to be God.

The Chalcedonian grammar undergirding Barth's doctrine of election is clearly spelt out. "The name of Jesus Christ has within itself the double reference: the One

---

32. *CD* II/2, 106.
33. *CD* II/2, 111.

called by this name is both very God and very man. Thus the simplest form of the dogma may be divided at once into the two assertions that Jesus Christ is the electing God, and that He is also elected man."[34]

Paul Jones is of the view that in referring to Christ as "very God," Barth "effectively discards the language of 'nature' in his mature Christology."[35] This is a misreading of Barth's theological vocabulary that I refuted in Chapter 3, and I will refrain from digressing to address it again here. Suffice it here to restate my thesis from Chapter 3: Barth retains the language of classical ontology (most significantly the terms *Natur* and *Wesen*) and combines it with Hegelian terminology (most notably the term *Bestimmung*) to express a basically Chalcedonian understanding of God's being-in-becoming. God-in-and-for-Godself determined Godself to become God-for-us without ceasing to be God-in-and-for-Godself.

This Chalcedonian grammar entails an abiding distinction between Christ's two natures in their inseparable unity. This grammar also applies to the two moments of election that *is* Jesus Christ. Jesus Christ is at once the subjective moment (Christ as electing God) and objective moment (Christ as elected human) of election.

In Jesus Christ who is the full actuality of election, there is no sublation of the subjective in the objective: Christ's two natures are united without confusion and without change. According to the *extra-Calvinisticum* to which Barth adheres, the Chalcedonian principle of abiding distinction is an expression of the Creator-creature distinction in the one unabridged person of Christ. The incommunicable attributes of God can be predicated of the man Jesus Christ only in accordance with the *genus idiomatum*, and there can never be any *communicatio idiomatum* in and through a *genus maiestaticum*.[36]

Barth applies this Reformed rendition of Chalcedon to the doctrine of election and insists that the subject of election remains unsublatably divine, and the object abidingly human. In other words, in saying that election is God's determination of

---

34. *CD* II/2, 103.

35. Paul Jones, *The Humanity of Christ: Christology in Karl Barth's Church Dogmatics* (London: T&T Clark, 2008), 28.

36. Piotr Malycz contends that Barth misunderstood the Lutheran doctrine of the *genus maiestaticum*, and that Barth's own doctrine is in fact completely in line with this Lutheran view of the *communicatio idiomatum*. Malycz may be right about Barth's misunderstanding of Lutheran doctrine. In a similar vein, Paul Gavrilyuk has also argued that Barth misunderstood the notion of *theosis* in Orthodox doctrine by confusing it with Ebionite Christology. Barth thinks that Luther deified the human nature of Christ by teaching the *genus maiestaticum*. Granted that Barth might be wrong about Luther, Malycz does not seem to appreciate fully Barth's strong commitment to the *extra Calvinisticum*. See Piotr Malycz, "Storming Heaven with Karl Barth? Barth's Unwitting Appropriation of the *Genus Maiestaticum* and What Lutherans Can Learn from It," *International Journal of Systematic Theology* 9 (2007): 73–92. Also see Paul Gavrilyuk, "The Retrieval of Deification: How a Once-Despised Archaism Became an Ecumenical Desideratum," *Modern Theology* 25 (2009): 647–59.

God's own being, Barth avoids what he sees as Hegelian monism and pantheism by stressing the Chalcedonian principle of abiding distinction as understood in terms of the *extra Calvinisticum*. Strictly speaking, the Son qua Son, according to his divine nature, is not the object of election, for "as the Son of the Father He has no need of any special election."[37] But "because ... He is the Son of God elected in His oneness with man," Jesus Christ is God's election of Godself.[38]

In other words, it is only in the sense of *communicatio idiomatum* in the *genus idiomatum* that God in the person of the Son is said to be the object of election. But the Son is the fullness of the Godhead. Therefore, just as Mary is said to be not merely the mother of God the Son but the mother of God, the object of election is God in the fullness of God's essence. Put another way: he who was elected *is* God, but he was not elected *as* God.

The Creator-creature distinction in the person and history of Jesus Christ as the being of God in the act of election serves as the ground on which Barth can speak of an analogy between God's primary and secondary modes of absoluteness, between the Trinity and the *imago Trinitatis*, without falling into what he sees as idealism's error of pantheistic speculation or idolatrous projection. "It is as God's election that we must understand the Word and decree and beginning of God over against the reality which is distinct from Himself. When we say this, we say that in His decision all God's doing, both 'inward' and 'outward,' rest upon His freedom."[39] God's *opera ad intra* and *opera ad extra interna*, in other words, are two modes of the same freedom of the love that is God's being.

"Even the fact that He is elected corresponds as closely as possible to His own electing," precisely because the subjectivity of the electing God remains unsublated in the objectivity and the actuality of election.[40] God's unsublatable subjectivity in God's unceasing absoluteness in election means that there is only inseparable unity-in-distinction and abiding distinction-in-unity between the subject and object of election, but there is no alienation or contradiction. In the perfect union of the subject and the object in the act of election as the secondary mode of God's being as the one who loves in freedom, "the inner glory of God emanates."[41]

Election as Interna Actio *of God's Being*

The unsublatable subjectivity of God's abiding absoluteness means that God does not need to be reconciled to Godself even when God becomes an other to Godself outside of God's own being. Yet, Hegel is right, in Barth's view, that world history has to be a history of reconciliation, and that it is this history that reflectively mediates to us the essential reality of God as the absolute. Even the secondary

---

37. *CD* II/2, 103.
38. *CD* II/2, 103.
39. *CD* II/2, 99; *KD* II/2, 107. Translation revised.
40. *CD* II/2, 105.
41. *CD* II/2, 121; *KD* II/2, 130. Translation revised.

absoluteness of God cannot be revealed to us immediately, be it in the form of intuitions or of verbal propositions, or what not. The primary absoluteness of God is speculatively revealed in and through God's secondary absoluteness, and God's secondary absoluteness in and through the covenantal history of reconciliation as a history enacted on the external basis of creation.

In the history of reconciliation, the sin of the world is actually negated through the execution of election as the sublation of reprobation at Golgotha. Golgotha is the external basis of election, and election the internal basis of the crucifixion. The history of Jesus Christ as a history of reconciliation is in this way the *speculum electionis*, and the eternal reality of election that *is* Jesus Christ is in turn the *speculum Trinitatis*.

Put another way, election as the second mode of God's being as the one who loves in freedom (and not as an arbitrary act of God's will) corresponds perfectly to the primary mode of God's absolute existence. But God's *opera ad extra interna*, unlike the *opera ad extra externa*, are eternal and absolute, and thus not immediately knowable to creatures. God's revelation, then, is not merely indirect in that it has to take on the form of an *ad extra* mode of God's being. Revelation has to be doubly indirect: God's *ad extra interna* mode of being has to be mirrored to us through God's *opera ad extra externa*.

With this speculative theology of double mediation, Barth criticizes Reformed orthodoxy for having adopted a "particular conception" of God from "the fathers and scholastics," namely, the "conception" according to which "God is everything in the way of aseity, simplicity, immutability, infinity, etc., but He is not ... the God who lives in concrete decision."[42] Here Barth is not denying the classical doctrines of aseity, simplicity, immutability, etc. His notion of God's primary absoluteness encompasses all these attributes. What Barth intends to say is that if God is indeed absolute in this way in God's primary mode of being, then we are required to speak of election as a secondary mode of being in which God *is* the God who lives in concrete decision, rather than an abstract decision detached from the concrete life of the triune God.

The classical Reformed "conception" of God, in other words, entails that election is not a mode of God's being, "not something which belongs to His proper and essential life, but only to His relationship with the world."[43] As such election cannot be a *speculum* that mediates to us knowledge of God's being that is unknowable *per essentiam*.

Barth commends the Reformed orthodox for having ranked election among the *opera Dei ad extra interna*. "It was illogical, but most fortunate, that theologians still dared to speak not only of the *opera Dei ad extra externa* but also, with reference to the divine decrees, of the *opera Dei ad extra interna*."[44] By ascribing election

---

42. *CD* II/2, 80.
43. *CD* II/2, 80.
44. *CD* II/2, 80.

to an internal aspect of God's *ad extra* activities, classical Reformed theologians "could speak ... of the concrete forms and directions and aims of the divine will and the divine being ... in spite of the fact that God, as *ens simplex et infinitum*, was not properly or by definition capable of such *opera ad extra interna*, of such *interna actio*."[45]

Again, what is illogical about the classical doctrine of election, in Barth's view, is not that the classical formulation of God's being in terms of aseity, simplicity, and immutability stands at odds with the revealed fact that God is the electing God in relation to God's people. Barth unequivocally affirms with classical theology "the eternity, freedom and immutability of God" as the ground of election.[46] The logical contradictions in the classical formulation of the doctrine arise from the fact that "the discussion of the eternity, freedom and immutability of God as the basis, meaning and dynamic of what takes place between Christ and His people ... comes in a sense too late. And when it is a matter of God's eternity, we obviously cannot afford to let the discussion come too late."[47]

The problem with classical Reformed formulations of election, as Barth sees it, is that the eternal decrees of God are relegated to the internal activity of God's will, the "*interna voluntatis divinae actio*," but excluded from God's being.[48] Something then "happened," so to speak, to God's being at a much later stage when, in accordance with God's eternal decrees, God became human without ceasing to be God. There then came to be a secondary mode of God's being as God-for-us, God incarnate, *Logos ensarkos*, in addition to God's primary mode of being qua immanent Trinity. In Barth's view, this repetition of God's *ad intra* mode of being in an *ad extra* reality comes too late in classical formulations of the doctrine of election.

The fact that God is the living God as Father, Son, and Holy Spirit means for Barth that divine aseity and immutability do not prevent God from establishing an *ad extra* mode of being-in-act prior to the creation of the world, for even within God's *ad intra* mode of being, God is self-existent and immutable in God's abiding subjectivity, objectivity, and *opera ad intra*. God can *become* and *be* God-for-us prior to the creation of the world without ceasing to be God-in-and-for-Godself. Election, on this view, should be understood as an eternal mode of God's being, rather than a mere decision to enter into this secondary mode of being at a later stage in creaturely history. "Strangely enough, they [classical theologians] did not feel driven to make such a deduction even by their doctrine of the Trinity."[49]

The Trinity, in other words, is for Barth the biblical ground of the doctrine of election, and he is surprised that classical theologians (according to his

---

45. *CD* II/2, 80.
46. *CD* II/2, 90.
47. *CD* II/2, 90.
48. *CD* II/2, 80.
49. *CD* II/2, 80.

misunderstanding) failed to make this connection.[50] Barth's ground-breaking insight is that election is not an act of God's will outside of God's being and yet somehow internal to an eternal reality of God. Election as an act of God's will cannot be detached from God's being as the subject and object of love-in-freedom.

Election is an *interna actio* of God's being: this is Barth's key insight. This *interna actio* is grounded in and made possible by the fact that God is the triune God. Barth agrees with classical theology that God is unknowable *per essentiam*. He is surprised, however, that classical theologians did not explore the implications of this axiom for the doctrine of election, the "implications of the fact that this triune being does not exist and cannot be known as a being which rests or moves purely within itself."[51]

Barth continues:

> God is not *in abstracto* Father, Son and Holy Ghost, the triune God. He is so with a definite purpose and reference; in virtue of the love and freedom in which in the bosom of His triune being He has foreordained Himself from and to all eternity. And when we treat of the doctrine of election, we have to do with this determination of His will, and *eo ipso* of His being and all His perfections. For how can we speak of the being of God without at once speaking of this *interna actio* of His being, i.e., the election? And how can we speak of the election without speaking of the concrete life of the very being of God?[52]

Barth's Christological doctrine of election, in other words, sets forth the innovative insight that the secondary mode of God's being was determined from all eternity—that God did not wait until the incarnation to establish this secondary mode of being. Put another way, the history of the incarnation is the *ad extra externa* aspect, the external ground, of election, and election the internal basis of the incarnation.

In this light, Barth's Christological reorientation of the doctrine of election consists in an attempt to follow through with the "general Reformation assertion that Christ is the *speculum electionis*."[53] Through the history of incarnation in which the world is reconciled to God, election as an eternal mode of God's being-in-act is speculatively revealed to us. This secondary mode of God's absolute being, in turn, mediates to us knowledge of God's primary absoluteness qua Trinity.

---

50. Reformed theologians of the seventeenth century did in fact make this connection by formulating the doctrine of *pactum salutis*, the eternal covenant between the persons of the Trinity as the ground of all God's decrees. Barth was aware of this doctrine, but his understanding thereof was significantly misled. See my *Karl Barth* (Phillipsburg: P&R, 2021), 118–21. Barth's misunderstandings of the *pactum* arise primarily from his misreading of Cocceius. See my *Karl Barth's Infralapsarian Theology* (Downders Grove: IVP Academic, 2016), 51.

51. *CD* II/2, 80.

52. *CD* II/2, 80.

53. *CD* II/2, 154–5.

Jesus Christ as Speculum Electionis: Impassibility of the Suffering God

Jesus Christ is *speculum electionis*: this is in a sense the core insight of Barth's Christological doctrine of election. In II/2, Barth fleshes out his notion of the twofold indirectness of the Word of God set forth in I/1 with this insight. The notion, in a nutshell, is as follows.

> This secularity, this twofold indirectness, is in fact an authentic and inalienable attribute of the Word of God. Revelation means incarnation of the Word of God. But incarnation means entry into this secularity. We are in this world and are through and through secular. If God did not speak to us in secular form, He would not speak to us at all. To evade the secularity of His Word is to evade Christ.[54]

This is stated in more concretely Christological terms in II/2:

> For these are two separate things: the Son of God in His oneness with the Son of Man, as foreordained from all eternity; and the universe which was created, and universal history which was willed for the sake of this oneness …, as foreordained from all eternity …. On the one hand, there is God's eternal election of grace, and, on the other, God's creation, reconciliation and redemption grounded in that election and ordained with reference to it.[55]

In light of the incarnation, election is not just God's self-determination as God-for-us. Surely it is this. But the depth of God's being-for-us is such that God, in God's secondary mode of being, would take on the sin of the world and defeat sin for the sake of God's covenant partner in Jesus Christ. Election as the emanation of God's inner love-in-freedom is determined in such a way that God is willing to become an object of God's own wrath as a reprobate.

> "The Word became flesh" (Jn. I^{14}). This formulation of the message of Christmas already includes within itself the message of Good Friday. For "all flesh is as grass." The election of the man Jesus means, then, that a wrath is kindled, a sentence pronounced and finally executed, a rejection actualized … From all eternity judgment has been foreseen—even in the emanation of God's inner glory.[56]

The message of Christmas as such reveals to us that as God's elect *apropos*, Christ took on the sin of all humankind and suffered God's judgment in a way that no other can suffer. In this sense—in the sense that Christ alone was crucified under God's judgment—there is "other than Him no reprobate."[57]

---

54. *CD* II/2, 168.
55. *CD* II/2, 104; *KD* II/2, 111. Translation revised.
56. *CD* II/2, 122; *KD* II/2, 131. Translation revised.
57. *CD* II/2, 353; *KD* II/2, 389. Translation revised.

Election is an emanation of God's love-in-freedom in the deepest way. God's eternal love is expressed as covenantal love pre-determined by election, and correspondingly as a love that becomes determinate through a history of the removal of sin by holy sacrifice. Election as revealed in the history of the incarnation is such that "the rejection which all men incurred, the wrath of God under which all men lie, the death which all men must die, God in His love for men transfers from all eternity to Him in whom He loves and elects them, and whom He elects as their head and in their place."[58]

Election as such is the sublation of sin and reprobation. Critically borrowing the Hegelian language of the sublation of the negative in the positive, Barth speaks of election as the "positive will" in which reprobation (the negative) as the negation of sin (the abstract) is sublated.[59] As the sin of the world is negated by a reprobation that is "sublated [*aufgehoben*] in the positive will," all humankind is elected in Jesus Christ.[60]

Barth's express intention in stating that election is the sublation of reprobation is to contend that election does not sublate the subjectivity of the absoluteness of God's being, in which God qua unsublatable subject is impossible. The church's confession of Jesus as Lord means that God's immutability is revealed through God's flesh-becoming; God's impassibility through suffering.

Impassibility, in other words, is an expression of God's unsublatable subjectivity. From the very outset, Barth makes it his business in the whole of II/2 to "expound … the Subject God" as "disclosed only in the name of Jesus Christ."[61] God's primary absoluteness grounds and makes possible God's suffering, because within God's primary absoluteness there are both objectivity and unsublatable subjectivity. Even within God's inner being, God is an object of God's own love, and in the pure actuality of love God never ceases to be the subject. When God became an other outside of Godself, God remained abidingly absolute. And even in the history of reconciliation that consists of God's *opera ad extra externa*, Christ never ceased to be the impassible God, the subject of election with the Father and the Holy Spirit, even at Golgotha where he was crucified as a reprobate.

Barth's doctrine of election is in line with the Chalcedonian tradition, in that this tradition is characteristically dialectical in asserting that God's impassibility is revealed through God's suffering. To say that Golgotha reveals to us that suffering is natural to God's being (as Jürgen Moltmann does) is, from a Barthian perspective, to miss the whole point of the biblical proclamation, "the Word became flesh" (Jn. 1:14), as understood and confessed by the Christian church.

According to Barth, election as God's *actio ad extra interna* is fully contingent upon God's free decision, as much as it became and is God's very own mode of being. In this secondary mode of existence, suffering is taken up into God's being in the deepest way: God shall forever remain the Lamb that was slain. Still, suffering

---

58. *CD* II/2, 123.
59. *CD* II/2, 175.
60. *CD* II/2, 275; *KD* II/2, 189. Translation revised.
61. *CD* II/2, 5–6.

is an *ad extra* addition to God's essence. It pertains to God's secondary mode of existence. Barth is unequivocal that Jesus Christ "is Himself primarily and properly the divine freedom itself in its operation *ad extra*."[62] This *ad extra* determination of God's mode of being as God crucified is entirely contingent upon God's will.

> From all eternity God could have excluded man from this covenant. He could have delivered him up to himself and allowed him to fall. He could have refused to will him at all. He could have avoided the compromising of His freedom by not willing to create him. He could have remained satisfied with Himself and with the impassible glory and blessedness of His own inner life. But He did not do so. He elected man as a covenant-partner. In His Son He elected Himself as the covenant-partner of man.[63]

In this passage Barth is clear that in God's "own inner life" God is impassible. He also states clearly that election is not a necessary aspect of God's being. God can be God without being the crucified God. The question is: does election somehow sublate God's primary absoluteness, so that in becoming the crucified God, God somehow ceased to be impassible?

Some passages in *CD* II/2 might seem to suggest such a view. For instance, Barth writes: "In giving Himself to this act He ordained the surrender of something, i.e., of His own impassibility in face of the whole world which because it is not willed by Him can only be the world of evil."[64] However, Barth makes it clear in this context: "In Himself God cannot be affected either by the possibility or by the reality of that will which opposes Him."[65]

In other words, God is impassible qua unsublatable subject in the primary absoluteness of God's being. Yet, it may seem that Barth wants to suggest that the impassibility of God's primary mode of being was somehow sublated by God's decision to become the "covenant-partner" of "a being which was not merely affected by evil but actually mastered by it."[66]

What must be noted, however, is that Barth's rhetoric of God's surrendering God's inner glory is quite familiar to the tradition that affirms the doctrine of impassibility. Such rhetoric is found in the New Testament itself (most notably Phil. 2:6-8). Classical theology uses this rhetoric and takes the surrendering or self-emptying as an *addition* to rather than alteration or abolishment of God's impassible essence. For Barth, the surrendering of impassibility pertains to God's secondary mode of being, in which God does not cease to be impassible in God's primary absoluteness.[67]

---

62. *CD* II/2, 105.
63. *CD* II/2, 167.
64. *CD* II/2, 164.
65. *CD* II/2, 164.
66. *CD* II/2, 164.
67. See Paul Gavrilyuk, *The Suffering of the Impassible God: The Dialectics of Patristic Thought* (Oxford: Oxford University Press, 2004).

In the English translation of *CD* II/1, there is one instance in which Barth appears to deny the impassibility of God. The short sentence reads: "God is not impassible."[68] This, however, is a bad translation. The original reads: "Gott ist nicht unberührbar."[69] Here Barth does not use the conventional words for "impassibility," such as *Affektlosigkeit*, *Leidenschaftslosigkeit*, or *Apathie*. The word *unberührbar* simply means "untouchable," and Barth does not give to it any technical definition.

In the context in which he states that "God is not untouchable," he clearly affirms the impassibility of God's essence *a se*, and clarifies that God's suffering pertains to an *ad extra* mode of God's being *in addition* to God's primary absoluteness.

> He is not untouchable [*unberührbar*]. He cannot be moved from outside by an extraneous power. But this does not mean he is not capable of moving Himself ... It can be only a question of compassion, free sympathy, with another's suffering. God finds no suffering in Himself. And no cause outside God can cause Him suffering if He does not will it so. But it is, in fact, a question of sympathy with the suffering of another in the full scope of God's own personal freedom.[70]

In other words, the *ad intra* subjectivity, objectivity, and activity of God's essential absoluteness grounds and makes possible God's *ad extra* suffering. Barth even expresses agreement with the classical Reformed theologian Amandus Polanus (1561–1610), "to the extent that ... he wishes to avoid the conception of a God who can be moved and stirred from without."[71]

This position, established in II/1 and solidified in II/2, is indeed one that Barth continues to hold in the latest part-volumes of the *Church Dogmatics*. Without digressing to discuss these later works, suffice it here to quote an important footnote from George Hunsinger on this subject.

> It is not correct to say, as Bruce L. McCormack does, that "Barth's later Christology leaves no remaining room for any doctrine of divine impassibility ..." For Barth, God is free to be relative without ceasing to be absolute, immanent without ceasing to be transcendent, lowly without ceasing to be exalted, and so on. For that is how God encounters us in Jesus Christ. God enters fully into human suffering and death in Christ without ceasing to be impassible and immortal in himself. Barth writes: "God gives himself, but he does not give himself away. He does not give up being God in becoming a creature, in becoming man. He does not cease to be God. He does not come into conflict with himself. He does not sin when in unity with the man Jesus he mingles with sinners and takes their place. And when he dies in his unity with this man, death does not gain any power over him" (IV/1, 185). Just as God takes human sin on himself without ceasing

---

68. *CD* II/1, 370.
69. *KD* II/1, 416.
70. *CD* II/1, 370. Translation revised.
71. *CD* II/1, 370.

to be holy, so he also takes suffering and death on himself without ceasing to be impassible and immortal. It is because God remains holy, impassible, and immortal in himself that sin, suffering, and death gain no power over him in Christ, and indeed that is how he triumphs over them once and for all.[72]

Purified Supralapsarianism: The Substitution of Decretum Absolutum *with Jesus Christ*

In light of the foregoing analysis, we can proceed to expound on Barth's famous proposal of a "purified supralapsarianism" in a long excursus from II/2, §33, where he brings his formulation of election as the sublation of reprobation to bear on the seventeenth-century debate between supra- and infralapsarians. This was a historic controversy among classical Reformed theologians over the question whether the object of double predestination (*obiectum praedestinationis*) is considered as fallen (*homo lapsus*) or yet to fall (*homo labilis*) in God's eternal councils. Both sides agreed that election is an eternal act of God *ad extra interna*, and that the act of predestination logically, ontologically, and chronologically preceded the actual creation and fall of the world. So, the question that supra- and infralapsarians debated over was: is election God's decision to save and reprobation God's decision to punish fallen humans? Supralapsarians answered this question in the negative, and asserted that the double decree of election and reprobation did not presuppose God's decree of the fall. Instead, God decided to allow creatures to fall into sin in order to fulfil the purpose of election and reprobation, which is to manifest God's glory in mercy and justice. Infralapsarians, by contrast, contended that election and reprobation logically presuppose God's eternal decree to permit the fall of humanity (but not the historical actuality of the fall).

In a previous monograph I discussed in detail Barth's misunderstandings of this historic debate and argued that his doctrine of election is in fact a basically infralapsarian one that consists of a complex combination of supra- and infralapsarian elements.[73] In light of the foregoing analyses, however, this thesis needs to be revised: I will now contend that Barth's doctrine of election is basically supralapsarian, albeit with strongly infralapsarian elements.

With regard to the *obiectum praedestinationis*, Barth considers Christ to be the elected human *apropos*. And as I have argued elsewhere, Barth consistently insisted on the sinlessness of Christ's human nature in his mature theology.[74] This would make Barth basically supralapsarian. With regard to the human race elected in and with Christ, however, he is in fact in line with infralapsarianism, although he does not realize this. He purports to hold to the view that the *obiectum praedestinationis*

---

72. George Hunsinger, *Evangelical, Catholic, and Reformed: Essays on Barth and Other Themes* (Grand Rapids: Eerdmans, 2015), 168n32.
73. See my *Barth's Infralapsarian Theology*.
74. See my *Barth's Ontology of Sin and Grace: Variations on a Theme of Augustine* (London: Routledge, 2018), 110–12.

is *homo labilis*, but then his definitions of *homo labilis* and *homo lapsus* are mistaken.⁷⁵ He thinks that the supralapsarian notion of "*homo labilis*" as the object of election refers to "man sinful and lost" in God's eternal plan, but not yet created or fallen in historical actuality.⁷⁶ This, however, is in fact what *homo lapsus* refers to in the Lapsarian Controversy. Barth takes "*homo lapsus*" to designate "man as already created and fallen" in historical actuality.⁷⁷ The infralapsarian position, on his misunderstanding, is that election and reprobation are based on God's foresight of humanity as actually created and fallen: "before God could decide in mercy and justice, there must have been a corresponding constitution of individuals and an actualisation of their existence."⁷⁸ With regard to the *obiectum praedestinationis*, then, Barth confuses the infralapsarian thesis with the argument set forth by the Remonstrants at the Synod of Dort, and the supralapsarian thesis with the infralapsarian. When he sides with the thesis that the *obiectum praedestinationis* is *homo labilis*, he is actually referring to *homo lapsus*.

It is specifically with regard to the logical order of God's eternal decrees (*ordo decretorum*) that my previous thesis is in need of significant revision: Barth's doctrine of election is basically supralapsarian, because election is for him a secondary mode of God's absolute being that determines the modes of existence of everything that is not God. There is no will of God in relation to anything *ad extra* apart from or prior to election. And because this ground-breaking assertion is so central to Barth's doctrine of election as a function of the doctrine of God as a whole, the question of the *obiectum praedestinationis* is really a secondary issue for him compared to the *ordo decretorum*.

Barth concedes that classical supralapsarianism was prone to attribute to God an arbitrary will, while infralapsarianism was more successful in avoiding the ascription of random exercises of *Willkür* to God. However, Barth finds in supralapsarianism a key insight that is crucial for a right view of God's freedom as perfect correspondence between essence and activity, rather than indeterministic arbitrariness. The key insight is the logical priority of election as determinative of everything else that God decides in the reality of God *ad extra interna*: "to this proper divine will and decree of God everything else that God wills is subordinate, as an interrelated means to its accomplishment."⁷⁹

I was right in my previous work that Barth's "purified supralapsarianism" consisted in his rejection of the assumption of *decretum Dei absolutum* in the classical Reformed doctrine of election. I was wrong, however, that his purification of the doctrine is primarily about the replacement of the *decretum absolutum* with his novel understanding of election as the sublation of reprobation: this replacement was the salient point of *Gottes Gnadenwahl*, but Barth takes it one step further in *CD* II/2.⁸⁰

---

75. For details, see my *Barth's Infralapsarian Theology*, 68–71.
76. *CD* II/2, 143.
77. *CD* II/2, 131.
78. *CD* II/2, 135.
79. *CD* II/2, 128.
80. See my *Barth's Infralapsarian Theology*, 65–6.

As we saw in an earlier quote, the "substitution of the election of Jesus Christ for the *decretum absolutum* is ... the decisive point in the amendment of the doctrine of predestination" in II/2.[81] Barth's emphasis here, as we saw, is that election is not merely an act of God's will apart from the triune love that is God's essence, but rather a secondary mode of God's absolute being as the one who loves in freedom.

In election, God is absolute and therefore free as the subject, object, and act of love *pro nobis*, just as God is absolutely free qua Trinity *a se*. There is no absolute decree of God above, behind, apart from, or prior to God's being. Election, then, is absolute not merely as a decree. Election is absolute in that Jesus Christ *is* election in its subjectivity, objectivity, and actuality.

Barth's purification of supralapsarianism is, in the current analysis, reflective of his concerted attempt to detach every last element of arbitrariness from the Christian conception of divine freedom. With Kant and Hegel, he refuses to define freedom as arbitrary exercises of *Willkür*. Against the Kantian view that freedom as autonomy is attainable by theoretical and practical uses of pure reason (however much divine assistance might be needed in this process) and the Hegelian notion of absolute freedom as the sublation of subjectivity in objectivity, Barth argues with the Augustinian tradition that God is absolutely free as unsublatable subject in the pure actuality of God's love. The freedom of God in election lies primarily in the fact that in election as an *ad extra interna* mode of being, God remains absolute as the unsublatable subject in the objectivity and activity of love.

Barth fleshes out classical supralapsarianism with the innovative insight that Jesus Christ is God's very own being in this secondary and self-determined mode of absolute existence as the one who loves in freedom. Accordingly, the God of his "purified Supralapsarianism is not the God who in holy self-seeking is so preoccupied with Himself and the revelation of His own glory ... He is the God who loves man. He is the God who in love makes man a companion"—without ceasing to be God.[82]

Conclusion

This chapter completes my portrait of Barth as a Christocentric speculative theologian. He is "speculative" in two related senses. First, in terms of intellectual-historical heritage, he undoubtedly belongs to the longstanding tradition of speculative theology instituted by Augustine, solidified by Anselm, and transformed or distorted by German idealism. Second, "speculation" best describes both the *Denkform* and the material contents of Barth's mature theology. His all-important notion of being-in-act, as we have seen, is a function of his speculative theology.

"Speculative theology" in this second sense refers to (1) how the subject God has revealed and continues to reveal Godself to us, and (2) how we come to

---

81. *CD* II/2, 162.
82. *CD* II/2, 142.

know God as unsublatable subject through God's self-revelation. In the classical tradition, revelation is described in terms of mirror (*speculum*), image (*imago*), and emanation (*emanatio*). Modern speculative philosophers like Fichte, Schelling, and Hegel added to these the key notions of identity (*Identität*), determination (*Bestimmung*), and absoluteness (*Absolutheit*). Hegel, in particular, inherited from the classical tradition the key notion of mediation (*Vermittlung*) and reinterpreted it as a process involving sublation (*Aufhebung*).

With the representatives of classical speculative theology, most notably Augustine, Anselm, and classical Reformed theologians, Barth insists that God is unknowable *per essentiam*. God is *ipsum esse*: in the language of modern speculative philosophy, God is immediately self-identical. Kant forcefully demonstrated God's unknowability *per essentiam* by a critique of immediacy unsuccessfully challenged by Fichte and the early Schelling. Barth relies on Augustine to argue in II/1 that God is immediately self-identical as Father, Son, and Holy Spirit, and speaks of God's *ipsum esse* in terms of the Hegelian notion of absoluteness as perfect communion of subjectivity, objectivity, and activity. This primary absoluteness of God, according to Barth, is not immediately but only speculatively knowable to human beings.

In II/2, Barth spells out the view that the *speculum* that mediates to us knowledge of God's triune essence is election. Election as a *speculative extension* or *emanation* (*Überfluss*) of God's triune love-in-freedom is as such not merely an *act* of God's will. A mere *act* of the will apart from nature is arbitrary. Agreeing with Augustine, Kant, and Hegel that freedom is not arbitrary exercise of the power of choice (*Willkür*), Barth insists that election is none other than Jesus Christ, who is at once the subject and object of this activity. Accordingly, election is the secondary mode of God's absolute being in Jesus Christ as the subject, object, and act of love-in-freedom, and is as such the *speculum Trinitatis*.

Election as Christ's eternal mode of being, however, is still unknowable to humans whose cognition is conditioned by spatio-temporality and finitude. Knowledge of the eternal history of election is mediated to us by the temporal history of Jesus Christ, who is in his work of reconciliation the *speculum electionis*. Christmas, which includes within itself Good Friday and Easter, is the external basis of election, and election the internal basis of the history of the incarnation. Election and the incarnation are two aspects of the same reality. In this way Golgotha mirrors to us the sublation of reprobation in eternal election.

Barth's speculative theology is *Christocentric* precisely in that Jesus Christ, the very unsublatable subject God, is the *speculum Dei* every step of the way. The history of God's covenant with us actualized on the basis of creation, namely, the birth, death, and resurrection of Jesus, as well as his promise of the Holy Spirit in between the times of his ascension and his second coming, mirrors to us God's covenantal love-in-freedom in election. Election as the secondary, *ad extra* mode of God's being in the free act of love in turn mirrors to us the primary absoluteness of God's triune essence *ad intra*.

God's self-revelation through this twofold mediation in the one Jesus Christ who is the very subject God becomes speculatively known to us through faith.

Faith is originally wrought in the man Jesus by the Holy Spirit and re-enacted *in nobis* by the same Holy Spirit. If election and its actualization in the history of the incarnation constitute the downward vector of revelation, then faith is the initiation of the upward vector.

Human knowledge of God is formed by faith that seeks understanding. With Anselm, Barth insisted against German idealism that God is that greater than which nothing can be conceived, and greater than can be conceived: the subject God is unsublatable and remains unsublated in both the *ad intra* and *ad extra* modes of God's abidingly absolute being. The infinitude and perfections of the divine nature, then, cannot be speculatively projected from the finitude and deficiencies of human nature. That is to say, no creature can in and of itself serve as *speculum Dei*.

What is properly called *speculum Dei* has to be none other than the subject God. Jesus Christ is the fullness of this divine subject. As the electing, the elected, and election, Jesus Christ is the subject God who remains unsublated in his own eternal objectivity and activity *ad extra interna*. Even at Golgotha that is the external basis of election, Christ suffered without ceasing to be the electing God, the unsublatable subject—the impassible God.

Faith in Jesus Christ as the unsublatable subject God who became *speculum Dei* in this twofold sense without ceasing to be the same subject is the Christocentric starting point of Barth's basically Anselmian mode of speculation. The Christocentric reorientation of Barth's speculative theology entails, *inter alia*, that everything positing itself as a this-worldly appearance of the divine must be regarded as the demonic, for there is other than Christ no *imago Dei apropos* in this world.

In Barth's day, the idolatrous assertion of historical divine appearances was expressed most domineeringly in Germany's mystical nationalism, echoed throughout Europe and beyond. His Christocentric speculative theology thus carried profound cultural and socio-political implications in his own *Sitz im Leben* and beyond. In the next chapter, I will frame my portrait of Barth as a Christocentric speculative theologian with an analysis of his theology of nationhood set forth in *Gottes Gnadenwahl*, which, as I hope to show, remains pertinent to the global-political and cultural context of our own day and age.

Chapter 7

FRAMING THE PICTURE: ELECTION AND NATIONHOOD—CHRISTOCENTRIC REFLECTIONS FROM 1936 TO 1938

My narrative of the intellectual-historical background of Barth's speculative theology in Chapter 2 has suggested that his adoption of a basically Anselmian *Denkform* was partly aimed at countering a popular nationalistic epic from the nineteenth century, which claimed Anselm as a forerunner of pantheistic German Christianity. This chapter will seek to frame my portrait of Barth as a speculative theologian within the political context of the 1930s. This framing is not at all intended to suggest that Barth's theology was driven by political concerns. Except in certain artworks from the Baroque period, it would indeed be odd to frame a portrait in such a way that the final result appears as if the picture were painted to fit a pre-existing frame.

The political framing of Barth's theological portrait in this chapter, then, serves to demonstrate that his view of nationhood, statehood, and nationalism was consistently guided by his Christocentric speculative theology, which sought to honor the Word of God and repudiate every form of idolatry. Just as he refused to let the philosophical tail wag the theological dog, he did not allow his theology to be governed by political or cultural circumstances. To use a phrase from an open letter that Barth wrote in 1932 to the Nazi theologian Emanuel Hirsch, Barth's erstwhile colleague in Göttingen: genuine theology is "a theology that, even in the face of politics, would not become politics, but would remain theology."[1]

I will probe into how Barth's Christocentric reorientation of his speculative theology in 1936, which I introduced in Chapter 4, served to repudiate Germany's mystical nationalism in its heyday. I will demonstrate how Barth's Christological doctrine of election in *Gottes Gnadenwahl* provided a basis for a sophisticated theology of nationhood, and how this theology serves to explain both his renunciation of German nationalism and his affirmation of German nationhood.

Part of this chapter has been accepted for publication elsewhere: Shao Kai Tseng, "Karl Barth on Election and Nationhood: Christological Reflections from 1936," *Scottish Journal of Theology* 75 4 (forthcoming).

1. Offener Brief Karl Barths, Bonn, April 17, 1932. In *GA* 35, 209.

As we saw in Chapter 4, it has been a large consensus among Barth scholars for over two decades that the theologian's Christological reformulation of the doctrine of election in *Gottes Gnadenwahl* marks, in one way or another, the beginning of the Christocentric phase of his theology. Lesser known is the fact that well before his famous discussion of nationhood in *CD* III/4, §54, "Freedom in Fellowship," Barth already published a self-contained passage on the same topic in *Gottes Gnadenwahl*.[2]

This passage is found in the questions and answers (*Fragebeantwortung*) appended to the main body of the volume, which consists of written lectures that Barth delivered in Hungary and Transylvania in September and October of 1936.[3] Under the fourth topic, "the relationship between providence and predestination," he devotes eight pages to addressing what appears to be the most frequently recurring question on his tour, "raised in Debrecen, Sárospatak, Cluj and Oradea: the gospel and folklore/nationhood [*Volkstum*]? The gospel and nationalism?"[4]

To appreciate the weight that Barth attaches to this question, it serves well to recall that he was forced to leave Germany in the previous year for his refusal to conform to the ideologies and policies of the National Socialist Party. Barth shared the view, popular among German-speaking Christian thinkers during the Second World War, that immanentizations of the Christian doctrines of election and providence under the Enlightenment principle of historical progress by modern German thinkers, most notably Hegel, were largely at fault for having provided theological and philosophical justifications for the rise of Germany's mystical nationalism in the name of German Christianity.[5]

Barth was appalled by the idolatrous notion of Christianity as civil religion (*Volksreligion*), and insisted against his compatriots that there is no such thing as "Swiss Christianity."[6] His repudiation of nationalism and civil religions in the late 1930s, however, did not amount to a negation of nationhood. He insisted that nationhood is integral to God's determination of human existence *in Christo*. It is an indispensable part of our human experience, and just like everything else in God's good yet fallen creation, nationhood must be sanctified. Nationhood survives and thrives only when its idolatrous status is mortified, making way for the universal lordship of Jesus Christ who reigns in and through the "*una sancta ecclesia.*"[7]

In this chapter, I will demonstrate that Barth's Christocentric reformulation of the doctrine of election in 1936 led to a view of nationhood as *one* indispensable dimension of the external basis of the communion of the elect, and the election of the community as *the* internal basis of nationhood. In my conclusion, I will offer a

---

2. See *CD* III/4, 285–323.
3. *Gottes Gnadenwahl*, 36–43.
4. *Gottes Gnadenwahl*, 36.
5. E.g. Karl Löwith, *From Hegel to Nietzsche: The Revolution in Nineteenth-Century Thought*, trans. David Green (New York: Columbia University Press, 1991).
6. *Gottes Gnadenwahl*, 40.
7. *Gottes Gnadenwahl*, 40.

discussion of his rather surprising suggestion of the vision of Christian countries by turning to his treatment of church-state relations in a work from roughly the same period, *Recthfertigung und Recht* (1938).[8]

Cultural-Historical Background: Pantheistic German Christianity

From Menschheitsideal to Weltdeutsch: *Germany's Mystical Nationalism*

In Chapter 2, we saw how Barth reacted to an intellectual-historical folklore that served to support the nationalistic view of pantheistic Christianity as Germany's *Volksreligion*. My narration of the intellectual-historical background of his speculative theology in that chapter drew primarily on *Protestant Theology in the Nineteenth Century*, completed in Basel shortly after the defeat of the Nazi regime and published in September 1946. On his own account, this book was "not a new book," but rather a rearrangement of written "lectures on the history modern Protestant theology" from the late 1920s and the early 1930s.

"When the Hitler régime dawned," Barth reports in the foreword, he "happened to be occupied with Rousseau."[9] Though Barth does not explicitly deal with German nationalism in this work, it is not difficult for the reader to discern in this thoroughly historical-theological work, just as in the *Barmen Theological Declaration* as a thoroughly dogmatic-theological statement, an implicit yet intense struggle against the pantheistic reinterpretation of Christianity in Germany's mystical nationalism.

To situate this mystical nationalism against its cultural-historical background, it would serve well to turn to the composer Richard Wagner (1813–83) and consider his popularity among Hitler and his ministers in light of the history of speculative theology that I narrated in Chapter 2. Interestingly, of all the great composers of the German-Austrian tradition, Wagner is the only one who remains forbidden in the state of Israel. The Jewish conductor Daniel Barenboim caused a nationwide protest when he performed Wagner in Israel in 2001. In 2015, the Israeli Public Broadcasting Corporation was forced to issue an official apology after playing an excerpt from Wagner's *Götterdämmerung* on radio, which stirred up a nationwide storm.

The association of Wagner with Germany's rise as a *Reich* is of course a gross distortion of what the composer stood for. World-leading *Germanistiker* Dieter Borchmeyer, in his highly acclaimed *Was ist deutsch?*, describes Wagner as one supreme expression of Germany's identity as a *Kulturnation*, alongside Johann Wolfgang von Goethe (1749–1832) and Thomas Mann (1875–1955).[10] Borchmeyer

---

8. Karl Barth, *Rechtfertigung und Recht, Christengemeinde und Bürgergemeinde, und Evangelium und Gesetz* (Zurich: TVZ, 1998).

9. *Protestant Theology*, xi.

10. See Dieter Borchmeyer, *Was ist deutsch? Die Suche einer Nation nach sich sebst* (Berlin: Rowohlt, 2017).

titled this work after a later essay by Wagner, *Was ist deutsch?* (1878). This work has definitively demonstrated, *inter alia*, that the quintessentially German *Menschheitsideal* in Wagner stands at odds with the nationalistic ethos that led to the two World Wars.

One question that remains after perusing Borchmeyer's magisterial volumes, articles, and published lectures is: granted that Third Reich propaganda fundamentally distorted Wagner's image, what was it about Wagner that made his compositions so dear to Hitler and his ministers?

Of course, plenty of academic work has been devoted to the study of the various dimensions of Wagner's relationship to German nationhood and nationalism—Borchmeyer himself acknowledges Mann's criticisms of Wagner's later works. On the other hand, it is also well established in the literature that Wagner, under the influence of Friedrich Schiller (1759–1805), saw in the common *Volk*, rather than the princes, the true essence of the German nation.[11] Borchmeyer demonstrates that Wagner remained well in line with Goethe's ideal of *Weltbürgertum*: "Wagner emphasized that 'Germans are not addicted to conquest and that the desire to rule over foreign peoples is un-German.'"[12]

Clearly, then, Wagner's political convictions did not cater to the interest of the Nazi Party in particular and German nationalism in general. A theological perspective is necessary to explain the intellectual-historical link between Wagner and German nationalism. Readers familiar with Wagner's operas will recall how he celebrates not only the paganistic origins of Teutonic pantheism through the grand futuristic *Ring des Nibelungen* cycle, but also incorporates medieval Christian legends into his pantheistic world of *Kunstreligion* through works like *Tannhäuser*.

Parsifal, a deeply psychological work that accentuates the inner activities of the characters, is another Wagnerian opera often understood as communicating a basically "religious" message.[13] Based on a legend by Wolfram von Eschenbach (ca. 1160/80–ca. 1220), the "religious" message of *Parsifal* is conveyed through a medieval European setting featuring a deeply mystical form of Christianity.

Wagner was by no means a "Christian" in any traditional sense of the term, but his works and writings exhibit a strong sense of "Christian" identity in a highly mystical and pantheistic way. Wagner was familiar with the writings of Lessing, Hegel, and Feuerbach at a relatively early phase of his career, and greeted their ideas with general approval, though he was never fond of David Strauss, whom

---

11. For example, Tim Blanning, "Richard Wager and the German Nation: The Prothero Lecture," *Transactions of the Royal Historical Society* 25 (2016): 95–112.

12. Borchmeyer, *Was ist deutsch? Die Suche einer Nation nach sich sebst*, 40.

13. See Ulrike Kiezle, "*Parsifal* and Religion: A Christian Music Drama?" in *A Companion to Wagner's Parsifal*, ed. William Kinderman and Katherine Syer (Rochester: Camden House, 2005), 81–130. Richard Bell, "Richard Wagner's Prose Sketches for Jesus of Nazareth," *Journal for the Study of the Historical Jesus* 15 (2017): 260–90.

he did not read until a much later stage.[14] Like the eighteenth- and nineteenth-century critics of religion, Wagner deemed the resurrection of Jesus incredible.

In 1848, Wagner drafted an opera titled *Jesus von Nazareth*, which was never finished. The sketches manifest very careful readings of the Synoptic Gospels, the Gospel of John, and the rest of the New Testament. What is especially interesting about the plot is that the resurrection of Jesus is omitted, while the promise of the Holy Spirit becomes the highlight of the whole opera. Wagner saw in Christianity a spirit of universal religion that transcended national and institutional boundaries. It was precisely this pantheistic reorientation of Christianity that lent itself to the mystical nationalism underlying Nazi ideology.

This theological perspective on Wagner of course does not contradict Borchmeyer's contention that leading cultural figures like Goethe, Schiller, and Wagner understood the essence of German identity in terms of cultural-nationhood rather than state-nationhood. Borchmeyer illuminates this fact with a plethora of literary, artistic, and musical works from the eighteenth and nineteenth centuries by some of the most representative figures on the German cultural scene. These works demonstrate that the leading *Gebildete* in Germany from the long nineteenth-century held to the "idea of the German [*Idee des Deutschen*]" not as "circumscribed [*abgegrenzten*] nationality, but rather a meta-national, cosmopolitan, purely human substance."[15]

It serves well to recall that one of Wagner's most celebrated operas, *Tristan und Isolde*, is based on an originally Irish tale. Wagner's operatic adaptation of this tragic love story is exemplary of what Borchmeyer considers to be the quintessentially German ideal of the purely human, *das Reinmenschliche*. Incidentally, William Shakespeare was among the few cultural figures deified in Wagner's *Kunstreligion*, alongside Beethoven and Schiller. Wagner's idea of the German, clearly, is not delimited in terms of ethnicity or statehood, but rather by the pure idea of universal humanity.

In fact, as Borchmeyer points out, "Wagner's idea of the German is not his invention; it refers to the idea of a German cultural nation as it emerged in the second half of the eighteenth century."[16] If Wagner's view of German nationhood can only be gathered from bits and pieces of his writings, then "Goethe's idea of world-literature as the culture of humanity [*Menschheitskultur*]" clearly espouses the ideal of "world-citizenship (*Weltbürgertum*) versus nation-state (*Nationalstaat*)."[17] Borchmeyer cites a eulogy from *Xenien* by Goethe and Schiller, titled *Das deutsche Reich*: "Germany? But where does she reside? I do not know where to find this country. /Where the learned begins, there ends the political."[18]

14. See.
15. Borchmeyer, *Was ist deutsch? Die Suche einer Nation nach sich sebst*, 45.
16. Borchmeyer, *Was ist deutsch? Die Suche einer Nation nach sich sebst*, 44.
17. Borchmeyer, *Was ist deutsch? Die Suche einer Nation nach sich sebst*, 44.
18. Borchmeyer, *Was ist deutsch? Die Suche einer Nation nach sich sebst*, 45. Translation mine henceforth.

Unfortunately, Germany's consciousness of her *Weltbürgertum*, expressed by the best of her cultural leaders in modernity, became increasingly distorted through the desire of the people in a long history of national humiliations to transform the *Kulturnation* into a *Staatsnation*. By the First World War, the term *Weltdeutsch*, which first emerged in the 1850s, had become a political slogan serving the purpose of German colonialism. The Second World War saw a host of Germany's best theological minds marrying the *Weltdeutsch* idea with mystical German Christianity.

While Borchmeyer blames the rise of Germany as a *Staatsnation* on contingent factors in socio-political events in history, there is in fact an intellectual-historical link, from a theological perspective, between Germany's mystical nationalism and figures like Goethe, Schiller, and Wagner. The Lutheran theologian Hans Schwarz describes this link as a long intellectual-historical continuum of attempts "to go behind Christianity to the Germanic roots and re-introduce the old Germanic religion which allegedly is true to the Germanic race."[19] The pantheistic narrative of German nationhood and German Christianity was part and parcel of the nationalistic view of the rise of the German nation—*Kulturnation* or *Staatsnation* all the same—as a divinely elected entity.

The view of German Christianity as a cultivated form of ancient Teutonic pantheism was explicitly presented in Heine's philosophical epic, which we discussed at some length in Chapter 2, notwithstanding his distaste for political visions of a *Staatsnation*. In fact, this view was already in the foreground on the intellectual scene in Germany by the latter half of the eighteenth century, albeit still under severe scrutiny and suppression. The famous pantheism controversy (*Pantheismusstreit*), initiated by the debate between Friedrich Jacobi (1743–1819) and Moses Mendelssohn (1729–86) on Gotthold Lessing's (1729–81) reception of Spinozist philosophy, significantly shaped the subsequent developments of German thought and culture.[20] The *Sturm und Drang* movement led by Goethe and Schiller, the romantic movement initiated by Novalis (1772–1801) and the Schlegel brothers (1767–1845 and 1772–1829), and the idealist turn in post-Kantian philosophy beginning with Johann Gottlieb Fichte (1762–1814) were all informed by this controversy in one way or another.

Fichte himself was dismissed from the University of Jena in a related controversy, when he was accused of atheism for what were taken as either pantheistic or deistic, idealistic or naturalistic, beliefs expressed in his 1798 essay, *Ueber den Grund unsers Glaubens an eine göttliche Weltregierung*. The most powerful attack came from none other than Jacobi, who famously coined the term "nihilism" to describe what he saw as the atheistic essence of Fichte's pantheistic or deistic reinterpretation of divine providence. One might wonder if Barth's assessment of

---

19. Hans Schwarz, "Paul Althaus (1888–1966)," in *Twentieth-Century Lutheran Theologians*, ed. Mark Mattes (Göttingen: Vandenhoeck & Ruprecht, 2013), 144.

20. See Benjamin Crowe, "On 'The Religion of the Visible Universe': Novalis and the Pantheism Controversy," *British Journal for the History of Philosophy* 16 (2008): 125–56.

Fichte's pantheistic speculation as one in which God is treated as "non-existent" (see Chapter 2) was not also under direct or indirect influence from the famous controversies in which Jacobi played a major role.

Incidentally, Heine's folkloric historiography also discusses these eighteenth-century controversies on pantheism in some detail. The ideas presented in this philosophical epic were very much "in the air" (as Sigurd Baark would put it) toward the end of the long nineteenth century. Regardless of how familiar Barth was with Heine's work, then, it well represents the intellectual air that Barth breathed during his student years.

This can be demonstrated by Barth's engagement with Goethe in 1913—before the break with liberalism. With an intellectual-historical perspective inherited from Adolf von Harnack (1851-1930), the early Barth interpreted Goethe in a deism-versus-pantheism framework, which was typical of nineteenth-century German historiographies of ideas and culture. At the time, Barth understood "the error of idealistic pantheism" to be "a dissolution of the notion of God's personality through the unilateral emphasis on the notion of God's sublimity. By contrast, deism errs in the dissolution of the notion of God's sublimity through the unilateral emphasis on the notion of God's personality, in such a way that the idea of God is ultimately watered down."[21]

Barth explicitly drew on Goethe's famous "caricature" of deism: "'What would be a God who only bumps in from the outside ...!'"[22] However, "Barth is in disagreement with the idealistic-pantheistic position of Goethe and his caricature of deism."[23]

Despite the distaste for *Staatsnation* among leading German cultural figures from the long nineteenth century like Goethe, Schiller, Heine, and Wagner, then, the pantheistic soil that they ploughed, coupled with immanentized reinventions of the Christian doctrines of election and providence by figures like G. W. F. Hegel (1770-1831) and Karl Marx (1818-83), eventually cultivated a mystical *Volksreligion* according to which the consummation of history is destined to be fulfilled in the German *Vaterland*.

The dominance of this narrative in the early twentieth century is partly reflected by the vehemence of the criticisms raised by its opponents. Even Paul Althaus (1888-1966), Barth's life-long friend and critic who scorned the democratic order of the Weimar Republic and signed the notorious *Ansbacher Ratschlag* in 1934, voiced his objections against Hitler's ideological encroachment on the churches. Althaus, once a naïve yet reserved supporter of the National Socialist regime, insisted amongst and against his compatriots that "national religion is national idolatry."[24] He refused to identify himself with the "German Christians—meaning

---

21. Thomas Xutong Qu, *Barth und Goethe: Die Goethe-Rezeption Karl Barths 1906-1921* (Neukirchen-Vluyn: Neukirchener, 2014), 96. Translation mine henceforth.
22. "Die weltanschaulichen Gedichte," in Goethe, *Werke*, Bd. 1, 357. Cited in Qu, 96.
23. Qu, 97.
24. Schwarz, "Paul Althaus (1888-1966)," 143.

those who fell prey to National Socialism."[25] Even Althaus was appalled by the German Christian doctrine that the Third Reich is the consummation of God's kingdom on earth.

In a very different manner, the celebrated *Meaning in History* by the Jewish Christian philosopher Karl Löwith (1897–1973) also reflects the popularity of the pantheistic core of Germany's mystical nationalism.[26] Already in an earlier work published during the Second World War, Löwith spelled out the view that Hegel was largely at fault for having provided theological and philosophical justifications for the rise of Germany's mystical nationalism.[27]

Löwith's *Meaning in History* is a classic that seeks to account for the rise of secularized views of divine providence that culminated in nineteenth-century German thinkers like Hegel and Marx. It is hardly a coincidence that Tillich, a contemporary of Barth and Löwith, also faults the "rational" reinterpretation of "providence" as "historical dialectics" advanced by "Hegel and Marx" for the "catastrophes of the twentieth century."[28]

Incidentally, this cultural-historical background was precisely the setting in which Barth developed his reinterpretation of Anselm, which we discussed in Chapter 2. Just as Löwith attempts to dissociate Augustine from Hegel in *Meaning in History*, Barth's *Anselm* is partly intended to claim Anselm against the nationalistic narrative that associated Anselm with what Barth deemed to be the idolatry of speculative identity in German idealism that culminated in Hegel.[29]

The way Löwith strived to dissociate the Christian doctrine of providence from modern philosophies of historical progress is characteristic of early twentieth-century German thinkers critical of the nationalistic myth of German Christianity as a *Volksreligion*. It does not require a "theologian of the Word" like Barth, so to speak, to recognize the fundamental differences between Christian and non-Christian views of election and providence. Even Tillich would stress that genuinely Christian, "paradoxical" faith in "God's permanent activity" in history and in the life of the individual must be strictly distinguished from "erroneous ... confidence in individual or historical providence."[30]

It is but a short step from believing that a certain cultural nation is a particular expression of some sacred *Menschheitsideal* to maintaining that the world ought to be reinvented in the particular image of this sanctified nation. The reversibility of the speculative identity between the sacred *Ideal* of humanity and a particular

25. Schwarz, "Paul Althaus (1888–1966)," 145.
26. Karl Löwith, *Meaning in History: The Theological Implications of the Philosophy of History* (Chicago: University of Chicago Press, 1957).
27. Löwith, *From Hegel to Nietzsche*. This volume was written in Japan 1939 while in exile from Germany and published in Switzerland in 1941.
28. Paul Tillich, *Systematic Theology, Volume I: Reason and Revelation; Being and God* (Chicago: Chicago University Press, 1951), 266.
29. Löwith, *Meaning in History*, 21.
30. Tillich, *Systematic Theology*, 267–9.

nation as its *imago* is very much the same as the reversibility, astutely observed by Feuerbach, of the Hegelian proposition, "humanity is Spirit."

In other words, the central idea espoused by Goethe, Schiller, and Wagner was that the German nation did not arise for her own sake. The German nation became determinate in history through her *Weltbürgertum*. Now that Germany as a *Kulturnation* has come to be the purest expression of the sacred ideal of humanity, she is called to cultivate the world so as to transform the world into her own likeness. Ruth Benedict, in her somewhat outdated yet still pertinent and celebrated *The Chrysanthemum and the Sword*, observes that this very German worldview was precisely what Japanese militarism adopted in the name of *Yamato Damashii* (大和魂: literally "Japanese *Geist*") in the wake of the Second World War.[31] Following Nazi Germany, militarist Japan saw herself as burdened with the duty to transform Asia in her own image as the purest expression of the sacred *Menschheitsideal*. The idea of German *Weltbürgertum*, on the view, was but a short step away from *Weltdeutsch* ideology.

Barth versus Althaus: The Need for Christocentrism

Of all the figures discussed above, Althaus represents an especially interesting case for our considerations from the perspective of speculative identity and extension. As a Lutheran theologian, Althaus in fact held to an ideal of universal humanhood that resonated deeply with Goethe and Wagner. Klaus Tanner cites Althaus and explains:

> According to Althaus, the "nationhood [*Volkheit*]" to which the members of the people [*Volk*] owe "unconditional loyalty" is "never given." It is "never what is, but what should be, the norm ... Nationhood is God's will over a people. When a nation contemplates before the unconditioned holy Lord, her nationhood, her mission, and her essence are enlightened as a synthesis of the eternal will of God above all humanity with the particular kind of people [*Volksart*]."[32]

The *Menschheitsideal* in Althaus, we must observe, was far from sufficient for preventing him from lending reserved and conditional support to German nationalism. Schwarz explains: "While a national religion is a national idolatry, Althaus is convinced that 'the nations are endowed with different callings by the Lord of history.'"[33] It is precisely at this juncture that we see a nationalistic distortion of the Christian doctrines of election and providence typical of German theologians sympathetic to the cause of the Third Reich.

---

31. See Ruth Benedict, *The Chrysanthemum and the Sword: Patterns of Japanese Culture* (New York: Mariner, 2005).

32. Klaus Tanner, *Die fromme Verstaatlichung des Gewissens: Zur Auseinandersetzung um die Legitimität der Weimarer Reichsverfassung in Staatsrechtswissenschaft und Theologie der zwanziger Jahre* (Göttingen: Vandenhoeck & Ruprecht, 1989), 254. Translation mine.

33. Schwarz, "Paul Althaus (1888–1966)," 143.

For Althaus, "the national heritage must seek out the church, but the church must also seek out the national heritage."[34] Althaus thus speaks of a *"Volkskirche"* instrumental to the cause of making Germany great again, so to speak (no pun intended).[35] With the other signatories of the *Ansbacher Ratschlag*, Althaus publicly expressed gratitude on behalf of the Christians in Germany for "the *Führer*" as God's providential gift to the nation, and professed a Christian "responsibility to cooperate in the work of our *Führer* according to our vocation and state."[36]

From the case of Althaus, then, we can see how the very noble notions of *Weltbürgertum* and *Menschheitsideal* that cultural luminaries like Goethe and Wagner epitomized were entirely powerless against the onslaught of German nationalism that based itself on distorting reinterpretations of election and providence. Barth saw Althaus's failure, along with the failure of other German theologians who (cautiously or not) embraced German nationalism, as one that ensued from a speculative view of revelation and history that was fundamentally erroneous.

In the early 1930s, Barth already discerned in Althaus a deeply flawed understanding of revelation and history, even though his references to Althaus in *CD* I/1-2 are for the most part appreciative. "The modern problem of 'revelation and history,' i.e., the question whether and how far man's time may be regarded at any definite point as the time of God's revelation," Barth urges, "rests upon a portentous failure to appreciate the nature of revelation."[37] The answer to this question must not find its starting point

> in the general phenomena of time, or, as it is preferably called, history ... To a man ... who actually stands in front of this phenomenon as in front of a wall and is unable to perceive anything of revelation at all (e.g., with P. Althaus ...), it may well be said it is the historical as such in its universality and relativity which is the necessary "offence" to revelation.[38]

In retrospect of the Second World War, Barth offers an in-depth analysis of the speculative view of revelation and history represented by Althaus, and how this widespread view among Christians in Germany bolstered the rise of the Third Reich. This passage from 1951 deserves to be quoted in its entirety.

> I now turn to P. Althaus (*Grundriss der Ethik*, 1914, p. 138): "The nations are indeed summoned to a common life and reciprocal responsibility." But if this interdependence is a norm overruling their relations, then the "living laws

---

34. Paul Althaus, *Kirche und Volkstum: Der völkische Wille im Lichte des Evangeliums* (Gütersloh: Bertelsmann, 1928), 27. Cited in Schwarz, 143.
35. Schwarz, "Paul Althaus (1888–1966)," 143.
36. *Ansbacher Ratschlag*, fifth thesis. Cited in Schwarz, "Paul Althaus (1888–1966)," 145.
37. *CD* I/2, 56.
38. *CD* I/2, 56–7.

of history entail that it should also have the form of opposition when one nation with its vocational question comes into collision in living history with the vocational question of another nation." Living history poses questions in which right is not merely opposed to wrong, or wrong to right, but right to right. "The law of conflict has a more elemental basis than the human will; it is to be associated with the sin of humanity; it thus stands or falls with history generally." Final decisions in the "truly great" questions are not to be sought in legal verdicts, since the historical right of a people depends on a power still to be demonstrated. This right must be determined in the venture of a historical act in which it concentrates its whole power upon its vocation. The inevitability of war rests on this foundation. It was in accordance with this kind of theological wisdom that in belief in "living history," in the "law of conflict," and in the determining of right by might, new "historical acts" were ventured in 1938, and the Second World War began.

Barth blames this theological "nonsense" on the almost official view of the historical determination of state-nationhood to which nineteenth-century thinkers gave rise (Hegel is certainly chief among them in Barth's view, though Barth does not mention any names here).[39] Theologians like Althaus and Adolf Schlatter gave "the impression that basically they have not yet outgrown the historical picture of so many nineteenth- and early twentieth-century historical text-books, which find the true essentials of universal and national history both ancient and modern in the campaigns, battles and conflicts waged on land and sea."[40]

This passage suggests that for Barth, the marriage of *Menschheitsideal* and *Weltbürgertum* with nationhood, which resulted in the political *Weltdeutsch* ideal, was a result of an essentially pantheistic view of the mediated, speculative identity between universal and national histories. As early as *CD* I/1, he had come to blame what he saw as the incipient pantheism in classical formulations of the *speculum Trinitatis* (see Chapter 5) as the root of Althaus's error in the doctrine of revelation.[41]

As we saw in Chapters 4–6, the Christocentric reorientation of the *speculum Trinitatis* and the doctrine of election was Barth's antidote to this last vestige of pantheism in the Anselm's speculative program. In this chapter, we will see how Barth appealed to Christocentrism in 1936 to rebuke heretical views of election, providence, revelation, and history, prevalent in German academic theology and philosophy as well as popular culture during the nineteenth and early twentieth centuries. Again, my interpretation of Barth's text will focus on his engagement with Hegel, for reasons already stated in the previous chapters, as well other reasons that we will discuss in this chapter.

39. *CD* III/4, 457–8.
40. *CD* III/4, 458.
41. *CD* I/1, 335.

Barth's Engagements with Hegel: A Brief Review

Actualistic Ontology

Barth's actualistic ontology is a topic discussed extensively in Chapter 3 of the present monograph. It serves well to review this topic briefly and highlight the points that are pertinent to this chapter. In recent scholarship, the term "actualistic ontology" has for the most part been associated with the view that being or essence is determined or constituted by activities, decisions, relationships, and histories. Proponents of this view read into Barth a basically idealistic notion of being-*as-act*. On this interpretation, Barth is described as treating election as the act by which God's triune essence is constituted.

Against this view, I have argued that Barth critically adopted a distinctively Hegelian grammar to (1) reinvigorate the form and substance of the *credo ut intelligam* program represented by Augustine and Anselm, and (2) correct what Barth saw as Hegel's mistake of subject-predicate reversal in ontological predications about God, a reversal that prioritizes activity over essence.

Barth's retainment of the originally substantialist language of essence (*Wesen*) and nature (*Natur*), I argued, is intended to safeguard theology from falling into Hegel's error of identifying essence or essentiality (*Wesentlichkeit*) with something consummate—something that is not yet determinate. Barth's distinction between *Wesen* (essential being) and *Sein* (existential being) serves to demonstrate how his actualistic ontology is tailored to a Hegelian grammar in order to overcome Hegel's idolatrous presuppositions.

Especially noteworthy, as I pointed out, is Barth's critical adoption of Hegel's terminological association of *Sein* with *Schein* (appearance). Barth emphatically rejects what he takes to be the Hegelian view that God's "being [*Sein*], speaking and acting" in history "are only an appearance [*Schein*]" of God's consummate essence.[42] Against Hegel, Barth differentiates strictly "between the divine" and the "appearance of the divine [*dem Schein-Göttlichen*]," and completely excludes the latter from his theology.[43]

This will be important for my exposition of Barth's doctrine of election and theology of nationhood. It was Hegel and the larger idealist tradition that gave rise to the basic contours of modern Germany's *Volksreligion*, a nationalistic mysticism that eventually came to justify the rise of the Third Reich as an immanent *Schein* of the divine.

Barth is at pains to emphasize in *Gottes Gnadenwahl* that Jesus Christ is himself the electing God, rather than a mere historical appearance of God in some Hegelian sense. This identification of Jesus Christ with the electing God—which Barth did not wait until 1942 to formulate—precludes the mystical view of

---

42. *CD* II/1, 496; *KD* II/1, 558. Translation revised.
43. *CD* II/1, 409; *KD* II/1, 461.

nations as appearances of the divine.⁴⁴ Because Christ has come, as Barth puts it in a passage written between 1937 and 1939, all creaturely entities and historical phenomena that posit themselves as divine appearances must be regarded as "the demonic."⁴⁵

Keyword: Bestimmung

An originally Hegelian notion worth revisiting here is one that pervades *Gottes Gnadenwahl* as well as Barth's earlier and later works, namely, "determination" (*Bestimmung*). This notion played a decisive role in the secularization of the doctrines of election and providence in nineteenth-century German thought and culture. Barth's use of this originally Hegelian term is partly intended to refute the idolatrous views of sacred historical destiny that arose from the various receptions and (mis)interpretations of Hegel.

By "determination," Hegel means the definition of a subject through a history of conflict and reconciliation with otherness. A thing is *determinate* (*bestimmt*) only in relation to an other in the dialectical process of sublation (*Aufhebung*: the negation of an abstract moment of logic in a dialectical moment for the purpose of elevating the logical subject to the moment of the positively rational).

We explained this notion by considering the proposition, "Confucius was a Chinese philosopher." In Confucius's time, the *subject* that subsequently came to be China was not yet *determinate* as a nation. International conflicts in modern times, including the Siege of Peking of 1900 by the International Legations, led to a determination of China's consciousness of herself as a nation in the same category as, say, Great Britain and Japan. But because the China of the early twentieth century and the ancient entity that was in the process of becoming China are the same *subject* of self-consciousness, it is correct, by virtue of a *logic of mediation*, as Hegel would have it, to say that Confucius was a Chinese philosopher. The identification of Confucius as a Chinese philosopher hinges upon the historical determination of China as China—it is an *identity* determined from the twentieth century and *mediated* through a long historical process to the ancient sage.

---

44. *Pace* Bruce McCormack and Matthias Gockel. See Bruce McCormack, "Seek God Where He May Be Found: A Response to Edwin Van Driel," *Scottish Journal of Theology* 60 (2007): 64; Matthias Gockel, *Barth and Schleiermacher on the Doctrine of Election* (Oxford: Oxford University Press, 2006), 167.

45. *CD* II/1, 409. *CD* II/1 was already underway in 1937 before the completion of I/2. Most of the materials in II/1 were written in 1938. The half-volume was completed in the summer of 1939 and published in 1940.

Election as Divine Determination of Human Existence

Election as God's Self-Determination

Again, Barth's Christocentric doctrine of election from 1936 is a topic that we already covered in a previous chapter. I will not repeat the arguments from Chapter 4 here. However, it is worth our while to review this topic and highlight some salient points pertinent to Barth's theology of nationhood.

In the very first sentence at the beginning of *Gottes Gnadenwahl*, Barth uses Hegelian terminology to restate the classical Reformed view of "election" as a function of "predestination [*Vorherbestimmung*]."[46] Throughout the text, he capitalizes on the Hegelian connotations of the etymologically Teutonic term *Vorherbestimmung* and uses it interchangeably with *Prädestination*. Barth explains in a subsequent paragraph in the same chapter: "God's grace ... is not just a determination [*Bestimmung*], but rather a pre-determination [*Vorherbestimmung*], *prae-destinatio*, of our human existence."[47]

To say that election is a *pre*-determination of human existence is to deny the historicist understanding of an immanently consummate determination of humankind to which Hegel, according to the mainstream view among German-speaking thinkers of Barth's generation, gave rise. Löwith is well representative of this intellectual-historical view when he describes Hegel's notion of historical "progress directed toward a final elaboration and consummation of the established principle of the whole course of history" as largely a result of "reinterpreting" through "Enlightenment" categories "the theological tradition according to which" history is determined by God's purpose in election and providence.[48]

Barth, too, interprets Hegel as positing a "final identity" between the human "Self" that thinks and God as the object that is thought.[49] On this popular interpretation, Hegel is taken as asserting that human existence remains indeterminate until the actualization of its consummate essentiality. There is no *pre*-determination of human existence. Human existence is determined by the absolute essentiality of Spirit from a consummate future, in much the same way Confucius was determined from the twentieth century to be a Chinese philosopher.

Many Christian thinkers of Barth's generation sympathized with Löwith's outspoken rejection of what they took to be the Hegelian view of the "possibility ... of imposing on history a reasoned order" and "of drawing out the workings of God."[50] This was in fact one reason why so many of them, Löwith included, embraced Barth's opposition to the anthropological grounding of theology, stated as early as the first edition of *Romans* II.[51]

---

46. *Gottes Gnadenwahl*, 4.
47. *Gottes Gnadenwahl*, 7.
48. Löwith, *Meaning in History*, 60.
49. *Protestant Theology*, 379.
50. Löwith, *Meaning in History*, v.
51. See Karl Löwith, *My Life in Germany before and after 1933* (London: Athlone, 1994), 26.

Barth, however, was not satisfied with a mere rejection of anthropological religion as the "summit of human possibility" distanced from God by an infinite qualitative difference.[52] As early as the two editions of *Romans*, he had embarked on a quest for genuinely theological grounds on which he could speak of God's determination of human existence through election and providence.

The ground-breaking insight in *Gottes Gnadenwahl* that allowed Barth to speak of a divine determination of human existence as *pre*-determination is that election is first and foremost a self-determination of God's own being as being-for-us. He stresses against Hegel and German idealism that this divine self-determination is not an *essential* act of God. As we saw in Chapters 5–6, Barth later explains in *CD* II/2 that the God-human relationship determined in the act of election "is a relation *ad extra*, undoubtedly; for both the man and the people represented in him [Christ] are creatures and not God."[53]

This self-determination is grounded in and made possible by God's immutably determinate and thus unsublatable being-in-and-for-Godself qua Trinity. Because election is an eternal act of God that determines God's own mode of being *ad extra*, it is, with respect to the creature, a *pre*-determination from eternity.

More concretely, election is in the very first instance an *ad extra* determination of God's own mode of being through the incarnation. Barth states in *Gottes Gnadenwahl*: "God began with himself and therefore ... from what is outside of us: it was by virtue of the decision and act of the eternal Son and Word that this man, conceived of the Holy Spirit and born of the Virgin Mary when He began to be human, began to be the Son and Word of God. This is election!"[54]

Note here that the identity between Jesus Christ and the "eternal Son" qua electing God—the subject of the "decision and act" of election—is *speculative* (i.e., mediated and mirrored) rather than *immediate*. Immediate identity between act and being resides in God's *ad intra* essence qua Trinity alone. Barth describes the "identity" between Jesus Christ and the electing God in the Hegelian language of *Bestimmung*.[55] The identity is, as the quote above indicates, determined "by virtue of the decision and act of the eternal Son." The logic of mediation, so to speak, underlying this speculative identity is analogous to the logic underlying the phrase, "Confucius was a Chinese philosopher": it is a *mediated* identity, a speculative extension.

It is correct, by virtue of God's *ad extra* self-determination, to say that Jesus Christ is the subject of election. Strictly speaking, however, "the subject of predestination is recognized as the triune God in His revelation in Jesus Christ."[56] As Sigurd Baark aptly puts it, the doctrine of the aseity of the triune God is for Barth an expression of "God's unsublatable subjectivity, which is revealed in Jesus

---

52. *Romans* II, 252.
53. *CD* II/2, 7.
54. *Gottes Gnadenwahl*, 15.
55. *Gottes Gnadenwahl*, 45.
56. *Gottes Gnadenwahl*, 44.

Christ" to be "identical with God's essence as the one who loves in freedom."[57] Barth's understanding of God's self-determination to be God-for-us without ceasing to be God-in-and-for-Godself allows him to speak of a pre-determination of human existence *in Christo* while avoiding what he saw as the Hegelian error of reducing God's absolute being and purpose to the rational concept of an immanent consummation of history.[58]

Election and Human Nature

Barth's speculative identification of election with the incarnation means that election as the *Vorherbestimmung* of human existence is not just a one-way traffic. As an ontological determination of human existence, it is not a divine exercise of "*decretum absolutum* abstracted from Christ," but rather a concrete determination in and by Jesus Christ who is himself the God self-determined to be *pro nobis*.[59]

In *CD* III/2, Barth describes this two-way traffic in terms of the covenant and speaks of "Man in His Determination as God's Covenant-Partner" in §45, where he stresses an "inner necessity with which Jesus is at one and the same time for God and for man."[60] In III/3, §50, Barth states that "in the incarnation," God as our covenant-partner "exposed Himself to nothingness even as His enemy and assailant. He did so in order to repel it and defeat it."[61] This means that the determination of our creaturely nature is one in which sin and nothingness are assumed in order to be defeated.

This narrative of the determination of human nature is already spelled out under the rubric of election and reprobation in *Gottes Gnadenwahl*. "It is in all seriousness that God made himself one with sinful and mortal man in Christ, and took upon himself the sin and death of this man … He has to be truly laden with humanity's total sin and burdened with humanity's total death."[62]

Just as Christ died in order to conquer death, reprobation must be understood as God's No that serves the purpose of the Yes. Election, then, must be understood as the total negation of sin through the "sublation" of "reprobation."[63] Thus, "even on the cross, Jesus Christ is the Elect of God."[64] The determination of Christ as

---

57. Sigurd Baark, *The Affirmations of Reason: On Karl Barth's Speculative Theology* (Cham: Palgrave Macmillan, 2018), 255–6.

58. For Barth's take on Hegel's philosophy of ultimate divine-human identity, see *Protestant Theology*, 370–407. I acknowledge that interpretations of Hegel diverge on this point. See Charles Taylor, *Hegel and Modern Society* (Cambridge: Cambridge University Press, 1979). In a similar vein: Michael Rosen, *Hegel's Dialectic and Its Criticism* (Cambridge: Cambridge University Press, 1982).

59. *Gottes Gnadenwahl*, 44.
60. *CD* III/2, 218–19.
61. *CD* III/3, 311.
62. *Gottes Gnadenwahl*, 16.
63. *Gottes Gnadenwahl*, 23.
64. *Gottes Gnadenwahl*, 21.

the elect is the essentiality that determined the whole sublatory process of double predestination.

Human nature, on this view, is the determination of human existence through Christ's triumph over sin. As such it is, in its present state of fallenness, a nature still under the sway of the ontologically impossible reality of nothingness.

Nationhood and the Determination of Human Existence

Election and Nationhood

On the basis of this view of election as God's ontological pre-determination of human existence, Barth proceeds to formulate a Christocentric theology of nationhood in the appendix to *Gottes Gnadenwahl*. He begins with a firm rejection of the notion of chosen peoples:

> If what is being asked here is whether the Bible allows us to speak of chosen peoples, I think everyone who knows Holy Scripture will agree with me that this is not allowed. There is according to Holy Scripture only one chosen people: the people of Israel. Beyond this people, Scripture only knows of the fellowship of the Church chosen from all peoples.[65]

This is not an endorsement of Jewish nationalism. Rather, Barth has in mind a view of Israel that he would later spell out in *CD* II/2, §34, "The Election of the Community." The "election of the many" through Israel and the church is the historical re-enactment of the election of the one Jesus Christ.[66] It is in this redemptive sense, rather than in any nationalistic sense, that Scripture speaks of Israel as God's chosen people. Thus Barth in *Gottes Gnadenwahl*: "The chosen people of God can be none other than the people of the community of salvation, the community that knows of no national boundaries, that is at once alien and at home in every nation."[67]

Barth's rejection of nationalism, however, does not amount to a denial of nationhood as a result of God's election. It is one question whether earthly nations can be understood as God's chosen peoples. It is quite "a different question" whether there is "an election of a certain person as a member of his nation."[68]

To the latter question, Barth's answer is clearly in the affirmative. He states that "national identity pertains to the general realm that we call human nature," qualifying that "this dimension of human nature" is by no means "the deepest and most central."[69] Barth would think that the attempt to dissolve national

---

65. *Gottes Gnadenwahl*, 36.
66. *CD* II/2, 195.
67. *Gottes Gnadenwahl*, 36.
68. *Gottes Gnadenwahl*, 36.
69. *Gottes Gnadenwahl*, 37.

consciousnesses and identities advocated by certain political ideologies in the West today, especially in the European Union, as dehumanizing. "The fact that one belongs to this or that nation and therefore to this or that culture," Barth urges, "is part of one's existence, as is the fact that one is either a man or a woman. This is so deeply rooted in a person's experience that we would not see him truly, if we refuse to see him in his capacity as a member of his nation."[70]

Barth's newly developed Christocentrism, as we saw, dictates that human nature must be understood as God's pre-determination of human existence through Christ's assumption of human flesh. This is also the case with nationhood as one dimension of human nature. "In the Bible, human nature is called flesh—*sarx*. Nationhood, along with all other determinations of human nature, belongs to this flesh."[71]

In view of Barth's Christological formulation of election as the sublation of reprobation, this identification of nationhood as a dimension of human flesh carries two implications. First, "Scripture identifies *sarx* as the condition of man, who is a sinner before God in his radical essence, and who in his totality has thus fallen into death and God's judgment. Nationhood belongs to this sinful man who has fallen into death."[72]

Second, the sublation of reprobation in election means that "we are at once at the bottom of this abyss as well as on top of the summit: the Word became flesh (Jn. 1:14)."[73] This means that "in the work of reconciliation, God did not consider our human nature too lowly to make it His own … In view of revelation, therefore, nationhood and culture become human greatness, as they have been taken on by God in their waywardness and sinfulness."[74]

In other words, the quintessential Christian proclamation, "God became human," entails that "we no longer need to look at our human essence *in abstracto* …, but rather we may gaze upon it by faith in Jesus Christ's human nature and thus see our ethnic essence as God's gift by grace, accepted and assumed in His condescension."[75] The history of the incarnation allows us to understand nationhood *concretely* as God's grace.

The terms "abstract" and "concrete" in Barth's usage fit into the larger framework of his speculative language of *Bestimmung*, and have their origins again in Hegelian philosophy. Abstraction is the detachment of the particular from the universal and vice versa, while concretion is the marriage of the particular with the universal. Although German idealism since Hegel has been for the most part emphatic on understanding human nature concretely, it has never been able to truly avoid abstract speculation.

---

70. *Gottes Gnadenwahl*, 36–7.
71. *Gottes Gnadenwahl*, 37.
72. *Gottes Gnadenwahl*, 37.
73. *Gottes Gnadenwahl*, 37.
74. *Gottes Gnadenwahl*, 37.
75. *Gottes Gnadenwahl*, 37.

As we saw in Chapter 4, genuinely concrete thinking, per Barth, is possible only in light of Jesus Christ's particular revelation of the triune God. When nationhood is abstracted from particular individuals, it becomes a tyrant that enslaves humanity through "paganism" in the form of "nationalism."[76] Christ alone, as a member of the Jewish nation, born into a particular family of Davidic descent in the specific city of Bethlehem at the beginning of Rome's imperial era under the reign of Caesar Augustus, died at a specific place called Golgotha under a particular man named Pontius Pilate to accomplish God's election of *all*. The universal truth of the gospel of Jesus Christ goes hand in hand with its particularity. Only in Jesus Christ are we able to understand our human nature, including the dimension of nationhood—which, to be sure, is by no means the most central dimension—concretely.[77]

Barth is emphatic that God's gracious election does not negate or annihilate nationhood, however much it is an aspect of sinful human flesh. National consciousness "belongs" to sinful "flesh," and the church professes faith in "the resurrection of the flesh."[78] National identity as a dimension of human nature is determined by the election of all in Jesus Christ, manifested in his death and resurrection.

And because in Barth's view, every person's national identity is pre-determined by God's grace in Christ, he is emphatic that Christians must be grateful for the divine gift of national identity. Addressing a Hungarian audience, Barth states: "As it pleased God to make me a man and not a woman, it pleased Him to make me Swiss and not Hungarian. I then try to understand this fact as coming from God's hand."[79]

More importantly, however, because God's eternal election is actualized here and now in the form of the community of God's chosen people on earth, Barth is emphatic on the ontological priority of the church over the nations. The church, and not the earthly nation, "is the first actual community in which we live," for "we are first predestined, and only then are we by God's providence created."[80] The providential gift of nationhood serves the purpose of communion in the body of Christ.

Put another way, nationhood is *an* external basis of the communion of the elect, and the election of the community is *the* internal basis of nationhood. There is no balanced equilibrium or dialectic between the church and the nation, as Althaus would have it. There is an irreversible order of subordination between the church and the nation. "National consciousness is necessary in the Christian Church in this particular order of subordination ... National consciousness can only be the consciousness of sinners whose sins are forgiven. Knowing this, we

---

76. *Gottes Gnadenwahl*, 40.
77. *Gottes Gnadenwahl*, 37.
78. *Gottes Gnadenwahl*, 40.
79. *Gottes Gnadenwahl*, 37.
80. *Gottes Gnadenwahl*, 40.

must acknowledge ... the primacy of baptism over birth. If this is acknowledged, then national consciousness may live."[81]

Civil Religions as Tyrannical Idolatry

Ontological priority of the community of the elect over earthly nations means for Barth that all forms of civil religions (*Volksreligionen*), which identify the nation as the community of the elect, are inevitably idolatrous. Speaking of his native land, he stresses that "there is no such thing as Swiss totality of life [*Lebenstotalität*], no Swiss religion, no Swiss Christianity."[82]

Barth's association of the notion of *Volksreligion* with the term *Lebenstotalität* is especially noteworthy. This term is closely associated with idealism and the phenomenological tradition in German philosophy. It was well in use in broader German culture by the second half of the eighteenth century, as evident in the proto-romantic *Sturm und Drang* movement. Wilhelm Dilthey (1833–1911) made the notion of *Lebenstotalität* central to the disciplines of historical studies and hermeneutics, including literary criticism. Broadly defined, the term designates the totality of social life as an expression of the collective consciousness of a society. *Lebenstotalität* as such is usually understood as an expression of social determinism in the sense that this totality is inescapable for individual members of society. Hegelian philosophy is partly responsible for enhancing the deterministic dimension of the notion of *Lebestotalität*. According to Hegel, collective human consciousness is determined by the consummate essentiality of *Volksreligionen* in the form of *Lebenstotalitäten*.

The god of civil religions who reigns through *Lebenstotalitäten*, argues Barth, is not the "Father of Christ," but rather a "god of the people [*Volksgott*]."[83] This is "a god of philosophical abstraction," be it that of absolute idealism, left-Hegelian materialism, religious naturalism, secular naturalism, religious historicism, secular historicism, or what not.[84] These are for Barth, as we saw in Chapter 2, little more than various expressions of essentially the same kind of pantheistic speculation. The *Volksgott* is a god of historical determinism created in the image of humanity, a tyrant that imposes *Lebestotalitäten* on its worshippers to strip away the freedoms of human individuals for the sake of some collective destiny in history.

Election and Freedom

Barth is emphatic that the biblical doctrine of election is not determinism. Election does not deprive human beings of freedom, but rather activates it. "Man in his free decision is the object of divine pre-decision: how should he be discharged from

---

81. *Gottes Gnadenwahl*, 40.
82. *Gottes Gnadenwahl*, 40.
83. *Gottes Gnadenwahl*, 37.
84. *Gottes Gnadenwahl*, 37.

this decision through God's pre-decision, and how could he not be irresistibly challenged and compelled thereby to make a totally determinate [*bestimmt*] decision?"[85]

Barth's use of Hegelian vocabulary here is again noteworthy. Recall that in Hegel's terminology, a thing becomes *determinate* only through a dialectical process of *sublation*. When Barth uses this Hegelian grammar to describe human freedom in terms of a "determinate decision," he has in mind an act of the human will that re-enacts the sublatory process of reprobation and election in Jesus Christ. Barth speaks of this ongoing re-enactment of double predestination *in nobis* as an "analogy" (*Gleichnis*) and "repetition" (*Wiederholung*) of what already took place *extra nos*: "He [the free human being] will choose faith, and his decision as such will become an analogy of the divine pre-decision and a repetition of the decree in Jesus Christ, through whom he has passed from God's left hand over to the right, from death to life, from fear to hope."[86]

Precisely because "God's will and God's sovereignty as such do not negate man in his freedom and responsibility," but rather grounds and activates this freedom and responsibility, Barth stresses that both "indeterminism and determinism are erroneous ways."[87] The doctrine of predestination "repudiates determinism just as it repudiates indeterminism."[88]

Here Barth is likely alluding to Kant's treatment of the debate between "determinism" and indeterministic "freedom" in early modern philosophy.[89] As Kant sees it, this futile metaphysical debate within the realm of theoretical reason necessarily results in an irresolvable antinomy between the deterministic view that "everything in the world happens solely in accordance with the laws of nature" and the indeterministic notion of "a lawless faculty of freedom."[90] The theoretical "question of transcendental freedom," per Kant, "concerns merely speculative knowledge" that can be "set aside if we are concerned with what is practical," even though "the abolition of transcendental freedom would also eliminate all practical freedom."[91] Knowledge of practical freedom is attainable through moral experience, which reveals that genuine freedom is neither deterministic nor indeterministic.

Moral experience, according to Kant's later works, "leads inescapably to religion, through which it expands to the idea of a powerful moral legislator, outside the human being."[92] Practical knowledge of God as supreme moral legislator *extra*

---

85. *Gottes Gnadenwahl*, 31.
86. *Gottes Gnadenwahl*, 31–2.
87. *Gottes Gnadenwahl*, 44.
88. *Gottes Gnadenwahl*, 11.
89. Immanuel Kant, *Critique of Pure Reason*, trans. Paul Guyer and Allen Wood (Cambridge: Cambridge University Press, 2007), A445/B473–A449/B477.
90. Kant, *Critique of Pure Reason*, A445/B473–A449/B477.
91. Kant, *Critique of Pure Reason*, A803/B831; A534/B562.
92. Immanuel Kant, *Religion within the Bounds of Bare Reason* trans. Werner Pluhar (Indianapolis: Hackett, 2009), 4.

nos gives rise to a view of freedom that is neither determined by nature nor separated from nature. Positive freedom, according to Kant, is *autonomy*, that is, the voluntary, non-coerced conformity of a person's maxims and actions to the divinely legislated law of morality in opposition to its "radically" evil "propensity."[93]

In the previous chapters we saw how Kant gave rise to a characteristically post-Kantian conception of freedom as emancipation from the arbitrariness of both determinism and indeterminism. Barth, too, adopts the formal patterns of Kant's formulation of positive freedom and fleshes it out Christologically in *Gottes Gnadenwahl*. As election in Christ "proclaims God's freedom and lordship, it removes itself from that which places the concept of necessity at the top of its system and proclaims this concept as the world-principle as far away as from that which attributes the same primacy to the concept of freedom."[94] In opposition to the indeterministic understanding of freedom as lawlessness of the will, as well as the deterministic view that divine ordinances negate human freedom, Barth insists that genuine human freedom is freedom delimited by divine election. "There can be no question that predestination delimits the responsibility and freedom of man."[95]

The truly free human being is the human being under the reign of grace. "We cannot even entertain the idea that we have any freedom other than that which is identical with the reign of grace."[96] This is not a general concept of grace, but rather God's particular grace for us in Jesus Christ. We are free only in conforming to Christ who, "as the Elect of God," embraced God's gracious election as he said "Yes to … reprobation by faith" at Golgotha.[97]

Only when we respond in the freedom of faith and obedience as such to God's double pre-determination of our human existence do we *actually* become elected in the present tense. On one hand, Christ's accomplished work at Golgotha has already freed us from the threat of reprobation. On the other hand, "our election in Jesus Christ takes place through the Holy Spirit" who creates "faith in us by a miracle in which we no longer understand ourselves."[98] This faith is borne in us by the "witness of His [Christ's] Holy Spirit," but because it is wrought *in nobis*, it is our "own faith insofar as it is obedience, the sinner's obedience."[99]

Freedom in Fellowship: The Church and the Nation

Barth's actualistic affirmation of individual human agency and freedom stands in sharp contrast to a predominant view of freedom to which Hegel and other German idealists gave rise. Whereas Barth defines freedom in terms of the Holy

93. Kant, *Religion*, 32, 56–7.
94. *Gottes Gnadenwahl*, 11.
95. *Gottes Gnadenwahl*, 44.
96. *Gottes Gnadenwahl*, 8.
97. *Gottes Gnadenwahl*, 22.
98. *Gottes Gnadenwahl*, 30.
99. *Gottes Gnadenwahl*, 32.

Spirit's actualization of faith *in nobis*, Hegel defines freedom as "self-actualization [*Selbstverwirklichung*]": "freedom is precisely ... to be at home with oneself in one's other, to be dependent upon oneself, to be the determining factor for oneself."[100] The sublation of individuality through confrontation and reconciliation with otherness [*Anderssein*] is required for the determinacy of such freedom. Hegel dismisses the "'expression, 'to think for oneself'" as a "pleonasm," in view of the obvious fact that "nobody can think for someone else."[101] The freedom to think for oneself is merely the freedom "of a subjectively non-determinate being-with-itself [*Beisichsein*]."[102] Determinate freedom—the absolute freedom of being-in-and-for-itself—entails relinquishing one's "subjective particularity" and individual volition in a "determining" process of reconciliation.[103]

The absolute freedom that Hegel envisions is a mediation between what he famously calls "subjective" and "objective" freedoms. His notion of subjective freedom is akin to Kant's understanding of the negative aspect of freedom as non-coercion of the will. The more difficult concept of objective freedom has been variously interpreted in line with Rousseau's notion of the general will, with communitarianism, or even with Marxism.[104] More often than not, Hegel is taken to be suggesting that individual freedoms must be negated in the process of reconciliation (a process of sublation rather than synthesis) in order to make way for absolute freedom.

The freedom of the absolute, according to Hegel himself, is concretely realized by the establishment of the modern state.[105] The highest duty of the modern state is rational cultivation (*Bildung*) of its citizens.[106] This cultivation requires policies that impose censorships on various freedoms such as the "freedom of the press."[107]

Hegel's association of right (*Recht*: also "justice" and "law") and freedom with the establishment of the modern state was popular among German thinkers up to the two World Wars. The patriotic lyrics of August Heinrich Hoffmann (1798–1874), later adopted as Germany's national anthem, also makes the political "unity" (*Einigkeit*) of the German *Vaterland* the pretext of "right and freedom" (*Recht und Freiheit*).

---

100. G. W. F. Hegel, *Encyclopedia of the Philosophical Sciences in Basic Outline, Part 1: Logic*, ed. and trans. Klaus Brinkmann and Daniel Dahlstrom (Cambridge: Cambridge University Press, 2010), 60.
   101. Hegel, *Encyclopedia of the Philosophical Sciences in Basic Outline, Part 1: Logic*, 57.
   102. Hegel, *Encyclopedia of the Philosophical Sciences in Basic Outline, Part 1: Logic*, 57.
   103. Hegel, *Encyclopedia of the Philosophical Sciences in Basic Outline, Part 1: Logic*, 60.
   104. There are different interpretations of Hegel's notion of objective freedom. For a Marxist interpretation, see Slavoj Žižek, *Less Than Nothing: Hegel and the Shadow of Dialectical Materialism* (New York: Penguin Random House, 2012), 149, 205–11.
   105. G. W. F. Hegel, *Elements of the Philosophy of Right*, ed. Allen Wood, trans. H. B. Nisbet (Cambridge: Cambridge University Press, 1991), 273–4.
   106. Hegel, *Philosophy of Right*, 356–8.
   107. Hegel, *Philosophy of Right*, 356. Translation revised.

The elevation of the modern nation-state to the status of a priestly mediator or even divine giver of right and freedom, according to the mainstream view among German-speaking thinkers of Barth's generation, was largely a result of Hegel's secularization of the Christian doctrine of providence.[108] For Hegel and modern German nationalists after him, idealist or not, the unification of the German nation as a state was necessary for the realization of absolute freedom in human society.

Furthermore, Hegel insists that religion is the most proper means through which the modern state should cultivate absolute freedom among its citizens. Thomas Lewis puts it well:

> With respect to the challenge of social cohesion, what is most striking is the way that … [the] final form of worldly realization of reconciliation enables modern Christianity to function as the *Volksreligion* for which Hegel has been searching … The church's vital pedagogical role requires that the religious community or its functional equivalent—an institution that instills a consciousness of the absolute in representational form—endures. Only through practices of this sort do individuals come to view themselves in the manner appropriate for participation in modern life—as free individuals. The appropriate religious upbringing cultivates a self-understanding that enables individuals to be at home in institutions that realize this conception of ourselves—i.e. for Hegel, modern political institutions.[109]

The striking similarity between the role of German Christianity in the Third Reich and Hegel's vision of the function of Christianity as the *Volksreligion* responsible for cultivating absolute "freedom" among members of the modern state is hardly surprising. Regardless of whether Hegel himself would have approved of Hitler's regime, his theory of freedom does strongly suggest that subjective particularity must be negated in the determination of absolute freedom, both in the church and in the state. This is not to say that Hegel's theory of freedom cannot be reinterpreted or modified in such a way that it continues to inform contemporary societies where various freedoms of the human individual are held to be sacrosanct. Yet, as far as Hegel's *Rezeptionsgeschichte* in Germany up to the 1930s is concerned, it seems fair to say that his philosophy, along with even more radically absolutist theories advanced by Fichte and Schelling, gave rise to a view of Germany's national consciousness as determined by the German *Geist* that inevitably dissolves the consciousness of the individual in the name of absolute freedom.

When Barth proclaims that our freedom is actualized in Jesus Christ by the Holy Spirit, he is issuing a resounding No to what was in his time popularly taken as the originally Hegelian view of freedom. National consciousness is not

---

108. So Löwith, *Meaning in History*, 60.
109. Thomas Lewis, *Religion, Modernity, and Politics in Hegel* (Oxford: Oxford University Press, 2011), 227.

God—it is neither immediately nor consummately divine—and it has no authority to determine the existence of the human individual. Genuine freedom, per Barth, is not Spirit's self-realization in human consciousness, but rather the going re-enactments of God's gracious election, which already took place *extra nos*, by the Holy Spirit *in nobis*.

The freedom imparted to human beings as such cannot be absolute freedom (that is, the freedom of a subject's being-in-and-for-itself). Genuine human freedom is freedom that corresponds to God's *promeity*, the secondary freedom and absoluteness of God *pro me* in Jesus Christ (*CD* II/1: see Chapter 5), and as such it can only be determined as freedom *for* God (and, thereby, *for* our fellow creatures, *CD* III/4). Human freedom cannot be freedom in-and-for-ourselves. Absolute freedom, the "freedom" of God's "primary absoluteness," pertains to God alone in God's triune aseity, that is, God-in-and-for-Godself, to which no human activity can directly correspond (see Chapters 5–6).[110]

Yet, because Jesus Christ as the ectype (*Nachbild*) of the triune God in the pattern of an *analogia relationis* (*CD* III/2) is himself the subject, object, and act of election, the love and freedom actualized *in nobis* by his grace through the Holy Spirit is speculatively and mediately an "analogy" and "repetition" of God's love and freedom in-and-for-Godself.[111] Within the triune God-in-and-for-Godself is an endless communion of the subject, object, and act of love in freedom, and there is no need of reconciliation of God to Godself. As creatures, however, human beings must be reconciled to God and to fellow creatures in a communion of diverse alterities. Only in this communion will subjective and objective freedoms be genuinely reconciled, such that both unity and diversity will thrive at the same time.

Barth is emphatic that no nation, or any earthly entity for that matter, is divinely chosen for the purpose of imparting the freedom given to us in Jesus Christ: "Scripture only knows of the fellowship of the Church chosen from all peoples."[112] This proclamation carries social implications diametrically opposed to the nationalisms that pervaded Europe since the nineteenth century. "The fact that one belongs to this or that nation" and thus one's "self-evident solidarity with" one's "countrymen," Barth urges, is not determined "by history or by … ethnic blood," but rather by God's gracious election and calling.[113]

Barth insists that the only divinely appointed means of grace through which the Holy Spirit calls us into freedom *in* Christ, which is originally the very freedom *of* Jesus Christ himself as God's elect, are the "Christian Church …, one holy baptism, and one proclamation of the divine Word."[114]

---

110. *CD* II/1, 317.
111. *Gottes Gnadenwahl*, 31–2. See *CD* III/2, 220.
112. *Gottes Gnadenwahl*, 36.
113. *Gottes Gnadenwahl*, 37–8.
114. *Gottes Gnadenwahl*, 39.

> In the Christian Church, we see beyond all national boundaries the communion of the Word, communion in grace. She is the first actual community in which we live … [W]e were first baptised even before we were born, first in the Church and then in the … nation, first brothers and sisters to all who belong and want to belong in the *communio sanctorum*, and then in the communion of our people.[115]

What this entails is that the church in every nation should stand in "solidarity" with her "countrymen, a solidarity that is at once critical."[116] The church is entrusted with the responsibility of "making God's will recognisable" in the national "edifice of error and conceit."[117]

This is not to say that the Christian should despise her own nation or ethnic culture. The church must understand the nation as an external basis of her existence on earth. Through proclamation of "Jesus Christ to [her] people, and along with Him the forgiveness of sins and hope of eternal life," the church "will seek out the best things in [her] people. In all circumstances the Church should refrain from being sceptical. She should be trustful and have the courage to take herself seriously—with ruthless seriousness—on their behalf, and then she shall serve her people."[118] That is, the church, by priestly repentance on behalf of and proclamation of the gospel to her nation through preaching of the Word and administration of the sacraments, shall impart to her people the love and freedom given to humankind through God's gracious election in Jesus Christ.

Conclusion: Barth's Vision of a Christian Country

This chapter has demonstrated the implications of Barth's Christocentric reorientation of the doctrine of election in 1936 for his theology of nationhood. By way of conclusion, and in light of the foregoing discussions, I will offer a brief account of his vision of a Christian country. I begin here with his own personal example of "critical solidarity" with his "countrymen."

Barth is well known for his staunch opposition to German nationalism during both World Wars. It does not require a Barth scholar to show that he deemed all forms of nationalism idolatrous. Yet, his specific criticisms of Swiss nationalism are seldom discussed even among experts on his thought.

Carys Moseley's 2013 monograph is among the very few comprehensive works in the English language, if not the only one, on Barth's theology of nationhood.[119] She traces the development of Barth's view on this subject from the years preceding the

---

115. *Gottes Gnadenwahl*, 40.
116. *Gottes Gnadenwahl*, 38.
117. *Gottes Gnadenwahl*, 38.
118. *Gottes Gnadenwahl*, 42–3.
119. See Carys Moseley, *Nations & Nationalism in the Theology of Karl Barth* (Oxford: Oxford University Press, 2013).

First World War up to the 1950s, supporting her findings with solid biographical information and textual evidences. The work succeeds in demonstrating, *inter alia*, that Barth's mature theology of nationhood, in which the dignity of the nations is affirmed while nationalism is repudiated, is firmly grounded in his Christocentric doctrine of election.

> Barth made a distinction between nationhood and the state throughout his career … By the time that his mature reflection on the subject was published in 1951, Barth had come to situate nationhood within the sphere of obedience to God. Nationhood is the product of human agency operating in relation to and under divine activity and moral guidance. More specifically nations relate to God as the electing God who has elected Israel and the Church.[120]

In particular, Moseley accentuates Barth's affirmations of Swiss nationhood. She rightly points out that Barth's "reaffirmation of Swiss political neutrality" during the Second World War was basically "a continuation of an attitude which Barth held towards Switzerland during the First World War."[121] Barth saw the Swiss state as playing different strategic roles in the two World Wars, but he remained supportive of the policy of neutrality during both periods.

Moseley's portrayal of Barth seems to suggest that he was a patriotic theologian who thought of "Switzerland" as "a contemporary example" of a "just state" that "replaced Israel as the exemplary polity, given that Israel was a state encompassing one nation, whereas Switzerland was a state encompassing several."[122] This portrayal is not wrong, but it is too one-sided. While Barth may well have affirmed the polity of Switzerland, he was sharply aware of one crucial implication of his own Christological doctrine of election: "Being a Switzer means being a sinner."[123]

This would imply that Barth's attitude toward Swiss neutrality is much more complex than described in Moseley's narrative. Moseley provides ample textual evidences to show that Barth was overall supportive of the neutrality of Switzerland as a *state*, and yet her account falls short of acknowledging Barth's theological exposition of neutrality as a sinful aspect of Switzerland's national consciousness.[124] This exposition is at once concrete and personal in *Gottes Gnadenwahl*.

> I will tell myself that as a Switzer and in solidarity with my countrymen, I stand under God's prosecution and judgment. The sin of the Swiss could be uniquely visible in Swiss neutrality. For four hundred years, the Swiss have actually been only guests and spectators in world history. They rejoice in their freedom and wisdom in view of other nations; they are by nature political Pharisees who

---

120. Moseley, *Nations & Nationalism in the Theology of Karl Barth*, 204.
121. Moseley, *Nations & Nationalism in the Theology of Karl Barth*, 145.
122. Moseley, *Nations & Nationalism in the Theology of Karl Barth*, 162.
123. *Gottes Gnadenwahl*, 39.
124. Moseley, *Nations & Nationalism in the Theology of Karl Barth*, 145, 162.

thank God for not being like the others. The Switzer sits in his little house and looks through his little window, and is pleased when others come and marvel at his beautiful and free Switzerland. Perhaps he would also be delighted to initiate good and helpful actions. He adopts German and French children during the war. He becomes the benefactor of mankind to everyone else. He knows of and loves no extreme problems, and thus no extreme political parties. Swiss politics feeds on compromises. The Switzer is a bourgeois person, and peace and security are his top priorities … In her national consciousness, God's judgment that looms over the world becomes clear to us.[125]

Barth proceeds on the next page to a criticism of Swiss nationalism:

God does not play favourites with His children. And my people do not have the right to possess some private access to heaven that allows them to behave arrogantly in history as if they were exceptional. This possibility—it would probably be what one might call nationalism—of a *religio helvetica* … died in baptism. If this were not the case, then Switzerland would become a pagan country again, even if she has a Christian Church in her midst. "Let thy most beautiful star shine here upon my earthly fatherland" (Gottfried Keller)—this is paganism, even if it is a call upon God!![126]

What is especially intriguing here is Barth's insinuation of a view of Switzerland as a Christian country. The question is, on Barth's view, what is it that makes a country non-pagan and therefore Christian? Obviously, as Barth suggests in the quote above, even a country like Switzerland, which, in the capacity of a state, recognizes official churches of the country (*Landeskirchen*), can be pagan as well.

While such a country can also be a Christian one, Barth completely rules out the possibility of Christendom as a theologically justifiable form of a Christian country. In a work from roughly the same period, *Rechtfertigung und Recht* (literal translation: *Justification and Right*, as in the "philosophy of *right*") of 1938, Barth urges that the state must not be "deified" in the sense of being treated as the "heavenly Jerusalem."[127] The speculative misidentification of Christian countries with Christendom can only be blasphemous. "Legitimization" of Jesus's claim to universal lordship "could not and can never be Pilate's business. In the question of truth, the state is neutral."[128] Universal priesthood of the believers and proclamation of the gospel of justification by faith pertain solely to the sphere of the church.

---

125. *Gottes Gnadenwahl*, 39.
126. *Gottes Gnadenwahl*, 40. Here Barth is paraphrasing the final line from Keller's poem, *An das Vaterland*: "Beten will ich dann zu Gott dem Herrn: 'Lasse strahlen deinen schönsten Stern/ Nieder auf mein irdisch Vaterland.'"
127. Barth, *Rechtfertigung und Recht*, 24. Translation mine henceforth.
128. Barth, *Rechtfertigung und Recht*, 12.

The state, just as the nation, however, is a determination of human existence *in Christo*. "The state as such" is ontologically determined as an "angelic power" that "belongs originally and finally to Jesus Christ," albeit in a way different than the church.[129] Anticipating his own notion of the "ontological impossibility" of nothingness discussed at length in *CD* III/1 and III/3, Barth states that both "deification" and "demonization" (in the sense of becoming a persecutor of the church) of the state are "impossible."[130] They are "impossible" not in that they cannot become present realities. It is a point of fact that these impossible possibilities are repeatedly actualized in what Hegel might call the contingent irrationalities of history. Rather, they are impossible in that they contradict the very essence of the state ontologically determined in Christ.

The essence of the state is determined in Christ in such a way that "from its own origin and in its concrete encounter with Christ and his church, it could indeed also—without itself becoming the church somehow ... —administer justice and protect the law, and then thereby—voluntarily or involuntarily, very directly and yet substantially—open up a secure avenue [*freie, gesicherte Bahn geben*] for the message of justification by faith."[131]

A country is genuinely Christian if and only if her actual mode of existence in the dimensions of statehood and nationhood conform to her ontological determinations in Christ. In this sense, and only in this sense, does Barth permit the talk of Christian countries. A Christian country, on this view, is not one that fashions herself as God's kingdom on earth, a "city upon the hill," so to speak. It is not a country that proclaims the truth of the gospel in the capacity of the state, but rather one that refrains from dictating the truth of God, while giving to the church sufficient freedoms and protections to allow her to proclaim the gospel through preaching of the Word and administration of the sacraments.

This is indeed how the Barth of 1936 describes Switzerland as a non-pagan and thus Christian country: "there is in Switzerland also a Christian Church ... There is also a remission of sins for Switzerland. Jesus Christ also died for us. We may allow ourselves to say that, and that is the best thing about being Swiss ... Even the Switzer can be baptised."[132]

Prophetic witness against the sins of one's own nation "does not abrogate gratitude and responsibility, but they are now incorporated into the knowledge that I am the accused and the convict. *Helveticus sum, homo sum, peccator sum.*"[133] The church in every country is called to bear the guilt of her people and repent for the sins of her nation. God's negation of sin in the reprobation of Jesus is re-enacted *in nobis* through the church's priestly repentance.

129. Barth, *Rechtfertigung und Recht*, 19.
130. Barth, *Rechtfertigung und Recht*, 24.
131. Barth, *Rechtfertigung und Recht*, 19.
132. *Gottes Gnadenwahl*, 39.
133. *Gottes Gnadenwahl*, 39.

The nations are for Barth *one* dimension of the external basis of the election of the ecclesial community, and the *communio sanctorum* is *the* internal basis of nationhood. In that sense, "true ... national consciousness can actually be nothing other than the consciousness of the baptised Christian in [the nation]."[134] Only through the very consciousness of the baptized sinner in the *una sancta ecclesia* will God's gracious election be manifested in and to the nations. God's kingdom on earth is not manifested through Christendom, but rather through genuinely Christian countries in which the church is separated from statehood and nationhood in such a way that the two sides serve one another as mutual bases, the one internal, and the other external. "Then the following shall come true: 'Seek first God's kingdom and His righteousness, and all these things shall be given to you.' That is how the future of our people may be fashioned: 'all these things shall be given to you.'"[135]

---

134. *Gottes Gnadenwahl*, 39.
135. *Gottes Gnadenwahl*, 43.

EPILOGUE

In this study I have painted a portrait of Barth as a Christocentric speculative theologian. "Speculative" in this context is a comprehensive term describing his theology as a whole, regulated simultaneously by what George Hunsinger calls an Anselmian moment and a Hegelian one. Barth's Christocentric reorientation of his speculative theology in 1936–42 is intended to uphold his seminal insistence on what Sigurd Baark calls the unsublatable subjectivity of God in revelation. Jesus Christ as the very subject God is the *speculum* of all that God is and does in eternity. The temporal history of the man Jesus as *speculum electionis* is at once the eternal history of the subject God who does not cease to be the electing God in becoming the elected human. As the electing, elected, and election, Jesus Christ is eternally the secondary mode of God's absolute being, and is as such the *speculum Trinitatis*. In Jesus Christ who *is* revelation, not merely as a divine act but as a mode of God's absolute being *ad extra*, that mediates to us speculative knowledge of the Trinity, the subject God remains ever unsublated. This Christocentric theology firmly excludes the kind of idolatrous speculation characteristic of German idealism as disclosed by Ludwig Feuerbach.

I framed this portrait of Barth in his discourse on nationhood and nationalism, and it would serve well for me to conclude this study by demonstrating the global significance of his theology from the perspective of my vocation as a Sino-Christian theologian. We may begin by observing an interesting pattern of his reception in Asia.

Barth's theology was introduced to Japan in an era of surging nationalism. Yoshio Inoue (井上 良雄, 1907–2003), who was accused in 1935 of having violated the Peace Preservation Laws enacted in imperial Japan for the suppression of left-wing resistance, was instrumental for the promotion of Barth's theology in the country. After the Second World War, Hajime Tanabe (田辺 元, 1885–1962), famed co-founder of the Kyoto School in philosophy, appealed to Barth for the development of a theory of guilt and repentance, termed "metanoetics" (懺悔道).

In contrast to Japan, the first introduction of Barth to academic theology in China by Tzu-ch'en Chao (趙紫宸, 1888–1979) in 1939 was met with large indifference. In the last two decades or so, however, there has been an explosion of interest in Barth studies among theologians and even lay believers in China. Noteworthy is the fact that the beginning of this phenomenon chronologically coincided with China's rise to the status of a leading global economic and military power. A closer look at the phenomenon—at the everyday discussions between my friends and colleagues in the Chinese Barth circle—reveals that there is indeed a causal relationship between sympathy toward Barth's theology and opposition to national and political idols.

In my native Taiwan, the theology of Barth first took root in Formosan Presbyterianism in the 1960s under the leadership of theologians like Choan-Seng Song (宋泉盛, born 1929) and Shoki Coe (黃彰輝, 1914–88). Song drew eclectically on the insights of Barth and Paul Tillich to develop a postcolonial indigenous theology akin to liberation theology in Latin America, while Coe gifted Formosan theology with a more evangelical form of Barthianism reminiscent of T. F. Torrance. Both, however, relied on the spirit of Barth's *Nein!* in calling Taiwanese Presbyterians to resistance against the totalitarian regime of the Chinese Nationalist Party under the deified Chiang Kai-shek.

I would venture to say that this pattern of Barth's *Rezeptionsgeschichte* in Asia is not by sheer coincidence, though I will refrain from writing another chapter to demonstrate this thesis here. Although Barth refused to allow the political tail to wag the theological dog, so to speak, his theological development as a whole was guided by a consistent attempt to ward off the temptations of speculative idolatry. And in his *Sitz im Leben*, it was primarily the insanity of German nationalism that disclosed to him the idolatrous nature of idealist speculation.

The question now is: can Barth's theology, developed against a very Western and German intellectual-historical background, be transposed to a different cultural and linguistic mode, and remain meaningful for Christians striving to stay faithful to the First, Second, and Third Commandments? Germany's nationalism, as we saw in this study, was deeply rooted in an idolatrous mode of speculation characteristic of Western civilization and modern German culture. Is there a similar kind of speculative idolatry in non-European cultures such as that of China?

My own cross-cultural identity and experience have revealed to me that the ostensibly European mode of idolatrous speculation that Barth resisted is in fact not peculiar to Western civilization. What Barth (sometimes misleadingly) labels as *analogia entis* is in fact prevalent in traditional Chinese ways of thinking as well.

This can be demonstrated by the well-known debate between Mencius and Gaozi (告子) on the moral inclinations of human nature. Gaozi is of the view that human beings are not naturally inclined toward either good or evil, and argues for this view with the analogy that streams of water do not necessarily flow eastward or westward. In response, Mencius argues that human nature is innately inclined toward the good, just as water naturally flows downward. The validity of this argument by analogy, which would be deemed fallacious in most Western systems of thought, finds its basis in a monistic ontology according to which the transcendent *Dao* (道) or *Li* (理) as a cosmic principle governs both the moral inclinations of human nature and physical phenomena such as the flow of water.

The neo-Confucian scholar Cheng Yi (程頤, 1033–1107) explains: "Question: 'does the "investigation of things" refer to things external, or to things within human nature?' Answer: 'There is no distinction, for all things before our eyes are things, and all things contain the *Li*, which makes fire hot and water cold. As for relations between the emperor and his servants, the father and the son—these are all *Li*'" (*Yishu* [遺書], Volume 19, translation mine).

On the basis of this monistic worldview, neo-Confucians of the Song Dynasty proposed to "attain knowledge [of *Li*] through the investigation of things" (格物致知), taking empirically cognizable phenomena to be *specula* of the transcendent *Li* of heaven. Zhu Xi's (朱熹, 1130–1200) classic statement of the attainment of knowledge takes on speculative characteristics akin to those of German idealism:

> What "attainment of knowledge by the investigation of things" means is that in order to establish knowledge in myself, I have to observe things exhaustively to understanding their *Li*. All spirits of the human mind possess knowledge, and all things under *Tian* [heaven] possess *Li*. The reason why [human] knowledge is yet incomplete is that *Li* has not yet been exhaustively studied. Therefore the *Great Learning* [大學] teaches that scholars must be required to investigate all things under *Tian* such that these things become exhaustively understood by scholarly knowledge of the *Li* that permeates these things … After long-term diligence, once the understanding becomes thorough and comprehensive, the external and internal, the fine and the rough aspects of all things will all enter into the totality of the great praxis of my mind and become perspicuous.
> (Zhu Xi, *The Great Learning by Chapter and Phrase* [大學章句], Chapter 15, translation mine)

With a survey of similar passages from Confucian classics, Huang Chun-Chieh comments that according to "the general understanding of East-Asian Confucianism," and not just neo-Confucianism of the Song, "humanity and all things in the natural universe constitute 'one substance' [一體: literally 'one body,' meaning 'one substance,' 'one entity,' or simply 'unity']."[1] Huang explains: "What 'one substance' means is that 'humanity' and 'nature' stand in … a relation in which they permeate one another, cohabiting and sharing in one another's cognition, forming a relation of mutual influence."[2]

In view of the current analysis, then, Mou Zongsan, despite his problematic interpretations of Kant and Hegel as well as his tendencies to distort classical Chinese texts, is right that there exist striking similarities between Confucian and Hegelian modes of speculation. Mou explains that according to Confucianism, the "*Li* permeates all things in the universe … How is it that a flower, a leaf, or a grain of sand can represent the universe …? This is because *Tian-Li* [天理: the cosmic

---

1. Huang Chun-Chieh [黃俊傑], "Humanistic Spirit in East-Asian Confucian Traditions [東亞儒家傳統中的人文精神]," in *Humanistic Spirit from Intercultural Perspectives: Confucianism, Buddhism, Christianity, and Judaism in Dialogue* [跨文化視野中的人文精神——儒、佛、耶、猶的觀點與對話芻議], ed. Hong-Hsin Lin [林鴻信] (Taipei: National Taiwan University Press, 2011), 12. Translation mine hereafter.
2. Huang, "Humanistic Spirit in East-Asian Confucian Traditions," 12.

or heavenly principle] is characterized by a kind of omnipresence that gives life to all things and inheres all things."³

Speculative human knowledge of *Tian-Li* is attainable according to the Confucian system, Mou comments, because it inheres all things in a way akin to Hegel's Spirit:

> According to Hegel's dialectical method, [it is meaningless] to speak of God apart from the Son ... The Father represents the objective principle of God-in-Godself, whereas the Son represents the subjective principle of God-for-Godself. [Similarly], to speak only of the substance of the *Dao* is only to speak of the objective significance of the *Dao* in itself. Without this substance of the *Dao*, the universe would be without foundation ... [However], to speak only of the objectivity of the substance of the *Dao* would lead to empty talk.⁴

Mou observes that the "real unification of subjectivity and objectivity" in the speculative epistemology of (neo-)Confucianism is similar to Hegel's dialectic in that both hold to the view that "subjectivity becomes true subjectivity through a process of objectification."⁵

Now, as we saw in this study, in the modern German context, in Barth's view, it was only a short step from Hegel to the idolatrous identification of the *Führer* and the *Reich* as a speculative *Schein-Göttlichen* or appearance of the divine. It would be interesting to observe that the Confucian notion of the objective inherence of a transcendent and self-existent heaven in nature, too, lent support to the traditional Chinese view of emperors as "sons of heaven" (天子). The heavenly principle which dictates that fire is hot and water is cold, proclaims Cheng Yi in a quote that we saw earlier, also governs the "relations between the emperor and his servants." It should not be surprising, given the foregoing discussions, that this sounds so reminiscent of the *Naturphilosophie* of German idealism and romanticism.

Traditionally, Confucians believed that obedience to the emperor was required by the *Dao* of heaven itself, for the emperor is to be revered as an embodiment of heaven, a *Schein-Göttlichen* so to speak. Jürgen Osterhammel, in his authoritative work on the history of disenchantment in Asia, demonstrates that according to traditional Confucian belief, the emperor's power as a speculative representation of heaven is "absolute and almost infinite."⁶ Those who submit to the Chinese emperor are "under heaven" (天下), while nations refusing to pay tribute to the son of heaven are ranked among the "barbarians" (夷). The case of Confucianism, then, shows that the kind of speculative idolatry underlying Third Reich ideology

---

3. Mou Zongsan [牟宗三], *Topics and Developments in Song-Ming Confucianism* [宋明儒學的問題與發展] (Taipei: Linking Books, 2003), 89–90. Translation mine henceforth.
4. Mou, *Topics and Developments in Song-Ming Confucianism*, 174–5.
5. Mou, *Topics and Developments in Song-Ming Confucianism*, 291.
6. Jürgen Osterhammel, *Die Entzauberung Asiens—Europa und die asiatischen Reiche im 18. Jahrhundert*. (Munich: C. H. Beck, 1998), 333–4. Translation mine.

is not at all peculiar to nations whose peoples still pride themselves in proclaiming, "*civis romanus sum*" or "*Ich bin ein Berliner.*"

I already addressed the topic of nationalistic idolatry in Chapter 7, and here I would like to bring the findings of this study to bear on the development of Christian theology in the Chinese language. Confucian worldviews, as demonstrated above, are laden with speculative conceptions of some transcendent reality in relation to the world, conceptions that are idolatrous from, dare I say, a genuinely Christian perspective. This has come to inform the Chinese language in profound ways like how Latin was shaped by Hellenistic philosophy. Uncritical uses of Chinese, just as uncritical uses of Greek or Latin, can easily lead to speculative idolatries.

As a Sino-Christian theologian, I take special care to discern the strengths and limits of my native language in my verbalization of theological reflections. Unlike Western languages, the lack of subject-object distinctions in Chinese often tends to lead to dissolutions of proper boundaries in social relationships and theological discourses. As the philosopher Chung-ying Cheng points out, the "strong Platonic and Cartesian tradition of subject-object and human person-God-dualism" undergirding Western languages reflect onto-hermeneutical underpinnings that are quite foreign to classical Chinese texts.[7]

The onto-hermeneutical differences between Western languages and classical Chinese can be demonstrated by a simple example. If I were to tell a friend that I miss him very much in classical Chinese, I would only need to say, "very miss" (甚念). This grammatical construct is not considered a proposition or predication in Western philosophy, and it does not constitute a complete sentence in English. Yet, this phrase, which is without a subject, an object, and any verb conjugation, suffices in the Chinese context for expressing the English sentence, "I miss you very much." To state the proposition with a subject and an object, as most contemporary Chinese speakers do, can be suggestive, from a more traditional Chinese viewpoint, of a kind of relational alienation that violates the supposed harmony of *Tian-Li*.

As a Christian theologian, I take my cue from Barth's critical adaptation of the languages of German idealism and classical Hellenism in my uses of Chinese expressions, classical or contemporary. I am not entirely dismissive of the onto-hermeneutical views underlying the Chinese language. I can agree with Hans Lenk's positive assessment that "in-depth and detailed study of classical philosophical texts of the Chinese tradition" may "offer a very important alternative example which facilitates the on-going demise of the epistemological imperialism of Cartesian dualism" and "the overstated philosophical relevance of the grammatical subject-object separation."[8]

---

7. Chung-ying Cheng, "Onto-Hermeneutical Vision and Analytic Discourse: Interpretation and Reconstruction in Chinese Philosophy," in *Two Roads to Wisdom? Chinese and Analytic Philosophical Traditions*, ed. Bo Mou (Chicago: Open Court, 2001), 101.

8. Hans Lenk, "Introduction," in *Epistemological Issues in Classical Chinese Philosophy*, ed. Hans Lenk and Gregor Paul (Albany: SUNY Press, 1993), 4.

However, I am also critical of the monistic-speculative presuppositions that inform the Chinese language as a whole. I am especially sensitive to how the lack of subject-object distinction and, therewith, the lack of the concept of being have led to difficulties in theological expressions in Sinophone Christianity. Among other things, the relative uncertainty of subject-object relations in the language, even in its contemporary and somewhat Westernized form, has been a significant hindrance to honoring the unsublatable subjectivity of God in Sinophone theology.

I think Barth would agree with me that both the monistic-relational ontology underlying the Chinese language and the dualistic substantialism embedded in Western languages are "speculative" in a bad sense. In the end of the day, both Western languages and Chinese are heavily burdened with what Barth liked to call "metaphysics," by which he meant all idolatrous modes of speculation that attempt to reach up to some transcendent reality apart from revelation in Christ. The god of "metaphysics" as such is the god of Feuerbachian projection. This kind of speculative metaphysics posits an identity of some sort between *my* thinking and *my* being as the starting point of a faith-seeking-understanding program. The deficiencies of *my* thinking and *my* being are treated as *specula* of God's perfections. What this suggests is that divine nature is no more than the perfection of human attributes. That Confucianism is also speculative in this idolatrous sense is evinced by the fact that contemporary Confucians like to speak of an "inner transcendence" (内在超越) within human nature.

The basically Anselmian mode of speculation that Barth developed is diametrically opposed to speculative idolatry. In his *credo ut intelligam* program, he begins with faith in the speculative identity between God's inner essence and God's being-in-revelation. He fleshes out this basically Anselmian *Denform* Christologically: the speculative identity between *Deus absconditus* and *Deus revelatus* is to be concretely understood as a mediated identity between God's *ad intra* mode of absolute being qua Trinity and *ad extra* mode of absolute being as the electing God, mirrored to us through the history of the elected man Jesus.

What we have not yet noted in this study is that both the form and substance of Barth's speculative theology allow and demand him to adopt *secular* language in his speech about God. In his case, as we saw in Chapter 3, the speculative terminologies of Hellenistic philosophy and German idealism serve as the primary vehicles through which he expresses his theological reflections.

We have seen in this study that according to Barth's speculative theology, human nature in all its dimensions is ontologically pre-determined (*vorherbestimmt*) from above (*von oben*) by the Word of God. Even before the Christocentric reorientation of his speculative theology, Barth insisted that verbal communication as a dimension of human nature is ontologically pre-determined to be genuinely theological speech. Speculative idolatries contradict the ontological determination of human language, and they are as such ontological impossibilities: "there is no genuinely profane speech. In the last resort there is only talk about God."[9]

---

9. *CD* I/1, 47.

However, we live in a world in which our pre-determined essence in Christ is presently threatened from below (*von unten*) by the reality of nothingness (*Nichtiges*). In his later theology Barth would retain his position in *CD* I/1 that the "place where God's Word is revealed is objectively and subjectively the cosmos in which sin reigns."[10] This implies that "the speech of God is and remains the mystery of God supremely in its secularity."[11]

In Chapter 7, we saw how Barth understands the central Christian proclamation, "the Word became flesh" (Jn. 1:14), as an affirmation of human nature in the dimension of nationhood. For Barth, this proclamation can be understood as an affirmation of secularity in general, designated by the term "flesh." This includes human nature in the dimension of verbal communication.

To take seriously the flesh of Jesus Christ is to affirm secular languages as part and parcel of fallen creation as the external basis on which God's revelation is enacted. "Revelation means incarnation of the Word of God. But incarnation means entry into this secularity. We are in this world and are through and through secular. If God did not speak to us in secular form, He would not speak to us at all. To evade the secularity of His Word is to evade Christ."[12]

This does not warrant us to adopt secular languages in speaking about God without being critical of their idolatrous nature or, better put, "un-nature."[13] As a matter of fact, "not all human talk is talk about God."[14] In the state of fallen secularity, "it is quite impossible to interpret human talk ... as talk about God."[15]

All dimensions of human nature in the condition of fallenness need to be reconciled to Christ. This is true of both nationhood and language. Barth did not forsake the metaphysical languages he inherited from his predecessors, but he did not adopt them uncritically either. Instead, he purified them of speculative idolatries and incorporated them into the church's confession of Jesus Christ as Lord.

From my perspective as a neo-Calvinist in the spirit of Herman Bavinck's Reformed eclecticism, Barth sets an excellent example for theologians who refuse to make theology a function of an arbitrarily invented language game of the church. I am firmly convinced that theology has to be articulated through Christocentric transformations of human languages that are in themselves secular, and recognize that the speculative-metaphysical or "onto-hermeneutical" characteristics of these languages reflect at once God's good creation and our own fallenness.

My hope as a Sino-Christian theologian is that, together with all the colleagues from different denominations and branches of the faith who share the same commitment to the one Lord Jesus Christ, we will develop a theology that is at once genuinely Sinophone and genuinely Christian. I can speak with confidence

---

10. *CD* I/1, 166.
11. *CD* I/1, 165.
12. *CD* I/1, 168.
13. *CD* IV/2, 26
14. *CD* I/1, 47.
15. *CD* I/1, 47.

that there is a large consensus among contemporary proponents of Sino-Christian theology to recognize our shared cultural and linguistic identity as a gift from God, a gift that is at once corrupted by the very particular sins and idolatries of our people and our history. We also acknowledge that our theological speech is called to be *in* but not *of* the world, such that our very Sinophone speech about God must be at once secular and sanctified through and through. In and with the very Word of God who became flesh, we hope to serve our people in the world that God so loved with the *una sancta ecclesia*.

As for myself, I pray that my development as a theologian will always be guided, informed, and protected by our Lord's high priestly prayer to the Father following his promise of the Holy Spirit. It would make sense, in my view, to appreciate Barth's speculative theology as a whole, with all its Christocentric revisions, as a *credo ut intelligam* explication of this prayer.

> But now I am coming to you, and these things I speak in the world, that they may have my joy fulfilled in themselves. I have given them your word, and the world has hated them because they are not of the world, just as I am not of the world. I do not ask that you take them out of the world, but that you keep them from the evil one … Sanctify them in the truth; your word is truth. As you sent me into the world, so I have sent them into the world. And for their sake I consecrate myself that they also may be sanctified in truth … O righteous Father, even though the world does not know you, I know you, and these know that you have sent me. I made known to them your name, and I will continue to make it known, that the love with which you have loved me may be in them, and I in them.
>
> (Jn. 17:13-26, ESV)

BIBLIOGRAPHY

Primary Sources by Karl Barth (German)

Anselm: Fides quaerens intellectum. Zurich: Theologischer Verlag Zürich, 1931.
Die christliche Dogmatik im Entwurf, 1. Band: Die Lehre vom Worte Gottes, Prolegomena zur christlichen Dogmatik, 1927. In *Gesamtausgabe* II.14. Zurich: Theologischer Verlag Zürich, 1982.
Gottes Gnadenwahl. Munich: Chr. Kaiser Verlag, 1936.
Die Kirchliche Dogmatik, 4 volumes in 12 parts (I/1–IV/4). Zollikon-Zurich: Evangelischer Verlag, 1932–67.
Die Protestantische Theologie im 19. Jahrhundert: Ihre Geschichte und ihre Vorgeschichte. Zurich: Theologischer Verlag Zürich, 1994.
Der Römerbrief 1922. Zurich: Theologischer Verlag Zürich, 1999.
Die Theologie Calvins 1922. In *Gesamtausgabe* II.23. Zurich: Theologischer Verlag Zürich, 1993.
Die Theologie der reformierten Bekenntnisschriften 1923. In *Gesamtausgabe* II.32. Zurich: Theologischer Verlag Zürich, 1998.
Rechtfertigung und Recht, Christengemeinde und Bürgergemeinde, and *Evangelium und Gesetz*. Zurich: Theologischer Verlag Zürich, 1998.
Unterricht in der christlichen Religion 1924–1926, 3 volumes. In *Gesamtausgabe* II.17, 20, and 38. Zurich: Theologischer Verlag Zürich, 1985, 1990, and 2003.

Primary Sources by Karl Barth (English Translation)

Anselm: Fides Quaerens Intellectum, translated by Ian Robertson. London: SCM, 1960.
Church Dogmatics. 4 vols. in 12 parts (I/1–IV/4), edited by Geoffrey W. Bromiley and Thomas F. Torrance, translated by Geoffrey W. Bromiley. Edinburgh: T & T Clark, 1936–75.
The Epistle to the Romans, translated by Edwyn Hoskyns. Oxford: Oxford University Press, 1933.
The Göttingen Dogmatics, Vol. 1: Instruction in the Christian Religion, edited by Hannelotte Reiffen, translated by Geoffrey Bromiley. Grand Rapids: Eerdmans, 1991.
Protestant Theology in the Nineteenth Century, translated by Brian Cozens and John Bowden. London: SCM, 2001.

Other Primary Sources

Althaus, Paul. *Kirche und Volkstum: Der völkische Wille im Lichte des Evangeliums*. Gütersloh: Bertelsmann, 1928.
Anselm of Canterbury. *St. Anselm: Basic Writings*, translated by Sidney Norton Deane. Chicago: Open Court, 1962.

Augustine of Hippo. *Confessions*, translated by Henry Chadwick. Oxford: Oxford University Press, 1991.
Augustine of Hippo. *De natura boni*. In *St. Augustin: The Writings against the Manicheans and against the Donatists*, edited by Philip Schaff, translated by Arthur Haddan. Edinburgh: T&T Clark, 1887.
Augustine of Hippo. *On the Free Choice of the Will*. In *On the Free Choice of the Will, On Grace and Free Choice, and Other Writings*, edited and translated by Peter King. Cambridge: Cambridge University Press, 2010.
Augustine of Hippo. *On the Holy Trinity*, edited by Philip Schaff, translated by Arthur Haddan. Edinburgh: T&T Clark, 1887.
Augustine of Hippo. *On Rebuke and Grace*. In *St. Augustin's Anti-Pelagian Works*, edited by Philip Schaff, translated by P. Holmes and R. Ernest. Edinburgh: T&T Clark, 1988.
Benedict, Ruth. *The Chrysanthemum and the Sword: Patterns of Japanese Culture*. New York: Mariner, 2005.
Bonhoeffer, Dietrich. *Act and Being*, edited by Hans-Richard Reuter and Wayne Whitson Floyd, translated by H. Martin Rumscheidt. Minneapolis: Fortress Press, 1996.
Brunner, Emil. *Dogmatics, vol. 1: The Christian Doctrine of God*, translated by Olive Wyon. Philadelphia: Westminster, 1950.
Bultmann, Rudolf. *History and Eschatology: The Presence of Eternity*. Waco: Baylor University Press, 2019.
Calvin, John. *Concerning the Eternal Predestination of God*, translated by J. K. S. Reid. Louisville: Westminster John Knox, 1961.
Calvin, John. *Institutes of the Christian Religion*, edited by John T. McNeill, translated by Ford Lewis Battles. Philadelphia: Westminster John Knox, 1960.
Calvin, John. *The Secret Providence of God*, translated by Paul Helm. Wheaton: Crossway, 2010.
Feuerbach, Ludwig. *The Essence of Christianity*, translated by George Eliot. New York: Prometheus, 1989.
Fichte, Johann Gottlieb. *The Science of Knowledge*, edited and translated by Peter Heath and John Lachs. Cambridge: Cambridge University Press, 1982.
Fichte, Johann Gottlieb. *The Vocation of Man*, translated by Peter Preuss. Indianapolis: Hackett, 1987.
Hegel, Georg Wilhelm Friedrich. *Elements of the Philosophy of Right*, edited by Allen Wood, translated by Hugh B. Nisbet. Cambridge: Cambridge University Press, 1991.
Hegel, Georg Wilhelm Friedrich. *The Encyclopaedia of Logic*, translated by T. F. Geraets, W. A. Suchting and H. S. Harris. Indianapolis: Hackett, 1991.
Hegel, Georg Wilhelm Friedrich. *Encyclopedia of the Philosophical Sciences in Basic Outline: Part I: Science of Logic*, edited and translated by Klaus Brinkmann and Daniel Dahlstrom. Cambridge: Cambridge University Press, 2010.
Hegel, Georg Wilhelm Friedrich. *Lectures on the History of Philosophy 1825–6: Volume I: Introduction and Oriental Philosophy*, edited and translated by Robert Brown. Oxford: Oxford University Press, 2009.
Hegel, Georg Wilhelm Friedrich. *Lectures on the History of Philosophy 1825–6: Volume II: Greek Philosophy*, edited and translated by Robert Brown. Oxford: Oxford University Press, 2009.
Hegel, Georg Wilhelm Friedrich. *Lectures on the History of Philosophy 1825–6: Volume III: Medieval and Modern Philosophy*, edited and translated by Robert Brown. Oxford: Oxford University Press, 2009.

Hegel, Georg Wilhelm Friedrich. *Lectures on the Philosophy of Religion: Volume I: Introduction and the Concept of Religion*, edited and translated by Peter Hodgson. Oxford: Oxford University Press, 2008.

Hegel, Georg Wilhelm Friedrich. *Lectures on the Philosophy of Religion: Volume II: Determinate Religion*, edited and translated by Peter Hodgson. Oxford: Oxford University Press, 2008.

Hegel, Georg Wilhelm Friedrich. *Lectures on the Philosophy of Religion: Volume III: Consummate Religion*, edited and translated by Peter Hodgson. Oxford: Oxford University Press, 2008.

Hegel, Georg Wilhelm Friedrich. *Phänomenologie des Geistes*. Hamburg: Meiner, 2011.

Hegel, Georg Wilhelm Friedrich. *Phenomenology of Spirit*, edited by Terry Pinkard and Michael Baur, translated by Michael Baur. Cambridge: Cambridge University Press, 2018.

Hegel, Georg Wilhelm Friedrich. *The Science of Logic*, edited and translated by George di Giovanni. Cambridge: Cambridge University Press, 2010.

Heine, Heinrich. *Zur Geschichte der Religion und Philosophie in Deutschland*. Augsburg: Jazzbee Verlag, 2012.

Heppe, Heinrich. *Die Dogmatik der Evangelisch-Reformierten Kirche*. Whitefish: Kessinger, 2010.

Jenson, Robert. *God after God: The God of the Past and the God of the Future, Seen in the Work of Karl Barth*. Minneapolis: Fortress, 2010.

Kant, Immanuel. *Critique of the Power of Judgment*, edited by Paul Guyer, translated by Paul Guyer and Eric Matthews. Cambridge: Cambridge University Press, 2000.

Kant, Immanuel. *Critique of Practical Reason*, edited and translated by Mary Gregor. Cambridge: Cambridge University Press, 1997.

Kant, Immanuel. *Critique of Pure Reason*, edited by Paul Guyer, translated by Paul Guyer and Allen Wood. Cambridge: Cambridge University Press, 2007.

Kant, Immanuel. *Groundwork of the Metaphysics of Morals*, edited and translated by Mary Gregor and Christine Korsgaard. Cambridge: Cambridge University Press, 2012.

Kant, Immanuel. *Kritik der reinen Vernunft*. Wiesbaden: Fourier Verlag, 2003.

Kant, Immanuel. *Prolegomena to Any Future Metaphysics*, edited and translated by Gary Hatfield. Cambridge: Cambridge University Press, 2004.

Kant, Immanuel. *Religion within the Bounds of Bare Reason*, translated by Werner Pluhar. Indianapolis: Hackett, 2009.

Kierkegaard, Søren. *Concluding Unscientific Postscript to the Philosophical Crumbs*, edited and translated by Alastair Hannay. Cambridge: Cambridge University Press, 2009.

Kierkegaard, Søren. *Sickness unto Death*, translated by Alastair Hannay. Radford: Wilder, 2008.

Maury, Pierre. "Erwählung und Glaube." *Theologische Studien* 8 (1940): 7–12.

Moltmann, Jürgen. *Der lebendige Gott und die Fülle des Lebens: Auch ein Beitrag zur gegenwärtigen Atheismusdebatte*. Gütersloh: Gütersloher, 2014.

Moltmann, Jürgen. "The Election of Grace: Barth on the Doctrine of Predestination." In *Reading the Gospels with Barth*, edited by Daniel Migliore. Grand Rapids: Eerdmans, 2017.

Moltmann, Jürgen. *The Trinity and the Kingdom*. Minneapolis: Fortress Press, 1993.

Moltmann, Jürgen. *The Way of Jesus Christ*. Minneapolis: Fortress Press, 1993.

Newman, John Henry. *Apologia Pro Vita Sua*. New York: Norton, 1968.

Novalis. *Werke*, edited by Gerhard Schulz. Munich: C. H. Beck, 1987.

Pannenberg, Wolfhart. *Problemgeschichte der neueren evangelischen Theologie in Deutschland: von Schleiermacher bis zu Barth und Tillich*. Göttingen: Vandenhoeck & Ruprecht, 1997.

Pannenberg, Wolfhart. *Revelation as History*. London: Macmillan & Co., 1969.
Pannenberg, Wolfhart. *Systematic Theology*, 3 volumes, translated by Geoffrey W. Bromiley. Grand Rapids: Eerdmans, 2009.
Schelling, Friedrich. *Philosophical Inquiries into the Nature of Human Freedom*, translated by James Gutmann. Chicago: Open Court, 2003.
Schiller, Friedrich. *Schiller: Theoretische Schriften: Text und Kommentar*, edited by Rolf-Peter Janz. Berlin: Deutscher Klassiker Verlag, 2008.
Schiller, Friedrich. *Über die ästhetische Erziehung des Menschen: In einer Reihe von Briefen*. Ditzingen: Reclam, 2000.
Schleiermacher, Friedrich. *The Christian Faith: A New Translation and Critical Edition*, translated by Terrence Tice, Catherine Kelsey and Edwina Lawler. Louisville: WJK, 2016.
Schleiermacher, Friedrich. *On Religion: Speeches to Its Cultured Despisers*, edited and translated by Richard Crouter. Cambridge: Cambridge University Press, 1988.
Schweizer, Alexander. *Die Glaubenslehre der evangelisch-reformieten Kirche, dargestellt und aus den Quellen belegt*, 2 volumes. Zurich: Orell, Füssli, 1844–7.
Strauss, David Friedrich. *The Life of Jesus Critically Examined*, 3 volumes, translated by George Eliot. London: Continuum, 2005.
Thomas, Aquinas. *Aquinas: Selected Philosophical Writings*, edited by Timothy McDermott. Oxford: Oxford University Press, 1993.
Thomas, Aquinas. *Summa Theologiae: Latin-English Edition, Prima Pars, Q1–64*. Scotts Valley: NovAntiqua, 2008.
Tillich, Paul. *Systematic Theology*, 3 volumes. Chicago: Chicago University Press, 1957.
Torrance, Thomas. *Space, Time and Resurrection*. Edinburgh: T&T Clark, 1976.
Torrance, Thomas. *Theology in Reconciliation*. Eugene: Wipf and Stock, 1996.

Secondary Sources

Allison, Henry. *Kant's Transcendental Idealism: An Interpretation and Defense*. New Haven: Yale University Press, 2004.
Amemiya, Eiichi, (雨宮栄一), Keiji Ogawa (小川圭治) and Heita Mori (森平太), eds. *Yoshio Inoue Studies* (井上良雄研究). Tokyo: Shinkyo Publishing, 2006.
Ameriks, Karl. *Interpreting Kant's Critiques*. Oxford: Oxford University Press, 2003.
Ameriks, Karl. *Kant and the Historical Turn: Philosophy as Critical Interpretation*. Oxford: Oxford University Press, 2006.
Anderson, Clifford. "A Theology of Experience? Karl Barth and the Transcendental Argument." In *Karl Barth and American Evangelicalism*, edited by Bruce McCormack and Clifford Anderson, 91–111. Grand Rapids: Eerdmans, 2010.
Baark, Sigurd. *The Affirmations of Reason: On Karl Barth's Speculative Theology*. Cham: Palgrave Macmillan, 2018.
Bartel, Cora. *Kierkegaard receptus I: Die theologiegeschichtliche Bedeutung der Kierkegaard-Rezeption Rudolf Bultmanns*. Göttingen: Vandenhoeck & Ruprecht, 2008.
Becker, Dieter. *Karl Barth und Martin Buber, Denker in dialogischer Nachbarschaft? Zur Bedeutung Martin Bubers für die Anthropologie Karl Barths*. Göttingen: Vandenhoeck & Ruprecht, 1986.
Beeke, Joel and Mark Jones. *A Puritan Theology: Doctrine for Life*. Grand Rapids: Reformation Heritage Books, 2012.
Beintker, Michael, ed. *Barth Handbuch*. Tübingen: Mohr Siebeck, 2016.

Beintker, Michael. *Die Dialektik in der "dialektischen Theologie" Karl Barths*. Munich: Chr. Kaiser Verlag, 1987.
Beintker, Michael. "Unterricht in der christlichen Religion." *Verkündigung und Forschung* 30 (1985): 45–9.
Bell, Richard. "Richard Wagner's Prose Sketches for Jesus of Nazareth." *Journal for the Study of the Historical Jesus* 15 (2017): 260–90.
Berkouwer, Gerrit C. *The Triumph of Grace in the Theology of Karl Barth*, translated by Harry Boer. London: Paternoster, 1956.
Billings, Todd. *Calvin, Participation, and the Gift: The Activity of Believers in Union with Christ*. Oxford: Oxford University Press, 2007.
Blanning, Tim. "Richard Wager and the German Nation: The Prothero Lecture." *Transactions of the Royal Historical Society* 25 (2016): 95–112.
Borchmeyer, Dieter. *Was heisst deutsche Musik: Speeches of Dieter Borchmeyer in China* (什么是德意志音乐:博希迈尔教授中国讲演录), translated into Chinese by Linjing Jiang (姜林静) and Mingfeng Yu (余民峰). Beijing: Commercial Press, 2020.
Borchmeyer, Dieter. *Was ist deutsch? Die Suche einer Nation nach sich sebst*. Berlin: Rowohlt, 2017.
Boersma, Gerald. *Augustine's Early Theology of Image: A Study in the Development of Pro-Nicene Theology*. Oxford: Oxford University Press, 2016.
Bradshaw, Timothy. "Karl Barth on the Trinity: A Family Resemblance." *Scottish Journal of Theology* 39 (1986): 145–64.
Buckley, James. "Barth and Rahner." In *The Wiley-Blackwell Companion to Karl Barth*, edited by George Hunsinger and Keith Johnson, 607–17. Oxford: Wiley-Blackwell, 2020.
Busch, Eberhard. *Die Anfänge des Theologen Karl Barth in seinen Göttingen Jahren*. Göttingen: Vandenhoek & Ruprecht, 1987.
Busch, Eberhard. *Karl Barth: His Life from Letters and Autobiographical Texts*, translated by John Bowden. London: SCM, 1975.
Busch, Eberhard. *Meine Zeit mit Karl Barth*. Göttingen: Vandenhoeck & Ruprecht, 2011.
Cary, Philip. *Augustine's Invention of the Inner Self: The Legacy of a Christian Platonist*. Oxford: Oxford University Press, 2003.
Chao, Tzu-ch'en (趙紫宸). *Barth's Religious Thought* (巴德的宗教思想). Shanghai: Youth Association Press (青年協會書局), 1939.
Collins, Paul. *Trinitarian Theology West and East: Karl Barth, the Cappadocian Fathers, and John Zizioulas*. Oxford: Oxford University Press, 2001.
Congdon, David. "*Apokatastasis* and Apostolicity: A Response to Oliver Crisp on the Question of Barth's Universalism." *Scottish Journal of Theology* 67 (2014): 464–80.
Cortez, Marc. "What Does It Mean to Call Karl Barth a 'Christocentric' Theologian?" *Scottish Journal of Theology* 60 (2007): 127–43.
Costas, Trinidad Pineiro. *Schillers Begriff des Erhabenen in der Tradition der Stoa und Rhetorik*. Bern: Peter Lang, 2005.
Crisp, Oliver. *Divinity and Humanity*. Cambridge: Cambridge University Press, 2007.
Crisp, Oliver. "Karl Barth and Jonathan Edwards on Reprobation (and Hell)." In *Engaging with Barth: Contemporary Evangelical Critiques*, edited by David Gibson and Daniel Strange, 300–22. Nottingham: Apollos, 2008.
Crowe, Benjamin. "On 'The Religion of the Visible Universe': Novalis and the Pantheism Controversy." *British Journal for the History of Philosophy* 16 (2008): 125–56.
Dempsey, Michael T., ed. *Trinity and Election in Contemporary Theology*. Grand Rapids: Eerdmans, 2011.

Emilsson, Eyjólfur. *Plotinus on Intellect*. Oxford: Oxford University Press, 2007.
Erickson, Millard. *Christian Theology*. Grand Rapids: Baker Academic, 2013.
Fesko, John. *The Covenant of Redemption: Origins, Development, and Reception*. Göttingen: Vandenhoeck & Ruprecht, 2016.
Fesko, John. *Reformed Apologetics: Retrieving the Classical Reformed Approach to Defending the Faith*. Grand Rapids: Baker, 2019.
Fiddes, Paul. *The Creative Suffering of God*. Oxford: Oxford University Press, 1988.
Firestone, Chris and Stephen Palmquist, eds. *Kant and the New Philosophy of Religion*. Bloomington: University of Indiana Press, 2006.
Fisher, Simon. *Revelatory Positivism? Barth's Earliest Theology and the Marburg School*. Oxford: Oxford University Press, 1988.
Frei, Hans. *Theology and Narrative*, edited by George Hunsinger and William Placher. Oxford: Oxford University Press, 1993.
Frick, Tyler. *Karl Barth's Ontology of Divine Grace: God's Decision Is God's Being*. Tübingen: Mohr Siebeck, 2021.
Furry, Timothy. "Analogous analogies? Thomas Aquinas and Karl Barth." *Scottish Journal of Theology* 63 (2010): 318–30.
Gavrilyuk, Paul. "The Retrieval of Deification: How a Once-Despised Archaism Became an Ecumenical Desideratum." *Modern Theology* 25 (2009): 647–59.
Gavrilyuk, Paul. *The Suffering of the Impassible God: The Dialectics of Patristic Thought*. Oxford: Oxford University Press, 2004.
Ge, Yonghua. "The Role of *creatio ex nihilo* in Augustine's *Confessions*." *Sino-Christian Studies* 22 (2016): 41–64.
Gérard, Gilbert. "Hegel, lecteur de la métaphysique d'Aristote. La substance en tant que sujet." *Revue de Métaphysique et de Morale* 74 (2012): 195–223.
Gioia, Luigi. *The Theological Epistemology of Augustine's* De Trinitate. Oxford: Oxford University Press, 2016.
Gockel, Matthias. *Barth and Schleiermacher on the Doctrine of Election*. Oxford: Oxford University Press, 2006.
Gockel, Matthias. "How to Read Karl Barth with Charity: A Critical Reply to George Hunsinger." *Modern Theology* 32 (2016): 259–67.
Greggs, Tom. *Barth, Origen, and Universal Salvation: Restoring Particularity*. Oxford: Oxford University Press, 2009.
Greggs, Tom. "'Jesus Is Victor': Passing the Impasse of Barth on Universalism". *Scottish Journal of Theology* 60 (2007): 196–212.
Green, Bradley. *Colin Gunton and the Failure of Augustine*. Eugene: Pickwick, 2011.
Green, Christopher. *Doxological Theology: Karl Barth on Divine Providence, Evil, and the Angels*. London: Bloomsbury, 2011.
Gunton, Colin. *Being and Becoming: The Doctrine of God in Charles Hartshorne and Karl Barth*. Oxford: Oxford University Press, 1978.
Grier, Michelle. *Kant's Doctrine of Transcendental Illusion*. Cambridge: Cambridge University Press, 2001.
Guyer, Paul *Kant and the Claims of Knowledge*. Cambridge: Cambridge University Press, 1987.
Guyer, Paul. *Kant's System of Nature and Freedom*. Oxford: Oxford University Press, 2005.
Hare, John. "Karl Barth, American Evangelicals, and Barth." In *Karl Barth and American Evangelicalism*, edited by Bruce McCormack and Clifford Anderson, 73–90. Grand Rapids: Eerdmans, 2011.
Hare, John. *The Moral Gap: Kantian Ethics, Human Limits, and God's Assistance*. Oxford: Oxford University Press, 1996.

Hattrell, Simon, ed. *Election, Barth, and the French Connection: How Pierre Maury Gave a "Decisive Impetus" to Karl Barth's Doctrine of Election*. Eugene: Wipf and Stock, 2016.
Healy, Nicholas M. "Karl Barth, German-Language Theology, and the Catholic Tradition." In *Trinity and Election in Contemporary Theology*, edited by Michael T. Dempsey, 229–43. Grand Rapids: Eerdmans, 2011.
Hector, Kevin. "Actualism and Incarnation: The High Christology of Friedrich Schleiermacher." *International Journal of Systematic Theology* 8 (2006): 307–22.
Hector, Kevin. "God's Triunity and Self-Determination: A Conversation with Karl Barth, Bruce McCormack and Paul Molnar." In *Trinity and Election in Contemporary Theology*, edited by Michael T. Dempsey, 29–46. Grand Rapids: Eerdmans, 2011.
Hector, Kevin. "Immutability, Necessity and Triunity: Towards a Resolution of the Trinity and Election Controversy." *Scottish Journal of Theology* 65 (2012): 64–81.
Hendry, George. "The Transcendental Method in the Theology of Karl Barth." *Scottish Journal of Theology* 37 (1984): 213–27.
Henry, Paul. *Plotin et l'Occident*. Louvain: Spicilegium Sacrum Lovaniense, 1934.
Hitchcock, Nathan. *Karl Barth and the Resurrection of the Flesh: The Loss of the Body in Participatory Eschatology*. Eugene: Wipf and Stock, 2013.
Holmes, Christopher R. J. "'A Specific Form of Relationship': On the Dogmatic Implication of Barth's Account of Election and Commandment for His Theological Ethics." In *Trinity and Election in Contemporary Theology*, edited by Michael T. Dempsey, 182–200. Grand Rapids: Eerdmans, 2011.
Houlgate, Stephen. *The Opening of Hegel's Logic: From Being to Infinity*. West Lafayette: Purdue University Press, 2006.
Hunsinger, George. *Disruptive Grace: Studies in the Theology of Karl Barth*. Grand Rapids: Eerdmans, 2000.
Hunsinger, George. "Election and the Trinity: Twenty-Five Theses on the Theology of Karl Barth." *Modern Theology* 24 (2008): 179–98.
Hunsinger, George. *Evangelical, Catholic, and Reformed: Doctrinal Essays on Barth and Related Themes*. Grand Rapids: Eerdmans, 2015.
Hunsinger, George. *How to Read Karl Barth*. Oxford: Oxford University Press, 1991.
Hunsinger, George. "Karl Barth's Christology: Its Basic Chalcedonian Character." In *The Cambridge Companion to Karl Barth*, edited by John Webster, 127–42. Cambridge: Cambridge University Press, 2000.
Hunsinger, George. "Karl Barth's *The Göttingen Dogmatics*." *Scottish Journal of Theology* 46 (1993): 371–82.
Hunsinger, George. *Reading Barth with Charity: A Hermeneutical Proposal*. Grand Rapids: Baker Academic, 2015.
Hunsinger, George. "Review of *Barth, Origen, and Universalism: Restoring Particularity* by Tom Greggs." *Modern Theology* 28 (2012): 356–8.
Hunsinger, George and Keith L. Johnson, eds. *The Wiley-Blackwell Companion to Karl Barth*, 2 volumes. Oxford: Wiley-Blackwell, 2020.
Inwood, Michael. *A Hegel Dictionary*. Oxford: Blackwell, 1992.
Jiang, Linjing. *Carl Schmidt als Literaturkritiker: Eine metakritische Untersuchung*. Vienna: Praesens, 2016.
Johnson, Adam J. *God's Being in Reconciliation: The Theological Basis of the Unity and Diversity of the Atonement in the Theology of Karl Barth*. London: T&T Clark, 2012.
Johnson, Keith E. *Rethinking the Trinity and Religious Pluralism: An Augustinian Assessment*. Downers Grove: IVP Academic, 2011.

Johnson, Keith L. *Karl Barth and the Analogia Entis*. London: T&T Clark, 2010.
Johnson, Keith L. "Natural Revelation in Creation and Covenant." In *Thomas Aquinas and Karl Barth: An Unofficial Catholic-Protestant Dialogue*, edited by Bruce McCormack and Thomas Joseph White, O.P., 129–56. Grand Rapids: Eerdmans, 2013.
Johnson, William Stacy. *The Mystery of God: Karl Barth and the Postmodern Foundations of Theology*. Louisville: Westminster John Knox, 1997.
Jones, Paul. *The Humanity of Christ: Christology in Karl Barth's Church Dogmatics*. London: T&T Clark, 2008.
Jones, Paul. "Obedience, Trinity and Election: Thinking with and beyond the *Church Dogmatics*." In *Trinity and Election in Contemporary Theology*, edited by Michael T. Dempsey, 138–61. Grand Rapids: Eerdmans, 2011.
Jones, Paul Dafydd and Paul Nimmo, eds. *The Oxford Handbook of Karl Barth*. Oxford: Oxford University Press, 2020.
Jüngel, Eberhard. *God's Being Is in Becoming: The Trinitarian Being of God in the Theology of Karl Barth*, translated by John Webster. Grand Rapids: Eerdmans, 2001.
Jüngel, Eberhard. *Gottes sein ist im Werden*. Tübingen: Mohr Siebeck, 1986.
Jüngel, Eberhard. "Von der Dialektik zur Analogie: Die Schule Kierkegaards und der Einspruch Petersons." In *Barth-Studien*, 127–79. Zurich: Benziger Verlag, 1982.
Kiezle, Ulrike. "*Parsifal* and Religion: A Christian Music Drama?" In *A Companion to Wagner's Parsifal*, edited William Kinderman and Katherine Syer, 81–130. Rochester: Camden House, 2005.
Kitamori, Kazoh. *Theologie des Schmerzes Gottes*, translated by Tsuneaki Kato and Paul Schneiss. Göttingen: Vandenhoeck & Ruprecht, 1972.
Krötke, Wolf. "The Humanity of the Human Person in Karl Barth's Anthropology." In *The Cambridge Companion to Karl Barth*, edited by John Webster, translated by Philip Ziegler, 159–76. Cambridge: Cambridge University Press, 2000.
Krötke, Wolf. *Sin and Nothingness in the Theology of Karl Barth*, edited and translated by Philip Ziegler and Christina-Maria Bammel. Princeton: Princeton Theological Seminary, 2005.
Langton, Rae. *Kantian Humility: Our Ignorance of Things in Themselves*. Oxford: Oxford University Press, 1998.
Lewis, Thomas. *Religion, Modernity, and Politics in Hegel*. Oxford: Oxford University Press, 2011.
Lenk, Hans and Gregor Paul, eds. *Epistemological Issues in Classical Chinese Philosophy*. Albany: SUNY Press, 1993.
Liao, Chin-Ping. "Tanabe Hajime's Religious Philosophy." *NCCU Philosophical Journal* 32 (2014): 57–91.
Lin, Hong-Hsin (林鴻信), ed. *Humanistic Spirit from Intercultural Perspectives: Confucianism, Buddhism, Christianity, and Judaism in Dialogue* (跨文化視野中的人文精神:儒、佛、耶、猶的觀點與對話芻議). Taipei: National Taiwan University Press, 2011.
Lindbeck, George. *The Nature of Doctrine: Religion and Theology in the Postliberal Age*. Louisville: Westminster John Knox, 1984.
Lohman, Johann. *Karl Barth und der Neukantianismus*. Berlin: de Gruyter, 1995.
Long, D. Stephen. *Saving Karl Barth: Hans Urs von Balthasar's Preoccupation*. Minneapolis: Fortress, 2014.
Longuenesse, Béatrice. *Hegel's Critique of Metaphysics*. Cambridge: Cambridge University Press, 2007.

Löwith, Karl. *From Hegel to Nietzsche: The Revolution in Nineteenth-Century Thought*, translated by David Green. New York: Columbia University Press, 1991.
Löwith, Karl. *Meaning in History*. Chicago: University of Chicago Press, 1949.
Löwith, Karl. *My Life in Germany before and after 1933*. London: Athlone, 1994.
Malycz, Piotr. "Storming Heaven with Karl Barth? Barth's Unwitting Appropriation of the *Genus Maiestaticum* and What Lutherans Can Learn from It." *International Journal of Systematic Theology* 9 (2007): 73–92.
Mangina, Joseph. *Karl Barth: Theologian of Christian Witness*. London: Westminster John Knox, 2004.
Marga, Amy. *Karl Barth's Dialogue with Catholicism in Göttingen and Münster: Its Significance for His Doctrine of God*. Tübingen: Mohr Siebeck, 2010.
Marshall, Bruce. *Christology in Conflict: The Identity of a Saviour in Rahner and Barth*. Oxford: Blackwell, 1987.
McCormack, Bruce. "Barths Grundsätzlicher 'Chalcedonianismus'?" *Zeitschrift für dialektische Theologie* 18 (2002): 138–73.
McCormack, Bruce. "Election and the Trinity: Theses in Response to George Hunsinger." *Scottish Journal of Theology* 63 (2010): 203–24.
McCormack, Bruce, ed. *Engaging the Doctrine of God: Contemporary Protestant Perspectives*. Grand Rapids: Baker, 2008.
McCormack, Bruce. "Grace and Being: The Role of God's Gracious Election in Karl Barth's Theological Ontology." In *The Cambridge Companion to Karl Barth*, edited by John Webster, 92–110. Cambridge: Cambridge University Press, 2000.
McCormack, Bruce. *The Humility of the Eternal Son: Reformed Kenoticism and the Repair of Chalcedon*. Cambridge: Cambridge University Press, 2021.
McCormack, Bruce. "Karl Barth's Christology as Resource for a Reformed Version of Kenoticism." *International Journal of Systematic Theology* 8 (2006): 243–51.
McCormack, Bruce. *Karl Barth's Critically Realistic Dialectical Theology*. Oxford: Clarendon Press, 1995.
McCormack, Bruce. "The Ontological Presuppositions of Barth's Doctrine of the Atonement." In *The Glory of the Atonement*, edited by Charles Hill and Frank James III, 346–66. Downers Grove: IVP, 2004.
McCormack, Bruce. *Orthodox and Modern: Studies in the Theology of Karl Barth*. Grand Rapids: Baker, 2008.
McCormack, Bruce. "Seek God Where He May Be Found: A Response to Edwin Chr. Van Driel." *Scottish Journal of Theology* 60 (2007): 62–79.
McCormack, Bruce. "The Sum of the Gospel: The Doctrine of Election in the Theologies of Alexander Schweizer and Karl Barth." In *Toward the Future of Reformed Theology: Tasks, Topics, Traditions*, edited by David Willis and Michael Welker, 470–93. Grand Rapids: Eerdmans, 1999.
McCormack, Bruce. "So That He May Be Merciful to All: Karl Barth and the Problem of Universalism." In *Karl Barth and American Evangelicalism*, edited by Bruce McCormack and Clifford Anderson, 227–49. Grand Rapids: Eerdmans, 2011.
McCormack, Bruce. *For Us and Our Salvation: Incarnation and Atonement in the Reformed Tradition*. Princeton: Princeton Theological Seminary, 1993.
McCormack, Bruce and Alexandra Parvân. "Immutability, (Im)passibility and Suffering: Steps towards a 'Psychological' Ontology of God." *Neue Zeitschrift für Systematische Theologie und Religionsphilosophie* 59 (2017): 1–25.

McDonald, Nathan. "The *Imago Dei* and Election: Reading Genesis 1: 26–28 and Old Testament Scholarship with Karl Barth." *International Journal of Systematic Theology* 10 (2008): 303–27.

McDonald, Suzanne. "Barth's 'Other' Doctrine of Election in the *Church Dogmatics*." *International Journal of Systematic Theology* 9 (2007): 134–47.

McDonald, Suzanne. "Evangelical Questioning of Election in Barth: A Pneumatological Perspective from the Reformed Heritage." In *Karl Barth and American Evangelicalism*, edited by Bruce McCormack and Clifford Anderson, 250–70. Grand Rapids: Eerdmans, 2010.

McDonald, Suzanne. *Re-Imaging Election: Divine Election as Representing God to Others & Others to God*. Grand Rapids: Eerdmans, 2010.

McDowell, John. "Learning Where to Place One's Hope: The Eschatological Significance of Election in Barth." *Scottish Journal of Theology* 53 (2000): 316–38.

McKenny, Gerald. *The Analogy of Grace: Karl Barth's Moral Theology*. Oxford: Oxford University Press, 2013.

McMaken, W. Travis. "Election and the Pattern of Exchange in Karl Barth's Doctrine of the Atonement." *Journal of Reformed Theology* 3 (2009): 202–18.

Menn, Stephen. *Descartes and Augustine*. Cambridge: Cambridge University Press, 1998.

Moltmann, Jürgen. "The Election of Grace: Barth on the Doctrine of Predestination." In *Reading the Gospels with Barth*, edited by Daniel Migliore, 1–15. Grand Rapids: Eerdmans, 2017.

Molnar, Paul. "Can the Electing God Be without Us? Some Implications of Bruce McCormack's Understanding of Barth's Doctrine of Election." *Neue Zeitschrift für Systematische Theologie und Religionsphilosophie* 49 (2007): 199–222.

Molnar, Paul. *Divine Freedom and the Doctrine of the Trinity: In Dialogue with Karl Barth and Contemporary Theology*. London: T&T Clark, 2017.

Molnar, Paul. "The Function of the Immanent Trinity in Karl Barth: Implications for Today." *Scottish Journal of Theology* 42 (1989): 367–99.

Molnar, Paul. "The Obedience of the Son in the Theology of Karl Barth and of Thomas F. Torrance." *Scottish Journal of Theology* 67 (2014): 50–69.

Molnar, Paul. "The Perils of Embracing a 'Historicized Christology.'" *Modern Theology* 30 (2014): 454–80.

Molnar, Paul. "A Response: Beyond Hegel with Karl Barth and T. F. Torrance." *Pro Ecclesia* 23 (2014): 165–73.

Molnar, Paul. "'Thy Word Is Truth': The Role of Faith in Reading Scripture Theologically with Karl Barth." *Scottish Journal of Theology* 63 (2010): 70–92.

Molnar, Paul. "The Trinity, Election and God's Ontological Freedom: A Response to Kevin Hector." *International Journal of Systematic Theology* 6 (2006): 294–306.

Molnar, Paul. "The Trinity and the Freedom of God." *Journal for Christian Theological Research* 8 (2003): 59–66.

Montagne, D. Paul. *Barth and Rationality: Critical Realism in Theology*. Eugene: Wipf and Stock, 2012.

Moseley, Carys. *Nations and Nationalism in the Theology of Karl Barth*. Oxford: Oxford University Press, 2013.

Mou, Bo, ed. *Two Roads to Wisdom? Chinese and Analytic Philosophical Traditions*. Chicago: Open Court, 2001.

Mou, Zongsan (牟宗三). *Topics and Developments in Song-Ming Confucianism* (宋明儒學的問題與發展). Taipei: Linking Books, 2003.

Muller, Richard. *Christ and the Decree: Christology and Predestination in Reformed Theology from Calvin to Perkins*. Grand Rapids: Baker, 1986.
Muller, Richard. *Dictionary of Latin and Greek Theological Terms Drawn Principally from Protestant Scholastic Theology*. Grand Rapids: Baker Academic, 1985.
Muller, Richard. *Post-Reformation Reformed Dogmatics*, vol. 1. Grand Rapids: Baker Academic, 2003.
Murphy, Francesca Aran. *God Is Not a Story: Realism Revisited*. Oxford: Oxford University Press, 2007.
Neder, Adam. *Participation in Christ: An Entry into Karl Barth's Church Dogmatics*. Louisville: Westminster John Knox, 2009.
Nimmo, Paul. "Barth and the Election-Trinity Debate: A Pneumatological View." In *Trinity and Election in Contemporary Theology*, edited by Michael T. Dempsey, 162–81. Grand Rapids: Eerdmans, 2011.
Nimmo, Paul. *Being in Action: The Theological Shape of Barth's Ethical Vision*. London: T&T Clark, 2007.
Nimmo, Paul. "Karl Barth and the *concursus Dei*: A Chalcedonianism Too Far?" *International Journal of Systematic Theology* 9 (2007): 58–72.
O' Connell, Robert. *The Origin of the Soul in St. Augustine's Later Works*. New York: Fordham University Press, 1987.
Osterhammel, Jürgen. *Die Entzauberung Asiens—Europa und die asiatischen Reiche im 18. Jahrhundert*. Munich: C. H. Beck, 1998.
Palmquist, Stephen. *Comprehensive Commentary on Kant's Religion within the Bounds of Bare Reason*. Oxford: Wiley-Blackwell, 2016.
Palmquist, Stephen. *Kant's Critical Religion: Volume Two of Kant's System of Perspectives*. London: Routledge, 2000.
Pattison, George. *God and Being: An Enquiry*. Oxford: Oxford University Press, 2011.
Pereboom, Derk. "Kant on Transcendental Freedom." *Philosophy and Phenomenological Research* 73 (2006): 537–67.
Pinkard, Terry. *Hegel's Naturalism: Mind Nature, and the Final Ends of Life*. Oxford: Oxford University Press, 2012.
Pinkard, Terry. "How to Move from Romanticism to Post-Romanticism: Schelling, Hegel, and Heine." *European Romantic Review* 21 (2010): 391–407.
Pippin, Robert. *Hegel's Idealism: The Satisfactions of Self-Consciousness*. Cambridge: Cambridge University Press, 1989.
Prestige, George Leonard. *God in Patristic Thought*. London: SPCK, 1959.
Price, Daniel. *Karl Barth's Anthropology in Light of Modern Thought*. Grand Rapids: Eerdmans, 2002.
Price, Robert B. *Letters of the Divine Word: The Perfections of God in Karl Barth's Church Dogmatics*. London: T&T Clark, 2011.
Rosen, Michael. *Hegel's Dialectic and Its Criticism*. Cambridge: Cambridge University Press, 1982.
Rosen, Michael. *The Shadow of God: Kant, Hegel, and the Passage from Heaven to History*. Cambridge: Harvard University Press, 2022.
Qu, Thomas Xutong. *Barth und Goethe: Die Goethe-Rezeption Karl Barths 1906–1921*. Neukirchen-Vluyn: Neukirchener, 2014.
Qu, Thomas Xutong. "Kritischer musste Kants Kritik sein: Eine nachkantische Interpretation von Barths Beziehung zu Kant unter besonderer Berücksichtigung der Religionskritik Barths." In *Gottes Gegenwarten: Festschrift für Günter Thomas zum 60.*

Geburtstag, edited by Markus Höfner and Benedikt Friedrich, 53–68. Leipzig: Evangelische Verlagsanstalt, 2020.

Rasmussen, Joel. "The Transformation of Metaphysics." In *The Oxford Handbook of Nineteenth-Century Christian Thought*, edited by Joel Rasmussen, Judith Wolfe and Johannes Zachhuber, 11–34. Oxford: Oxford University Press, 2017.

Rigsby, Curtis. "Nishida on God, Barth and Christianity." *Asian Philosophy* 19 (2009): 119–57.

Rist, John M. *Augustine: Ancient Thought Baptized*. Cambridge: Cambridge University Press, 1994.

Rodin, R. Scott. *Evil and Theodicy in the Theology of Karl Barth*. New York: Peter Lang, 1997.

Rombs, Ronnie. *Saint Augustine and the Fall of the Soul: Beyond O'Connell and His Critics*. Washington, DC: Catholic University of America Press, 2006.

Schwarz, Hans. "Paul Althaus (1888–1966)." In *Twentieth-Century Lutheran Theologians*, edited by Mark Mattes, 136–54. Göttingen: Vandenhoeck & Ruprecht, 2013.

Seibt, Johanna. "Particulars." In *Theory and Applications of Ontology: Philosophical Perspectives*, edited by Johanna Seibt and Roberto Poli, 23–55. New York: Springer, 2010.

Smith, Aaron T. "God's Self-Specification: His Being Is His Electing." *Scottish Journal of Theology* 62 (2009): 1–25.

Smith, Brett. "Augustine's Natural Law Theory in *De libero arbitrio*." *Irish Theological Quarterly* 80 (2015): 111–35.

Song, Choan-Seng. *The Relation of Divine Revelation and Man's Religion in the Theologies of Karl Barth and Paul Tillich*. Ph.D. dissertation, Union Theological Seminary, 1964.

Soskice, Janet. "Athens and Jerusalem, Alexandria, and Edessa: Is There a Metaphysics of Scripture?" *International Journal of Systematic Theology* 8 (2006): 149–92.

Sparby, Terje. *Hegel's Conception of the Determinate Negation*. Leiden: Brill, 2015.

Spencer, Archie. *The Analogy of Faith: The Quest for God's Speakability*. Downers Grove: IVP Academic, 2015.

Spiekermann, Ingrid. *Gotteserkenntnis: Ein Beitrag zur Grundfrage der neuen Theologie Karl Barths*. Munich: Chr. Kaiser Verlag, 1985.

Stratis, Justin. *God's Being towards Fellowship: Schleiermacher, Barth and the Meaning of "God is Love."* London: Bloomsbury, 2019.

Stratis, Justin. "Speculating about Divinity? God's Immanent Life and Actualistic Ontology." *International Journal of Systematic Theology* 12 (2010): 20–32.

Strawson, Peter F. *The Bounds of Sense: An Essay on Kant's* Critique of Pure Reason. London: Routledge, 1975.

Sumner, Darren. *Karl Barth and the Incarnation: Christology and the Humility of God*. London: Bloomsbury, 2014.

Swinburne, Richard. *Providence and the Problem of Evil*. Oxford: Clarendon Press, 1998.

Takizawa, Katsumi. "Über die Möglichkeit des Glaubens." *Evangelische Theologie* 2 (1935): 376–402.

Tanner, Kathryn. "Creation and Providence." In *The Cambridge Companion to Karl Barth*, edited by John Webster, 111–26. Cambridge: Cambridge University Press, 2000.

Tanner, Klaus. *Die fromme Verstaatlichung des Gewissens: Zur Auseinandersetzung um die Legitimität der Weimarer Reichsverfassung in Staatsrechtswissenschaft und Theologie der zwanziger Jahre*. Göttingen: Vandenhoeck & Ruprecht, 1989.

Taylor, Charles. *Hegel and Modern Society*. Cambridge: Cambridge University Press, 1979.

Taylor, Charles. *A Secular Age*. Cambridge: Harvard University Press, 2007.

Teske, Ronald. "Augustine's Use of 'Substantia' in Speaking about God." *Modern Schoolmen* 62 (1985): 147–63.
Theiler, Willy. *Porphyrios und Augustin*. Halle: Niemeyer, 1933.
Tietz, Christiane. "Karl Barth and Charlotte von Kirschbaum." *Theology Today* 74 (2017): 86–111.
Tietz, Christiane. *Karl Barth: Ein Leben im Widerspruch*. Munich: C. H. Beck, 2019.
Tietz, Christiane. *Karl Barth: A Life in Conflict*, translated by Victoria Barnett. Oxford: Oxford University Press, 2021.
Torchia, Joseph. *Creatio ex nihilo and the Theology of St. Augustine: The Anti-Manichaean Polemic and Beyond*. New York: Peter Lang, 1999.
Torrance, Thomas F. *Karl Barth, Biblical and Evangelical Theologian*. Edinburgh: T&T Clark, 1990.
Torrance, Thomas F. *Karl Barth: An Introduction to His Early Theology 1910–1931*. Edinburgh: T&T Clark, 1962.
Tseng, Shao Kai. "Barth and Actualistic Ontology." In *The Wiley-Blackwell Companion to Karl Barth*, edited by George Hunsinger and Keith Johnson, 739–51. Oxford: Wiley-Blackwell, 2020.
Tseng, Shao Kai. *Barth's Ontology of Sin and Grace: Variations on a Theme of Augustine*. London: Routledge, 2019.
Tseng, Shao Kai. "The Christocentric Reorientation of Karl Barth's Actualistic Ontology in *Gottes Gnadenwahl* (1936)." *Sino-Christian Studies* 31 (2021): 149–90.
Tseng, Shao Kai. "Church." In *The Oxford Handbook of Nineteenth-Century Christian Thought*, edited by Joel Rasmussen, Judith Wolfe and Johannes Zachhuber, 610–27. Oxford: Oxford University Press, 2017.
Tseng, Shao Kai. "Condemnation and Universal Salvation: Karl Barth's 'Reverent Agnosticism' Revisited." *Scottish Journal of Theology* 71 (2018): 324–38.
Tseng, Shao Kai. *Immanuel Kant*. Phillipsburg: P&R, 2020.
Tseng, Shao Kai. *Karl Barth*. Phillipsburg: P&R, 2021.
Tseng, Shao Kai. "Karl Barths aktualistische Ontologie: Ihre Substanzgrammatik des Seins und Prozessgrammatik des Werdens." *Neue Zeitschrift für Systematische Theologie und Religionsphilosophie* 61 (2019): 32–50.
Tseng, Shao Kai. *Karl Barth's Infralapsarian Theology: Origins and Development, 1920–1953*. Downers Grove: IVP Academic, 2016.
Tseng, Shao Kai. "Non Potest Non Peccare: Karl Barth on Original Sin and the Bondage of the Will." *Neue Zeitschrift für Systematische Theologies und Religionsphilosophie* 60 (2018): 185–207.
Turchin, Sean. "Introducing Christianity into Christendom: Investigating the Affinity between Søren Kierkegaard and the Early Thought of Karl Barth." Ph.D. Thesis, University of Edinburgh, 2011.
Turchin, Sean. "Kierkegaard's Echo in the Early Theology of Karl Barth." *Kierkegaard Studies Yearbook* (2012): 323–36.
Van Asselt, Willem. *The Federal Theology of Johannes Cocceius (1603–1669)*, translated by Raymond Blacketer. Leiden: Brill, 2001.
Van Asselt, Willem. "On the Maccovius Affair." In *Revisiting the Synod of Dordt*, edited by Aza Goudriaan and Fred van Lieburg. Leiden: Brill, 2006.
Van Driel, Edwin. *Incarnation Anyway: Arguments for Supralapsarian Christology*. Oxford: Oxford University Press, 2008.
Van Driel, Edwin. "Karl Barth on the Eternal Existence of Jesus Christ." *Scottish Journal of Theology* 60 (2007): 45–61.

Walker, Ralph. "Kant and Transcendental Arguments." In *The Cambridge Companion to Kant and Modern Philosophy*, edited by Paul Guyer, 238–68. Cambridge: Cambridge University Press, 2006.

Watson, Gordon. "Karl Barth and St. Anselm's Theological Programme." *Scottish Journal of Theology* 30 (1977): 31–45.

Webster, John. *Barth's Moral Theology: Human Action in Barth's Thought*. London: T&T Clark, 1998.

Webster, John. *Karl Barth*. New York: Continuum, 2004.

Weihrauch, Bianca. *Friedrich Schillers Philosophisches Konzept des Erhabenen und seine Bedeutung für die Literaturtheorie*. Norderstedt: GRIN, 2016.

Weinrich, Michael. *Karl Barth*. Göttingen: Vandenhoeck & Ruprecht, 2019.

Weinrich, Michael. "Trinität." In *Barth Handbuch*, edited by Michael Beintker, 289–95. Tübingen: Mohr Siebeck, 2016.

Wigley, Stephen. "The von Balthasar Thesis: A Re-Examination of von Balthasar's Study of Barth in the Light of Bruce McCormack." *Scottish Journal of Theology* 56 (2003): 345–59.

Wittman, Tyler. *God and Creation in the Theology of Thomas Aquinas and Karl Barth*. Cambridge: Cambridge University Press, 2018.

Wood, Allen. *Kant's Rational Theology*. Ithaca: Cornell University Press, 1978.

Wüthrich, Matthias. *Gott und das Nichtige: zur Rede vom Nichtigen ausgehend von Karl Barths* KD §50. Zurich: Theologischer Verlag Zürich, 2006.

Zachhuber, Johannes. "The Historical Turn." In *The Oxford Handbook of Nineteenth-Century Christian Thought*, edited by Joel Rasmussen, Judith Wolffe and Johannes Zachhuber, 53–71. Oxford: Oxford University Press, 2017.

Zachhuber, Johannes. *Theology as Science in Nineteenth-Century Germany*. Oxford: Oxford University Press, 2013.

Žižek, Slavoj. *Less Than Nothing: Hegel and the Shadow of Dialectical Materialism*. New York: Penguin Random House, 2012.

Zizioulas, John. "Human Capacity and Human Incapacity: A Theological Exploration of Personhood." *Scottish Journal of Theology* 28 (1975): 401–47.

INDEX

absolute (adjective)
   being of God qua Trinity 4, 8–9, 15–18, 20, 22, 48–9, 58, 60, 80, 84, 90, 96–7, 106, 108–10, 113, 135, 143, 152, 154, 157, 169–77, 179–81, 183–201, 218, 227, 238
   decree of God (*see decretum absolutum*)
   freedom (Hegelian notion) (*see* freedom: absolute)
   idealism (Hegelian doctrine) 39, 43, 109, 222
absolute, the (Hegelian notion) 14–15, 36, 39, 43, 48, 67, 70–2, 79, 87, 97–8, 101–3, 109, 114–15, 131, 134, 139, 151–2, 166–9, 216, 225–6, 238
absoluteness of God's being
   primary (*see* absolute being of God qua Trinity)
   secondary 8–9, 18, 20, 22, 48–9, 58, 60, 76, 84, 96–7, 106, 109–10, 118, 147, 154, 157, 169–77, 183–201, 227, 233 (*see also* election: as mode of God's absolute being)
actualism 12–13, 15–16, 19, 45–9, 81–5, 87–91, 95–7, 109, 126–9, 142–8, 181–4
   in German idealism 47, 91, 143–4, 161
   Hermann Cohen and 46–7, 84–6, 90–1, 96, 114, 126
   in romanticism 161
actuality/efficacy (*Wirklichkeit*), Hegelian notion of 97–8, 134
actus purus (pure act; pure actuality) 90, 97, 106–8, 112, 115, 159, 168, 176, 194
Althaus, Paul 208–13, 221
analogy
   archetype-ectype 118, 173–4, 227
   Barth's turn from dialectics to 3, 27–30, 55, 153, 182
   of being (*analogia entis*) 86, 93, 106, 176, 234

   in classical Chinese philosophy 234–7
   of faith (*analogia fidei*) 7, 29, 31, 94, 133
   of relations (*analogia relationis*) 9, 94, 106–7, 176, 227 (*see also imago Dei*; *speculum electionis*; *speculum Trinitatis*)
Anselm of Canterbury 1, 3, 5–9, 14–16, 19, 22, 27–30, 52–62, 67, 72–81, 87–90, 149–57, 201, 203, 210, 213–14. *See also* speculation: Anselmian
antinomy, Kantian 223, 164–5
apokatastasis 140–2, 145
appearance (*Erscheinung*)
   Hegelian notion 134, 102
   Kantian notion 12, 38, 42–3, 96, 99–100
appearance (*Schein*, Hegelian notion) 9, 48–9, 70, 95–8, 114, 117–18, 130, 172, 177, 214–15, 236
arbitrariness 18–20, 108, 118, 128, 166–7, 169–72, 181, 184–5, 190, 198–200, 224. *See also* caprice; determinism; indeterminism; nature and freedom; *Willkür*
Aristotle 90–3, 97, 159
art religion (*Kunstreligion*) 206–7
aseity, divine. *See* God: aseity
Athanasius 120
Augustine of Hippo 19, 59–61, 73, 75, 85, 89–90, 92–5, 104–8, 110, 120, 134, 148, 150–64, 169–70, 177, 179, 199–200, 210, 214. *See also* speculation: Augustinian
autonomy (*Autonomie*), Kantian formula of 165, 199, 224

Baark, Sigurd 1–6, 16, 25–6, 28–30, 37, 41, 43–6, 52, 55–6, 59, 68, 79–81, 83, 113, 119, 153, 183, 217–18, 233
Balthasar, Hans Urs von 3, 27–30, 36–7, 54–5, 77, 153, 182

Bavinck, Herman 155
being
   actual/existential (*Sein/Dasein*) 15–16, 19, 48, 92, 95–8, 105, 107–8, 112, 114–15, 214
   essential (*Wesen*) 13, 16, 48–9, 76, 91–9, 104–5, 111–15, 118, 144, 177, 179, 184, 186, 188, 214
   Hegelian notion 4, 15–16, 33, 48–9, 79, 110–15, 135–6, 151–2, 169, 179, 214–15, 218, 225 (*see also* essence/essentiality)
being-for-us (*Für-uns-Sein*). *See* God: promeity
being-in-act (*Sein-in-der-Tat*) 8, 15, 17–18, 35, 45–9, 58, 83, 87, 90, 96–7, 109, 118, 127, 142–7, 160–3, 176, 191, 199
being-in-and-for-itself (*An-und-für-sich-Sein*). *See* absolute, the
being itself (*ipsum esse*) 7, 74, 93, 150, 158–9, 161–3, 177, 200. *See also* God: aseity
Benedict, Ruth 211
Beza, Theodore 137
Bonhoeffer, Dietrich 35, 47
Borchmeyer, Dieter 205–8
Brunner, Emil 35
Bultmann, Rudolf 23

Calvin, John 57, 60, 119, 127–8, 134, 137, 148, 182
caprice (*Willkür*, Barthian term) 107, 112, 169, 184, 198–9. *See also Willkür*
categorical imperative (Kantian doctrine) 40, 64, 165
Catholicism, Roman 61, 73
causality/causation 18, 57, 92, 97, 164–6, 128, 184, 196
Chalcedon (conciliar tradition) 16, 22, 85, 89, 103, 114–15, 155, 160, 185–99
Chao, Tzu-ch'en (趙紫宸) 233
Cheng, Yi (程頤) 234
Christocentrism, theological 1, 4, 6, 9, 15–17, 19, 25–6, 34, 39, 45, 52, 80–1, 108, 112, 119, 121, 127, 129, 132, 137, 142, 144, 146–9, 153–4, 157, 170, 175–7, 179, 181–2, 199–201, 203–4, 211, 213, 216, 219–20, 228–9, 233, 238–40

Christomonism 143–4
church 7, 12, 23, 40, 78, 80, 85, 98, 127, 159–60, 177, 185–8, 194
   and nation 204, 212, 219, 221, 224–32
   and state 205, 209, 230–2
civil religion (*Volksreligion*) 12, 53, 73, 204–5, 209–10, 214, 222, 226
classical theism 89, 97, 155–7, 168
Coccejus, Johannes 192, 120
Coe, Shoki (黃彰輝) 234
cogito ergo sum (Cartesian dictum) 6, 14, 57, 61, 63–4, 68–9, 78–9, 99, 101, 117, 150
Cohen, Hermann 46–7, 84, 86, 90–1, 96, 114, 126, 161
communicatio idiomatum 132, 188n36, 188–9
Confucianism 234–8
consciousness (*Bewusstsein*)
   Fichtean notion 68
   German idealist renditions 113, 133, 139, 226–7
   Hegelian notion 39, 44–5, 70, 72, 78–9, 102, 139, 167, 215, 226–7
   modern historical 10–11
   modern national 208, 215, 219–22, 226–7, 229–32
   (neo-)Kantian notion 41, 45
   romantic notion 65–6
   Schleiermacherian notion 31, 67
Constantinople, Council of (381) 89, 92, 160
constitution (*Beschaffenheit* and *Konstitution*, Kantian notions) 40, 99, 103, 107, 165
consubstantiality (*homoousion*) 106–7, 160, 187
consummate (*vollendet*, Hegelian adjective)
   determinacy 102
   essentiality 48, 72, 214–16
   identity 39, 48, 71–2, 114, 131, 152
   moment of logic 70, 98, 114
   religion, Christianity as 222
consummation (*Vollendung*), historical 11, 23, 33, 50 133–5, 139, 187, 209–10, 216, 218, 227
correspondence (*Entsprechung*) 9, 13, 18–19, 90, 98, 104–6, 109–14, 125, 129, 113, 142, 157, 161, 171–6, 180–1, 185–6, 189–90, 194, 198, 227

covenant 4, 98, 103–4, 107–10, 112, 174–6, 179, 181–2, 193–5, 200
   as internal basis of creation 122, 169, 171, 175, 190, 200, 218
   of redemption (*pactum salutis*) 192n50
creation
   doctrine of 80, 104, 150, 158, 174–5, 177
   as external basis of the covenant 103, 122, 173–5, 190, 200
Creator-creature distinction 33, 71, 77, 96, 111, 114, 129, 131, 144, 155, 171–3
critical realism 2–4, 42, 50, 50n107, 96, 124

decretum absolutum 80, 109, 118, 121, 123, 125, 127, 137–9, 142, 145, 180–1, 183, 186, 189–92, 197–9, 218, 223
Descartes, René 5–7, 13–15, 19, 22, 29, 52–3, 55–6, 58, 61–4, 67–70, 72–3, 75–9, 86, 101, 150, 163
determinacy (*Bestimmtheit*) 90, 101–2, 133–7, 225. *See also* determination (*Bestimmung*)
determination (*Bestimmung*) 15–18, 20–2, 46–8, 79, 85, 87, 91–2, 102–5, 107–13, 135–7, 139, 157–8, 169, 172, 181–2, 184–5, 187–8, 192–3, 195, 204, 215–20, 224, 231. *See also* election: as divine self-determination; predestination: as pre-determination
   German idealist notion 68–9, 102, 102n61, 200
   Hegelian notion 21–2, 48, 70–1, 79, 99–103, 109–11, 114, 133–4, 152, 172, 215–16, 220, 226
   determination (*das Bestimmen*)
   Kantian notion of 21, 63–4, 99–101
   Leibnizian-Wolffian notion of 100
determinism (metaphysical theory) 20, 164, 167, 170–1, 180, 222–4. *See also* antinomy, Kantian; arbitrariness; freedom: absolute; freedom: transcendental; indeterminism; *Willkür*
dignity (*Würde*) 64–5, 165, 229. *See also* autonomy
Dilthey, Wilhelm 222

Eckhart von Hochheim (Meister Eckhart) 151
emanation (*Überfluss*) 22, 60, 73, 84, 97, 109–10, 118, 126, 157–9, 162, 176, 179–81, 193–4, 200
   (neo-)Platonist notion 84, 90, 151, 157–9, 200
empirical realism (classical Kantianism) 5, 12–13, 32, 41–3, 47, 114. *See also* transcendental idealism
election
   of the community 23, 204–5, 219–22, 226–8, 232
   as determination of human nature (*see* predestination)
   as divine self-determination (*Selbstbestimmung*) 17–18, 20–3, 84, 99, 102–3, 107–13, 118, 129, 135–7, 169, 181–5, 188, 193, 216–18
   as *opera Dei ad extra interna* 18, 110, 118, 129, 180, 184, 189–91, 194, 197–9, 201
   and reprobation (*see decretum absolutum*; predestination: double)
   as secondary mode of God's absolute being 18, 58, 76, 106, 108–10, 129, 136, 147, 154, 171, 173, 175–6, 181, 186–7, 190–5, 199–202, 217, 238
essence/essentiality (*Wesen/Wesentlichkeit*)
   Barth's definition 91–108 (*see also* being: essential)
   Hegelian notion 48, 78, 86, 88, 91, 98, 134–5, 139, 168, 214, 216, 222
extension, speculative 6–9, 16, 40, 52, 57–8, 60, 66, 75–9, 83–4, 86, 90, 92, 96, 107, 110, 112, 118, 124, 126, 130, 140, 200, 211, 217
extra-Calvinisticum 13, 121–2, 132–3, 188–9

faith seeking understanding (*fides quaerens intellectum*) 3, 6, 13, 27, 52–3, 58–9, 67–9, 71–2, 79–80, 87, 92, 94, 117, 124, 214, 238, 240
fallenness 105, 121, 125, 140, 197–8, 204, 219–20, 239
feeling (*Gefühl*) 65–7, 140
Feuerbach, Ludwig 7, 11, 37, 61, 74, 77–8, 115, 117, 150–1, 155, 206, 211, 233, 238

Fichte, Johann Gottlieb 5, 10, 12, 14, 21, 32–3, 43–4, 47–8, 55, 58, 62, 67–70, 73, 102, 130, 166, 200, 208–9, 226
First World War 208, 229
finitum non capax infiniti 13, 57–9, 121, 152. *See also extra-Calvinisticum*
freedom
  absolute (Hegelian doctrine) 45, 108–9, 166–8, 174, 224–6
  in fellowship 171–6, 181, 204, 224–8
  God's absolute 18, 20, 108–9, 133, 143, 147, 154 168–9, 171, 173, 179–80, 184–7, 199, 227
  God's essence as one who loves in 15, 17–20, 79, 84, 106, 108–9, 133, 147, 153–4, 168–77, 179–81, 184–7, 189–90, 192–4, 199–200, 218, 227 (*see also* aseity)
  human 122, 166–9, 173–5, 204, 223–4, 227–8
  as post-Kantian theme 20, 23, 44–5, 64–5, 107–8, 143, 164–71, 173–4, 184, 198–200, 222, 224–7
  of speech 225, 231
  transcendental (Kantian doctrine) 18–20, 109, 124, 164–6, 171, 184, 222–4 (*see also* antinomy, Kantian; determinism; indeterminism; nature and freedom; *Willkür*)

Gaozi (告子) 234
German idealism 1, 3–5, 16–18, 20, 27, 32–3, 40, 44–5, 49–50, 52–3, 55, 72–6, 79, 86, 118, 129–30, 138, 143–4, 147, 150, 154–5, 166, 169, 174, 184, 199, 201, 210, 217, 220, 224, 233, 235–8
God
  as absolute being (*see* absolute: being of God qua Trinity)
  aseity 8, 18, 80, 84, 90, 93, 98, 108–10, 112, 150, 161, 168, 171, 173, 176–7, 184–5, 190–1, 196, 217, 227 (*see also* being itself)
  essential unknowability 9, 13, 57–60, 75, 93, 117, 151, 161, 190–2, 200
  immutability 7, 17–18, 33, 72, 90–1, 93, 97–8, 110, 112–13, 118, 124–6, 129, 131, 133, 136, 143–4, 147, 160–1, 163, 171, 174, 176, 190–1, 194, 217

  impassibility 18, 89, 110, 130, 132, 155, 160, 193–7, 201
  incomprehensibility 57, 156–64
  inconceivability 7–8, 15, 57, 59–60, 72, 75–7, 79–80, 90, 106, 113, 124, 133, 150, 154, 157, 201
  as the infinite (romantic notion) 65–7, 130, 140
  infinitude 7, 13, 27–8, 57, 59–61, 77–8, 121, 132, 150, 152, 168, 190–1, 201, 217
  promeity 8, 17, 80, 85, 98, 108–10, 112, 171, 173–4, 176–7, 185, 199, 218, 227
  simplicity 93, 115, 158–61, 190–1
  transcendence 32–3, 50, 57, 71, 89, 115, 117, 124, 129, 147, 155, 158–61, 172–3, 196
  unsublatable subjectivity 1, 4, 9, 15–18, 48, 72, 75, 79–80, 84–7, 90, 93, 97, 110, 112–15, 125–6, 133, 135–6, 142–3, 147–8, 152, 154, 175–6, 179, 183, 185, 187–9, 194–5, 199, 200–1, 217, 233, 238
Goethe, Johann Wolfgang von 205–9, 211–12

Harnack, Adolf von 50, 75, 89, 155–6, 209
Hartshorne, Charles 33, 88n11
Hegel, G. W. F. 1, 3–7, 10–16, 19, 21–3, 27, 29, 32–3, 36–7, 39, 43–5, 48–9, 51–6, 58, 61–2, 66–79, 85–8, 90, 95–103, 105, 108–11, 113–15, 117–18, 130–1, 133–6, 138–40, 142–4, 147–8, 150–2, 154–7, 161, 163, 166–9, 171–6, 179, 184, 187–9, 194, 199–200, 204, 206, 209–11, 213–18, 220, 222–6, 231, 235–6
Heine, Heinrich 14, 72–5, 151, 163, 208–9
Herder, Gottfried 11
Herrmann, Wilhelm 46, 50
Hirsch, Emanuel 203
historicism (metaphysics) 21, 23, 34–5, 50, 92, 94, 102, 155, 216, 222
Hitler, Adolf 10, 205–6, 226, 236
Hoffmann, August Heinrich 225

Holy Spirit 22, 43, 90, 98, 103, 105, 107–8, 111–13, 122, 124, 128, 130–3, 138, 143, 145, 146, 152–3, 159–62, 170–1, 176–7, 180–1, 187, 191, 194, 200–1, 207, 217, 224, 226–7, 240
Hume, David 57
Hunsinger, George 4, 15, 18, 29, 31, 36–7, 85–7, 97, 107–8, 110, 112, 144, 155, 168, 196–7, 233

idealism
   absolute (*see* absolute: idealism)
   Berkeleian 38, 43, 115
   empirical 32
   German (*see* German idealism)
   transcendental (*see* transcendental idealism)
identity, immediate
   Anselmian-Barthian formulation 7–9, 52, 57–8, 75–6, 84–5, 91, 98, 103, 108, 118, 126, 129–33, 145, 150, 171–7, 200, 217–18
   Cartesian formulation 6, 14, 58, 63, 101, 148, 150
   in classical theology 103, 108, 118, 158–9, 163
   in post-Kantian German philosophy 47–8, 65, 68–9, 83, 86, 99, 117–18, 130–1, 163, 200
identity, national 205–7, 201–11, 213, 215–16, 219–22
identity, speculative
   Anselmian-Barthian formulation 4, 6–9, 15, 17, 20, 21–2, 39–40, 45, 52–5, 57–8, 60, 75–80, 84, 95, 103, 113, 117–18, 125–6, 129–33, 136, 144, 148, 150, 157, 171–7, 182–3, 186–7, 200, 215–18, 238
   Cartesian formulation 6, 14
   in classical theology 86, 103, 106, 118, 131–2, 151–2, 158–9, 163
   Hegelian formulation 7, 11, 14, 21, 30, 52–5, 58, 69–72, 87–8, 91, 102, 114, 131, 148, 152, 167, 172, 200, 214–16
   in post-Kantian German philosophy 48, 67, 72–5, 83, 86, 117–18, 151–2, 163, 200, 210–11

idolatry, speculative (Feuerbachian notion) 4, 7, 32, 45, 48, 52–4, 61, 78, 108, 117, 122, 154–5, 177, 189, 201, 203–4, 209–11, 214–15, 222, 228, 233–4, 236–40
image, speculative 6–8, 13, 15, 40, 56, 118, 122, 200, 210–11
imago Dei 8, 84–5, 90, 92–4, 105–7, 117–18, 122, 124, 129–30, 150–4, 161, 170, 174–5, 201. *See also speculum Trinitatis*
imago Trinitatis. *See speculum Trinitatis*
immediacy (*Unmittelbarkeit*)
   Barth's treatment 129–33
   in early-modern rationalism 6, 61–2, 70
   in German idealism 70, 130–1, 200
   Hegel's critique of 70–1
   Kant's critique of 62–4, 101, 130, 200
   in romanticism 66–7
immutability, divine. *See* God: immutability
impassibility, divine. *See* God: impassibility
incarnation 9, 17–19, 23, 46, 96, 103, 107, 111, 118, 125, 129–37, 134–5, 143, 145, 161–3, 172–3, 175, 183, 186–7, 191–4, 200–1, 217–18, 220–1, 239
incomprehensibility, divine. *See* God: incomprehensibility
inconceivability, divine. *See* God: inconceivability
indeterminism (metaphysical theory) 20, 164, 167, 171, 180, 183–4, 198, 223–4. *See also* antinomy, Kantian; arbitrariness; determinism; freedom; *Willkür*
infinitude, divine. *See* God: infinitude
Inoue, Yoshio (井上 良雄) 233
intellect (*intellectio*) 6, 13, 42, 59, 71, 86, 89–90, 92–3, 106, 140, 150–1
intellectualism 149–52, 156, 180
intuition (*Anschauung*) 38–9, 43, 66, 99–100, 144, 190. *See also* worldview

Jacobi, Friedrich 208–9
Jenson, Robert 34–5
Jüngel, Eberhard 18–19, 108–9, 113, 135, 143

Kant, Immanuel 4–6, 10–14, 18, 20, 25–6, 28, 37–45, 47, 49, 51–3, 55, 57–8, 61–6, 68–70, 72–4, 76–7, 86, 96, 99–102, 109, 114–15, 124–5, 127, 130, 142, 164–9, 184, 199–200, 223–5, 235
Keller, Gottfried 230, 230n126
Kierkegaard, Søren 28–9, 63–4, 114
Kitamori, Kazoh (北森 嘉蔵) 155
Knox, John 120–1
Kulturnation 205, 208, 211. *See also* Staatsnation

lapsarian controversy 120–1, 192, 197–9
Lebenstotalität 167, 222
Leibniz, G. W. 21, 62, 73, 76, 100, 102
Lessing, Gotthold 208
logic of mediation (Hegelian method) 4, 16, 22, 62, 70–1, 97, 102–3, 118, 172, 215, 217
Logos asarkos. See immanent Trinity
Logos incarnandus 183
Löwith, Karl 11, 23, 204, 210, 216, 226
Luther, Martin 139, 148
Lutheranism 188n36, 208, 211–13

Mann, Thomas 205
Marburg neo-Kantianism 2–3, 12–13, 19, 28, 37–8, 40–2, 44–50, 74, 84, 96, 115, 124, 127
Marx, Karl 10, 155, 209–10
Marxism 23, 225
Maury, Pierre 119–21, 129, 137–8, 147, 182
McCormack, Bruce L. 1–4, 10–13, 18–21, 25–9, 35–8, 40–55, 60, 63, 83–6, 91, 96, 103, 108, 111, 119–20, 124, 126, 132–3, 135, 148, 152–4, 169, 176–7, 180, 182–4, 196, 215
mediation (*Vermittlung*, German idealist notion) 4, 14, 21–2, 70–1, 80, 87, 102–3, 131, 200, 215, 225
mediation of Christ 8–9, 103, 113, 117–18, 132–3, 162, 170, 173, 185, 189–90, 192, 200, 217, 233
Mencius 234
Mendelssohn, Moses 208
Menschheitsideal 205–6, 210–13
metaphysics 5–6, 14–16, 23, 29, 39, 41, 44–5, 49–52, 51n114, 55, 61–2, 64–73, 79, 85–98, 100, 109–11, 114–15, 123–4, 127–31, 134, 137–8, 141, 143, 147–8, 155, 158, 164–5, 170, 184, 223, 238–9
Molnar, Paul 30–1, 36–7, 44, 88, 111
Moltmann, Jürgen 33, 36, 89, 155, 194
Mou, Zongsan (牟宗三) 235

Nachdenken (speculative method) 13, 17, 58, 71–2, 105, 124–5, 163. *See also* reflection
natural theology 15, 31, 86, 115
naturalism
   positivistic 51
   religious 222
   versus pantheism (intellectual-historical theme) 74
nature (*natura/Natur*)
   Barth's definition 15–16, 31, 43, 45–9, 79, 83, 90–8, 103–7, 172–6, 197, 214, 218–21
   in classical Chinese philosophy 234–9
   in German idealism and romanticism 73–4, 78, 89, 102–3, 143, 164–8, 201, 236
   Kantian view 68, 164–8, 200, 223–4, 164–5
   revisionist view of Barth's use of the term 2, 45–6, 84–5, 88, 91–4, 188
   substantialist definition 11–14, 88, 90–8
nature and freedom (metaphysical problem) 20, 154, 164–8, 223–4, 164–5. *See also* antinomy, Kantian; arbitrariness; determinism; freedom: absolute; freedom: transcendental; indeterminism; *Willkür*
nationalism, modern 4–5, 11, 14, 22–3, 56, 72, 154, 177, 201, 203–8, 210–14, 129, 221, 226–30, 233–4, 237
Naturphilosophie 73–4, 236
Nazism 203, 204–7, 209–11
(neo-)Platonism 22, 84, 89–90, 93, 99, 104, 106, 110, 151, 156–9, 163, 176, 237
Newman, John Henry 30
Nicaea, Council of (325) 89–90, 92–3, 151, 159–61
nothingness (*das Nichtige*) 98, 105, 218–19, 231, 239
Novalis 14, 65–6, 208

ontological impossibility 98, 219, 231, 238–9
ontology
　actualistic 45–9, 84–115
　of classical Western theology 92–5, 157–64
　as general metaphysics 15–16, 85–7
　Nicene-Chalcedonian 159–61
organicism 102, 138–9

panentheism 73, 176
Pannenberg, Wolfhart 32–6, 155
pantheism 5, 12, 29, 53, 55–6, 69, 71–5, 79, 149–51, 154–6, 163, 176, 189, 203, 205–10, 213, 222
　versus deism (intellectual-historical theme) 75, 209
　versus naturalism (intellectual-historical theme) 74
pantheism controversy (*Pantheismusstreit*) 208
particularism 17, 60, 92, 140–2, 158
phenomenalism (Kant interpretation) 5, 12–14, 32, 39, 41–4, 48, 51, 66, 114
physiocracy 91, 164. See also nature and freedom
Plato 57, 93, 97, 99
Plotinus 90, 93, 151, 156, 159–60
Polanus, Amandus 196
Porphyry 156, 159
post-Kantian paradigm (Barth interpretation) 3–4, 12, 19, 25–6, 36–52, 83–9, 91, 99, 123–9
postulate, (neo-)Kantian 39, 123–5, 129, 168
preamble of faith (*praeambula fidei*) 15, 31. See also regula fidei
predestination
　doctrine of 34, 119–25, 127–30, 134, 137–9, 141, 144–8, 181–2, 185, 197, 199, 204, 216, 217, 219, 223–4
　double 34, 103, 119–24, 128–9, 134–9, 141–2, 145–6, 148, 180, 190, 193–4, 197–8, 218–20, 223–4, 231 (*see also decretum absolutum*)
　as pre-determination (*Vorherbestimmung*) 22–3, 123, 139, 194, 216–21, 224, 238–9
principle (*Prinzip*: Kantian notion) 38, 99, 123

constitutive 39–40, 99, 123–4, 165
regulative 40, 64, 123–4, 165
process philosophy 33, 88, 155
promeity, divine. See God: promeity
providence 11, 22–3, 180, 204, 208–13, 215–17, 221, 226

Rahner, Karl 36, 154
rational, the/rationality (*das Vernünftige/die Vernünftigkeit*, Hegelian notions) 45, 79, 97, 102, 134, 218
Realdialektik 4, 19, 28–9, 42
reason (*Vernunft*, Kantian notion)
　practical use of 39–40, 62, 124, 165–8, 199, 223
　theoretical use of 10, 39–41, 43, 62, 64, 100–1, 123–4, 164–5, 199, 223
reconciliation (*Versöhnung*)
　Christ's work of 104–5, 110, 127, 136, 144, 171, 175, 189–90, 192–4, 200, 220, 227, 239
　Hegelian notion of 14, 21, 102, 109–10, 167–9, 174, 215, 225–6
reflection (speculative method) 6–7, 13, 15, 17, 19, 40, 57–8, 60, 63, 65–6, 70–2, 79–80, 101–2, 117–18, 124–5, 129, 166, 174–5, 181, 189. See also *Nachdenken*
Reformed theology, classical 57, 59, 120–1, 127, 137, 141, 152, 180, 183, 188, 190–2, 196–200, 216
regula fidei 15, 31, 39–40, 94
relationalism (ontology) 21, 94, 102
religion 16, 53, 66–7, 72–4, 78, 151, 165–6, 204–11, 214, 217, 222–4, 226. See also art religion; civil religion
repetition (*Wiederholung*), actualistic 171, 173, 191, 223, 227
reprobation. See predestination: double
revisionism (Barth interpretation) 18n42, 18–19, 84, 87–8, 91, 94, 99, 103, 107, 110–11, 114, 119, 154–7, 169, 181–4. See also post-Kantian paradigm
Ritschl, Albrecht 37, 50–2, 86, 156
romanticism 52, 65–7, 73–4, 150, 208, 222, 236
Rosen, Michael E. 12, 18, 20, 71, 164, 166, 170, 218n58
Rousseau, Jean-Jacques 205, 225

Schelling, Friedrich 10, 12, 21, 32–3, 44, 47, 67, 70, 73, 75, 86, 130, 143, 166, 174, 200, 226
Schiller, Friedrich 14, 64–5, 206–9, 211
Schleiermacher, Friedrich 10, 14, 30–3, 37, 45, 47, 49–51, 65–7, 78, 130, 139–44, 147, 161
Second World War 74, 204, 208, 210–13, 229, 233
simplicity, divine. *See* God: simplicity
sin 98, 104–5, 121–2, 128–9, 136–7, 139, 141, 175, 190, 193–4, 196–7, 213, 218–21, 229, 231, 239
Song, Choan-Seng (宋泉盛) 234
speculation
    Anselmian 1–9, 16–17, 22, 39–40, 44, 52–61, 67, 75–81, 83, 87, 94, 110–14, 121, 124, 128, 147, 149–54, 157, 177, 201, 203, 210, 214, 238
    Augustinian 16, 59, 105–7, 110, 150–64, 168–70, 174–7, 179, 199–200, 210, 214
    Cartesian 1, 5–9, 13–15, 22, 53–6, 61–4, 67–72, 76–9, 101, 131, 121, 124, 126, 128, 148–50, 163
    in classical theology 1, 3, 6–8, 13, 14, 16, 56–61, 91–5, 74–5, 97–8, 115, 121, 127, 151, 156–7, 168, 180–1, 191–2, 213
    Hegelian 1, 5–9, 13–15, 22, 52–3, 56, 61, 67–75, 79, 85–7, 97, 102–5, 111, 114–15, 139, 148–50, 210
    idealist and romantic modes of 4–5, 49, 52, 57, 60, 64–9, 72–5, 79, 83–5, 87, 108, 122, 127, 139, 147, 234
    model of Barth interpretation 1–9, 13–15, 25–6, 53–61, 75–81
    Platonist 89–90, 93, 151, 156–9, 163, 176
speculum electionis 4, 9, 17, 20, 23, 60, 117–18, 120–3, 128, 146, 190, 192–3, 200, 234
speculum Trinitatis 4, 8–9, 16, 19–20, 58–60, 85, 90, 93–4, 105–6, 108, 113, 149–54, 157, 161–4, 173–7, 179–81, 189–90, 200, 213, 233
Spinoza, Baruch 164, 208
Staatsnation 208–9
Suárez, Francisco 100

sublation (*Aufhebung*, Hegelian notion) 14, 16, 18, 71, 102, 122, 135, 137–42, 146, 187–8, 190, 194, 197–200, 215, 218, 220, 223, 225
supralapsarianism, purified 197–9
Strauss, David Friedrich 11, 74, 77–8, 206
Sturm und Drang 208, 222
substantialism 15, 46, 84–5, 87–92, 94–5, 98, 111, 114–15, 117, 126–7, 138, 155–7, 161, 214, 238

Tanabe, Hajime (田辺 元) 233
Taylor, Charles 12, 71, 218n58
Theotokos 103, 118, 160, 187, 189
Third Reich 177, 205–6, 210–12, 214, 226, 236
Thomas Aquinas 57, 86, 92–3, 97, 150, 152, 156, 159
Tillich, Paul 74–5, 210, 234
Torrance, Thomas F. 3, 28–32, 36–7, 234
traditionalism (Barth interpretation) 36–7
transcendence
    in classical Chinese philosophy 234–8
    in modern German philosophy 33, 71, 124, 155, 172
    in Platonism 158–60
transcendence, divine. *See* God: transcendence
transcendental idealism (Kantian doctrine) 10, 12–13, 38–9, 41–3, 51, 96, 100, 114, 124, 127, 130, 166
    two-aspect interpretation of 38, 43 (*see also* empirical realism)
    two-object interpretation of 12–13, 38n60, 38n61, 38–9, 41–3, 43n84 (*see also* phenomenalism)
transcendental (Kantian adjective)
    argument 38–9
    cognitions 39–40, 96, 100
    concepts 40
    critique 100, 130
    Denkform and method 2–3, 13, 37–40, 58, 96, 124–7, 176–7
    freedom (*see* freedom: transcendental)
    idealism (*see* transcendental idealism)
    theology 39–40, 62
Trinity
    economic 2, 25
    image of (*see speculum Trinitatis*)

immanent 2, 8, 18, 22, 25, 35, 46, 98, 111–12, 131, 154–5, 172, 183, 191 (*see also* absolute: being of God qua Trinity)
   logical (Hegelian doctrine) 16, 114–15, 143, 152, 187
Troeltsch, Ernst 50–1

universalism 140–2. *See also* apokatastasis
unknowability *per essentiam*, divine. *See* God: essential unknowability
unsublatable subjectivity. *See* God: unsublatable subjectivity

vestigium Trinitatis. *See speculum Trinitatis*
voluntarism 180, 183–4

Wagner, Richard 205–9, 211–12
worldview (*Weltanschuung*) 73, 140, 211, 235, 237. *See also* intuition
Weltbürgertum (cultural ideal) 206–8, 211–13
Weltdeutsch (ideological slogan) 205, 208, 211, 213
Willkür (Kantian and post-Kantian notion) 18, 20, 109, 165–6, 169–71, 184, 198–200
Whitehead, Alfred North 33, 88n11, 155
Wolff, Christian 21, 62, 76, 86, 100–1

Zhu, Xi (朱熹) 235

www.ingramcontent.com/pod-product-compliance
Lightning Source LLC
Chambersburg PA
CBHW062122300426
44115CB00012BA/1780